That Every Man Be Armed

The great object is, that every man be armed. . . .

—Patrick Henry, 1788

A well regulated Militia, being necessary to the security of a free State, the right of the people to keep and bear Arms, shall not be infringed.

—Second Amendment,
U.S. Constitution

No State shall make or enforce any law which shall abridge the privileges or immunities of citizens of the United States; nor shall any State deprive any person of life, liberty, or property, without due process of law; nor deny to any person within its jurisdiction the equal protection of the laws.

—from the Fourteenth Amendment

That Every Man Be Armed

The Evolution of a Constitutional Right

Stephen P. Halbrook

University of New Mexico Press
Albuquerque

Portions of this book have previously appeared
as follows: "The Jurisprudence of the Second and
Fourteenth Amendments," *George Mason University
Law Review* 4 (1981): 1–69; "The Fourteenth Amend-
ment and the Right to Keep and Bear Arms: The
Intent of the Framers," Report of the Subcommit-
tee on the Constitution, Committee on the Judiciary,
The Right to Keep and Bear Arms, U.S. Senate, 97th
Cong., 2d Sess. (1982): 68–82; "To Keep and Bear
Their Private Arms: The Adoption of the Second
Amendment, 1787–1791," *Northern Kentucky Law Re-
view* 10 (1982): 13–39; and "Tort Liability for the
Manufacture, Sale and Ownership of Handguns?"
Hamline Law Review 6 (1983): 351–82.

Library of Congress Cataloging in Publication Data

Halbrook, Stephen P.
   That every man be armed.

   Bibliography: p.
   Includes index.
   1. Firearms—Law and legislation—United States.
I. Title.
KF3941.H35   1984   344.73'0533   84-13127

To my Children:
May they ever live free.

Contents

Preface

Between 1981 and 1984, handgun bans were enacted in Morton Grove, Evanston, and Oak Park, all suburbs of Chicago. In the same period, bans on pistols and revolvers were defeated in Skokie and a half dozen other Chicago suburbs. On the west coast, San Francisco sought to prohibit possession of handguns in 1982, but the ordinance was promptly stricken down by the courts. Simultaneously, California voters defeated Proposition 15, a referendum proposal to freeze the number of handguns in that state, by a two-to-one margin.

In recent years, public debate on the issue of "gun control" has sharply escalated. One group, the prohibitionists, opposes the constitutional right of private possession of firearms (especially handguns) and proposes that possession of firearms should be confined to the military and the police. Other groups believe that the Second Amendment means what it says: "the right of the people to keep and bear arms, shall not be infringed." The battles between these prohibitionists and constitutionalists are being waged in local, state, and national legislatures, and in the courts all around the country.

For an issue as hotly debated as firearms prohibition, one would think that a wealth of information and history on whether the Constitution guarantees an individual right to possess guns would be available in the public forum. Given all that has been written on free speech and religion, unreasonable search and seizure, cruel and unusual punishment, and other topics in the Bill of Rights, the lack of attention to the meaning of the Second Amendment seems inexplicable.

If a court held that "the people" mentioned in the First Amendment are a select group of orators, or that small printing presses and cheap handbills could be outlawed as long as expensive newspapers are published, outraged civil libertarians would quickly disprove these restrictive views by reference to history. The original records would likewise refute an attempt to exclude search and seizure in the bedroom from Fourth Amendment protection of "houses" on the rationales that a disproportionate number of crimes are committed in bedrooms and that some other rooms of the house would still retain Fourth Amendment protection.

Firearms prohibitionists are currently making arguments comparable to the above farfetched hypothetical cases. It seems that select military forces, not "the people," have a right to keep and bear arms. Even if individuals hold this right, some kinds of arms (such as handguns) are supposedly not really "arms" at all, and can be banned without infringing on anyone's rights. Yet if the Bill of Rights has any meaning at all, it must be based on the linguistic usage of those who wrote it. Thus, the validity of the prohibitionist argument must be tested by the historical evolution of the constitutional right in question, particularly as it was known and understood by the framers and ratifiers of the American Bill of Rights.

The philosophical origins of the Bill of Rights, including the Second Amendment, may be found in the Greek and Roman classics and in English Whig thought. The English common law and the Declaration of Rights of 1689 were more immediate influences on the Founding Fathers. Following an analysis of these sources of the right to keep and bear arms, this study will provide the most extensive analysis yet published of the American Revolution and the adoption of the Second Amendment. The records of the Documentary History of the Ratification of the Constitution, currently being edited by John P. Kaminski and Caspare J. Saladino at the University of Wisconsin, were examined for this purpose. The Bill of Rights collection maintained in that project, probably the most complete in the world on the subject, contains not one iota of evidence that the Second Amendment was intended to guarantee solely and exclusively a collective right and not an individual right.

Antebellum interpretations of the nature of the right to keep and bear arms not only provide the legal views and public attitudes which prevailed during the adoption of the Bill of Rights, but they also illuminate the already emerging debate concerning the abolition of slavery in all forms. One badge of slavery, the absence of any right to keep and carry weapons, reappeared in the post–Civil War black codes. The intention that the Fourteenth Amendment would protect freedmen and all citizens from state infringement of the right to keep and bear arms pervades the political debates of Reconstruction. Inexplicably, the courts and commentators alike have been immersed in ignorant bliss on this original intention. It seems beyond imagination that the highest courts of the land would make sweeping judgments denying that the Fourteenth Amendment incorporates the Second Amendment, when this was precisely the undisputed original understanding.

After investigating the philosophical, common law, and historical backgrounds of the right to keep and bear arms, this work analyzes the state and federal court opinions on this topic during the last century, concluding with some reflections on public policy.

While this book is the most comprehensive constitutional history of the right to keep and bear arms published to date, it may represent only the tip of an iceberg. Many original sources remain hidden in old records, correspondence, and newspapers. The astonishing fact about these sources is their unanimity in recognizing the right of the American citizen to have arms, a fundamental right never seriously questioned until fairly recent times.

At the opening of its fall 1983 term, the U.S. Supreme Court declined to review the first total handgun ban in American history, which had been enacted by Morton Grove, Illinois, two years before. When the ban was first tested, U.S. District Judge Bernard Decker stringently interpreted the nature of the Second Amendment right to keep and bear arms so as to uphold the ban.[1] Decker was the same judge who years earlier had invoked the absolute protection of the First Amendment in support of the right of Nazis to march in Skokie, Illinois, a predominently Jewish community.[2]

In a 2 to 1 decision, the U.S. Court of Appeals for the Seventh Circuit upheld the Morton Grove handgun ban. Even though the framers of the Illinois Constitution had "intended to include handguns in the class of protected arms,"[3] the majority reasoned, "a ban on handguns does not violate that right."[4] As to the intended meaning of the federal constitutional guarantee, "the debate surrounding the adoption of the second and fourteenth amendments . . . has no relevance on the resolution of the controversy before us."[5]

Thus, the court of appeals was willing to allow a ban on keeping arms by the common citizens of Morton Grove. By contrast, the same court was unwilling to allow a ban on marches by Nazis in the nearby community of Skokie. Judge Harlington Wood, who joined in the opinion to uphold Morton Grove's ban, concurred in protecting Nazi rights against Skokie's ban under this logic: "Any exception, however, to the First Amendment which we might be tempted to fashion would not 'die away.' It would remain a dangerous and unmanageable precedent in our free and open society."[6] In Orwellian language, some Bill of Rights provisions are more equal than others.

The dissenting opinion in the court of appeals in the Morton Grove case relied on the traditional view that "a man's home is his castle."[7] "The Morton Grove Ordinance, by prohibiting the possession of a handgun within the confines of the home, violates both the fundamental right to privacy and the fundamental right to defend the home against unlawful intrusion within the parameters of the criminal law."[8] In banning pistols, Morton Grove assumed the role of Big Brother in George Orwell's *1984*.[9]

The lack of a Supreme Court review of the Morton Grove ordinance will encourage firearms bans in other localities throughout the country. This, in turn, will spawn new legal challenges and additional court decisions. Eventually, gun prohibitions will assume sufficiently widespread proportions as to be ripe for Supreme Court review. The highest court is bound not by judicial precedent but by the intent of the framers of the Constitution. If and when it looks into the understanding of our forefathers who wrote the Bill of Rights and the Fourteenth Amendment, the Court will discover a rich history that is only beginning to be told.

A number of people have assisted and encouraged me in various ways in writing this book. None of them are responsible for its shortcomings, and everyone who has sparked a useful contribution to the subject is not named here. However, for their helpful comments on portions of the manuscript, I thank David I. Caplan, George S. Knight, Bernice Glatzer Rosenthal, Richard E. Gardiner, Sue Wimmershoff-Caplan, Robert J. Dowlut, and Davis E. Keeler. And for actually preparing the manuscript, thanks are due to Margaret R. Vogt and Marguerite E. Wagner. For assistance during all phases of publishing, I thank the staff of the University of New Mexico Press and my editor, David V. Holtby.

That Every Man Be Armed

Introduction:
Firearms Prohibition
and Constitutional Rights

The United States Supreme Court has recently reiterated that the right to keep and bear arms is one of many other "specific guarantees . . . provided in the Constitution." More specifically, the Court listed these rights: "the freedom of speech, press, and religion; the right to keep and bear arms; the freedom from unreasonable searches and seizures; and so on."[1] *Moore* v. *East Cleveland* (1977), the opinion in which this language appears, clarifies little else about a subject the high court has rarely spoken on—the right to keep and bear arms. *Moore* seems to place the right recognized in the Second Amendment on a level of equal significance as the rights protected by the First and Fourth Amendments. Posed in a discussion of the rights incorporated into the Fourteenth Amendment, the opinion also appears to imply that the right to have arms is protected from state infringement. On the other hand, in 1969 the Supreme Court dismissed an appeal seeking to invalidate New Jersey's Gun Control Act for want of a "substantive federal question."[2] Of course, that act did not prohibit the possession of arms but only required a police permit to buy them, a permit available to all law-abiding citizens.

In its entire history, the Supreme Court has spoken only rarely and sketchily on the meaning and applicability of the right to keep and bear arms. But the rapidly escalating and comprehensive forms of firearms control, regulation, and prohibition at both federal and state levels must at some point provoke a more definitive response from the Court. Since, after all, the Bill of Rights guarantees this right, at some point the Court may no longer be able to avoid defining more comprehensively the meaning of the Second Amendment and determining whether the Fourteenth Amendment guards the right from state infringement. The objective of this study is to provide the basis for just such a definition and determination, and thereby to contribute a comprehensive jurisprudence of the right to keep and bear arms.

Both federal and state courts may perhaps indefinitely defer decisions on matters such as the nature and scope of the Third Amendment's proscription of the peacetime quartering of soldiers, for no case or controversy seems likely

3

to arise from the question.[3] However, increasingly restrictive forms of gun-control legislation, which have been or may be enacted, prompt the exposition of the constitutional limits of such legislation. The possible conflict of the escalating firearms control legislation at both state and federal levels with both constitutional and statutory provisions as well as with common law makes resolution of the nature of the right to have arms imperative. This right needs to be defined not only in terms of the requirements of the Second and Fourteenth Amendments (and possibly the Ninth and Tenth), but also in terms of state constitutions and civil rights laws that contain no explicit provisions protecting the right to possess arms or that have provisions which differ in wording from the Second Amendment. Indeed, the definitional parameters of a right to keep and bear arms protected by the Fourteenth Amendment, if such right exists, may differ from state provisions even where the language of those provisions is identical with the Second Amendment, since federal standards for protection of fundamental rights may be held to be more stringent than standards set by states.[4]

The federal gun-control legislation of 1968 provides severe penalities only for acts that are *mala prohibita* (evil only by reason of a legislative act) and not for those that are *mala in se* (inherently evil).[5] A nonfirearms dealer who sells or gives any firearms to a resident of a state other than his own commits a felony. Technically, a father who presents the family rifle to his son who resides in another state is subject to imprisonment of five years and a fine of five thousand dollars.[6] Generally, arms can be bought, sold, or otherwise transferred by nonlicensed persons only within one's home state. Persons who engage in the business of buying or selling arms or ammunition must acquire a federal firearms license. However, what constitutes engaging in such business has never been clearly defined; accordingly, innocent-minded citizens have been arrested by agents of the Bureau of Alcohol, Tobacco, and Firearms.[7] Possession of shotguns with barrels of less than eighteen inches, guns that fire more than once with a single depression of the trigger, and other arms which are harmless in themselves may subject a person to ten years' imprisonment and a ten-thousand-dollar fine.[8] An absolute prohibition of mere possession of firearms applies to persons under indictment for or convicted of a felony, to veterans who received dishonorable discharges, to mental incompetents, to illegal aliens, to citizens who renounced their citizenship, and to users of unlawful drugs including marijuana.[9]

The states and some localities have passed a variety of regulations concerning the possession, ownership, and carrying of firearms.[10] Little uniformity exists in regard to whether permits to purchase and/or carry, as well as registration and/or licensing, are required. Some states, such as New Mexico, Georgia, Oregon and Virginia, have very liberal policies in respect to the freedom to purchase, possess, and carry firearms. In these states, few regulations exist other than the prohibition of sale to minors and the requirement that a permit be acquired for carrying a concealed weapon outside of one's home. While Florida prohibits carrying pistols and even rifles, even though unloaded, unless engaged in such activities as hunting or target practice,[11] California makes it unlawful to carry loaded guns only if they are not carried for a legitimate purpose.[12] Yet in Florida a handgun carried in a glove compartment is not readily accessible and thus not concealed,[13] while in California a handgun carried in a trunk is considered to be concealed.[14] Most states prohibit convicted felons from possessing firearms. Some states require that the crime have been violent; others remove the disability after a certain number of years. Exceptional cases exist in Texas, which permits possession at one's residence,[15] and Oregon, which does not disarm persons convicted of felonies related to marijuana possession.[16]

Should the U.S. Supreme Court render a significant and extensive opinion concerning the right to keep and bear arms, as it seems bound to do in the future, it may concern the arms prohibition laws of New York City, Massachusetts, or Washington, D.C., which involve the most stringent control over a traditional liberty that, after all, the Bill of Rights guarantees. But the most likely candidate for Supreme Court review is a total ban on all handguns such as the ban enacted by the Village of Morton Grove, Illinois, in 1981, and which the Court declined to review in 1983. The passage of similar legislation around the country and the litigation that will ensue may eventually ripen the issue for Supreme Court review.

In New York City, which requires burdensome licensing procedures for the possession of arms, it is common knowledge that licenses to carry handguns are usually not granted except to the rich and the well-connected. Massachusetts requires a firearm identification card or license to possess any type of arm, including a BB gun. One who illegally carries a handgun on his person or under his control in a vehicle risks a *mandatory* sentence of one-year imprisonment (a sentence not required for manslaughter), while anyone who merely possesses a shotgun with a barrel of less than eighteen inches, a harmless act in itself, may receive life imprisonment.[17] And in the District of Columbia, no person may possess a handgun not registered as of February 5, 1977. All guns, except those at a place of business, must be disassembled or locked, thereby preventing the protection of a family at home; and any arm that may fire over twelve shots without reloading, including common boyhood-type .22 caliber rifles, is considered a machine gun.[18] Some other states and localities require identification cards for possession of firearms, limit the number of firearms an individual may possess, define BB guns as "guns" in the normal sense (and thereby prohibit their possession by minors and felons), and/or prohibit sale of blank guns used for track and other sporting events.

The objective of this study is to provide a broad jurisprudential view of the right to keep and bear arms, and it will begin with a review of some of the important philosophical influences on the Founding Fathers, followed by an analysis of the English political theory and constitutional and common law regarding the right to possess arms. The theory and praxis of the American Revolution and the debate over the adoption of the Constitution illuminate the concept of the armed people. Next, the development of the right to keep and bear arms in the nineteenth century is assessed through an investigation of antebellum state cases, the experiences of the War between the States and Reconstruction—as expressed in the congressional debates over the Fourteenth Amendment and civil rights legislation—and a review of nineteenth-century U.S. Supreme Court cases that discussed the Second Amendment. In examining twentieth-century thought concerning the nature of the individual right, if any, to have firearms, the study proceeds to investigate state and federal court opinions decided both before and after *United States* v. *Miller* (1939),[19] the meaning of the *Miller* case itself, and federal cases since the federal gun-control legislation of 1968. A critical analysis of judicial policy and logic, as well as of the future of the right to keep and bear arms, concludes the study.

1

The Elementary Books of Public Right

The right of the citizen to keep arms has roots deep in history. The American Revolution was sparked at Lexington and Concord, and in Virginia, by British attempts to disarm the individual and hence the militia. Thomas Jefferson once wrote that the authority of the Declaration of Independence rested "on the harmonizing sentiments of the day, whether expressed in conversation, in letters, printed essays, or in the elementary books of public right, as Aristotle, Cicero, Locke, Sidney, & c."[1] These sentiments, which attacked standing mercenary armies and vindicated the use of armed force to oppose tyranny, were also reflected in the Bill of Rights and indeed provide a jurisprudential commentary thereon.[2] Aristotle, Cicero, John Locke, and Algernon Sidney provided the philosophical justification of the armed sovereignty of the populace. On the other hand, Plato, Jean Bodin, Thomas Hobbes, and Sir Robert Filmer set forth the classical argument in favor of monarchial absolutism. Also among the "elementary books of public right" referred to by Jefferson were the works of Niccolò Machiavelli and James Harrington, whose analyses of the Roman republic and strategy of popular freedom clearly influenced the Whigs of 1688 and 1776; and of Jean Jacques Rousseau, the intellectual harbinger of the French Revolution. Montesquieu, Beccaria, Burgh, and Adam Smith were influential in the areas of legal theory, criminology, and political economy.

While relying to a great extent on Cicero, "the greatest orator, statesman, and philosopher of Rome"[3] (in the words of John Adams), the founders of this nation based their thinking on the role of the Roman militia in great measure on Machiavelli. Machiavelli's influence was clear in George Mason's speech to the Fairfax Independent Militia Company,[4] which was composed of volunteers who supplied their own arms and elected their own officers. When, according to Mason, the "essential maxims" of the Roman commonwealth were undermined, "their army no longer considered themselves the soldiers of the Republic, but as the troops of Marius or Sylla, of Pompey or of Caesar of Marc Antony or of Octavius."[5] John Adams praised

Machiavelli for his constitutional model for Florence (which included a popular militia) wherein "the sovereign power is lodged, both of right and in fact, in the citizens themselves."[6] Considering such influences, it is no wonder that the Second Amendment "affirms the relation between a popular militia and popular freedom in language directly descended from that of Machiavelli. . . ."[7]

For constitutional principles of government, the founders of our republic relied most on the seventeenth-century English republicans, who themselves had been deeply influenced by Aristotle, Cicero, and Machiavelli. Jefferson saw to it that Locke and Sidney would be required reading at the University of Virginia, for "as to the general principles of liberty and the rights of man, in nature and in society, the doctrines of Locke, in his 'Essay concerning the true original extent and end of civil government', and of Sidney in his 'Discourses on Government', may be considered as those generally approved by your fellow citizens of this, and the United States."[8] Relying on Locke to deny any governmental right to be absolutely arbitrary,[9] Samuel Adams related: "Mr. Locke has often been quoted in the present dispute between Britain and her colonies, and very much to our purpose."[10] Like the Declaration of Independence, the Virginia Declaration of Rights of 1776, written by George Mason, contains specific phrases from Locke as well as from *Cato's Letters*.[11] The same philosophers appeared in the last will and testament of Josiah Quincy, Jr. who left "to my son when he shall arrive to the age of fifteen years, Algernon Sidney's works, John Locke's works, . . . and *Cato's Letters*. May the spirit of liberty rest upon him!"[12]

In summary, the two categorical imperatives of the Second Amendment—that a militia of the body of the people is necessary to guarantee a free state and that all of the people all of the time (not just when called for organized militia duty) have a right to keep arms—derive from the classical philosophical texts concerning the experiences of ancient Greece and Rome and seventeenth-century England. Aristotle, Cicero, Machiavelli, and the English Whigs provided an armed populace with the philosophical vindication to counter oppression, which found expression in the Declaration of Independence and the Bill of Rights. In this sense, the people's right to have their own arms was based on the philosophical and political writings of the greatest intellectuals of the past two thousand years.

An appreciation of the significance of these elementary books of public right is indispensable to a correct understanding of the meaning of the Bill of Rights, in general, and of the Second Amendment, in particular. Furthermore, an understanding of the authoritarian absolutism of Plato, Bodin, Hobbes,[13] and Filmer is as necessary as an understanding of classical libertarian republicanism in order to know what America's founders rejected as well as what they accepted. Those who drafted and supported the Bill of Rights followed the libertarian tradition of Aristotle, Cicero, and Sidney, and they rejected the authoritarian, if not totalitarian, tradition of Plato, Caesar, and Filmer. These two basic traditions in political philosophy have consistently enunciated opposing approaches to the question of people and arms, with the authoritarians rejecting the idea of an armed populace in favor of a helpless and obedient populace and the libertarian republicans accepting the armed populace and limiting the government by the consent of that armed populace.

The Citizen as Arms Bearer
in Greek Polity:
Plato and Aristotle

Speaking as Socrates in the *Republic*, Plato provided a comprehensive analysis of the social and political consequences of individual ownership of arms versus a state monopoly of arms. To refute the definition of justice as fulfilling promises and paying debts, Socrates suggested, in a counterexample, that one ought not "to return a deposit of arms or of any thing else to one who asks for it when he is not in his right senses; and yet a deposit cannot be denied to be a debt."[14] Since the return should not be made to one "not in his right mind," repayment of a debt was not necessarily justice because "a friend ought always to do good to a friend and never evil."[15] By implication, individual possession of weapons by sane individuals was ethically acceptable to Socrates. Yet Socrates's own definition of justice as the fulfillment of one's proper function—at least as propounded by the more conservative Plato—rejected as degenerate the egalitarian democracy that an armed populace would predictably instate.[16]

An essential element of Plato's explanation of political transformation in the *Republic* related to the tendencies of the unjust state to win privilege through "armed force" and of the "armed multitude" to abolish the unjust state in question. According to Plato, oligarchy arises when privilege based on wealth is fixed by statute. "This measure is carried through by armed force, unless they have already set up their constitution by terrorism." The abuse resulting from the state monopoly of violence leads to a disunited state wherein the rich and poor continuously plot against each other. If a war with outside forces arises, the oligarchs are faced with the following dilemma: "Either they must call out the common people or not. If they do, they will have more to fear from the armed multitude than from the enemy; and if they do not, in the day of battle these oligarchs will find themselves only too literally a government of the few."[17]

The development of an oligarchy into a democracy requires that the common people be armed. Former members of the ruling class who lose their wealth and power "long for a revolution; . . . these drones are armed and can sting."[18] Finally, "whether by force of arms or because the other party is terrorized into giving way," the poor majority overcomes and establishes a democracy which grants the people "an equal share in civil rights and government. . . . Liberty and free speech are rife everywhere; anyone is allowed to do what he likes."[19] While Plato attacks democracy for exhibiting characteristics which today would be considered laudable, some of his remarks are nevertheless directed against a social order that retains political inequality and therefore cannot be considered a complete democracy. Thus, after the old oligarchy is replaced by a society progressing toward democracy, a strong leader arises who "begins stirring up one war after another,[20] in order that the people may feel their need of a leader, and also be so impoverished by taxation that they will be forced to think of nothing but winning their daily bread, instead of plotting against him."[21] Finally, the despot wins complete victory by reestablishing the state monopoly of arms:

> Then, to be sure, the people will learn what sort of a creature it has bred and nursed to greatness in its bosom, until now the child is too strong for the parent to drive out.
> Do you mean that the despot will dare to lay hands on this father of his and beat him if he resists?
> Yes, when once he has disarmed him.[22]

While Plato portrays tyranny as the ultimate degeneration of the state, his ideal state—the reign of the philosopher king—actually resembles tyranny. Both despotism and the ideal monarchy involve rule by one person, with the only difference being the alleged good intentions of the ideal monarch—a dubious check on despotism. Plato himself suggested that a young, educated despot may become the philosopher king.[23] After attacking the democratic ideal where "one man is trader, legislator, and warrior all in one,"[24] Plato devised a normative social structure with the ruling philosophers at the top, the soldier auxiliaries in the middle, and the working masses at the bottom. This pyramid sets the royal elite over the professional warriors and requires the "inferior multitude" to "mind their own business."[25] The stage is thereby set for a tyranny, having monopolized the means of force, to exploit the majority.[26]

Plato's practical proposals for totalitarianism are set forth in the *Laws*, which anticipates a state of just over five thousand citizens plus numerous slaves.[27] While at one point designating warriors as a specialized class,[28] Plato elsewhere anticipates that the Director of Children and other instructors will discipline all girls, boys, women, and men with compulsory military exercises.[29] In discussing the Pyrrhic (war-dance), pankration (fighting with hands and feet), and armed contests, Plato would mandate that "the techniques of fighting" are "skills which all citizens, male and female, must take care to acquire."[30] While the possession by the citizens of martial skills would suggest a mode for some form of popular control, the overwhelming power of the Guardians of the Laws would provide for state domination over every aspect of life. Unlike Aristotle, Plato nowhere hints that the citizens would have their own arms. Instead, arms seem to be placed in the citizen's hands only for the temporary purpose of military exercise once per month.[31]

While failing to foresee that martial arts learned by the citizens may contribute to the protection of popular liberty, the *Laws* insists that "freedom from control must be uncompromisingly eliminated from the life of all men . . . ." By following the militarist examples of Sparta and Crete rather than the freer civilization of Athens, Plato hopes that "no one, man or woman, must ever be left without someone in charge of him; nobody must get into the habit of acting above and independently, either in sham fighting or the real thing, and in peace and war alike we must give our constant attention and obedience to our leader. . . ."[32] Rather than use their arms to protect their interests against the despotism, the people may use arms solely at the state's command: "Everyone is to have the same friends and enemies as the state."[33] In sum, in the *Laws*, as in the *Republic*, Plato advocates an authoritarian state wherein arms and people function solely as grist for the ruling elite.

In the *Politics*, Aristotle critically analyzes the elitist, authoritarian regime advocated by Plato. As opposed to the strict division between rulers, warriors, and workers in the Socratic dialogue, Aristotle's concept of polity included a large middle class in which each citizen fulfilled all three functions of self-legislation, arms bearing, and working. According to Aristotle, "there are many things which Socrates left undetermined; are farmers and craftsmen to have no share in government . . .? Are they or are they not to possess arms . . .?"[34] In accord with his broad philosophical ideal of the golden mean, Aristotle expresses a keen awareness of the true basis of political equality: "The whole constitutional set-up is intended to be neither democracy nor oligarchy but mid-way between the two—what is sometimes called 'polity,' *the members of which are those who bear arms.*"[35] Aristotle proceeded to attack again the constitution of Plato's *Laws* because, despite its suffrage, it was oligarchical—and one of its salient features was a disarmed populace.

Aristotle found the monopolization of arms bearing in the hands of one class to be an objectionable feature of the "Best State" advocated by Hippodamus. "Hippodamus planned a city with a population of ten thousand, divided into three parts, one of skilled workers, one of agriculturalists, and a third to bear arms and secure defense."[36] The legal restriction of arms bearing to a given class entrusted with defense would lead to oppression by that class: "the farmers have no arms, the workers have neither land nor arms;

this makes them virtually the servants of those who do possess arms. In these circumstances the equal sharing of offices and honours becomes an impossibility."[37] The possession of arms is a requisite for true citizenship and participation in the polity, but since "those who possess arms must be superior in power to both the other sections," the constitution proposed by Hippodamus would breed inequality and discontent.[38]

In analyzing the elusive concept of the constitutional kingship, Aristotle commented on its opposite, tyranny, which was founded on a professional standing army. Thus, "a king's bodyguard is composed of citizens carrying arms, a tyrant's of foreign mercenaries."[39] The citizens protect the king, but they need protection from the tyrant. Even the armed force of the monarch must not be "strong enough to overpower . . . the whole population."[40]

Since all true citizens possess arms, the arms bearers are not limited to those who defend the state in war. Just after referring to "the class which will defend in time of war,"[41] Aristotle declares that "it is quite normal for the same persons to be found bearing arms and tilling the soil."[42] By contrast, "oligarchial devices" exist in "regulations . . . made about carrying arms" to the effect that "it is lawful for the poor not to possess arms; the rich are fined if they do not have them." Since arms were essential to the polity for full participation, "in principle citizenship ought to be reserved for those who can afford to carry arms."[43] Yet Aristotle immediately went on to recognize the ill treatment of the poor that would result from such a property qualification. In a polity, each citizen is to possess his own arms, which are not supplied or owned by the state.

As Plato had perceived in the *Republic*, Aristotle also saw that a prerequisite to the transition from an oligarchy to a popular constitution is the arming of the people, who would overpower the oligarch's troops.[44] Furthermore, tyranny derives from the oligarchy's "mistrust of the people; hence they deprive them of arms, ill-treat the lower class, and keep them from residing in the capital. These are common to oligarchy and tyranny."[45] War, taxation, and public works keep the people poor and preoccupied, perpetuating the power of the tyrant. "It is also in the interests of a tyrant to keep his subjects poor, so that they may not be able to afford the cost of protecting themselves by arms and be so occupied with their daily tasks that they have no time for rebellion."[46]

While recognizing the political implications of material factors, including territory and military technology, Aristotle contended that conditions promoting the use of cavalry and hoplites would result in an oligarchy because of the high costs of horses and heavy armor. "But the light-armed infantry and service in ships are democratic. And so in practice, wherever these form a large proportion of the population, the oligarchs, if there is a struggle, fight at a disadvantage."[47] The possession of light arms by the people allows them to overcome oligarchy: "It is by the use of light infantry in civil wars that the masses get the better of the rich; their mobility and light equipment give them an advantage over cavalry and the heavy-armed."[48]

Every city requires food, tools, and arms. "Arms are included because members of the constitution must carry them even among themselves, both for internal government in the event of civil disobedience and to repel external aggression."[49] In polity and democracy—in contrast with oligarchy and tyranny— the members of the constitution are many and all have arms. Whether they comprise the few or the many, those with arms are sovereign: "For those who possess and can wield arms are in a position to decide whether the constitution is to continue or not."[50] Because no free man submits to a tyrant and since rule without consent is neither rightful nor legal,[51] Aristotle deemed arms possession a requisite to obtain or to maintain the status of being a freeman and citizen.

In the *Athenian Constitution*, Aristotle described the manner in which Peisistratus seized power by force and set up a tyranny by disarming the Athenians. Sent into exile for establishing a tyranny, Peisistratus hired soldiers and returned.

> Winning the battle of Pallenis, he seized the government and disarmed the people; and now he held the tyranny firmly, and he took Naxos and appointed Lygdamis ruler. The way in which he disarmed the people was this: he held an armed muster at the Temple of Theseus, and began to hold an Assembly, but he lowered his voice a little, and when they said they could not hear him, he told them to come up to the forecourt of the Acropolis, in order that his voice might carry better; and while he used up time making a speech, the men told off for this purpose gathered up the arms,[52] locked them up in the neighbouring buildings of the Temple of Theseus, and came and informed Peisistratus.[53]

Peisistratus then told the people that henceforth only he would manage public affairs.

Peisistratus was tyrant for almost two decades and was succeeded by his sons, Hippias and Hipparchus. After Hipparchus was killed in a procession, Hippias resorted to torture and execution. "But the current story that Hippias made the people in the procession fall out away from their arms and searched for those that retained their daggers is not true, for in those days they did not walk in the procession armed, but this custom was instituted later by the democracy."[54] In short, the Athenians were disarmed under tyranny and armed under democracy.

Aristotle also described the similar methods resorted to by the Thirty Tyrants to perpetuate their power. Under their rule, only three thousand persons who favored the tyranny qualified for citizenship. Opposition naturally arose from the majority of the people deprived of citizenship. The multitude found an able spokesman in Theramenes, who the Thirty feared would lead the people to destroy the oligarchy.[55] After losing an expedition against armed exiles, the Thirty "decided to disarm the others and to destroy Theramenes," in part by giving themselves "absolute powers to execute any citizens not members of the roll of Three Thousand. . . ."[56] "Theramenes having been put out of the way, they disarmed everybody except the Three Thousand, and in the rest of their proceedings went much further in the direction of cruelty and rascality."[57] The Thirty eventually met a violent end due to the success of the armed refugees.

In sum, in the theory and praxis of Athenian politics as expounded by Plato and Aristotle, an armed populace means polity and direct democracy, while a disarmed populace is the essential element of oligarchy and tyranny. Moreover, Aristotle's concept of individual autonomy through personal arms in a polity may be viewed in light of the nature which impels mankind to develop and possess defensive weapons. This natural tendency, according to his account in *Parts of Animals*, stems from the human's anatomy:

> Now it must be wrong to say, as some do, that the structure of man is not good, in fact, that it is worse than that of any other animal. Their grounds are: that man is barefoot, unclothed, and void of any weapon of force. Against this we may say that all the other animals have just one method of defence and cannot change it for another: they are forced to sleep and perform all their actions with their shoes on the whole time, as one might say; they can never take off this defensive equipment of theirs, nor can they change their weapon, whatever it may be. For man, on the other hand, many means of defence are available, and he can change them at any time, and above all he can choose what weapon he will have and where. Take the hand: this is as good as a talon, or a claw, or a horn, or again, a spear or a sword, or any other weapon or tool: it can be all of these, because it can seize and hold them all. And Nature has admirably contrived the actual shape of the hand so as to fit in with this arrangement.[58]

From Republic to Empire in Rome:
Cicero versus Caesar

Roman philosophy and history embodied significant lessons concerning the social and political characteristics of armed and disarmed populaces. On the one hand, Roman citizenship, particularly during the republican epoch, included a right to keep and bear arms for individual or collective self-defense. On the other hand, aggression against both "barbarians" and Roman citizens by Roman tyrants and empire builders was coupled with the policy of disarming and then eliminating their opponents.

The use of deception to disarm the populace to be conquered was a technique that early Roman aggressors learned well from Greek tyrants. Tullus Hostilius, the third Roman king, entered Alba under false pretenses, with the intention of razing the city to its foundations. According to Dionysius of Halicarnassus, he "ordered all the [Alban] troops to come to an assembly after first laying aside their arms."[59] Roman troops, "swords concealed under their garments," surrounded the Albans, who were informed by Tullus that the city would be destroyed. "Upon this, a tumult arose in the assembly and, some of them rushing to arms, those who surrounded the multitude, upon a given signal, held up their swords."[60] Opponents were then slain and the city razed.

The institution of an armed populace, whose members would provide and keep their own arms, was initiated by Servius Tullius, the sixth Roman king. "Formerly the right to bear arms had belonged solely to the patricians. Now plebeians were given a place in the army, which was to be reclassified according to every man's property, i.e., his ability to *provide himself* a more or less complete equipment for the field."[61] According to Livy, all the citizens "capable of bearing arms" registered in a census,[62] and "these men were required to provide" their own swords, spears, and other armor.[63] In *De Re Publica*, Cicero relates that Servius organized a "large group of knights from the main body of the people" and that "the rest of the population" was divided into centuries.[64] Thus, even before the overthrow of the monarchy and the establishment of the republic, the right to keep and bear arms belonged to patrician and plebeian alike.

Marcus Tullius Cicero, the great philosopher, senator, and lawyer, set forth the most complete discussion in the Roman republican tradition of the natural right to have and use arms for public defense against tyranny and for private defense against attack. By contrast, the connection between standing armies, the disarmament of peoples, and foreign and domestic tyranny is well exemplified in the writings of Julius Caesar. Analysis in a chronological context of the orations and philosophical writings of Cicero, and secondarily of Caesar's account of the Gallic and civil wars, demonstrates the identification of the armed citizen with the Roman republic and of the standing army with the empire.

Cicero delivered two orations involving arms in the turbulent year 63 B.C. First, he defended Gauis Rabirius, who was prosecuted for the murder of Lucius Appuleius Santurnius. Saturninus was an ally of Gaius Marius, who replaced Rome's citizen army with mercenaries and was an uncle and political teacher of Caesar.[65] Saturnius was killed in 100 B.C. for attempting a coup d'etat to destroy the Roman constitution. Now, forty years later, Caesar instigated the prosecution of Rabirius for murder, and Cicero acted as defense counsel.

While he had not killed Saturninus, like many other citizens "Rabirius took up arms with the intention of killing Saturninus." Yet neither the attempt nor the fatal act against the would-be tyrant was unlawful:

> For there is surely no difference between the man who kills and the man who takes up arms for the purpose of killing. If it was a crime to kill Saturninus, then to take up arms against him could not fail to be a crime as well. But if you agree that the taking up of arms was lawful, then you are obliged to agree that the killing was lawful as well.[66]

To counter the forces of Saturninus, the consuls

> ordered every citizen who had the welfare of the state at heart to take up arms and follow their lead. Everyone obeyed. Weapons were taken from the temples and the public arsenals, and Gaius Marius distributed them among the populace.[67]

Interestingly, Saturninus had originally depended on the backing of Gaius Marius and his mercenaries.

After Saturninus had seized the capitol, "every single other Roman citizen who existed . . . proceeded to take up arms in the same cause."[68] Many noteworthy individuals "armed themselves to protect our country in its peril,"[69] and men of all ranks "took up arms to defend the freedom of every one of us."[70]

The prosecution of Rabirius was eventually stopped, but Cicero applied similar principles in another oration, during the same year, against Lucius Sergius Catilina. Catilina had also sought to abolish the republic. Cicero personally had assembled forces and bodyguards to protect the people and himself from Catilina.[71] For Cicero, having and using arms to protect the republic was honorable; thus, he praises "the courage to strike down a dangerous Roman citizen more fiercely even than they struck down the bitterest of foreign foes."[72] But having arms specifically to be used for assassination was criminal: "You were illegally carrying arms. You had got together a group determined to strike down the leading men of the state. . . ."[73]

In 53 B.C. Cicero again defended a fellow republican, Titus Annius Milo, on trial for murdering Publius Clodius Pulcher, a protégé of Caesar and Pompeius. Milo and Clodius were political enemies who, accompanied by some of their respective followers, clashed on the Appian Way. Rioting followed the death of Clodius. Pompeius used the disorder to strengthen his personal power, and Milo came to trial in a politically charged atmosphere.

Cicero argued that Milo's acts, viewed with both Roman law and natural law, were in self-defense and constituted justifiable homicide:

Besides, the Twelve Tables themselves ordained that a thief by night may be killed under any circumstances—and that he may be killed also by day if he attempts to defend himself with a weapon. That being so, it is impossible to argue that every act of homicide must necessarily deserve punishment, since in certain circumstances the laws themselves place a sword in our hands to inflict death upon our fellow-men.

There are, in fact, many occasions on which homicide is justifiable. In particular, when violence is needed in order to repel violence, such an act is not merely justified but unavoidable.[74]

Examples cited by Cicero to justify "the swords we carry" included the right to resist indecent assault by a military superior as much as by the bandit and brigand.[75]

Cicero proceeded to set forth an elaborate justification of the right to bear and use arms in individual self-defense:

> And indeed, gentlemen, there exists a law, not written down anywhere but inborn in our hearts; a law which comes to us not by training or custom or reading but by derivation and absorption and adoption from nature itself; a law which has come to us not from theory but from practice, not by instruction but by natural intuition. I refer to the law which lays it down that, if our lives are endangered by plots or violence or armed robbers or enemies, any and every method of protecting ourselves is morally right. When weapons reduce them to silence, the laws no longer expect one to await their pronouncements. For people who decide to wait for these will have to wait for justice, too—and meanwhile they must suffer injustice first. Indeed, even the wisdom of the law itself, by a sort of tacit implication, permits self-defence, because it does not actually forbid men to kill; what it does, instead, is to forbid the bearing of a weapon with the intention to kill. When, therefore, an inquiry passes beyond the mere question of the weapon and starts to consider the motive, a man who has used arms in self-defence is not regarded as having carried them with a homicidal aim.[76]

After tracing detail by detail the manner in which Clodius's followers had attacked Milo, Cicero again returned to a philosophical vindication of the right of self-defense and, by implication, the right to keep and bear arms. "Civilized people are taught by logic, barbarians by necessity, communities by tradition; and the lesson is inculcated even in wild beasts by nature itself. They learn that they have to defend their own bodies and persons and lives from violence of any and every kind by all the means within their power."[77] If one cannot kill a robber in self-defense, reasoned Cicero, then it would follow that the robber or, if he was unsuccessful, the court should kill the victim.[78] While the politically motivated court did in fact find Milo guilty, it exiled rather than executed him. Caesar carried out the latter punishment in the year that he crossed the Rubicon.

The crossing of the Rubicon in 49 B.C. was the symbolic result of the abolition by Gaius Marius of the citizen soldier, a tradition dating back to Servius Tullius, and its replacement by professional mercenaries. If Roman citizens lost interest in military service as policy became more imperialistic, the same cause made it possible for mercenaries to loot foreign lands. The demise of the citizen militiaman, who provided his own weapons, and the transition to the standing army heralded the end of the republic and liberty and the beginning of the institution of the empire and tyranny. In particular, Caesar's conquest of Gaul became the conquest of Rome.

Caesar's account of the Gallic wars contains numerous instances which buttress the obvious proposition that the deprivation of the right to bear arms is a requisite for conquest. Caesar recognized the difficulty in conquering an armed people. Among the Gauls, an armed convention "marks the beginning of a war; and by a general law all grown men are accustomed to assemble at it in arms. . . ."[79] "All men capable of bearing arms" would meet in one location.[80] When he defeated the Gauls, Caesar routinely received all arms and hostages— "all the arms were collected from the town";[81] "there could be no terms of surrender save on delivery of arms";[82] Caesar "cut off the hands of all who had borne arms";[83] and he "slew a great number of them and stripped all of their arms."[84]

The Roman senate belatedly concluded that the tyranny of Rome would be the result of the conquest of Gaul. It resolved "that Caesar should disband his army" or be considered a traitor to the republic.[85] However, it was too late. Caesar responded by illegally bringing his army across the Rubicon, thereby invoking, in his own words, "the declaration and decision of the senate by which the Roman people are called to arms. . . ."[86] In his account of the ensuing civil war, Caesar refers to the armed participation of the body of citizens and even slaves,[87] and to the levy or seizure of private persons and arms.[88]

Caesar consolidated his dictatorship by finally defeating the Pompeian forces in 45 B.C. However, Caesar himself was slain by the Roman senators a year later. Cicero's *De officiis*, a treatise on ethics, defended the killing of Caesar. Cicero referred to "that king who with the Roman People's army brought the Roman People themselves into subjection,"[89] justified tyrannicide,[90] and predicted that tyrants who rule by armed force are bound to be overthrown by those who seek freedom.[91]

The armed citizen was the last hope of the republic, according to Cicero's last orations in the senate, the *Philippics*, a series of orations directed against Marcus Antonius. According to Cicero, Antonius "is an enemy against whom arms have rightly been taken up."[92] In response to Antonius's threat to enter

Rome with his army, an illegal act, Cicero queried: "What did this mean but a threat to the Roman people of slavery?"[93] Antonius "should be compelled by arms."[94] Arguing against Calenus, Cicero asked: "do you call slavery peace? Our ancestors indeed took up arms not only to win freedom, but also empire; you think our arms should be thrown away to make us slaves. What juster reason is there for the waging of war than to repel slavery?"[95] Again, it "is for the liberty of the Roman people . . . they see they must struggle in arms."[96] This argument—"We are all of us carried along by a fiery zeal to recover our liberty; our arms cannot be wrested from our hands,"[97]—was a politico-military ideal but an inaccurate prediction, for both Cicero and the Roman republic, in part due to the inferiority of their arms, were killed within the year by Caesar's standing army.[98]

The year 43 B.C. marked the death of the republic and the end of the superiority of the armed citizenry over the standing army. However, the keeping of arms by individuals continued to be recognized as a natural and legal right of the Roman citizen under the empire. After having fought at Brutus's side at Philippi in 42 B.C., Horace expressed in poetic form what was actually a legal rule:

> But my pen will never jab without a provocation at anyone on earth, for it protects me like a sword kept in the sheath. Why should I ever pull it out if no criminal attacks me? Jupiter, Father and King, may my weapon stay unused and perish from rust, and no one injure me.[99]

At the turn of the eras, Ovid wrote: *"Armaque in armatos sumere iura sinunt"* ("The laws allow arms to be taken against an armed foe").[100] These words were to be repeated sixteen hundred years later in the definitive expression of the English common law.[101] And two centuries into the Christian era, the influential Ulpian repeated the provision of natural law that "one may repel arms with arms."[102]

The development of defensive arms were viewed through the Roman philosophy of nature as a part of the growth of civilization. The poet Lucretius mused: "Tilling of fields, walls, laws, and arms, and roads . . .—all these arts were learned by practice and the mind's experience, as men walked forward step by step."[103] And Galen, the distinguished physician, stated in his anatomical treatise completed in 165 A.D.:

> Now to man—for he is an intelligent animal and, alone of all creatures on earth, godlike—in place of any and every defensive weapon, [Nature] gave hands, instruments necessary for every art and useful in peace no less than in war. Hence he did not need horns as a natural endowment, since, whenever he desired, he could grasp in his hand a weapon better

than a horn; for certainly swords and spears are larger weapons than horns and better suited for inflicting wounds. Neither did he need hoofs, for clubs and rocks can crush more forcibly than any hoof. Furthermore, nothing can be accomplished with either horns or hoofs without coming to close quarters, but a man's weapons are effective at a distance as well as near by, javelins and darts excelling horns, and rocks and clubs excelling hoofs. . . . Such is the hand of man as an instrument of defense.[104]

Roman law reflected this philosophy of nature for centuries to come. The sixth century *Institutes* of Justinian reiterated the same rule of law previously enunciated as an established principle by Cicero in defense of Titus Annius Milo—that carrying or using arms in self-defense is justifiable, but "the bearing of a weapon with the intention to kill" is criminal.[105] The *Lex Cornelia de sicariis*, passed in 81 B.C.,[106] was still recognized as established law over six hundred years later in the *Institutes*, which state:

> The lex Cornelia on assassination pursues those persons, who commit this crime, with the sword of vengeance, and also all who *carry weapons for the purpose of homicide*. By a 'weapon', as is remarked by Gaius in his commentary on the statute of the Twelve Tables, is ordinarily meant some missile shot from a bow, but it also signifies anything thrown with the hand; so that stones and pieces of wood or iron are included in the term. *'Telum'*, in fact, or 'weapon', . . . means anything thrown to a distance . . . 'namely spears, bows and arrows, slings, and large numbers of stones.' *Sicarius*, or assassin, is derived from *sica*, a long steel knife.[107]

Justinian also referred to another ancient law: "The lex Julia, relating to public or private violence, deals with those persons who use force armed or unarmed."[108] The mainstay of the republic, the use of arms to ward off tyranny, declined with the rise of the empire. The increasing use of mercenaries and consequent helplessness of the populace in the face of attacks by the armed barbaric hordes would lead to the fall of Rome.

Machiavellian Interlude:
Freedom and the Popular Militia

In his most important work, *Discourses on the First Ten Books of Titus Livy* (1531), Niccolò Machiavelli treats at length the relation between arms and politics. In expressing his clear preference for republics over principalities, Machiavelli draws on the Roman experience to show that an armed populace has *virtù*, while a disarmed people is subject to the whims of *fortuna*. Princes tend to degenerate into tyrants, and throughout history "the masses, therefore,

. . . took up arms against the prince. . . ."[109] Although a large armed population such as the Roman plebs may be hard to control, an unarmed populace is
at the mercy of any attacker.[110] For defensive purposes, a people unaccus-
tomed to the use of arms is to be preferred over mercenaries; of the liberators
of Thebes, Machiavelli says, "such was their virtue that they did not hesitate
to put the populace under arms" to defeat the Spartans.[111]

Machiavelli praised the Roman senate for urging the Latins and the Hernici
to defend themselves, "because on other occasions the same senate had forbidden these people to arm in their own defense. . . ."[112] To uphold a republic or a kingdom, one must "arm oneself with one's own subjects. . . ."[113]
Thus, "the Romans encountered in all parts of the world, however small, a
combination of well-armed republics, extremely obstinate in the defense of
their liberty. . . ."[114] Under its sixth king, "There dwelt in Rome eighty
thousand men bearing arms," and later Rome "was able to put under arms
two hundred and eighty thousand men, whereas Sparta and Athens could
never muster twenty thousand each."[115] An armed populace is ideal for a
defensive war:

> For either I have my country well equipped with arms, as the Romans
> had and the Swiss have; or I have a country ill equipped with arms, as
> the Carthaginians had, and as have the king of France and the Italians
> today. In the latter case the enemy should be kept at a distance. . . .[116]
> But when states are strongly armed, as Rome was and the Swiss are,
> the more difficult it is to overcome them the nearer they are to their
> homes: for such bodies can bring more forces together to resist attack
> than they can to attack others. . . . In attacking a foreign country, [the
> Romans] never sent out armies of more than fifty thousand men; but for
> home defense they put under arms against the Gauls after the first Punic
> war eighteen hundred thousand.[117]
> In conclusion, therefore, I say again that a ruler who has his people
> well armed and equipped for war, should always wait at home to wage
> war. . . .[118]

Machiavelli blamed the foreigners' subjugation of Italy on the princes who
neglected the militia, which lost official status and became independent. "It
occurred to the militia that their reputation would be made if they had the
armed forces while the rulers had none."[119] Here Machiavelli separates the
militia from the rulers and advocates a strong militia to liberate Italy.

Although rulers built fortresses, in part due to fear of their own subjects,
the people would nonetheless rebel. "For if you reduce them to poverty,
'though despoiled, they still have arms', and, if you disarm them, 'their fury
will provide them with arms.' "[120] Still, Machiavelli refers to the Florentines,
Venetians, and French as people forced to pay tribute and despoiled by their

rulers: "This all comes from depriving the people of arms. . . ."[121] "Such are the inconveniences, then, that arise from depriving your people of arms . . . . For he who lives in the aforesaid way treats ill the subjects who reside within his domain. . . ."[122]

According to Machiavelli, Caesar had destroyed the liberty of the Roman republic by engaging in conquests and developing a standing army of professionals.[123] No longer could the populace check the empire's power by refusing to enlist for the wars,[124] and the slavery imposed abroad prompted slavery at home. The demise of the armed citizen meant the end of civic virtue and with it the end of the people's control over their destiny:

> If a city be armed and disciplined as Rome was, and all its citizens, alike in their private and official capacity, have a chance to put alike their virtue and the power of fortune to the test of experience, it will be found that always and in all circumstances they will be of the same mind and will maintain their dignity in the same way. But, when they are not familiar with arms and merely trust to the whim of fortune, not to their own virtue, they will change with the changes of fortune. . . .[125]

As an advocate of a popular militia instead of a professional standing army, Machiavelli was particularly qualified to examine the subject in *The Art of War* (1521), for he had successfully organized and led a citizen militia in the early sixteenth century. In praising the Roman republican example of part-time common soldiers, who "entered voluntarily into the service," while working in other occupations, Machiavelli lauds "the important privilege accorded Roman citizens of not being forced into the army against their will."[126] The demise of the republic was also the demise of the armed populace: "For Augustus, and after him Tiberius, more interested in establishing and increasing their own power than in promoting the public good, began to disarm the Roman people (in order to make them more passive under their tyranny) and to keep the same armies continually on foot within the confines of the Empire."[127] Similarly, the Venetians employed foreign troops "to prevent any of their own citizens from staging a coup," while the French king "disarmed all his subjects in order to rule them more easily."[128]

Although some elements of conscription were included in Machiavelli's militia ordinance adopted by Florence in 1506,[129] he recognized that "compulsion makes men mutinous and discontented; but both experience and courage are acquired by arming, exercising, and disciplining men properly. . . ."[130] It is a "legally armed" citizenry which has kept governments "free and incorrupt." "Rome remained free for four hundred years and Sparta eight hundred, although their citizens were armed all that time; but many other states that have been disarmed have lost their liberties in less than forty years."[131] The danger was a potential tyrant who "has nobody to deal with but an unarmed and defenseless multitude";[132] thus, "tyranny and usurpation are not the result of arming the citizens,"[133] but arise in part from the failure to arm them.

Machiavelli's argument was that "a state ought to depend upon only those troops composed of its own subjects; that those subjects cannot be better raised than by a citizens' militia. . . ." Possession by the citizens of their own weapons provided a sure response to any danger. "If you ever read the institutions established by the first kings of Rome, particularly by Servius Tullius, you must remember that the *classi* he formed were the basis of a citizens' militia which might be quickly raised at any sudden emergency for the defense of the state."[134] Servius "divided the Romans into six classes. . . . The class to which a citizen belonged determined the kind of *weapon he would furnish*, and hence his particular military role."[135]

All men capable of bearing arms would be armed and exercised, but militiamen would continue to follow their usual occupations and hold maneuvers only on holidays.[136] Private citizens bearing their own arms constituted the "regular and well-ordered militia [without which] people cannot live in security."[137] Machiavelli rejected the argument that an armed people would create tumults: "For men who are well disciplined will always be as cautious of violating the laws when they have arms in their hands as when they have not. . . ." The institution of the militia transforms factions who "may have arms and leaders of their own" into a unified people.[138] Promoting civic education by arming everyone, the militia would be kept nonaggressive by maintaining power in its members rather than in their leaders:

So that by establishing a good and well-ordered militia, divisions are extinguished, peace restored, and some people who were unarmed and dispirited, but united, continue in union and become warlike and courageous; others who were brave and had arms in their hands, but were previously given to faction and discord, become united and turn against the enemies of their country those arms and that courage which they used to exert against each other.

But to prevent a militia from injuring others or overturning the laws and liberties of its country (which can only be effected by the power and iniquity of the commanders), it is necessary to take care that the commanders do not acquire too great an authority over their men.[139]

Living during a time when firearms appeared on the scene, Machiavelli commented on the utility of the new weaponry. In addition to pikes and broadswords, infantrymen "also have harquebusiers among them, instead of the slingers and bowmen employed by the ancients."[140] The harquebusier was a rather short matchlock shoulder arm. "These arms and this sort of armor were invented and are still used by the Germans, particularly by the Swiss;

since they are poor, yet anxious to defend their liberties against the ambition of the German princes—who are rich and can afford to keep cavalry. . . ."[141] For infantry exercises, Machiavelli recommended physical conditioning "and using the crossbow, longbow, and harquebus—the last, you know, is a new, but very useful weapon. To these exercises I would accustom all the youth in the country. . . ."[142] Machiavelli added that "every inhabitant" would declare the class in which he would enroll, depending on the type of weapon he preferred.[143]

In *The Prince* (1532) Machiavelli explicitly analyzed the relation between an armed people and freedom in these terms:

> [A]n armed republic submits less easily to the rule of one of its citizens than a republic armed by foreign forces.
> Rome and Sparta were for many centuries well armed and free. The Swiss are well armed and enjoy great freedom.[144]
> Among other evils caused by being disarmed, it renders you contemptible. . . . [It] is not reasonable to suppose that one who is armed will obey willingly one who is unarmed; or that any unarmed man will remain safe among armed servants.[145]

This realist position cogently applied to an unarmed people and an armed state, which would thereby not long remain a "servant" of the people. Thus, the wise prince should permit his subjects to be armed. "But when you disarm them, you commence to offend them and show that you distrust them either through cowardice or lack of confidence, and both of these opinions generate hatred against you."[146] On the other hand, Machiavelli advised the imperialist ruler that a conquered state should be disarmed.[147] Still, "the best fortress is to be found in the love of the people, for although you may have fortresses they will not save you if you are hated by the people. Then once the people have taken up arms against you, there will never be lacking foreigners to assist them."[148] Revolutionaries from Cromwell to Jefferson heeded Machiavelli's maxim that "all armed prophets have conquered and unarmed ones failed."[149] In the final analysis, states are founded on "good laws and good arms. . . . [T]here cannot be good laws where there are not good arms. . . ."[150]

Absolutism Versus Republicanism in the Seventeenth Century

Seventeenth-century absolutism found an able defender in Jean Bodin, whose *Six Bookes of a Commonweale* (1606) provided intellectual swords for the monarchists Sir Robert Filmer and Thomas Hobbes and a target for republicans Algernon Sidney and John Locke. Bodin saw deprivation of arms among the lower classes as necessary to maintain the feudal status quo. Early in the *Six Bookes,* Bodin recognizes the connection between slavery and the monopolization of arms by the ruling class: "Now this fear that Cities and Commonweales had of their slaves, was the cause that they never durst suffer them to bear arms, or to be enrolled in their musters, and that upon pain of death. . . ."[151]

The fact that the ruler was not subject to the law was for Bodin a principle especially pertinent to the prevention of revolution through weapons control. "But so sometimes things fall out, as that the law may be good, just, and reasonable, and yet the prince to be no way subject or bound thereto: as if he should forbid all his subjects, except his guard and garrison soldiers, upon pain of death to carry weapons, so to take away the fears of murders and seditions; he in this case ought not to be subject to his own law, but to the contrary, to be well armed for the defense of the good, and punishment of the evil."[152] For Bodin, "good" meant the perpetuation of absolutism, and "evil" meant, in part, popular sovereignty.

The *Six Bookes* devoted much attention to preventing seditions, which Bodin attributed to the possession of arms by commoners and to free speech by orators. Simply put, Bodin trusted rulers, but not the ruled, with arms, as if rulers were inherently morally superior. His object was to prevent "sedition", that is, the liberation of the people from absolute rulers. "Another and the most visual way to prevent sedition, is to take away the subjects arms: howbeit that the princes of Italy, and of the East cannot endure that they should at all have arms; as do the people of the North and the West. . . ."[153] The practice of wearing a sword in peacetime, "which by our laws, as also by the manners and customs of the Germans and Englishmen is not only lawful; but by the laws and decrees of the Swiss even necessarily commanded: the cause of an infinite number of murders, he which weareth a sword, a dagger, or a pistol. . . ." While ignoring the more numerous homicides caused by rulers as well as the use of arms for self-defense,[154] Bodin appears to exaggerate those murders committed by commoners. "The Turks herein go yet farther, not only in punishing with all severity the seditious and mutinous people, but also by forbidding them to bear arms. . . ."[155] In these words Bodin praises one of history's worst despotisms.

The absolute ruler, according to Bodin, must be prepared to deprive the subject of arms and ideas in order to prevent social change. "But beside the causes of seditions and rebellions, which we have before spoken of, there is yet another, which dependeth on the immoderate liberty of speech given to orators, who direct and guide the peoples hearts and minds according to their own pleasure."[156] Using several historical examples to show how arms and speech had "translated the sovereignty from the nobility into the people, and changed the Aristocracy into a Democratic or Popular estate," Bodin complained that "we have seen all Germany in arms . . . after that the mutinous preachers had stirred up the people against the nobility."[157] Bodin clearly recognized that the spread of arms and ideas among the general population would doom monarchial absolutism.

Bodin devotes considerable attention to the issue of whether subjects should be trained in arms for purposes of foreign wars. In referring to the bloodshed inflicted by soldiers, Bodin pacifically states that "I see no reason why we should instruct citizens in this cruel and execrable kind of life, or to arm them. . . ."[158] Elsewhere, Bodin curiously alludes to the necessity of foreign wars for defense and offense, as well as to prevent civil war, and asserts that "it is needful to accustom the subjects to arms. . . ."[159] While all Romans were bound to bear arms,[160] Bodin sees such military discipline as a form of social control rather than a tool of popular rule as long as foreign enemies exist or are invented.[161] Yet for war Bodin favored a specialized army. He followed the Egyptians and Plato in arguing that it should be illegal for most subjects "to use and bear arms"[162] and that society should be divided into distinct classes with only the few trained to use arms.[163]

While failing to be concerned that a disarmed populace may be vanquished by its rulers, Bodin conceded that conquerors "disarm the vanquished." "For we may not think ever to keep that people in subjection which hath always lived in liberty, if they be not disarmed."[164]

A more liberal version of the rights of individuals was represented by Hugo Grotius, whose *On the Law of War and Peace* (1625) justified armed force, whether carried out solely for defense by persons or by states. Relying extensively on the republican classics, Grotius upholds, early in this work, the natural character of using weapons to preserve life and limb:

> for all animals are provided by nature with means for the very purpose of self-defence. See Xenophon, Ovid, Horace, Lucretius. Galen observes that man is an animal born for peace and war, not born with weapons, but with hands by which weapons can be acquired. And we see infants, without teaching, use their hands for weapons. See Aristotle.[165]

Grotius relies on Aristotle for the proposition that "every one ought to use arms for himself, if he has received an injury, or to help relatives, benefactors, allies who are injured."[166] Also cited as authoritative are Cicero's oration for Milo, "in which he appeals to the testimony of nature for the right of self-defence,"[167] and Ovid's dictum, *"armaque in armotos sumere jura sinunt."*[168] To the argument that "none should wear arms," Grotius replied, "If the right of inflicting capital punishments, and of defending the citizens by arms against robbers and plunderers, was taken away, then would follow a vast license of crime and a deluge of evils. . . ."[169]

Bodin's considerable influence on the English proponents of monarchy is clear in Thomas Hobbes' *Leviathan* (1651) and Sir Robert Filmer's *Patriarcha* (1680). While, unlike Bodin, neither Filmer nor Hobbes specifically advocated the complete disarming of private individuals, both presuppose a state monopoly of the means of violence sufficient to maintain absolute power. In contrast to Filmer's naive theory of the divine right of kings,[170] Hobbes provided a considerably more sophisticated doctrine which conceded that in the final analysis each person must guarantee his own survival if the king fails to do so. Roughly equal mental and physical powers, and competition over the same objects of desire, according to Hobbes, led in a state of nature to "continuall feare, and danger of violent death; and the life of man, solitary, poore, nasty, brutish, and short."[171] This condition of war of all against all allegedly is done away with when there exists "a common Power to keep them all in awe,"[172] that is, a state supremacy of force. Yet Hobbes also recognized that the state only institutionalized at the national level the war of all against all: "Yet in all times, Kings, and Persons of Soveraigne authority, because of their Independency, are in continual jealousies, and in the state and posture of Gladiators; having their weapons pointing, and their eyes fixed on one another; that is, their Forts, Garrisons, and Guns upon the Frontiers of their Kingdomes. . . ."[173] The wars, genocide, and potential nuclear holocaust which characterize the twentieth century suggest that states cause lives to be nasty, brutish, and short, while such violent capacity is unknown in stateless societies.[174]

While he attacked Aristotle and Cicero for defending the right to overthrow tyranny by armed force, Hobbes nonetheless realistically concluded that each individual must ultimately be his own protector. The "summe of the Right of Nature" is, "by all means we can, to defend our selves."[175] "A man cannot lay down the right of resisting them, that assault him by force, to take away his life. . . ."[176] In short, the individual never actually allows the state to enjoy a complete monopoly of coercion; "when taking a journey, he arms himself . . . and this when he knows there bee Laws, and publike Officers, armed, to revenge all injuries shall bee done him. . . ."[177] Individuals never actually relinquish the right of armed self-defense. "A covenant not to defend my selfe from force, by force, is always voyd."[178] In discussing the commonwealth, Hobbes added that "Covenants, without the Sword, are but Words, and of no strength to secure a man at all."[179] Should the people disagree about whether a breach of the Covenant has occurred, "there is, in this case, no Judge to decide the controversie: it returns therefore to the Sword again; and every man recovereth the right of Protecting himself by his own strength. . . ."[180] Hobbes defends the right to protect oneself by any means necessary whenever a criminal or even the state threatens self-preservation. "For the right men have by Nature to protect themselves, when none else can protect them, can by no Covenant be relinquished."[181]

James Harrington went far beyond Hobbes in recognizing the right of the people not only to defend themselves but also to resist an oppressive monarchy. The decisive proponent of the armed freeholder, Harrington's mid-seventeenth-century discourses transmitted classical republicanism to the Whigs of 1688. "A commonwealth whose arms are in the hands of her servants,"[182]—the ideal of *Oceana,* Harrington's most enduring work—expressed the lessons of the English civil war.

In the *Prerogative of Popular Government,* Harrington held it "impossible that a party should come to overbalance the people, having their arms in their own hands."[183] A citizenry "trained up unto their arms, which they use not for the defense of slavery but of liberty," composes "the vastest body of a well disciplined militia that is possible in nature."[184] "Men accustomed unto their arms and their liberties will never endure the yoke."[185] The "distribution of arms" among the citizens prevents a monarch from overcoming a republic.[186] "The arms of the commonwealth are both numerous, and in posture of readiness, but they consist of her citizens," Harrington amplified in *The Art of Lawgiving.*[187]

John Locke's refutation of Filmer and Hobbes in his *Two Treatises on Civil Government* (1689) did not dispute Hobbes' concession that self-defense is a fundamental natural right. According to Locke, in the state of nature each individual is equal and independent, and the social contract must thus be based on the consent of each member of the political society. In being sovereign, the people may alter or abolish oppressive government, which obviously presupposes the means to do so. Each individual has an equal right to his own life, liberty, and property, and may defend his natural rights against any person or group, "it being reasonable and just I should have a right to destroy that which threatens me with destruction."[188] The initiation of force by an aggressor puts one in a state of war with another and justifies self-defense. "For quitting reason, which is the rule given between man and man, and using force, the way of beasts, he becomes liable to be destroyed by him he uses force against, as any savage ravenous beast that is dangerous to his being."[189]

The individual rights of independence, equality, and self-defense come from nature and antedate government, an institution with delegated power only and which may be resumed by the individuals in whom ultimate sovereignty resides. It could hardly be assumed that the people would voluntarily disarm themselves and permit themselves to be dictated to by a smaller body of armed men who compose the state; for life, liberty, and estate would be in greater peril from an unchecked and organized armed force than from disorganized individuals in the state of nature. Locke rejected the absolute arbitrary power of government stemming from a disarmed populace:

> It cannot be supposed that they should intend, had they a power so to do, to give to any one, or more, an absolute arbitrary power over their persons and estates, and put a force into the magistrate's hand to execute his unlimited will arbitrarily upon them. This were to put themselves into a worse condition than the state of nature, wherein they had a liberty to defend their right against the injuries of others and were upon equal terms of force to maintain it, whether invaded by a single man or many in combination. Whereas, by supposing they have given up themselves to the absolute power and will of a legislator, they have *disarmed themselves, and armed him, to make prey of them when he pleases*. . . . For then mankind will be in a far worse condition than in the state of nature, if they shall have armed one, or a few men, with the joint power of a multitude to force them to obey at pleasure the exorbitant and unlimited decrees of their sudden thoughts, or unrestrained, and, till that moment, unknown wills, without having any measures set down which may guide and justify their actions.[190]

Locke's primary contribution in the minds of the Englishmen of 1688 and the Americans of 1776 was his argument that tyranny may rightfully be resisted with arms in the same manner as private aggression. While "force is to be opposed to nothing but to unjust and unlawful force,"[191] private persons "have a right to defend themselves and recover by force what by unlawful force is taken from them. . . ."[192] One may kill an aggressor where there is insufficient time to appeal to law, for "the law could not restore life to my dead carcass."[193] Because they are illegal, tyranny and usurpation may be resisted by force, and governments founded thereon may be dissolved in the same manner that people may resist robbers or pirates.[194] As even the promonarchist Barclay conceded: "Self-defense is a part of the law of nature; nor can it be denied the community, even against the king himself."[195] It goes without saying that the rights of the people to resume delegated power, to return to the state of nature, and to set up new guards for their security presuppose their sovereignty in fact, that is, their condition of being armed.

Algernon Sidney's *Discourses Concerning Government* (published posthumously in 1698) was used as evidence against him in a trial for treason that resulted in his beheading by Charles II in 1683. Sidney boldly attacked royal absolutism and inspired the English and American republicans who spearheaded the revolutions of 1688 and 1776. Paralleling Locke's *Treatises of Civil Government*, Sidney's *Discourse* upheld the natural freedom of individuals, constitutional liberty, and the right to resist tyranny. Like Machiavelli, Sidney lauded the popular sovereignty of republican Rome based on an armed citizenry and deplored the seizure of power by Caesar and his corrupt standing army. Rome could never have reached its height "if the People had not been exercised in arms. . . . Such men as these were not to be used like Slaves, or oppressed by the unmerciful hand of Usurers."[196]

While the absolute monarch seeks to render his subjects powerless,[197] "in a popular or mixed Government every man is concerned," which means that everyone participates in politics and that "the body of the People is the public defense, and every man is armed and disciplined. . . ."[198] The entrustment of defense to "the body of the People"—a phrase which reappears in the Virginia Declaration of Rights (1776) and in similar works of America's founders—entailed "every man" being armed and disciplined in civic virtue. When every man among them had been armed, the Romans "had as many soldiers to fight for their Country as there were freemen in it."[199] Among the Greeks, "there was not a Citizen of *Athens* able to bear arms," who did not join in the defense against invasion.[200]

Sidney cites numerous examples to demonstrate that people "by the use of Arms" maintain their defense [201] and that "no numbers of men, though naturally valiant, are able to defend themselves, unless they be well arm'd, disciplin'd and conducted."[202] An armed populace may maintain its independence longest; the defeat of a mercenary army is decisive, but among an armed people "when one head is cut off, many rise up in the place of it."[203] An armed populace maintained the ancient liberty of the Italians, whose cities were conquered by the Romans only "when all those who were able to bear arms had been slain. . . ."[204] And the Spaniards who defended themselves against the Romans "generally kill'd themselves when they were master'd and disarm'd, *Nullam sine armis vitam esse rati.*"[205]

Only an armed people can maintain freedom from foreign invasion as well as from domestic tyranny. "Peace is seldom made, and never kept, unless the Subject retain such a Power in his hands, as may oblige the Prince to stand to what is agreed. . . ."[206] Seizure of supreme power by a tyrant justifies sedition. "The Laws which they overthrow can give them no protection; and every man is a soldier against him who is a public Enemy."[207] Should no right to resist tyranny exist, "twere better for every man to stand in his own defense, than to enter into societies." Sedition is an extraordinary but righteous mode "of delivering an oppressed People from the violence of a wicked Magistrate, who having armed a Crew of lewd Villains," kills his opponents and confiscates their property.[208] "Nay, all Laws must fall, human Societies that subsist by them be dissolved, and all innocent persons be exposed to the violence of the most wicked, if men might not justly defend themselves against injustice by their own natural right, when the ways prescribed by public authority cannot be taken."[209]

Sidney based his realist theory of arms and freedom on the premise that "Swords were given to men, that none might be Slaves, but such as know not how to use them."[210] In attacking Sir Robert Filmer's argument that subjects must not disobey any commands or examine whether wars are just or unjust, Sidney used as counterexamples the Turks' slaugher of the Christians and the fact that "the King of *France* may when he pleases, arm one part of his Protestant Subjects to the destruction of the other. . . ."[211]

The arms question is central to Sidney's critique of royal absolutism in England. Monarchy orginally did not exist there. The Britons who fiercely defended their liberty from Roman conquest "could no otherwise be subdued, than by the slaughter of all the inhabitants that were able to bear arms." The people themselves rather than leaders made the laws, and "that no force might be put upon them they met arm'd in their general Assemblies. . . ."[212] Even after the establishment of monarchy following the Norman conquest, the people were expected to have arms. In referring to the ancient nobility as "composed of such men as have been ennobled by bearing Arms in the defense or enlargement of the Commonwealth," Sidney mentions the obligation "according to their several degrees and proportions, to provide and maintain Horses, Arms and Men for the same uses. . . ." Because he described this nobility as "such Gentlemen and Lords of Mannors, as we now call Commoners, together with the Freeholders,"[213] Sidney thus assumes the commoner's right to maintain and bear his own arms. In referring to the subversion of the English constitution in his own times, Sidney wrote: "The Law was plain, but it has been industriously rendered perplex: They who were to have upheld it are overthrown, that which might have been easily performed when the people were armed, and had a great, strong, virtuous and powerful Nobility to lead them, is made difficult, now they are disarmed, and that Nobility abolished."[214]

Like Locke, Sidney held that each individual is naturally free; that by the law of nature each person has a right to his own life, liberty, goods, and lands; and that tyrannical governments may rightfully be abolished.[215] Ultimately, each person must guarantee his own freedom. The ancients "carried their Liberty in their own breasts, and had Hands and Swords to defend it."[216] "Let the danger be never so great, there is a possibility of safety while men have life, hands, arms, and courage to use them; but that people must certainly perish, who tamely suffer themselves to be oppressed. . . ." Following Machiavelli, Sidney prefers civil war to tyranny.[217] Citing Pontius the Samnite, Sidney argued that *"those arms were just and pious that were necessary, and necessary when there was no hope of safety by any other way. This is the voice of*

mankind, and is dislike'd only by those Princes, who fear the deserved punishments may fall upon them. . . ."[218] For such bold words Sidney lost his
head, but England's absolute monarchs soon lost their thrones forever.

Arms, Militia, and Penal Reform in
Eighteenth-Century Liberal Thought

The question of arms figured prominently in eighteenth-century political
economy and criminology. The danger to liberty of standing armies and the
alternative of an armed populace was stressed in the writings of John Trenchard, Thomas Gordon, Jean Jacques Rousseau, James Burgh, and Adam
Smith. Similarly, the liberal tradition expressed itself in the arguments against
barbaric punishment and for penal reform set forth by Charles Montesquieu
and Cesare Beccaria, who attacked the treatment of the personal right to bear
arms as a criminal offense.

Among the English Whigs influenced by Algernon Sidney were John Trenchard and Thomas Gordon, whose joint essays known as *Cato's Letters* (1721–
22) influenced American critics of standing armies and were highly regarded
by John Adams and Thomas Jefferson.[219] Trenchard and Gordon stated their
views concisely in an attack on arbitrary power: "Our Armies formerly were
only a Number of the People armed occasionally; and Armies of the People
are the only Armies which are not formidable to the People."[220] In contending that only civil liberty produces military virtue, the two Whigs observed
that "when a tyrant's Army is beaten, his Country is conquered: He has no
Resource; his Subjects having neither Arms nor Courage, nor Reason to fight
for him. . . ." By contrast, "in Attacks upon a free State, every Man has
something to defend in it."[221] "The Exercise of despotic Power is the unre-
lenting War of an armed Tyrant Upon his unarmed Subjects," Trenchard
and Gordon boldly asserted.[222]

The Continental philosophical tradition that stressed an armed popular sovereignty found expression in the thought of Rousseau. In *The Social Contract*
(1762), Rousseau upheld Machiavellian republicanism by contending that "in
a State truly free, the citizens do all with their own arms and nothing with
their money. . . ."[223] And in *Discourse On Political Economy* (1758), Rousseau
reflected: "Having become enemies of the peoples for whose happiness they
were responsible, tyrants established standing armies, in appearance to repress
foreigners and in fact to oppress the inhabitants." Viewing the citizen's army
or militia as protective of freedom at home and nonaggressive abroad, Rousseau attributed the demise of ancient Roman liberty to the growth of a murderous standing army and foresaw the pernicious effects of standing armies
for the next two centuries: "To maintain them [standing armies], it is no less

necessary to oppress the peoples. And in recent times, these dangerous establishments have been growing so rapidly in all our countries that one can foresee only the future depopulation of Europe and, sooner or later, the ruin of the people who inhabit it."[224]

One of the most influential Whig treatises in the American colonies was James Burgh's *Political Disquisitions* (1774).[225] Over one hundred pages of the work are devoted to stressing the virtues of an armed people over a standing army. Burgh's lengthy use of historical examples, classic and Whig literature, and parliamentary debates to support his thesis defy detailed summarization here. He reminded his readers of Aristotle's dictum that those who have arms are masters of the state,[226] of Andrew Fletcher's argument that possession of arms distinguishes freemen from slaves,[227] and of many other sources which argued the virtues of having arms. Burgh's work is antiwar, anti-army and anticolonialism.[228]

"Nothing will make a nation so unconquerable as a militia, or every man's being trained to arms," according to Burgh.[229] The militia was not a government organization but a people with arms and with knowledge of how to use them. "And if the generality of housekeepers were only half-disciplined, a designing prince, or ministry, would hardly dare to provoke the people by an open attack on their liberties. . . . But without the people's having some knowledge of arms, I see not what is to secure them against slavery. . . ."[230] Thus, the militia should not be commanded by the crown.[231] "A militia-man is a free citizen; a soldier, a slave for life."[232] Burgh concludes by giving the following aid and comfort to "our brave American children":

> The confidence, which a standing *army* gives a minister, puts him upon carrying things with a higher hand, than he would attempt to do, if the people were armed, and the court unarmed, that is, if there were no land-force in the nation, but a militia. Had we at this time no standing army, we should not think of *forcing* money out of the pockets of three millions of our subjects. . . . [Burgh goes on to list deprivation of jury trial, lack of representation, and other grievances of the Americans.] There is no end to observations on the difference between the measures likely to be pursued by a minister backed by a standing *army*, and those of a court awed by the fear of an *armed people*.[233]

Adam Smith expressed the liberal consensus in his *Wealth of Nations* (1776):

> Men of republican principles have been jealous of a standing army as dangerous to liberty. It certainly is so, wherever the interest of the general and that of the principal officers are not necessarily connected with the support of the constitution of the state. The standing army of Caesar

destroyed the Roman republic. The standing army of Cromwell turned the long parliament out of doors.[234]

Among nations of hunters, shepherds, and husbandmen "every man is a warrior,"[235] just as in the republics of Greece and Rome "the trade of a soldier was not a separate, distinct trade."[236] "Each citizen . . . seems to have practised his exercises either separately and independently, or with such of his equals as he liked best. . . ."[237] Even under feudalism, ordinances provided that "the citizens of every district should practise archery as well as several other military exercises. . . ."[238] "In a militia, the character of the labourer, artificer, or tradesman, predominates over that of the soldier: in a standing army, that of the soldier predominates over every other character. . . ."[239]

Economic conditions related to the industrial revolution—particularly the lack of leisure in which an artificer or manufacturer could engage in martial exercises—acted as an unseen hand in the gradual displacement of the militia by the standing army.[240] While there is an "irresistible superiority which the militia of a barbarous, has over that of a civilized nation,"[241] firearms and the standing army would make the "civilized" state superior.[242] Yet Smith conceded that "the American militia may become in every respect a match for that standing army" of England.[243] Anticolonial struggles from 1776 to the present have demonstrated the superiority of "barbarous" peoples armed with firearms over standing armies of "civilized" imperialists.

At the same time that political economists were assessing the merits of an armed populace over a standing army, legal theorists questioned criminal laws that punished the mere bearing of arms without any aggressive intent. Referring to "the natural right of self-defense," Montesquieu in *The Spirit of the Laws* (1748) asked, "Who does not see that self-defense is a duty superior to every precept?"[244] Montesquieu attacked Plato's proscription of the use of arms by slaves: "If a slave, says Plato, defends himself, and kills a freeman, he ought to be treated as a parricide. This is a civil law which punishes self-defense, though dictated by nature."[245]

Criminal laws that interfered with self-defense by punishing harmless conduct would be doubly unreasonable. "It is unreasonable . . . to oblige a man not to attempt the defense of his own life."[246] The misuse of arms for aggressive violence, rather than their use in self-defense, should be punished: "Hence it follows, that the laws of an Italian republic [Venice], where bearing fire-arms is punished as a capital crime and where it is not more fatal to make an ill use of them than to carry them, is not agreeable to the nature of things."[247]

Influenced in part by Montesquieu, Cesare Beccaria initiated the modern movement for reform of the criminal laws with the publication of *On Crimes and Punishments* in 1764. In applying a utilitarian standard to renounce torture and even the death penalty, while at the same time supporting appropriate punishment for crimes against property and especially the person, Beccaria earned the reputation of being the father of penal reform. Of laws that punished the mere possession of firearms, Beccaria wrote:

> False is the idea of utility that sacrifices a thousand real advantages for one imaginary or trifling inconvenience; that would take fire from men because it burns, and water because one may drown in it; that has no remedy for evils, except destruction. The laws that forbid the carrying of arms are laws of such a nature. They disarm those only who are neither inclined nor determined to commit crimes. Can it be supposed that those who have the courage to violate the most sacred laws of humanity, the most important of the code, will respect the less important and arbitrary ones, which can be violated with ease and impunity, and which, if strictly obeyed, would put an end to personal liberty—so dear to men, so dear to the enlightened legislator—and subject innocent persons to all the vexations that the guilty alone ought to suffer? Such laws make things worse for the assaulted and better for the assailants; they serve rather to encourage than to prevent homicides, for an unarmed man may be attacked with greater confidence than an armed man. They ought to be designated as laws not preventive but fearful of crimes, produced by the tumultuous impression of a few isolated facts, and not by thoughtful consideration of the inconveniences and advantages of a universal decree.[248]

Thus, for Beccaria, it was unreasonable to punish one for mere possession of an inanimate object, particularly an arm which the law-abiding individual could use for self-defense. One who would disobey laws against murder would surely disobey laws against carrying arms, and murder could be committed more easily if the victim obeyed the latter proscription. In sum, Beccaria argues that laws against carrying arms belong in the dark ages of penology, along with the rack and the screw, while personal liberty and an enlightened approach to crime and punishment necessitate recognition of the right to keep and carry arms. After all, disarming a potential victim of murder may be capital punishment of the victim, a form of cruel and unusual punishment far worse than that inflicted upon the offender.[249]

2

The Common Law
of England

English legal history has often embodied a classic tension between those ancient customs and judicial decisions known as the common law and the
instruments of monarchial absolutism expressed in statutory law and royal
proclamations. This tension reflects a recurring political struggle between the
commoner, who insisted that his rights be recognized from time immemorial,
and the king, who sought to consolidate his power through royal decree supported by a Parliament under his control. Not surprisingly, the issue of whether
the individual possessed any right to have and use arms for defense of person
and property figured prominently in the conflict between commoner and king.

Despite requirements by early English monarchs that subjects be armed
for defense of the realm, the kings best known for arbitrary absolutism sought
to deprive the lower economic classes, various religious groups, and colonized
peoples of weapons so as to perpetuate and enhance the economic and political power of the dominant classes. Magna Charta, the English Declaration of
Rights of 1689, and the American Declaration of Independence were the most
prominent documents that resulted from the revolts against the various forms
of oppression inherent in monarchial absolutism. The right of the individual
to have and carry arms, recognized in such documents as the Declaration of
Rights, found expression in the common law in numerous judicial decisions
and in the commentaries of Blackstone and other jurists.

The Tradition of the Armed Freeman

The laws of the ancient English kings proscribed violent acts with arms,
from brandishing to murder, but recognized as rightful the mere possession
and carrying of arms. The laws of Alfred (871–899) prohibited fighting or drawing a weapon in the king's hall,[1] lending a weapon with evil intent to another
for purposes of murder,[2] the use by a sword polisher of another's weapon to
commit a crime,[3] and disturbing a public meeting by drawing a weapon.[4]

The Laws of Cnut (1020–1023) not only considered armed self-defense a right and duty, fining those who failed to follow the hue and cry,[5] but also directed that "if anyone illegally disarms a man, he is [to] compensate him with *heals-fang*,"[6] a fine. Unlike later feudal game legislation, under Cnut "every man is to be entitled to his hunting in wood and field on his own land."[7]

Because of the preference that an armed people, rather than a standing army, be entrusted with the power of defense, the keeping and bearing of arms came to be considered as not simply a right but a duty. In carrying out the popular reform of expelling plundering mercenaries, Henry II in the twelfth century rested the public defense on the feudal array and the national militia, which could be used neither for domestic or foreign aggression.[8] Thus, the Assize of Arms of 1181 provided:

1. Let every holder of a knight's fee have a hauberk, a helmet, a shield and a lance. And let every knight have as many hauberks, helmets, shields and lances, as he has knight's fees in his demesne.
2. Also, let every free layman, who holds chattels of rent to the value of 16 marks, have a hauberk, a helmet, a shield and a lance. Also, let every free layman who holds chattels or rent worth 10 marks have an 'aubergel' and a headpiece of iron, and a lance.
3. Also, let all burgesses and the whole body of freemen have quilted doublets and a headpiece of iron, and a lance.
4. Moreover, let each and every one of them swear that before the Feast of St. Hilary he will possess these arms and will bear allegiance to the lord king, Henry namely the son of the Empress Maud, and that he will bear these arms in his service according to his order and in allegiance to the lord king and his realm. And let none of those who hold these arms sell them or pledge them or offer them, or in any other way alienate them; neither let a lord in any way deprive his men of them either by forfeiture of gift, or as surety or in any other manner.
5. If anyone bearing these arms shall have died, let his arms remain for his heir.[9]

Contrary to the typical feudal practice of disarming the lower classes to prevent economic reform or popular revolution, the Assize of Arms even precluded the lords from depriving freemen of arms. The assize was intended to "re-arm the national forces of the fyrd. It directed that the whole free population, the *communa liberorum hominum*, should furnish themselves with arms."[10] The armed freemen were known as *jurati ad arma*.[11] Not unexpectedly, however, the monarch did not fully trust the people. While the order that the lower classes provide themselves with less expensive weapons took due account of their economic condition, the assize went further in prohibiting their possession of more arms than was appropriate for their class; in this way, they were certain to remain in a low economic condition where they could not threaten the monopoly of land and political power of the king and landlord class. As the assize stated:

> 6. Let every burgess who has more arms than he ought to have according to this assize, sell them or give them away or otherwise bestow them on such a man as will retain them for the service of the lord king of England. And let none of them keep more arms than he ought to have according to this assize.[12]

The assize also contained the following discriminatory provision: "7. Item, let no Jew keep in his possession a hauberk or an 'aubergel', but let him sell or give them away or otherwise dispose of them that they may remain in the king's service."[13] Since the hauberk (a tunic of chain mail) and the aubergel (breastplate) were pieces of defensive armor, this invidious restriction did not, in itself, amount to the complete disarming of Jews by law. Nevertheless, a shortage of weapons in the hands of Jews enabled a riotous mob in 1189 to annihilate the entire Jewish community of York.[14] Despite its limitations, the Assize of Arms of Henry II not only recognized as a legal right, but imposed as a legal duty, the individual possession of arms by English subjects.

Following the demise of Henry II, King John came to power and oppressed and disarmed nobles and commoners alike, which led to the revolt of 1215. The right of barons to correct the king by force was imposed on John in §61 of Magna Charta (1215),[15] and their ability to do so was guaranteed by the reaffirmation in §§29, 37, and 51 of the militia system set forth in the Assize of Arms of Henry II.[16] The barons caused John to project "a general league of 'communa' of the population in arms" for the public defense.[17] This policy related to the domestic duties not only of the watch and ward and the hue and cry, but also of the possession of arms to resist governmental oppression.

Henry III issued edicts in 1230 and 1252 in further support of the Assize of Arms.[18] Later, the 1285 Statute of Winchester of Edward I provided:

> That every Man have in his house Harness for to keep the Peace after the ancient Assize; that is to say, Every Man between fifteen years of age, and sixty years, shall be assessed and sworn to Armor according to the quantity of their Lands and Goods; that is to wit [from] Fifteen Pounds Lands, and Goods Forty Marks, an Hauberke, [a Breast-plate] of Iron, a Sword, a Knife, and an Horse; and [from] Ten Pounds of Lands, and Twenty Marks Goods, an Hauberke, [a Breast-plate of Iron,] a Sword, and a Knife; and from Forty Shillings Land and more, unto One hundred Shillings of Land, a Sword, a Bow and Arrows, and a Knife; and he that hath less than Forty Shillings yearly, shall be sworn to [keep Gis-armes,] Knives, and other [less Weapons]; and he that hath less than

Twenty Marks in Goods, shall have Swords, Knives, and other [less Weapons]; and all other that may, shall have Bows and Arrows out of the Forest, and in the Forest Bows and [Boults.]^{19}

Unlike the Assize of Arms of Henry II, the Statute of Winchester of Edward I contained no provision that sought to prohibit one from having more weapons than his estate allowed.

These acts of Henry III and Edward I encompassed "the whole population capable of bearing arms" and in them "the maintenance of the 'jurati ad arma' is closely connected with the conservation of the peace, according to the idea that this force was primarily a weapon of defense, not of aggression."[20] Without a standing army, Henry III and Edward I were forced to concede that "the parliament should be the whole nation in council . . . and thus the host should be again the whole nation in arms."[21] In summary, the existence of a populace armed with swords, shields, knives, and bows and arrows provided the physical might to ward off not only foreign aggression but monarchial despotism as well.

Gun Control Laws of the Absolute Monarchs

As the firearm began to replace the bow, the death knell of feudalism was struck when serfs and burghers began to acquire the new instrument. From the time that firearms were introduced in Tudor England and until the Glorious Revolution, they were used primarily by peasants principally for hunting.[22] The king feared an instrument that signified the economic and political independence of the poor and middle classes, and legislation was promptly passed that barred the keeping and using of arms by all but wealthy landowners.[23] Just as the fifteenth- and sixteenth-century statutes of Henry VII, Henry VIII, and James II sought to disarm the aspiring bourgeois and peasant classes, subsequent British colonial policy in Scotland, Ireland, and America rightly perceived that conquest depended upon armless and hence defenseless indigenous populations. Consequently, England's arms control legislation encompassed discrimination by race, religion, nationality, and economic class.

Feudal legislation had long existed that sought to restrict the hunting of game to the king and the landed gentry.[24] To force serfs to work for the landlords, Henry VII in 1485 passed legislation against hunting for the specific purpose of discouraging rebellion.[25] Henry VII's legislation of 1503 against hunting deer with crossbows,[26] which allegedly caused "great destruction of the King's Deer," provided that "no person within this Realm, without the King's special license . . . shall occupy or shoot in any crossbow, but if he shoot out of a house for the lawful defense of the same, except he be a Lord or that he or other persons to his use have land and tenements of Freehold to the yearly value of two hundred Marks. . . ." Nor could Lords allow their servants to shoot with their crossbows.[27] While aimed at hunting and revolution, the act did not seek to deprive the people of arms to defend their houses, a right which had existed from time immemorial.

Even Henry VIII, the embodiment of arbitrary despotism, recognized the ancient tradition of an armed populace by legislating in 1511 that "every man . . . do use and exercise shooting in longbows, and also to have a bow and arrows ready continually in his house to use himself and do use himself in shooting. . . ."[28] At the same time, however, he sought to increase the property qualification for using crossbows, providing that "no person but if he be a Lord or have lands or tenements of Freehold or other to his use to the yearly value of CCC marks of all charges shoot in any Crossbow otherwise than in the said Act as expressed for defense of his house. . . ."[29]

Within three years the conservative monarch, faced with the escalating effects of technological revolution in weaponry, enacted further legislation that included the use of firearms in the proscription. Complaining that "the commonalty and poor people of the realm" were neglecting archery for unlawful games—a euphemism for political meetings— the king again decreed that every man keep in his house and practice shooting long bows.[30] In companion legislation he admitted that his was a losing battle as the commoners were using not only crossbows but also "handgonnes" on a widening scale:

> Whereas the King's Subjects daily delight themselves in shooting of Crossbows . . . [and] many and diverse not regarding or fearing the penalties of the [previously enacted] statute use daily to shoot in Crossbows and handgonnes. . . . Wherefore . . . no person from henceforth [shall] shoot in any Crossbow and handgonne . . . unless he or other to his use have lands and tenements in the yearly value of CCC marks. . . . And that no man . . . [may] keep in his house or elsewhere any Crossbow or handgonne upon pain of imprisonment . . . unless that he or other to his use have land and tenements to the yearly value of CCC marks. . . .[31]

Exceptions were made for those granted licenses by the king and for inhabitants of towns near the sea or near Scotland.

By 1523, apparently sensing the inevitably of mass acquisition of the new weaponry, Henry VIII reduced the property qualification from three hundred marks (or £ 200) to £ 100 and restricted punishment to a fine and seizure of the weapon. Qualified persons could "lawfully use and shoot in Crossbows and Handguns . . . and to retain and keep the same," although lords were warned not to permit their tenants and servants to violate the act.[32] A more comprehensive act ten years later rejected the legal doctrine of constructive possession by providing that housekeepers were not liable for the possession by their lodgers of crossbows and handguns. The act also permitted gunners in the king's wages and residents of certain counties to keep crossbows and handguns in their homes for use "against thieves, Scotts, and other the King's enemies. . . ."[33]

By the time of the act of 1541[34] all persons could lawfully keep firearms subject to length requirements. Alleging that "persons have used and yet do daily use to ride and go in the King's highways and elsewhere, having with them Crossbows and little handguns," the act prohibited handguns of less than one yard in length and hagbutts of less than three-quarters of a yard. Persons not meeting the property qualification of £ 100 could not "carry or have, in his or their journey going or riding in the King's highway or elsewhere, any Crossbow or Gun charged or furnished with powder, fire or touche for the same. . . ." Yet anyone could shoot a handgun, demyhake, or hagbutt in town "at a butt or bank of earth in place convenient, or for the defense of his person or house. . . ." Gentlemen, yeomen, servingmen, and all inhabitants of cities and towns could "have and keep in every of their houses," and shoot at butts with, handguns, hagbutts, and demyhakes of the requisite length. The maximum punishment for possession of a short handgun by a person worth less than £ 100 was a fine of £ 10.[35]

That unenforceable laws should be rendered weaker rather than stronger was the demonstrated lesson. If imprisonment would not deter unqualified persons from having and using firearms, a mere fine would then be imposed. If the poor and middle classes carried arms contrary to the property qualification, realistic legislation would then allow more persons in these classes to possess arms legally. If the poorest acquired firearms despite any law, then the king would fine them only for short firearms. Finally, as had been true since ancient times, every person would be allowed to practice with arms and to use them to protect the person and home. Aside from the continual privilege of only the nobility to take game with guns or otherwise, little remained of the gun-control legislation of Henry VIII after thirty years of failure. Perhaps he recognized that acquisition of firearms by commoners was the death knell of England's absolute monarchs. As the most absolute of them all, Henry VIII was powerless to prevent it.

The initial wave of the English Revolution (1642–1660) sparked by Cromwell was unsuccessful in instituting equal rights for commoners, including the right to be armed. Both Cromwell and Charles II (1660 – 1685) favored a "new militia" which was closer to a standing army, select militia, or national guard than a militia composed of the whole people.[36]

> The original common law liability of every man between fifteen and sixty to keep arms according to his estate . . . had been put under a new basis, first by a statute of Philip and Mary's reign, and, later by statutes

of Charles II's reign. Under Charles II's statutes the liability to supply men, horses, and arms was placed upon the owners of property; and the lord lieutenants and their deputies were empowered to levy a rate for this purpose.[37]

Indeed, in 1662 Charles II passed a militia bill which empowered certain officials "to search for and seize all arms in the custody or possession of any person or persons whom the said lieutenant or any two or more of their deputies shall judge dangerous to the peace of the kingdom. . . ."[38] In 1670, for the first time in English history, Charles II sought to deprive all commoners of all firearms by legislation:

> That all and every Person and Persons not having Lands and Tenements . . . of the clear yearly Value of one hundred Pounds *per annum* . . . or having Lease or Leases . . . of the clear yearly Value of one hundred and fifty Pounds, other than the Son and Heir Degree . . . are hereby declared to be persons by the Laws of this Realm not allowed to keep . . . any Guns, Bows . . . or other Engines aforesaid; but shall be and are hereby prohibited to have, keep or use the same.[39]

A clear function of the act was to preserve game for the elite, thereby preventing the "divers idle, disorderly and mean Persons"[40] from securing sustenance and forcing them to continue in a position of serfdom for the benefit of the landlord class. Since it sought to disarm all but the landed aristocracy, the act was also aimed at the aspiring bourgeoisie, the burghers and professionals who supported progressive republicanism and opposed feudal domination. Passed not only to further economic exploitation, the act functioned also to enhance its necessary concomitant—political domination. As Blackstone observed, "prevention of popular insurrections and resistance to the government, by disarming the bulk of the people . . . is a reason oftener meant, than avowed, by the makers of the forest and game laws."[41] In sum, the landlord monopoly of the means of production rested on its monopoly of the means of violence, that is, the instruments which could bag animals and people alike. Thus, James II (1685–1688) carried on the same policy of increasing the size of the standing army and disarming the populace, particularly Protestants.[42]

That Subjects May Have Arms for Their Defense: The Glorious Revolution and Bill of Rights

A paramount aim of the Glorious Revolution of 1688 was to abolish the standing army of James II and to reinstate the right of Protestants to keep and carry arms. Following the abdication of England's last absolute monarch, Par-

liament enacted a bill of rights that the new limited monarch William and
Mary recognized as a condition of rule. The provisions of this English Bill of
Rights were to be reflected a century later in the first ten amendments of the
U.S. Constitution.

On January 28, 1689, a historic debate ensued in the House of Commons
concerning the proposed abdication of James II. Lord Somers's notes of the
debate clearly demonstrate the perceived abuses under the Militia Act of
1662, which had allowed arbitrary searches and seizures of the arms of private citizens. Thus, Sergeant Maynard complained: "An Act of Parliament
was made to disarm all Englishmen, whom the Lieutenant should suspect,
by day or by night, by force or otherwise."[43] Mr. Finch thought that no man
would be safe under the king, adding, "The constitution being limited, there
is a good foundation for defensive arms."[44]

Sir William Williams was concerned "Whether the power over [the militia
resided] in the crown or people?"[45] "Militia bill.—Power to disarm all England. —Now done in Ireland," lamented Sir Richard Temple.[46] Mr. Boscawen's attack on the ministry's arbitrary power indicates that the members
of Parliament themselves had no immunity: "Imprisoning without reason;
disarming.—Himself disarmed."[47] "An abominable thing to disarm the nation,
to set up a standing army," Sergeant Maynard agreed.[48] And Mr. Sachverel
brooded: "No man knows what he can call his own . . . Disarmed and imprisoned without cause."[49]

The deprivation of the arms of individual Englishmen constituted a major
complaint. No one suggested that "all Englishmen" really meant Protestant
militia companies or that Mr. Boscawen, who complained because he had
personally been disarmed, was a member of a formal militia company. On the
contrary, the remarks in the House of Commons indicate both that every citizen had a right to have arms and that power over the militia was lodged in the
people and not in the crown. All of the members of Commons who complained
about the people being disarmed were appointed to committees to draft the
Bill of Rights.[50]

Less than a week after the above discussion, the House agreed to a declaration of liberties that included the following provision: "It is necessary for the
public Safety, that the Subjects which are Protestants, should provide and
keep Arms for Their common Defence: And that the Arms, which have been
seized, and taken from them, be restored."[51] The declaration was afterward
expanded to include a list of grievances against James II, accusing him of
subverting the liberties of the kingdom in part "by causing several good
Subjects, being Protestants, to be disarmed. . . ."[52] Further, the declaration
of rights provision was altered to read: "That the Subjects, which are Protestants, may provide and keep Arms, for their common Defense. . . ."[53] The
substitution of "may" for "should" clarifies that the provision recognized a
right rather than imposed a duty.

The House of Lords passed an amended version of the declaration, which Mr. Somers read in Commons for its approval, along with reasons given for the changes. To the charge that James II had caused Protestants to be disarmed was added the following: "at the same time that Papists were both armed and employed, contrary to Law." "Reason.—This is a further Aggravation fit to be added to this Clause."[54] This indicates that, in the minds of the Lords, the disarmament of the Protestants was an aggravation in itself, but insult was added to injury by the circumstance that Papists were armed while Protestants were disarmed. The new language in no way suggests that it would not have been an aggravation had Protestants and Papists alike been disarmed.

The Lords also amended the rights provision in the following three ways: "instead of 'provide and keep,' read, 'have,' and leave out 'common;' and after 'Defence,' add, 'suitable to their Condition, and as allowed by law.' "[55] The first change appears to have been made purely for the sake of brevity. However, the deletion of "common" is of substantive import, in that it clarifies that the provision protects the right to have arms for both individual and common defense. The third alteration qualified the right somewhat so as to allow game laws that imposed property qualifications on using arms to hunt.[56]

As adopted, the English Bill of Rights complained that James II attempted to subvert "the Laws and Liberties of this Kingdom":

> 5. By raising and keeping a Standing Army within the Kingdom in Time of Peace, without Consent of Parliament, and quartering Soldiers contrary to Law.
> 6. By causing several good Subjects, being Protestants, to be disarmed, at the same Time when Papists were both armed and employed, contrary to law.[57]

The act accordingly declared thirteen "true, ancient and indubitable rights," including the following:

> 6. That the raising or keeping a standing Army within the Kingdom in Time of Peace, unless it be with Consent of Parliament, is against Law.
> 7. That the Subjects which are Protestants, may have Arms for their Defence suitable to their Condition, and as are allowed by Law.[58]

To vindicate the absolute rights of Englishmen, according to Blackstone, the Bill of Rights signified that subjects were entitled to justice in the courts, to petition the king, "and, lastly, to the right of having and using arms for self-preservation and defense."[59] In short, the philosophical justifications of the right of individual and collective self-defense, including revolution against oppressive government, became recognized as a part of the English common-law guarantee of an arms-bearing population.

By the plain words of the English Bill of Rights, the right of Protestants to carry arms applied to Protestants as individuals. This right was not limited to maintenance of militias or organized armed forces. Nor did it intend to disarm Catholics as individuals, but only to break up a standing army dominated by Catholic supporters of James II.[60] In the words of Sir William Holdsworth, the king "had allowed Papists to be officers in his army, and refused Protestants the right to carry arms."[61] The Bill of Rights complained of "the denial of the right of the subject to petition the king; and of refusal to allow Protestants the right to carry arms for self-defense. . . ."[62]

The Bill of Rights included only two individual rights—those of bearing arms and petition—while the remaining contents of the declaration constituted restrictions on the crown. In *The Declaration of the Rights of Man and of Citizens* (1901), Georg Jellinek clarified the Bill of Rights as follows:

> When one looks through the [English] Bill of Rights carefully, one finds but slight mention there of individual rights. That laws should not be suspended, that there should be no dispensation from them, that special courts should not be erected, that cruel punishments should not be inflicted, that jurors ought to be duly impanelled and returned, that taxes should not be levied without a law, nor a standing army kept without consent of Parliament, that parliamentary elections should be free, and Parliament be held frequently,—all these are not *rights of the individual,* but duties of the government. *Of the thirteen articles of the Bill of Rights only two contain stipulations that are expressed in the form of the rights of the subject* . . . [:] The right to address petitions to the kings (5), and *the right of Protestant subjects to carry arms for their own defense* suitable to their condition (7).[63]

These rights to petition and to keep and bear arms, the only individual rights recognized in the English Bill of Rights, reappeared exactly a hundred years later in a more absolute form as Articles I and II of the American Bill of Rights.

Less than a decade after its adoption, the Bill of Rights provision on standing armies came to be expounded in detail by the Whigs who had given birth to it. During the years 1697–1699, the king's ministers argued without success to persuade Parliament that temporary standing armies would not violate the Bill of Rights. The most significant Whig attacks on the monarch's proposals were penned by John Trenchard, Walter Moyle, and Andrew Fletcher,[64] who appealed to ancient laws on the duty to have arms and the Bill of Rights provisions against standing armies and the right to have arms. Thus, their expositions further bear out the true import of those provisions.

Trenchard, with the assistance of Parliament member Moyle, published in 1697 *An Argument Showing that a Standing Army is Inconsistent with a Free Govern-*

ment. This popular pamphlet, while centering narrowly on the army issue, included these words: "For the detestable Policies of the last Reigns were with the utmost Art and Application to disarm the People, and make the Militia useless. . . ."[65] "Why may not the Laws for shooting in Crossbows be changed into Firelocks, and a competent Number of them be kept in every parish for the young Men to exercise with. . . .?"[66]

Andrew Fletcher, the Scottish Whig who was sentenced to death in 1686, and who joined William of Orange at the Hague in 1688, treated the right-to-arms issue in more detail in *A Discourse of Government with Relation to Militias* (1698). Fletcher supported a constitution which "put the sword into the hands of the subject,"[67] for "he that is armed, is always, master of the purse of him that is unarmed."[68] "And I cannot see, why arms should be denied to any man who is not a slave, since they are the only true badges of liberty. . . ."[69]

Since the political objective of an armed populace was to prevent tyranny, Fletcher favored a militia comprised of all the people and independent of the crown. "We have quitted our ancient security, and put the militia into the power of the king."[70] Fletcher described a militia not subject to the authority of the chief executive as a "well-regulated" militia. "Let us now consider whether we may not be able to defend ourselves by well-regulated militias against any foreign force, though never so formidable: that these nations may be free from the fears of invasion from abroad, as well as from the danger of slavery at home."[71]

Fletcher had occasion to expand on these sentiments a half-decade later when he proposed limitations on royal prerogative before the Scottish parliament. Reducing monarchial power required a populace capable of enforcing its will:

> The possession of arms is the distinction between a freeman and a slave. He who has nothing, and belongs to another, must be defended by him, and needs no arms: but he who thinks he is his own master, and has anything he may call his own, ought to have arms to defend himself and what he possesses, or else he lives precariously and at discretion. And though for a while those who have the sword in their power abstain from doing him injury; yet, by degrees, he will be awed into submission to every arbitrary command. Our ancestors, by being always armed, and frequently in action, defended themselves against the Romans, Danes and English; and maintained their liberty against encroachments of their own princes.[72]

A final pamphlet is worthy of consideration because it discusses the English tradition of being armed in light of the new firearms technology. Published only a dozen years after the adoption of the Bill of Rights, the author of *The Claims of the People of England*, identified only as a member of the Country party, asserted that the people have "Just Claim to the use of Arms for the defense of their King and Themselves under Him. . . ."[73] In citing statutes of Henry VIII, the author stated:

> 'Tis true, the Law forbad Cross-bows that the Game might be preserved; but they ventured their Game to the Long-bow, as they may now to the Bullet and Musket with equal Security. . . . May not the People be trusted to guard the King, their Landlords, and themselves? . . . Madmen indeed ought not to be trusted with Weapons. But the care we took of our selves in preserving our Rights against the Incroachments of our late King, . . . may challenge that an old Right of handling Arms be trusted to us. . . .[74]

The Country party author specifically anticipated that each person would purchase his own firearms: "May not the Method of Bows and Arrows be accommodated to Guns and Ball? This new Artillery is somewhat more chargeable [i.e., expensive]; but are not the greatest part of the People able to bear the Charge themselves?"[75] He rejected the argument that "arming the People" would lead to tumults, which were instead caused by scarcity of food and work.[76] A just stability would follow from a populace accustomed to handling arms. "For if it be granted that an armed People will support a just and legal administration both in State and Church, 'tis no great harm if the People, by the help of their Arms, should happen to defend themselves against Tyranny and Oppression."[77]

Such were the sentiments of the Whigs who had successfully promoted the Glorious Revolution and adopted the Bill of Rights. Their recognition that having arms was an individual right went uncontradicted. Over a century later, the same conclusion was reached in *Rex* v. *Dewhurst,*[78] a case arising out of an armed meeting protesting against a massacre and advocating parliamentary reform. In instructing the jury, the court referred to and interpreted the Bill of Rights provision as follows:

> "The subjects which are Protestants may have arms for their defence suitable to their condition, and as allowed by law."
> But are arms suitable to the condition of people in the ordinary class of life, and are they allowed by law? A man has a clear right to protect himself when he is going singly or in a small party upon the road where he is travelling or going for the ordinary purposes of business. But I have no difficulty in saying you have no right to carry arms to a public meeting, if the number of arms which are so carried are calculated to produce terror and alarm. . . .[79]

In summary, while a person could not legally terrorize others, the private individual's right to have and bear arms was an essential feature of the English Bill of Rights.

The Common-Law Liberty to Have Arms:
From Coke to Blackstone

The common-law right to keep, carry, and use arms was attested to by well-established judicial precedent and by the leading commentators both before and after the 1688 Glorious Revolution. The jurisprudence of the right to have arms for self-defense and other lawful purposes developed primarily in response to prosecutions of those who rode armed to terrify the king's subjects and who possessed arms in violation of the game laws. In response to these prosecutions, which were based on statutes supportive of monarchial power and unequal privilege, the courts acquitted defendants whose only alleged offense was the bare possession of firearms since having arms per se was a liberty allowed by the common law.

The 1328 Statute of Northampton of Edward III, passed during the violence of the early fourteenth century, provided that no person other than the king's servants and ministers shall "come before the King's Justices . . . with force and arms, nor bring no force in affray of the peace, nor to go nor ride armed by night nor by day, in Fairs, Markets, nor in the presence of the Justices or other Ministers, nor in no part elsewhere. . . ."[80] The statute did not seek a disarmed populace, who were expected to respond to "a Cry made for Arms to keep the Peace,"[81] but sought to consolidate the monarch's power against roving bands of knights. "For in those days this deed of Chivalry was at random, whereupon great peril ensued," in the words of Sir Edward Coke.[82] According to Coke, whose *Institutes of the Laws of England* first appeared in 1628 to defend the common law against royal infringement, the statute contemplated armed self-defense against those using force in affray of the peace:

> And yet in some cases a man may not only use force and arms, but assemble company also. As any may assemble his friends and neighbors, to keep his house against those that come to rob, or kill him, or to offer him violence in it, and is by construction excepted out of this Act; and the Sheriff, etc., ought not to deal with him upon this Act; for a man's house is his Castle, and *domus sua cuique est tutissimum refugium* [a person's own house is his ultimate refuge]; for where shall a man be safe, if it be not in his house. And in this sense it is truly said,
> *Armaque in Armatos sumere jura sinunt* [and the laws permit the taking up of arms against armed persons].[83]

Whether the Statute of Northampton precluded going or riding armed peacefully[84] was resolved in *Rex* v. *Knight,* a case decided in 1686. The criminal information in that case alleged that Sir John Knight "did walk about the streets armed with guns" and that he went into a church with a gun, thereby "going or riding armed in affray of peace."[85] Counsel for the defendant contended: "This statute was made to prevent the people's being oppressed by great men; but this is a private matter, and not within the statute."[86] "The Chief Justice said, that the meaning of the statute . . . was to punish people who go armed *to terrify the King's subjects.*"[87] The chief justice further held: "But tho' this statute be almost gone in desuetudinem [disuse], yet where the crime shall appear to be malo animo [with evil intent], it will come within the Act (tho' now there be a general connivance to gentlemen to ride armed for their security). . . ."[88] Knight was found not guilty because he was not armed to terrify the king's subjects or in affray of the peace.

William Hawkins, in an exposition of affrays in his *Treatise of the Pleas of the Crown*, commented as follows:

> no wearing of arms is within the meaning of the statute unless it be accompanied with such circumstances as are apt to terrify the people; from when it seems clearly to follow, that persons of quality are in no danger of offending against this statute by wearing common weapons, or having their usual number of attendants with them for their ornament or defence, in such places, and upon such occasions, in which it is the common fashion to make use of them, without causing the least suspicion of an intention to commit any act of violence or disturbance of the peace. And from the same ground it also follows, that persons armed with privy coats of mail, to the intent to defend themselves against their adversaries, are not within the meaning of the statute, because they do nothing *in terrorem populi.*[89]

Rightly having and using arms for the defense of oneself or of others found further exposition in the law of justifiable homicide. Hawkins wrote:

> If those who are engaged in a riot or a forcible entry, or detainer, stand in their defense, and continue the force in opposition to the command of justice of peace, & c. or resist such justice endeavouring to arrest them the killing may be justified; and so perhaps may the killing of dangerous rioters by any private persons, who cannot otherwise suppress them or defend themselves from them, inasmuch as *every private person seems to be authorized by law to arm himself* for the purposes aforesaid.[90]

In recognizing the right of Protestants to "have arms for their defense,"[91] the English Bill of Rights laid to rest any doubt that all persons, not just "gentlemen" or "persons of quality" (euphemisms for the privileged classes), could "ride armed for their security."[92] As late as the early twentieth century it was held that even an Irishman could not be convicted under the Statute of Northampton for walking down a public road while armed with a loaded revolver:

Without referring to old principles, which are admitted by all, we think that the statutable misdemeanour is to ride or go armed *without lawful occasion in terrorem populi*. . . .

. . . . The words "in affray of the peace" in the statute, being read forward into the "going armed," render the former words part of the description of the statutable offence. The indictment, therefore, omits two essential elements of the offence—(1) That the going armed was without lawful occasion; and (2) that the act was *in terrorem populi*.[93]

Only a decade before this decision, the meaning of going armed to the terror of the people, as well as the distinction between statutes (such as that of Edward III) and common law, were clarified. "Not only was the offense charged against the prisoner one under the Statute of Edward III, but also under the common law, by which he was liable to punishment for making himself a public nuisance by firing a revolver in a public place, with the result that the public were frightened or terrorized."[94]

The right of commoners to keep and carry arms found recognition in prosecutions not only under the Statute of Northampton but also under the game laws. The Glorious Revolution succeeded in forcing the now limited monarchy to confirm the right to have arms for self-defense. But game laws, which were still being developed, continued to exact harsh penalties on commoners for hunting with guns or with other weapons or traps. The game laws reflected class struggle in the countryside between hungry peasants, who never accepted the landlord's right to the wild game, and landlords and their agents, who were armed with general powers of arrest, search, and seizure. Extending even to unqualified freeholders hunting on their own land, penalties ranged from whippings to capital punishment itself. Not suprisingly, abolition of the game laws was high on the agenda of reformers and radicals.[95] Despite the oppressive character of the game laws, a series of eighteenth-century judicial decisions held that the mere possession of guns created no presumption of an illegal purpose and that, to the contrary, it was a common-law right.

Resolution of the issue of whether keeping or using a gun was contrary to law because it might be used as an instrument to destroy game was prompted by prosecutions under An Act for the Better Preservation of the Game of 1706: "If any person or persons not qualified by the Laws of this Realm so do shall keep or use any Greyhounds . . . [or other dogs] or any other Engine to kill and destroy the Game," the punishment would be a fine of £ 5 or three months' imprisonment.[96] In affirming a conviction for the bare keeping of a lurcher, *Rex* v. *Filer* relied on precedent wherein "a difference was taken as to keeping a dog which could only be to destroy the game, and the keeping of a gun, which a man might do for the defence of his house."[97] The court's narrow view of dogs did not extend to its conception of the uses of guns. And in *Bluet* v. *Needs,* an action for debt against an attorney who had allegedly used a gun to kill game, the court held that "it is a matter of evidence, whether a gun be an engine to kill and destroy game."[98]

That keeping a gun could not be a crime was the reason for the decision in *Rex* v. *Gardner,*[99] wherein counsel for the defendant argued that "it might as well have been said, he kept a cane contrary to the statute, being an engine to destroy game; for it does not appear that he actually did kill any game. And to charge only that he kept a gun is improper, for it includes every man that keeps a gun."[100] The court put "great weight in the objection to this conviction,"[101] which it quashed on the ground that the law did "not extend to prohibit a man from keeping a gun for his necessary defense, but only from making that forbidden use of it."[102] "Farmers are generally obliged to keep a gun, and are no more within the Act for doing so than they are for keeping a cabbage-net. . . ."[103] "[A] gun differs from nets and dogs, which can only be kept for an ill purpose,"[104] and "is an instrument proper, and frequently necessary to be kept and use for other purposes, as the killing of noxious vermin, or the like. . . ."[105] The court referred to the game act not only of Anne[106] but also of Charles II, which had specifically prohibited commoners from having guns.[107] The court stated that *"as these acts restrain the liberty which was allowed by the common law,* and are also penal, they ought not to be extended further than they must necessarily be."[108] The characterization of the right to keep guns and dogs as liberties allowed by the common law is highly significant.

After *Gardner,* the English decisions all agreed that keeping a gun was no offense. In *Malloch* v. *Eastly,* involving a conviction for killing a pheasant beyond the boundaries of one's manor, "all the Court agreed, that the mere having a gun was no offence within the game laws, for a man may keep a gun for the defense of his house and family, but the party must use the gun to kill game before he can incur any penalty; and they said this point was settled and determined."[109]

The court held similarly in *Wingfield* v. *Stratford,*[110] an action of trover against the lord of a manor whose gamekeeper seized the plaintiff's gun as an engine possessed by an unqualified person for the killing of game: "And the Court held, that a gun is not necessarily to be taken to be an engine to kill game, as it does not appear upon this record that the plaintiff killed game with it; he might use it to shoot crows, or destroy vermin. . . ."[111] The court also held:

> It is not to be imagined, that it was the intention of the Legislature . . . to disarm all the people of England. . . . As a gun may be kept for the defense of a man's house, and for divers other lawful purposes, it was necessary to alledge . . . that the gun had been used for killing the game.[112]

Because of the "difference betwixt a gun and the other things expressly mentioned in the statute which can only be kept for bad purposes," the court rendered judgment for the plaintiff.[113]

The line of eighteenth-century decisions in point ended with two cases which clarify that possession of a dog established a rebuttable presumption that it was kept or used in violation of the game laws, while possession of a gun established a rebuttable presumption that it was kept or used lawfully. While defense counsel's argument in *Rex* v. *Hartley*—that "dogs are more commonly kept for this very purpose, the protection of houses, than guns are"—fell on deaf ears, the justices observed that "a gun may be used for other purposes, as the protection of a man's house,"[114] but that "it is incumbent upon the defendent to shew that [the greyhound] is kept for another purpose; as that in the present case, it is a house-dog, a favourite dog, or a particular species of greyhound."[115] And while the court in *Rex* v. *Thompson*[116] affirmed the defendant's conviction for having "kept and used a gun to kill and destroy game," the court averred that "the act of keeping a gun was in itself ambiguous, and that it must be shewn to be kept for the purpose of killing game. . . ."[117] "[It] is not an offense to keep or use a gun, unless it be kept or used for the purpose of killing game. . . ."[118]

Although Charles II had sought, prior to the Glorious Revolution of 1688, an absolute prohibition of possession of guns by commoners, English common-law cases occurring both before and after 1688, as well as the Bill of Rights of 1689, recognized the right of all to keep and bear arms for various legal purposes. Blackstone summarized well the function of the game laws to force serfs to work for landlords by depriving them of alternative food sources and of arms for revolt:

3. For prevention of idleness and dissipation in husbandmen, artificers, and others of lower rank; which would be the unavoidable consequence of universal license. 4. For prevention of popular insurrections and resistance to the government, by disarming the bulk of the people: which last is a reason oftener meant, than avowed, by the makers of forest or game laws.[119]

The American jurist St. George Tucker commented concerning this passage: "Whoever examines the forest, and game laws in the British code, will readily perceive that the right of keeping arms is effectually taken away from the people of England."[120] While this statement is accurate with respect to the game statute of Charles II, judicial construction in the eighteenth century consistently supported the right of all Englishmen to have guns despite the game laws.

Perhaps Blackstone best summarized the nature and function of the right to have arms as one of "the rights of persons." In referring to "the principal absolute rights which appertain to every Englishman," Blackstone cautioned:

> But in vain would these rights be declared, ascertained, and protected by the dead letter of the laws, if the constitution had provided no other method to secure their actual enjoyment. It has, therefore, established certain other auxiliary subordinate rights of the subject, which serve principally as outworks or barriers, to protect and maintain inviolate the three great and primary rights, of personal security, personal liberty, and private property.[121]

After discussing various rights, including the right to petition the government, Blackstone added:

> The fifth and last auxiliary right of the subjects, that I shall at present mention, is that of having arms for their defence suitable to their condition and degree, and such as are allowed by law. Which is also declared by the same statute 1 W.&M. st.2 c.2 [the Bill of Rights], and it is indeed, a public allowance under due restrictions, of the natural right of resistance and self-preservation, when the sanctions of society and laws are found insufficient to restrain the violence of oppression.
>
> In these several articles consist the rights, or, as they are frequently termed, the liberties of Englishmen. . . . So long as these remain inviolate, the subject is perfectly free; for every species of compulsive tyranny and oppression must act in opposition to one or other of these rights, having no other object upon which it can possibly be employed. . . . And, lastly, to vindicate these rights, when actually violated or attacked, the subjects of England are entitled, in the first place, to the regular administration and free course of justice in the courts of law; next, to the right of petitioning the king and parliament for redress of grievances; and, lastly, to the right of having and using arms for self-preservation and defense.[122]

The common law, as established in ancient tradition, the 1689 Bill of Rights, and judicial construction, defined the rights of all Englishmen, and was accepted as basic by the English settlers of America. Yet legislation continued to be passed in the eighteenth century to disarm the Irish and the Scots, exempting only those who could be expected to support English domination. As homes were searched for arms and offenders shot on sight, arms prohibition continued to enhance colonialist conquest.[123] When the British monarch adopted similar policies against the Americans who believed they were guaranteed common-law rights, including the right to keep and carry arms, the Americans sought to preserve their ancient liberties through the armed overthrow of British colonialism.

3

The American Revolution
and the Second Amendment

Strongly influenced by the philosophical classics and vigorously insisting on their common-law rights, the Americans who participated in the Revolution of 1776 and adopted the Bill of Rights held the individual right to have and use arms against tyranny to be fundamental. British firearms control policies that had been originally established to disarm and thereby conquer Indians came to be applied against the settlers themselves, first in Bacon's Rebellion of 1676 and again, a century later, in the great Revolution that ended colonial rule. In the minds of the American revolutionaries, the right to keep and bear arms for individual self-defense included the right to combine into independent militias for defense against the official colonial standing army and militias. After the armed populace had won the Revolution and the Consititution had been proposed, the Federalists promised that the new government would have no power to disarm the people. The anti-Federalists predicted that a standing army and select militia would come to overpower the people. In 1791, the American federal Bill of Rights was ratified, in part, as a formal recognition that private individuals would never be disarmed.

Poore Endebted Discontented and Armed:
Bacon's Rebellion of 1676

The American revolutionary war against British colonialism had roots in Bacon's rebellion, which took place a century before 1776. English commoners who settled in America were subject to some of the same forms of abuse that had been perpetrated on their counterparts in England by the Restoration monarchs. In 1671, at the same time that Charles II passed legislation to disarm indigenous Englishmen, his government in Virginia, headed by Sir William Berkeley, passed legislation to disarm indigenous Americans. Thus, arms control laws in the English experience served not only to subjugate domestically the poor and middle classes and religious groups, but also to conquer and colonize the Scots, the Irish, the American Indians, and finally the English settlers in America.

It was apparently unnecessary to pass legislation specifically for disarming Indians, since bounties were being paid for their heads.[1] Still, that carrying arms for defense was seen as both a right and a duty for English settlers in Virginia is clear in the enactment "that in going to churches and court in these times of danger, all people be enjoined and required to go armed for their greate[r] security."[2]

But any Englishman who dared to sell arms to the wrong Indians received, upon conviction, the death penalty:

> Whereas the country by sad experience have found that the traders with Indians by their avarice have so armed the Indians with powder, shot and guns. . . . Be it enacted . . . that if any person . . . shall presume to trade, truck, barter, sell or utter, directly or indirectly, to or with any Indians any powder, shot or arms . . . shall suffer death without benefit of clergy. . . .[3]

The act created an irrebutable presumption of such trade for any person living in any Indian town or more than three miles outside the English plantations who possessed any arms or ammunition other than one gun and ten charges of powder and shot.[4] In addition to death, the penalty included forfeiture of estate, half of which went to the state and the other half to the informer.[5]

The attempt to create a monopoly of arms in the hands of colonists was a double-edged sword, for colonists included landed royalists and commoners alike. The struggle against the monarchy through much of the seventeenth century in England also took place in English America. A central feature of the anti-monarchist cause, an armed commonalty, was the indispensable element in Bacon's Rebellion of 1676. As Sir William Berkeley, the royal governor, complained: "How miserable that man is who governs a people when six parts of seaven at least are Poore Endebted Discontented and Armed."[6] The "distribution of weaponry" among the poor exemplified in Berkeley's statement set the stage for a "politics of consent" in the coming century.[7]

The arms of the commoners directed against monarchial and colonial oppression set a precedent that was followed a century later. "A repetition of abuses such as those of which Bacon and his adherents complained, and an accumulation of oppressive acts on the part of the British government, without doubt, produced the American revolution. . . ."[8] Yet Bacon's laws also provided for the prosecution of "barbarous Indians" ("as enemies") who "shall refuse upon demand to deliver up into the hands of the English all such arms and ammunition of what kind or nature soever (bows and arrows only excepted) and also to deliver such hostages as shall from time to time be required of them. . . ."[9]

While Berkeley eventually crushed Bacon's Rebellion, he passed only feeble legislation restricting the right to bear arms. A series of acts in 1677 sanctioned the execution of rebels and of any one who spoke, wrote, or published "any matter or thing tending to rebellion," and provided for whipping anyone who spoke or wrote disrespectfully of those in authority.[10] Yet so fundamental was the right to have arms that to assemble with arms in numbers of five persons or more was the only offense decreed:

> And whereas by a branch of an act of assembly under Bacon made in March last, liberty is granted to all persons to carry their arms wheresoever they go, which liberty hath been found to be very prejudicial to the peace and welfare of this colony [a euphemism for royal administration]. Be it therefore enacted . . . that if any person or persons shall . . . presume to assemble together in arms to the number of five or upwards without being legally called together in arms the number of five or upwards, they be held deemed and adjudged as riotous and mutinous. . . .[11]

While Berkeley's collective gun-control policies existed for no other reason than to prevent the attainment of political power by commoners, so fundamental were firearms to the lives and livelihoods of the individual subjects that the royal administration conceded the right of every man to possess arms as an individual. The book of record of Samuel Wiseman, principal clerk to the king's commissioners, contains the following entry regarding the complaints of the people of James City County:

> Grievance: They ask that for their own defence they may be free to keep guns, buy ammunition and have their confiscated arms restored.

> Answer: The restraint was only during the rebellion. Now every man may bear arms. They think, where possible, confiscated arms should be restored to their former owners. The meaner sort rely on their arms to get part of their livelihood.[12]

Yet the Glorious Revolution of 1688 soon overthrew the Restoration monarchy in England and American alike, and "the right to bear arms in concert, which Bacon's succesive manifestos had justified,"[13] remained in the American consciousness. "A hundred years later, the collective right to bear arms that had been affirmed in Bacon's manifestos were again asserted in Virginia. This time, the rebellion turned into a revolution whose limited de facto success endured to receive lasting de jure recognition."[14] In short, the emerging American worldview and praxis entailed not only the right of individuals to keep and bear arms, but also the right to have and use arms in concert to defend their freedom against an oppressive government.

The American Revolution: Armed Citizens
Against Standing Army

Like other Bill of Rights freedoms, the personal right to keep and bear arms
gained consititutional recognition, in great part, from the abuses of power
that led to the Americn Revolution. Indeed, independence was attainable
only because the colonists owned and were expert in the use of firearms.

When, in 1768, British military forces were increased in Boston to quash
dissent, the town officially called upon the people to be armed for defense.
A *Journal of the Times* (1768–1769), printed in newspapers all over America
and England and circulated more widely than any other colonial writing except
Dickinson's *Letters*, defended the measure as follows: "It is certainly beyond
human art and sophistry, to prove that the British subjects, to whom the
privilege of possessing arms is expressly recognized by the [English] Bill of
Rights, . . . are guilty of an *illegal act*, in calling upon one another to be provided with them, as the *law directs*."[15] An armed populace was lauded in a
later issue of the *Journal* as necessary for protection from military abuses:

> Instances of the licentious and outrageous behavior of the *military
> conservators* of the peace still multiply upon us, some of which are of such
> nature, and have been carried to so great lengths, as must serve fully to
> evince that a late vote of this town, calling upon the inhabitants to pro-
> vide themselves with arms for their defence, was a measure as *prudent*
> as it was *legal*. . . . It is a natural right which the people have reserved to
> themselves, confirmed by the Bill of Rights, to keep arms for their own
> defence; and as Mr. Blackstone observes, it is to be made use of when
> the sanctions of society and law are found insufficient to restrain the vio-
> lence of oppression.[16]

The Boston Massacre in 1770 dramatically illustrated to Americans the cor-
rectness of the classical and Whig view that standing armies are dangerous to
liberty.[17] While the individuals shot down by the British troops were substantially unarmed, ironically both defenders and critics of the soldiers recognized
that the individuals in the crowd fired upon had a legal right to be armed. As
defense counsel for one of the soldiers, John Adams began his opening statement to the court by citing Becarria,[18] whose liberal criminological theory
asserted the right to carry arms.[19] Adams summarized Hawkins's comment in
Pleas of the Crown concerning the right of private persons to arm themselves
against rioters: "Here every private person is authorized to arm himself, and
on the strength of this authority, I do not deny the inhabitants had a right to
arm themselves at that time, for their defense, not for offence. . . ."[20] However, Adams contended that the soldiers were assaulted by the citizens, who
threw snowballs and other deadly objects. In this and other cases, Adams

cited numerous common-law cases and authorities in support of "self-defence, the primary canon of the law of nature."[21]

Samuel Adams wrote scathing attacks on the role of the soldiers in the Boston Massacre. While agreeing with his cousin John that the law recognized the right to carry arms for defense, he held that the superiorly armed troops were the aggressors. One of those slain, Mr. Attucks,

> was leaning upon his stick when he fell, which certainly was not a *threatning* posture: It may be supposed that he had as good right, *by the law of the land*, to carry a stick for his own and his neighbor's defence, in a time of such danger, as the Soldier who shot him had, to be arm'd with musquet and ball, for the defence of himself and his friend the Centinel: And if he at any time, *lifted up* his weapon of *defence*, it was surely, not more than a Soldiers *levelling* his gun charg'd with death at the multitude: If he had killed a *Soldier*, he might have been hanged for it, *and as a traitor too;* for even to attack a Soldier on his post, was pronounc'd *treason:* The Soldier shot *Attucks*, who was at *a distance* from him, and killed him,—and he was convicted of *Manslaughter*.[22]

In contrast to this recognition of the right of individuals to be armed for defense in the immediate vicinity of a confrontation between citizens and soldiers, modern practice in similar situations is for the state's standing armed forces to search for and to seize arms without any probable cause.

By 1775 the military occupation of Boston completely cut off its citizens from their compatriots outside the city. General Gage refused to allow inhabitants to leave unless they turned in their arms. Frothingham's contemporary account points out that, pursuant to Gage's order, "on the 27th of April the people delivered to the selectmen 1778 fire-arms [muskets], 634 pistols, 973 bayonets, and 38 blunderbusses. . . ." Thousands applied for passes to leave the city, and each pass given by Gage stated: "No arms nor ammunition is allowed to pass."[23] Incidentally, this arms seizure indicated the widespread possession of pistols as an American arm as the Revolution approached.[24] The following newspaper account, published months earlier, typifies the colonists' attempts to evade such restrictions: " A few days ago a number of small arms and a box of files, which were transporting from this place to Salem, were seized on Boston Neck, by order of lieutenant Johnston."[25]

Gage's seizure of privately owned arms in Boston would be castigated in the Declaration of Causes of Taking up Arms of 6 July 1775, which was drafted by John Hancock and Thomas Jefferson. Gage agreed to allow Bostonians to leave town after they "deposited their arms with their own magistrates," according to the Declaration:

They accordingly delivered up their arms; but in open violation of honour, in defiance of the obligation of treaties, which even savage nations esteemed sacred, the Governour ordered the arms deposited as aforesaid, that they might be preserved for their owners, to be seized by a body of soldiers; detained the greatest part of the inhabitants in the town, and compelled the few who were permitted to retire, to leave their most valuable effects behind.[26]

As the size and repressive character of the standing army increased, many Americans began to arm and to organize themselves into independent militias. In 1774, George Mason and George Washington organized the Fairfax County Militia Association, which was not subject to the control of the royal governor and which in fact arose, in part, as a defense force against the regular militia. "Threat'ned with the Destruction of our Civil-rights, & Liberty," (as stated in the resolution drafted by Mason), the members of this independent company of volunteers, who elected their own officers, pledged that "we will, each of us, constantly keep by us" a firelock, six pounds of gun powder, and twenty pounds of lead.[27]

In praising the Fairfax County model, a writer from Georgia implored that "the English troops in our front, and our governors forbid giving assent to militia laws, make it high time that we enter into *associations* for learning the use of arms, and to choose officers. . . ."[28] A South Carolina writer urged: "The inhabitants of this colony . . . ought therefore never to be without the most ample supply of arms and ammunition." He added that they should prepare "for the defence of this valuable country, by a diligent application to acquire a thorough knowledge of the use of arms and ammunition. . . ."[29]

Simultaneously, in New England, Samuel Adams urged "our Friends to provide themselves without Delay with Arms & Ammunition, get well instructed in the military Art, embody themselves & prepare a complete Set of Rules that they may be ready in Case they are called to defend themselves against the violent Attacks of Despotism. Surely the Laws of Self Preservation will warrant it in this Time of Danger & doubtful Expectation." In another communication, Adams agreed that "we may all be soon under the necessity of keeping *Shooting Irons*."[30]

In the meantime, George III wanted to know why the rebels had not been disarmed by General Gage, who replied in a letter to Lord Dartmouth in late 1774: "Your Lordship's ideas of disarming certain provinces . . . neither is nor has been practicable without having recourse to force, and being master of the country."[31] Indeed, by then the provinces swarmed with thousand of what were called *"minute men,* i.e., to be ready at a minute's warning with a fortnight's provision, and ammunition and arms."[32] Rumors that Americans planned to seize cannon and arms in Boston prompted the following letter from Governor Wentworth to General Gage: "This event too plainly proves the imbecility of this government to carry into execution his majesty's order in council, for seizing and detaining arms and ammunition imported into this province, without some strong ship of war in this harbour. . . ."[33]

The cry for independent militias, composed of citizens who would keep their own arms, spread through the colonies at the end of 1774 and during the beginning of 1775. The New Castle County (Delaware) committee resolved that "a well regulated Militia, composed of the gentlemen, freeholders, and other freemen, is the natural strength and stable security of a free Government," recommending that the inhabitants associate themselves into militia companies.[34] The Maryland provincial convention passed a similar resolution, adding that a freeman's militia "will obviate the pretence of a necessity for taxing us on that account [that is, for defense], and render it unnecessary to keep any Standing Army, (ever dangerous to liberty), in this Province. . . ."[35]; In a similar resolution, apparently drafted by George Mason, the Fairfax County (Virginia) committee concurred with the Maryland committee and "recommended to such of the inhabitants of this County as are from sixteen to fifty years of age . . . that they provide themselves with good Firelocks. . . ."[36]

In early 1775, George Mason continued to formulate the concept of the armed people as militia. In his Fairfax County Militia Plan "For Embodying the People," Mason reiterated that "a well regulated Militia, composed of the Gentlemen, Freeholders, and other Freemen" was necessary to protect "our antient Laws & Liberty" from the standing army.[37] "And we do each of us, for ourselves respectively, promise and engage to keep a good Fire-lock in proper Order, & to furnish Ourselves as soon as possible with, & always keep by us, one Pound of Gunpowder, four Pounds of Lead, one Dozen Gun-Flints, & a pair of Bullet-Moulds, with a Cartouch Box, or powder-horn, and Bag for Balls."[38]

A broader philosophical basis for the guarantee of self-sovereignty through the keeping of arms was provided by Mason in his Remarks on Annual Elections for the Fairfax Independent Company, which asserts as fundamental that "all men are by nature born equally free and independent."[39] While it should be formed to protect the weak, government is the source of "the most arbitrary and despotic powers this day upon earth," and thus by "frequently appealing to the body of the people" libery is secured.[40] The Roman experience proved that mercenaries destroy freedom, while the people must be introduced to "the use of arms and discipline" in order to "act in defence of their invaded liberty."[41] In summary, for Mason a "well regulated militia" consisted in the body of the people organizing themselves into independent companies, each member furnishing and keeping his own firearms, always ready to resist the standing army of a despotic state.

The 1774–1775 period was characterized by governmental attempts to disarm rebellious Americans through arbitrary searches and seizures and a ban on exports of arms and ammunition from England to the colonies. In the address of Massachusetts to the Mohawk Indians, Samuel Adams wrote that the British

> told us we shall have no more guns, no powder to use, and kill our wolves and other game, nor to send to you for you to kill your victuals with, and to get skins to trade with us, to buy your blankets and what you want. How can you live without powder and guns? But we hope to supply you soon with both, of our own making.[42]

Elsewhere, Adams warned that "it is always dangerous to the liberties of the people to have an army stationed among them, over which they have no control," even potentially the continental army.[43] "The Militia is composed of free Citizens. There is therefore no Danger of their making use of their Power to the destruction of their own Rights, or suffering others to invade them."[44]

Patrick Henry's "liberty or death" oration to the Virginia convention directly confronted the political import of an armed versus a disarmed populace. After offering several resolutions, including one which declared "that a well regulated militia, composed of gentlemen and yeoman, is the natural strength and only security of a free government,"[45] Henry implored:

> They tell us . . . that we are weak—unable to cope with so formidable an adversary. But when shall we be stronger? . . . *Will it be when we are totally disarmed*, and when a British guard shall be stationed in every house? . . . *Three million people, armed* in the holy cause of liberty . . . are invincible by any force which our enemy can send against us.[46]

The British attempt to seize or destroy the arms and ammunition at Lexington triggered the revolutionary shot heard around the world. At the same time, in Virginia, Lord Dunmore seized the gunpowder stored at Williamsburg. Yet the governor could not muster the regular Williamsburg militia against the "Hanover independent militia company" led by Patrick Henry, who, though unable to recapture the powder, forced restitution therefor.[47] In a proclamation similar to the one issued in Bacon's Rebellion, Lord Dunmore complained that Henry and his followers "have taken up arms and styling themselves an Independent Company, have . . . put themselves in a posture for war."[48] The governor soon saw it necessary to generalize this complaint in a letter to the British colonial minister: "Every County is now Arming a Company of men whom they call an independent Company for the avowed purpose of protecting their Committee, and to be employed against Government if occasion require."[49]

The patriots called upon all the people to arm themselves and to join the struggle. In his "Thoughts on Defensive War" (1775), Thomas Paine sought to persuade religious pacifists by employing the following reasoning:

> The supposed quietude of a good man allures the ruffian; while on the other hand, arms like laws discourage and keep the invader and the plunderer in awe, and preserve order in the world as well as property. The balance of power is the scale of peace. The same balance would be preserved were all the world destitute of arms, for all would be alike; but since some *will not*, others *dare not* lay them aside. . . . Horrid mischief would ensue were one half the world deprived of the use of them; . . . the weak will become a prey to the strong.[50]

Reports of seizures of arms by the British, and of attempts of Americans to obtain arms, fill the newspapers of the mid-1770s.[51] In 1776, a typical issue of the *Virginia Gazette* noted: "They write from St. Maloes, that the Commander in Chief of the maritime department there had ordered four American vessels laden with muskets, pistols, swords, bayonets, & c. to reland their cargoes and proceed home in ballast." The seizure of American arms on a vessel at St. John's, Antiqua, was also reported.[52] When the British fleet descended on Martha's Vineyard in 1778, its commanders demanded "all the arms, ammunition, and accoutrements on the island. . . ."[53] Despite their relative inaccuracy, pistols were common arms that were eagerly sought after on the civilian market[54] and used with effect in the Revolution's battles.[55]

An armed populace composed of partisans, militias, independent companies, and the continental army won the American Revolution.[56] Henry Lee, lieutenant colonel commandant of the partisan legion, a relative of Algernon Sidney and father of Robert E. Lee, clarified in his *Memoirs of the War* the reality of the American Revolution as an armed people's war. While the Americans were inferior in arms "imputable to our poverty"[57] and to British repression,[58] and despite their character as "a corps of peasants . . . defectively armed with fowling pieces, and muskets without bayonets," [59] "the American war presents examples of first-rate courage occasionally exhibited by corps of militia, and often with the highest success."[60] Such was the effectiveness of "armed citizens vying with our best soldiers"[61] that "our upper militia were never alarmed in meeting with equal numbers of British infantry"[62] and it was "chiefly undisciplined militia" that forced the surrender of Burgoyne's veterans in 1777.[63] A mass of farmers, mountaineers, and other commoners provided the arms and backbone to defeat the British: "every man capable of bearing arms must use them in aid or in opposition to the country of his birth. In the choice to be made, no hesitation existed in the great mass of the people. . . ."[64] With the spread of "the spirit of revolt" there was "a general rising of the people"—"our citizens rose in mass . . . and . . . armed themselves. . . ."[65] In theory and in practice, the American Revolution had both as an objective and as an indispensable means the individual right to keep, bear, and use arms to check governmental oppression.

Various colonies passed declarations of rights during the Revolution that explicitly recognized the individual right to have arms. The Virginia Declaration of Rights of 1776, which came from Mason's pen, included the provision "that a well regulated Militia, composed of the body of the People, trained to Arms, is the proper, natural, and safe Defence of a free State. . . ."[66] Thomas Jefferson proposed that the Virginia Constitution contain the provision, "No freeman shall be debarred the use of arms,"[67] and in the Declaration of Independence he vindicated the imperative of an armed uprising of the people, in times of oppression, against the standing army and the established government.

The Pennsylvania Declaration of 1776 stated "that the people have a right to bear arms for the defence of themselves and the state; and as standing armies in the time of peace are dangerous to liberty, they ought not to be kept up. . . ."[68] North Carolina's Declaration of Rights, drafted during the same year, asserted "that the people have a right to bear arms, for the defense of the State,"[69]—a subtle way of claiming not only the individual right to personal defense but also the right to overthrow the established (British) government by protecting the state against it. The Vermont Declaration of Rights of 1777 maintained "that the people have a right to bear arms for the defence of themselves and the State."[70]

The Massachusetts Declaration of Rights of 1780 provided that "the people have a right to keep and bear arms for the common defence."[71] The phrase "common defence" precluded any construction that arms could be used only for individual self-defense but not for common defense against governmental despotism. Both private and general defense had already been recognized in Article I of the declaration, which included among the unalienable rights those of "defending their lives and liberties; . . . and protecting property. . . ." Even so, because Massachusetts had felt the impact of British disarmament measures more than the other colonies, some objected to the clause as too narrow. The town of Northampton resolved:

> We also judge that the people's right to keep and bear arms, declared in the seventeenth article of the same declaration is not expressed with that ample and manly openness and latitude which the importance of the right merits; and therefore propose that it should run in this or some such like manner, to wit, The people have a right to keep and bear arms as well for their own as the common defence. Which mode of expression we are of opinion would harmonize much better with the first article than the form of expression used in the said seventeenth article.[72]

Similarly, the town of Williamsburg proposed the following alteration:

> Upon reading the 17th Article in the Bill of Rights. Voted that these
> words their Own be inserted which makes it read thus; that the people
> have a right to keep and to bear Arms for their Own and the Common
> defence.
>
> Voted Nemine Contradic. ———
>
> Our reasons gentlemen for making this Addition Are these. 1st that we
> esteem it an essential privilege to keep Arms in Our houses for Our Own
> Defense and while we Continue honest and Lawful subjects of Govern-
> ment we Ought Never to be deprived of them.
>
> Reas. 2 That the legislature in some future period may Confine all the
> fire Arms to some publick Magazine and thereby deprive the people of
> the benefit of the use of them.[73]

The objection to including what some believed to be a limitation on the
right to keep and bear arms explains why, nine years later, the U.S. Senate
rejected a proposal to add "for the common defense" at the end of what became the Second Amendment.[74] And while those who made this objection
somehow foresaw restrictive judicial interpretations that were never suggested
until the twentieth century, the framers of the Massachusetts declaration never
intended a narrow construction. In fact, it was drafted by John Adams, who
had defended the right to carry arms for self-defense and, in his study of American state constitutions, wrote that "arms in the hands of citizens [may] be
used at individual discretion . . . in private self-defence. . . ."[75]

Promilitia and anti–standing army sentiments were expressed in the Delaware and Maryland Declarations of Rights of 1776[76] and in the New Hampshire Bill of Rights of 1783.[77] The remaining six states adopted no declarations
of rights at that time.[78] Even so, two of these states later demanded protection for the right to keep and bear arms in the federal Constitution.[79] Before
the proposal of the Constitution, the newly independent colonies had existed
in a state of nature with each other, and with the defeat of the British, no one
feared that the natural and common-law right to have arms was any longer
in danger.

The Controversy over Ratification
of the Constitution

After the Constitution was submitted for ratification in 1787, political writings and debates in state conventions revealed two basic positions: the
Federalist view that a Bill of Rights was unnecessary because the proposed

government had no positive grant of power to deprive individuals of rights, and the anti-Federalist contention that a formal declaration would enhance protection of those rights. On the subject of arms, the Federalists promised that the people, far from ever being disarmed, would be sufficiently armed to check an oppressive standing army. The anti-Federalists feared that the body of the people as militia would be overpowered by a "select" or elite militia or standing army, unless there was a specific recognition of the individual right to keep and bear arms.[80]

While their sojourns abroad prevented their active involvement in the Constitution's ratification process, John Adams and Thomas Jefferson, the future leaders of the Federalist and Republican parties, respectively, reiterated in 1787 their preferences for an armed populace. In his defense of American State constitutions, John Adams relied on classical sources, in the context of an analysis of quotations from Marchamont Nedham's *The Right Constitution of a Commonwealth* (1656), to vindicate a militia of all the people:

> "That the people be continually trained up in the exercise of arms, and the militia lodged only in the people's hands, or that part of them which are most firm to the interest of liberty, that so the power may rest fully in the disposition of their supreme assemblies." The limitation to "That part most firm to the interest of liberty," was inserted here, no doubt, to reserve the right of disarming all the friends of Charles Stuart, the nobles and bishops. Without stopping to enquire into the justice, policy, or necessity of this, the rule in general is excellent. . . . One consequence was, according to [Nedham], "that nothing could at any time be imposed upon the people but by their consent. . . . As Aristotle tells us, in his fourth book of Politics, the Grecian states ever had special care to place the use and exercise of arms in the people, because the commonwealth is theirs who hold the arms: the sword and sovereignty ever walk hand in hand together." This is perfectly just. "Rome, and the territories about it, were trained up perpetually in arms, and the whole commonwealth, by this means, became one formal militia."[81]

After agreeing that all the continental European states achieved absolutism by following the Caesarian precedent of erecting "praetorian bands, instead of a public militia,"[82] the aristocratic Adams rejected the very right which won independence from England: "To suppose arms in the hands of citizens, to be used at individual discretion, except in private self-defence, or by partial orders of towns . . . is a dissolution of the government."[83] Note the exception for "private self-defense," a then universally recognized fundamental right. But for the more radical Thomas Jefferson, individual discretion was acceptable in the use of arms not simply for private but for public defense as well. Writing in 1787, Jefferson stressed the inexorable connection between the right to have and use arms and the right to revolution, as follows:

> God forbid we should ever be twenty years without such a rebellion. . . . And what country can preserve its liberties, if its rulers are not warned from time to time, that this people preserve the spirit of resistance? Let them take arms. . . . The tree of liberty must be refreshed from time to time, with the blood of partriots and tyrants.[84]

The Federalist Promise:
To Trust the People with Arms

The Federalists were actually in close agreement with Jefferson on the right to arms as a penumbra of the right to revolution. Thus, in *The Federalist*, No. 28, Hamilton wrote: "If the representatives of the people betray their constituents, there is then no recourse left but in the exertion of that original right of self-defense which is paramount to all positive forms of government. . . ."[85] And in No. 29, Hamilton expounded the argument that it would be wrong for a government to require

> the great body of yeomanry and of the other classes of citizens to be under arms for the purpose of going through military exercises and evolutions, as often as might be necessary to acquire the degree of perfection which would entitle them to the character of a well regulated militia. . . .
> Little more can reasonably be aimed at with respect to the people at large than to have them properly armed and equipped. . . .
> . . . This will not only lessen the call for military establishments, but if circumstances should at any time oblige the government to form an army of any magnitude that army can never be formidable to the liberties of the people while there is a large body of citizens, little if at all inferior to them in discipline and the use of arms, who stand ready to defend their rights and those of their fellow citizens.[86]

In *The Federalist*, No. 46, Madison, in contending that "the ultimate authority . . . resides in the people alone,"[87] predicted that encroachments by the federal government would provoke "plans of resistance" and an "appeal to a trial of force."[88] To a regular army of the United States government "would be opposed a militia amounting to near half a million citizens with arms in their hands." Alluding to "the advantage of being armed, which the Americans possess over the people of almost every other nation," Madison continued "Notwithstanding the military establishments in the several kingdoms of Europe, which are carried as far as the public resources will bear, the governments are afraid to trust the people with arms."[89] If the people were armed and organized into militia, "the throne of every tyranny in Europe would be speedily overturned in spite of the legions which surround it."[90]

The Constitution's proponents agreed that it conferred no federal power to deprive the people of their rights, because there was no explicit grant of such power and because the state declarations of right would prevail.[91] The existence of an armed populace, superior in its forces even to a standing army, and not a paper bill of rights, would check despotism. Noah Webster, a famous and influential Federalist, promised that even without a bill of rights, the American people would remain armed to such an extent as to be superior to any standing army raised by the federal government:

> Another source of power in government is a military force. But this, to be efficient, must be superior to any force that exists among the people, or which they can command; for otherwise this force would be annihilated, on the first exercise of acts of oppression. Before a standing army can rule, the people must be disarmed; as they are in almost every kingdom in Europe. The supreme power in America cannot enforce unjust laws by the sword; because the whole body of the people are armed, and constitute a force superior to any band of regular troops that can be, on any pretence, raised in the United States. A military force, at the command of Congress, can execute no laws, but such as the people perceive to be just and constitutional; for they will possess the power, and jealousy will instantly inspire the inclination, to resist the execution of a law which appears to them unjust and oppressive.[92]

Tench Coxe, a friend of Madison and a prominent Federalist, argued in his influential "An Amerian Citizen" that, should tyranny threaten, the "friends to liberty . . . using those arms which Providence has put into their hands, will make a solemn appeal to 'the power above.' "[93] Coxe also wrote: "The militia, who are in fact the effective part of the people at large, will render many troops quite unnecessary. They will form a powerful check upon the regular troops, and will generally be sufficient to over-awe them. . . ."[94] Writing as "A Pennsylvanian," Coxe went into even more detail as follows:

> The power of the sword, say the minority of Pennsylvania, is in the hands of Congress. My friends and countrymen, it is not so, for THE POWERS OF THE SWORD ARE IN THE HANDS OF THE YEOMANRY OF AMERICA FROM SIXTEEN TO SIXTY. The militia of these free commonwealths, entitled and accustomed to their arms, when compared with any possible army, must be *tremendous and irresistable.* Who are the militia? *are they not ourselves.* Is it feared, then, that we shall turn our arms *each man against his own bosom.* Congress have no power to disarm the militia. Their swords, and every other terrible implement of the soldier, are *the birth-right of an American.* . . .[T]he unlimited power

of the sword is not in the hands of either the *federal or state governments,* but, where I trust in God it will ever remain, *in the hands of the people.*[95]

Thus, the Constitution's proponents promised that the individual right to keep and bear arms would be not simply a paper right but a fact which would render an armed citizenry more powerful than any standing army, and consequently a bill of rights was unnecessary. Naturally, the virtues of an armed populace or general militia were stressed in terms of its political value for a free society, since the ratification process involved political issues. Nonetheless the right to have weapons for nonpolitical purposes, such as self-protection or hunting—but never for aggression—appeared so obviously to be the heritage of free people as never to be questioned. In the words of "Philodemos": "Every free man has *a right to the use of the* press, so he has to *the use of his arms.*" But if he commits libel, "he abuses his privilege, as unquestionably as if he were to plunge his sword into the bosom of a fellow citizen. . . ."[96] Punishment, not "previous restraints," was the remedy for misuse of either right.

Anti-Federalist Fears:
The People Disarmed, A Select Militia

The anti-federalists feared that without the protection of a bill of rights the creation of a select militia or standing army would result in the disarmament of the whole people as militia and in the consequent oppression of the populace. This fear had been expressed by the prediction of Oliver Ellsworth in the federal Convention that creation of "a select militia . . . would be followed by a ruinous declension of the great body of the militia."[97] Anti-Federalist spokesman John Dewitt contended:

> It is asserted by the most respectable writers upon government, that a well regulated militia, composed of the yeomanry of the country, have ever been considered as the bulwark of a free people. Tyrants have never placed any confidence on a militia composed of freemen.[98]

DeWitt predicted that Congress "at their pleasure may arm or disarm all or any part of the freemen of the United States, so that when their army is sufficiently numerous, they may put it out of the power of the freemen militia of America to assert and defend their liberties. . . ."[99]

George Clinton, governor of New York, writing as "Cato," predicted a permanent force because of "the fear of dismemberment of some of its parts, and the necessity to enforce the execution of revenue laws (a fruitful source of oppression). . . ."[100] "A Federal Republican" foresaw an army used "to suppress those struggles which may sometimes happen among a free people, and which tyranny will impiously brand with the name of sedition."[101] The anticipation by some federalists, particularly James Wilson, of a small standing army led to a particularly fearful reaction by anti-Federalists. "Freedom revolts at the idea,"[102] according to Elbridge Gerry, for the militia would become a federal force which "may either be employed to extort the enormous sums that will be necessary to support the civil list—to maintain the regalia of power—and the splendour of the most useless part of the community, or they may be sent into foreign countries for the fulfillment of treaties. . . ."[103] Praising the Swiss militia model, "A Democratic Federalist" rejected Wilson's argument for a standing army, "that great support of tyrants,"[104] with the following reasoning:

> Had we a standing army when the British invaded our peaceful shores? Was it a standing army that gained the battles of Lexington and Bunker Hill, and took the ill-fated Burgoyne? Is not a well-regulated militia sufficient for every purpose of internal defense? And which of you, my fellow citizens, is afraid of any invasion from foreign powers that our brave militia would not be able immediately to repel?[105]

The most influential writings stating the case against ratification of the Constitution without a bill of rights consisted of Richard Henry Lee's *Letters from the Federal Farmer* (1787–1788). Since most of Lee's proposals for specific provisions of a bill of rights were subsequently adopted in the Bill of Rights, and some with almost identical wording, the *Letters* provide an excellent commentary on the meaning of the provisions of the Bill of Rights, in general, and the Second Amendment, in particular. In predicting the early employment of a standing army through taxation, Lee contended:

> It is true, the yeomanry of the country possess the lands, the weight of property, possess arms, and are too strong a body of men to be openly offended—and, therefore, it is urged, they will take care of themselves, that men who shall govern will not dare pay any disrespect to their opinions. It is easily perceived, that if they have not their proper negative upon passing laws in congress, or on the passage of laws relative to taxes and armies, they may in twenty or thirty years be by means imperceptible to them, totally deprived of that boasted weight and strength: This may be done in a great measure by congress; if desposed to do it, by modelling the militia. Should one fifth or one eighth part of the men capable of bearing arms, be made a select militia, as has been proposed, and those the young and ardent part of the community, possessed of but little or no property, and all the others put upon a plan that will render them of no importance, the former will answer all the purposes of an army, while the latter will be defenceless. . . . I see no provision made

for calling out the *posse comitatus* for executing the laws of the union, but provision is made for congress to call forth the militia for the execution of them—and the militia in general, or any select part of it, may be called out under military officers, instead of the sheriff to enforce an execution of federal laws, in the first instance, and thereby introduce an entire military execution of the laws.[106]

In his second series of *Letters*, Lee classified as "fundamental rights" the rights of free press, petition, and religion; the rights to speedy trial, trial by jury, confrontation of accusers and against self-incrimination; the right not to be subject to "unreasonable searches or seizures of his person, papers or effects"; and, in addition to the right to refuse quartering of soldiers, "the militia ought always to be armed and disciplined, and the usual defense of the country. . . ."[107] Since these rights were all to be recognized in the Bill of Rights, Lee's concept of the militia warrants further examination:

A militia, when properly formed, are in fact the people themselves, and render regular troops in a great measure unnecessary. . . . [T]he constitution ought to secure a genuine [militia] and guard against a select militia, by providing that the militia shall always be kept well organized, armed, and disciplined, and include . . . all men capable of bearing arms; and that all regulations tending to render this general militia useless and defenceless, by establishing select corps of militia, or distinct bodies of military men, not having permanent interests and attachments in the community to be avoided.[108]

Thus, Lee feared that Congress, through its "power to provide for organizing, arming, and disciplining the militia" under Article I, § 8 of the proposed Constitution, would establish a "select militia" apart from the people that would be used as an instrument of domination by the federal government. The contemporary argument that it is impractical to view the militia as the whole body of the people, and that the militia consists of the select corps now known as the National Guard, also existed during Lee's time. He refuted it in these terms:

But, say gentlemen, the general militia are for the most part employed at home in their private concerns, cannot well be called out, or be depended upon; that we must have a select militia; that is, as I understand it, particular corps or bodies of young men, and of men who have but little to do at home, particularly armed and disciplined in some measure, at the public expense, and always ready to take the field. These corps, not much unlike regular troops, will ever produce an inattention to the general militia; and the consequence has ever been, and always must be, that the substantial men, having families and property, will generally be without arms, without knowing the use of them, and defenseless;

whereas, *to preserve liberty, it is essential that the whole body of the people always possess arms, and be taught alike, especially when young, how to use them;* nor does it follow from this, that all promiscuously must go into actual service on every occasion. The mind that aims at a select militia, must be influenced by a truly anti-republican principle; and when we see many men disposed to practice upon it, whenever they can prevail, no wonder true republicans are for carefully guarding against it.[109]

Richard Henry Lee's view that a well-regulated militia was the armed populace rather than a select group, or "Prussian militia,"[110] was reiterated by proponents and opponents of a bill of rights. As "M. T. Cicero" wrote to "The Citizens of America":

Whenever, therefore, the profession of arms becomes a distinct order in the state . . . the end of the social compact is defeated. . . .

No free government was ever founded, or ever preserved its liberty, without uniting the characters of the citizen and soldier in those destined for the defence of the state. . . . Such are a well regulated militia, composed of the freeholders, citizen and husbandman, who take up arms to preserve their property, as individuals, and their rights as freemen.[111]

The armed citizens would defend not only against foreign aggression but also against domestic tyranny. Another commentator declared, "The government is only just and perfectly free . . . where there is also a dernier resort, or real power left in the community to defend themselves against any attack on their liberties."[112]

While the view continued to be expressed that "a bill of rights as long as my arm" had no place in the Constitution,[113] a correspondent of the opposite persuasion noted that throughout his state people were "repairing and cleaning their arms, and every young fellow who is able to do it, is providing himself with a rifle or musket, and ammunition"; but civil war, he added, would be averted by adoption of a bill of rights.[114] If these views reflect the resultant compromise that a bill of rights would guarantee broad rights without being overly detailed, they also indicate that the demand for a bill of rights was as strong as the demand for independence had been a decade before. And consistent throughout that debate was the general understanding of the right to keep and bear arms as an individual right.[115]

Demands in the State Conventions for a Written Guarantee that Every Man be Armed

In the debates in the state conventions over the ratification of the Constitution, the existence of an armed citizenry was presumed by Federalists and anti-Federalists alike as essential to prevent despotism. Issues that divided the delegates included whether a written bill of rights guaranteeing the right to keep and bear arms among other individual rights should be added to the Constitution, and whether a provision guarding against standing armies or select militias was necessary. In the Pennsylvania convention, John Smilie warned:

> Congress may give us a select militia which will, in fact, be a standing army—or Congress, afraid of a general militia, may say there shall be no militia at all.
> When a select militia is formed; the people in general may be disarmed.[116]

This argument thus inherently assumed that the right to keep and bear arms[117] would be protected by the people combining into general militias to prevent being disarmed by select forces. In response, James Wilson contended that the Constitution already allowed for the ultimate force in the people: "In its principles, it is surely democratical; for, however wide and various the firearms of power may appear, they may all be traced to one source, the people."[118]

In the Massachusetts convention, William Symmes warned that the new government at some point "shall be too firmly fixed in the saddle to be overthrown by any thing but a general insurrection."[119] Yet fears of standing armies were groundless, affirmed Theodore Sedwick, who queried, "[i]f raised, whether they could subdue a nation of freemen, who know how to prize liberty, and who have arms in their hands?"[120] In New York, Thomas Tredwell feared that "we may now surrender, with a little ink, what it may cost seas of blood to regain."[121] And in the North Carolina convention, William Lenoir worried that Congress can

> disarm the militia. If they were armed, they would be a resource against great oppressions. . . . If the laws of the Union were oppressive, they could not carry them into effect, if the people were possessed of proper means of defence.[122]

But it was Patrick Henry who, in the Virginia convention, expounded most thoroughly the dual rights to arms and resistance to oppression:

> Guard with jealous attention the public liberty. Suspect every one who approaches that jewel. Unfortunately, nothing will preserve it but downright force. Whenever you give up that force, you are ruined.[123]

Fearful of the power of Congress over both a standing army and the militia,

Henry asked, "Have we the means of resisting disciplined armies, when our only defence, the militia, is put into the hands of Congress?"[124] Furthermore, "of what service would militia be to you when, most probably, you will not have a single musket in the state? for, as arms are to be provided by Congress, they may or may not furnish them."[125] The attempt to meet such objections prompted the adoption of the Second Amendment, which sought to guarantee the revolutionary ideal expressed by Henry in these words: "The great object is, that every man be armed. . . . Everyone who is able may have a gun."[126] Henry's objection to federal control over arsenals within the states would apply equally to control over private arms:

> Are we at last brought to such a humiliating and debasing degradation, that we cannot be trusted with arms for our own defense? Where is the difference between having our arms in our own possession and under our own direction, and having them under the management of Congress? If our defence be the *real* object of having those arms, in whose hands can they be trusted with more propriety, or equal safety to us, as in our own hands?[127]

George Mason buttressed Henry's arguments by pointing out that pro-British strategists resolved "to disarm the people; that it was the best and most effectual way to enslave them . . . by totally disusing and neglecting the militia."[128] Mason also clarified that under prevailing practice the militia included all people, rich and poor. "Who are the militia? They consist now of the whole people, except a few public officers."[129] Throughout the debates, Madison sought to portray the observations of Henry and Mason as exaggerations and to emphasize that a standing army would be unnecessary because of the existence of militias[130]—in short, to assure that the people would remain armed. And Zachriah Johnson argued that the new Constitution could never result in religious or other oppression because "the people are not to be disarmed of their weapons. They are left in full possession of them."[131]

The objections of the anti-Federalist pamphleteers and orators, particularly George Mason and Richard Henry Lee, prompted the state-ratifying conventions to recommend certain declarations of rights which became the immediate source of the federal Bill of Rights. Each and every recommendation that mentioned the right to keep and bear arms clearly intended an individual right. The individual character of the right is also evident in those proposals made in the conventions wherein a majority of delegates voted against a comprehensive bill of rights. The latter was the case in the Massachusetts convention in regard to the proposals of Samuel Adams "that the said Constitution be never construed to authorize Congress to infringe the just liberty of the press, or the rights of conscience; or to prevent the people of the United States, who are peaceable citizens, from keeping their own arms. . . ."[132] Similarly, the proposals adopted by the Pennsylvania minority included the following: "That the people have a right to bear arms for the defense of themselves, their state, or the United States, and for killing game, and no law shall be enacted for disarming the people except for crimes committed or in a case of real danger of public injury from individuals. . . ."[133]

New Hampshire was the first state to ratify the Constitution and to recommend that it include a bill of rights, including a provision that "Congress shall never disarm any citizen, unless such as are or have been in actual rebellion."[134] Not only are these words in no way dependent on militia uses, but the provision is separated from another article against standing armies by a provision concerning freedom of religion.[135] The New Hampshire convention was the first wherein a majority proposed explicit recognition of the individual right that was later expressed in the Second Amendment.[136] The New Hampshire and Pennsylvania proposals for the right to keep and bear arms were viewed as among "those amendments which particularly concern several personal rights and liberties."[137]

George Mason's pen was at work in Virginia, where the following provision was suggested: "That the people have a right to keep and bear arms; that a well-regulated militia, composed of the body of the people trained to arms, is the proper, natural, and safe defence of a free state; that standing armies, in time of peace, are dangerous to liberty, and therefore ought to be avoided. . . ."[138] These three propositions appear independent of one another. The first, a general protection of the individual right to have arms for any and all lawful purposes, is in no way dependent on the militia clause that follows. Madison's draft of the Second Amendment, as it was later proposed with the Bill of Rights in Congress, relied specifically on the recommendation by the Virginia convention.[139]

The New York convention predicated its ratification of the Constitution on the following interconnected propositions:

> That the powers of government may be reassumed by the people whensoever it shall become necessary to their happiness. . . .
> That the people have a right to keep and bear arms; that a well regulated militia, including the body of the people *capable of bearing arms*, is the proper, natural, and safe defence of a free state.[140]

Explicit in this language are the two independent declarations that individuals have a right to be armed and that the militia is the armed people. Similar language was adopted by the conventions of Rhode Island[141] and North Carolina.[142]

To Keep and Bear Their Private Arms:
The Adoption of the Bill of Rights

Madison's Proposed Amendments:
Guarantees of Personal Liberty

In acknowledgment of the conditions under which the state conventions ratified the Constitution, and in response to popular demand for a written declaration of individual freedoms, the first U.S. Congress in 1789 submitted for ratification by the states the amendments to the Constitution that became the Bill of Rights. Relying on the Virginia Declaration of Rights and on the amendments proposed by the state conventions,[143] James Madison proposed in the House of Representatives, on 8 June 1789, a bill of rights that included the following: "The right of the people to keep and bear arms shall not be infringed; a well armed, and well regulated militia being the best security of a free country: but no person religiously scrupulous of bearing arms shall be compelled to render military service in person."[144] That Madison intended an individual right is clear not only from this wording, but also from his notes for his speech proposing the amendment: "They [the proposed amendments] relate first to private rights—fallacy on both sides—especy as to English Decln. of Rights—l. mere act of parlt. 2. no freedom of press—Conscience . . . attainders—arms to protest[an]ts."[145] Madison's proposals were all referred to a House Committee on Amendments.

Madison's colleagues clearly understood the proposal to be protective of individual rights. Representative Fisher Ames of Massachusetts wrote: "Mr. Madison has introduced his long expected amendments. . . . It contains a bill of rights . . . the right of the people to bear arms."[146] Ames wrote to another correspondent, as follows: "The rights of conscience, of bearing arms, of changing the government, are declared to be inherent in the people."[147] Senator William Grayson of Virginia informed Patrick Henry: "Last Monday a string of amendments were presented to the lower House; these altogether respected *personal liberty*. . . ."[148]

Ten days after the Bill of Rights was proposed in the House, Tench Coxe published his "Remarks on the First Part of the Amendments to the Federal Constitution," under the pen name "A Pennsylvanian," in the Philadelphia *Federal Gazette*.[149] Probably the most complete exposition of the Bill of Rights to be published during its ratification period, the "Remarks" included the following: "As civil rulers, not having their duty to the people duly before them, may attempt to tyrannize, and as the military forces which must be occasionally raised to defend our country, might pervert their power to the injury of their fellow-citizens, the people are confirmed by the next article in their right to keep and bear their private arms." In short, what is now the

Second Amendment was designed to guarantee the right of the people to have "their private arms" to prevent tyranny and to overpower an abusive standing army or select militia.

Coxe sent a copy of his article to Madison along with a letter of the same date. "It has appeared to me that a few well tempered observations on these propositions might have a good effect. . . . It may perhaps be of use in the present turn of the public opinions in New York state that they should be republished there."[150] Madison wrote back, acknowledging "your favor of the 18th instant. The printed remarks inclosed in it are already I find in the Gazettes here [New York]." Far from disagreeing that the amendment protected the possession and use of "private arms," Madison explained that ratification of the amendments "will however be greatly favored by explanatory strictures of a healing tendency, and is therefore already indebted to the co-operation of your pen."[151]

Coxe's defense of the amendments was widely reprinted.[152] A search of the literature of the time reveals that no writer disputed or contradicted Coxe's analysis that what became the Second Amendment protected the right of the people to keep and bear "their private arms." The only dispute was over whether a bill of rights was even necessary to protect such fundamental rights. Thus, "One of the People" replied to Coxe's article with a response called "On a Bill of Rights," which held "the very idea of a bill of rights" to be "a dishonorable one to freemen." "What should we think of a gentleman, who, upon hiring a waiting-man, should say to him 'my friend, please take notice, before we come together, that I shall always claim the liberty of eating when and what I please, of fishing and hunting upon my own ground, of keeping as many horses and hounds as I can maintain, and of speaking and writing any sentiments upon all subjects." Thus, as a mere servant, the government had no power to interfere with individual liberties in any manner without a specific delegation. "[A] master reserves to himself . . . every thing else which he has not committed to the care of those servants."[153]

The House Committee on Amendments took up Madison's proposed amendments and subsequently reported the guarantee in this form: "A well regulated militia, composed of the body of the people, being the best security of free state, the right of the people to keep and bear arms shall not be infringed; but no person religiously scrupulous shall be compelled to bear arms."[154] The House debated this proposal on the seventeenth and twentieth of August 1789. Elbridge Gerry clarified that the purpose of the amendment was protection from oppressive government, and thus the government should not be in a position to exclude the people from bearing arms:

> This declaration of rights, I take it, is intended to secure the people
> against the mal-administration of the Government; if we could suppose

that, in all cases, the rights of the people would be attended to, the occasion for guards of this kind would be removed. Now, I am apprehensive, sir, that this clause would give an opportunity to the people in power to destroy the constitution itself. They can declare who are those religiously scrupulous, and prevent them from bearing arms.

What, sir, is the use of militia? It is to prevent the establishment of a standing army, the bane of liberty. Now, it must be evident, that, under this provision, together with their other powers, Congress could take such measures with respect to a militia, as to make a standing army necessary. Whenever Government mean to invade the rights and liberties of the people, they always attempt to destroy the militia, in order to raise an army upon their ruins. This was actually done by Great Britain at the commencement of the late revolution. They used every means in their power to prevent the establishment of an effective militia to the eastward. The Assembly of Massachusetts, seeing the rapid progress that administration were making to divest them of their inherent privileges, endeavored to counteract them by the organization of the militia; but they were always defeated by the influence of the Crown.[155]

Representative Gerry argued that the federal government should have no authority to categorize any individual as unqualified under the amendment to bear arms. "Now, if we give a discretionary power to exclude those from militia duty who have religious scruples, we may as well make no provisions on this head."[156] Keeping and bearing arms was a right of "the people," none of whom should thereby be disarmed under any pretense, such as the government's determination that they are religiously scrupulous or perhaps that they are not active members of a select militia (for example, the National Guard).

In reply, Representative Jackson "did not expect that all the people of the United States would turn Quakers or Moravians; consequently, one part would have to defend the other in case of invasion." The reference to "all the people" indicated again the centrality of the armed populace for defense against foreign attack. After further discussion, Gerry objected to the wording of the first part of the proposed amendment:

A well regulated militia being the best security of a free State, admitted an idea that a standing army was a secondary one. It ought to read, "a well regulated militia, trained to arms;" in which case it would become the duty of the Government to provide this security, and furnish a greater certainty of its being done.[157]

Gerry's words exhibit again the general sentiment that security rested on a generally—rather than a selectively—armed populace. The lack of a second to his proposal suggests that the congressmen were satisfied that the simple fact of citizens keeping and bearing arms would constitute a sufficiently well-regulated militia to secure a free state, and thus there was no need to make it, in Gerry's words, "the duty of the Government to provide this security. . . ."

Further debate on the exemption of religiously scrupulous persons from being compelled to bear arms highlights the sentiment that not only bearing but also merely keeping arms by all people was considered both a right and a duty to prevent standing armies. Representative Scott objected that the exemption would mean that "a militia can never be depended upon. This would lead to the violation of another article in the constitution, which secures to the people the right of keeping arms, and in this case recourse must be had to a standing army."[158] "What justice can there be in compelling them to bear arms," queried Representative Boudinot. "Now, by striking out the clause, people may be led to believe that there is an intention in the General Government to compel all its citizens to bear arms."[159] The proposed amendment was finally accepted after the insertion of the words "in person" at the end of the clause.[160]

In the meantime, debate over the proposed amendments raged in the newspapers. The underlying fear against a government monopoly of arms was expressed thusly: "Power should be widely diffused. . . . The monopoly of power, is the most dangerous of all monopolies."[161] The understanding that the keeping and bearing of private arms contributed to a well-regulated militia was represented in the following editorial:

> A late writer . . . on the necessity and importance of maintaining a well regulated militia, makes the following remarks:—A citizen, as a militia man is to perform duties which are different from the usual transactions of civil society. . . . [W]e consider the extreme importance of every military duty in time of war, and the necessity of acquiring an habitual exercise of them in time of peace. . . .[162]

At the same time, the Second Amendment was not intended only to protect the citizens having arms in their militia capacity. Rather, it originated in part from Samual Adams's proposal (which contained no militia clause) that Congress could not disarm any peacable citizens:

> It may well be remembered, that the following "amendments" to the new constitution of these United States, were introduced to the convention of this commonwealth by . . . SAMUEL ADAMS. . . . [E]very one of the intended alterations but one [that is, proscription of standing armies] have been already reported by the committee of the House of Representatives, and most probably will be adopted by the federal legislature. In justice therefore for that long tried Republican, and his numer-

ous friends, you gentlemen, are requested to republish his intended
alterations, in the same paper, that exhibits to the public, the amendments which the committee have adopted, in order that they may be compared together. . . .

"And that the said constitution be never construed to authorize congress . . . to prevent the people of the United States, who are peaceable
citizens, from keeping their own arms. . . ."[163]

Many of the proposed amendments were subjected to criticism. But the
Second Amendment was apparently never attacked, aside from one editorial
that argued the inefficiency of the militia clause but never questioned the
right-to-bear-arms clause. After quoting the language of the proposal as it was
approved by the House, the well-known anti-Federalist "Centinel" opined:

It is remarkable that this article only makes the observation, 'that a
well regulated militia, composed of the body of the people, is the best
security of a free state;' it does not ordain, or constitutionally provide
for, the establishment of such a one. The absolute command vested by
other sections in Congress over the militia, are not in the least abridged
by this amendment. The militia may still be subjected to martial law
. . . , may still be marched from state to state and made the unwilling
instruments of crushing the last efforts of expiring liberty.[164]

This indicates the understanding that the militia clause was merely declaratory and did not protect state rights to maintain militias to any appreciable
degree. That anti-Federalists of "Centinel's" persuasion never attacked the
right-to-bear-arms clause demonstrates that it recognized a full and complete
guarantee of individual rights to have and use private arms. Surely a storm of
protest would have ensued had anyone hinted that the right applied only to the
much feared select militia.

From the Senate to the States:
The Adoption of the Second Amendment

When the Senate came to consider the proposed amendments in early September 1789, it became evident that, while the right of individuals to keep
and bear arms would not be questioned, attempts to strengthen recognition
of state rights over militias and to proscribe standing armies would fail.
Amendments mandating avoidance of standing armies were rejected[165] as was
a proposal "that each state respectively, shall have the power to provide for
organizing, arming and discipling its own militia, whensoever Congress shall
omit or neglect to provide for the same."[166]

The form of the amendment adopted by the Senate, and approved by both houses on 25 September 1789, was the same that subsequently became the second article of the Bill of Rights: "A well regulated Militia, being necessary to the security of a free State, the right of the people to keep and bear Arms, shall not be infringed." In comparing the initial House version with the final Senate version, the House redundantly mentions "the people" twice—once in defining "militia" as the "body of the people", and again as the entity with the right to keep and bear arms. The Senate more succinctly avoided repetition by deleting the well-recognized definition of militia as "the body of the people." The Senate also deleted the phrase that "no person religiously scrupulous shall be compelled to bear arms"—perhaps because the amendment depicts the keeping and bearing of arms as an individual "right" (and not as a duty) for both public and private purposes, and perhaps to preclude any constitutional authority of the government to "compel" individuals (even those without religious scruples) to bear arms for any purpose. Finally, the Senate specifically rejected a proposal to add "for the common defense" after "to keep and bear arms,"[167] thereby precluding any construction that the right was restricted to militia purposes and to common defense against foreign aggression or domestic tyranny.

The Senate's deletion of the well-recognized definition of "militia" as "the body of the people" implied nothing more than its wish to be concise. But its rejection of the proposal to limit the amendment's recognition of the right to bear arms "for the common defence" meant to preclude any limitation on the individual right to have arms, for example, for self-defense or hunting. This is evident in the joint recommendation by the Senate and House of the amendments to the states. "The conventions of a number of the states having, at the time of their adopting the constitution, expressed a desire, in order to prevent misconstruction or abuse of its powers, that further declaratory and restrictive clauses should be added"[168]—this was the language of Congress that prefaced the proposed amendments when they were submitted to the states. In short, Congress modeled the Bill of Rights—including the Second Amendment's implicit definition of the militia as the whole people and the explicit guarantee to "the people," of the right to have arms— on the proposals submitted by the states, which, in turn, adopted the articles of amendment as a part of the Constitution.

The adoption of the amendments by the states was by no means a foregone conclusion, and the ratification struggle ensued through 1791. Three positions emerged during the controversy: (1) the proposed amendments were adequate, (2) further guarantees were needed, and (3) freemen had no need of a bill of rights. None of the proponents of these three different positions ever called into question the basic and individual right of keeping and bearing arms. As it was commonly understood, the proposed Bill of Rights sought to guarantee personal and unalienable rights, but the people also retained unenumerated rights.[169] Patrick Henry, Richard Henry Lee, and others were pleased with the Bill of Rights as far as it went, but they wanted guarantees against standing armies and direct taxes.[170] Since these same prominent anti-Federalists were among the most vocal in calling for a guarantee that would recognize the individual right to have arms, it is inconceivable that they did not object to what became the Second Amendment if anyone understood it to fail to protect personal rights.

The view that the rights of freemen were too numerous to enumerate in a bill of rights was coupled with the argument that the ultimate protection of American liberty would be provided by the armed populace rather than by a paper bill of rights. Nicholas Collins, a bill of rights opponent, argued in his "Remarks on the Amendments" that the American people would be sufficiently armed to overpower an oppressive standing army. "While the people have property, arms in their hands, and only a spark of noble spirit, the most corrupt Congress must be mad to form any project of tyranny."[171] On the other hand, the proamendment view held that both the existence of a bill of rights *and* an armed populace to enforce it were necessary to provide complementary safeguards. The following editorial advances this view. It assumes not only that keeping and bearing arms would contribute to a well-regulated militia, but also that militia exercises would demonstrate, in effect, the people's strength and thereby dissuade the government from infringing upon the right to keep and bear arms:

> The right of the people to keep and bear arms has been recognized by the General Government; but the best security of that right after all is, the military spirit, that taste for martial exercises, which has always distinguished the free citizens of these States; From various parts of the Continent the most pleasing accounts are published of reviews and parades in large and small assemblies of the militia. . . . Such men form the best barrier to the Liberties of America.[172]

While many people flexed their muscles by engaging in armed marches formed to ward off tyranny and secure the right to keep and bear arms, the debate over ratification of the Bill of Rights raged throughout 1790. Some reiterated that no bill of rights could enumerate the rights of the peaceable citizen, "which are as numerous as sands upon the sea shore. . . ."[173] President Washington reminded members of the House of Representatives that "a free people ought not only to be armed, but disciplined. . . ."[174] Still, right-to-arms provisions were not necessarily associated with the citizen's militia but were also coupled with different provisions. For instance, a widely published proposed bill of rights for Pennsylvania included a militia clause in a separate article from the following: "That the right of the citizens to bear arms in defence of themselves and the State, and to assemble peaceably together. . . shall not be questioned."[175]

During the ratification period the view prevailed that the armed citizenry would prevent tyranny. Theodorick Bland wrote Patrick Henry that "I have founded my hopes to the single object of securing (in terrorem) the great and essential rights of freemen from the encroachments of Power—so far as to authorize resistance when they should be either openly attacked or insidiously undermined."[176] While the proposed amendments continued to be criticized for the lack of a provision on standing armies,[177] no one questioned the right-to-bear-arms amendment.[178] Two days before Rhode Island ratified the Bill of Rights, newspapers in that state republished its declaration of natural rights, which had been included in its recent ratification of the Constitution: "That the people have a right to keep and bear arms: That a well-regulated militia, including the body of the people capable of bearing arms, is the proper, natural and safe defense of a free state. . . ."[179]

As more and more states adopted the amendments and as the great debate began to dwindle, even the opponents of a standing-army provision conceded that an armed citizenry, constituted as a well-regulated militia, would prevent oppression from that quarter. As "A Framer" argued in a plea addressed "To The Yeomany of Pennsylvania":

> Under every government the dernier resort of the people, is an appeal to the sword; whether to defend themselves against the open attacks of a foreign enemy, or to check the insidious encroachments of domestic foes. Whenever a people . . . entrust the defence of their country to a regular, standing army, composed of mercenaries, the power of that country will remain under the direction of the most wealthy citizens. . . .[Y]our liberties will be safe as long as you support a well regulated militia.[180]

In recent years it has been suggested that the Second Amendment protects the "collective" right of states to maintain militias, while it does not protect the right of "the people" to keep and bear arms. If anyone entertained this notion in the period during which the Constitution and Bill of Rights were debated and ratified, it remains one of the most closely guarded secrets of the eighteenth century, for no known writing surviving from the period between 1787 and 1791 states such a thesis. The phrase "the people" meant the same thing in the Second Amendment as it did in the First, Fourth, Ninth and Tenth Amendments—that is, each and every free person. A select militia defined as the only privileged class entitled to keep and bear arms was considered an anathema to a free society, in the same way that Americans denounced select spokesmen approved by the government as the only class entitled to freedom of the press. Nor were those who adopted the Bill of Rights willing to clutter it with details—such as nonpolitical justifications for the right to bear arms (for example, for self-protection and for hunting)—or with a list of what everyone knew to be common arms, such as muskets, scatterguns, pistols, and swords. In the light of present-day developments, perhaps the most striking insight of those who originally opposed the attempt to summarize all the rights of a freeman in a bill of rights was that, no matter how it was worded, artful misconstruction would be employed to limit and to destroy the very rights that needed to be protected.

A Linguistic Analysis of the Second Amendment

A purely logical analysis of the words of the Second Amendment and its relation to the Bill of Rights in its entirety demonstrates consistency with the historical context and with the intent of the framers. While some freedoms are relative—for instance, the Fourth Amendment's proscription only of "unreasonable" searches and seizures—others are guaranteed against any interference whatever:

> The kind of protection that particular rights enshrined in the Bill of Rights receive is not identical. Some are guaranteed in the most absolute and imperative terms. The first amendment specifies that Congress *shall* make *no* law "respecting an establishment of religion, . . . or abridging the freedom of speech. . . ." The second amendment prescribes that the right of the people to keep and bear arms *shall* not be infringed.[181]

In addition to its absolute character, the Second Amendment is written in a universal form, which suggests that it provides protection against both federal and state infringement. In contrast to the language of the First Amendment, which states only that "Congress shall make no law," the Second Amendment provides generally that the right "shall not be infringed." Well aware that the First Amendment applied only to the federal system, Madison had supported an amendment that "no State shall infringe the equal rights of conscience, nor the freedom of speech. . . ."[182] Thus, there is strong support for the proposition that the absolute and universal language of the Second Amendment precludes any federal or state infringement whatever.

While some guarantees in the Bill of Rights provide a more absolute and universal protection than others, all have in common the reasonable assumption that "the people" means exactly what the term says. The holistic argument that "the people" in the Second Amendment means the collective people in their role as the select militias of the state governments ignores the "metaphysical difficulty of how something can exist in the whole without existing in any of its parts."[183] The curious linguistic stipulation that "the people" signifies the state governments but does not refer to private individuals is inconsistent with other provisions of the Bill of Rights. The First, Second, and Fourth Amendments refer, respectively, to "the right of the people" to assemble and petition government, to keep and bear arms, and to be secure against unreasonable searches and seizures. The Ninth Amendment, a further guarantee, *inter alia*, of the individual right to keep and carry arms, also conceives of "the people" as comprising all individuals: "The enumeration in the Constitution, of certain rights, shall not be construed to deny or disparage others retained by the people." Finally, the Tenth Amendment not only clearly distinguishes between the states and the people, but it further supports the traditional right to possess weapons since Congress was delegated no power to regulate this right: "The powers not delegated to the United States by the Constitution, nor prohibited by it to the States, are reserved to the States respectively, or to the people."

If the framers had meant only to guarantee the right of states to have militias and of their organized militiamen to keep and bear arms, they would surely have worded the Second Amendment differently. Language such as "the right of the select militia to keep and bear arms" would have sufficed. It is unlikely that the framers would have intended to commit blatantly the fallacy of equivocation by shifting the meaning of "the people" from amendment to amendment, or that they would have risked the fallacy of ambiguity by defining the phrase "the people" in the Second Amendment in such an unusual manner, that is, as "those people in a select state militia." Such a bizarre interpretation would also commit the fallacies of division and of composition in reverse by holding that the right exists in the whole but not in its parts or that it fails to exist in the parts but does exist in the whole.

It goes without saying that Article I, § 8 of the Constitution had already provided for the existence and armament of the organized militia, and it would have been redundant for the Second Amendment to have done the same.

Still another interpretation of the Second Amendment, which opposes any right of "the people" to have arms, reasons thus: The right to have arms is dependent on a militia being necessary for the security of a free state, but despite the clear words of the amendment and the aversions of the framers, today the standing army allegedly protects freedom. This interpretation appears to reduce the amendment to a conditional or hypothetical syllogism, with its first premise as follows: If a well-regulated militia is necessary to the security of a free state (p), then the right to the people to keep and bear arms shall not be infringed (q); that is, p implies q. Standing alone, p and q constitute, respectively, the second premise and the conclusion of the syllogism, which appears thus:

$$p \supset q$$
$$\underline{p}$$
$$\therefore \quad q$$

and is valid by reason of *modus ponens*.

Yet the denial of the antecedent, should it be expressed in the second premise, fails to imply the denial of the consequent in the conclusion; that is, even if a militia is not necessary for the existence of a free state, the people still have the right to keep and bear arms.[184] The fallacy of denying the antecedent is committed in this form:

$$p \supset q$$
$$\underline{-p}$$
$$\therefore \quad -q$$

In sum, the syntax of the proposition that makes up the Second Amendment necessitates the construction that the right to keep and bear arms is absolute and is not dependent on the needs of the militia; the contrary view, that government may restrict this right, commits the fallacy of denying the antecedent and is therefore a misconstruction.

Despite the clear wording of the Second Amendment and the intent of its framers, critics of an armed populace have attempted to use the phraseology of the provision to deny any right to keep and bear arms to "the people" by resorting to the illogical reasoning analyzed above. It was precisely this form of artful misconstruction, employed by those who wished to expand governmental power by denying individual rights, that led some of the Founding Fathers to argue against the adoption of a bill of rights. In the words of James Madison:

> It has been objected also against a bill of rights, that, by enumerating particular exceptions to the grant of power, it would disparage those rights which were not placed in that enumeration; and it might follow, by implication, that those rights which were not singled out, were intended to be assigned into the hands of the General Government, and were consequently insecure. This is one of the most plausible arguments I have ever heard urged against the admission of a bill of rights into this system: but, I conceive, that it may be guarded against.[185]

Rather than have no bill of rights, Madison's solution was to add the provision that became the Ninth Amendment: "The enumeration in the constitution, of certain rights, shall not be construed to deny or disparage others retained by the people." As recognition of the "inherent natural rights of the individual,"[186] the Ninth Amendment presupposes the existence of personal, not collective, rights, which stem from natural law and common law.[187] Thus, even if the Second Amendment's reference to "the people" meant "select militiamen," or if its reference to "arms" meant only "militia-type arms," the Ninth Amendment's guarantee of all preexisting unenumerated rights would encompass the natural and common-law rights of the individual to keep and carry arms for such purposes as self-defense and hunting.[188]

The Federalist argument that a bill of rights was unnecessary, since the federal government had only limited delegated powers, would imply that the government would be powerless to pass legislation interfering with the individual right to possess arms. The further prediction that an enumeration of rights would be used to restrict those very rights by misconstruction or to deny the existence of unenumerated rights has certainly been applicable to the right to keep and bear arms. Nonetheless, the intent of the state conventions that requested adoption of a bill of rights and of the framers in Congress—who were all influenced by the classical vindications of natural rights, by English common law, and by the American revolutionary experience—was that the Second Amendment recognized the absolute individual right to keep arms in the home and to carry them in public.

4

Antebellum Interpretations

In the period of American history extending from the adoption of the Constitution to the War between the States, the act of keeping and bearing arms was treated as a virtually unquestioned right of each individual citizen. The fundamental right to have arms was based, in part, on the political lessons of the Revolutionary experience. "None but an armed nation can dispense with a standing army," Jefferson wrote in 1803. "To keep ours armed and disciplined, is therefore at all times important."[1] And in 1814, Jefferson observed that "we cannot be defended but by making every citizen a soldier, as the Greeks and Romans who had no standing armies."[2] In addition to the deterrence of aggression from a domestic or foreign tyranny, the individual possession of arms,[3] and particularly of firearms, functioned to provide a basic means of self-defense as well as a means of subsistence for hunters.

That the Second Amendment recognized an individual right to keep and bear arms was not an issue for partisan politics, and the courts consistently so held. The only exception to this rule appeared in the context of slavery. Specifically, in order to disarm slaves as well as black freemen, certain courts originated the view that the guarantee was limited to citizens rather than to all of the people and that the Second Amendment did not apply to the states. The exceptions were aberrations intended to prevent black liberation. Most commentaries and courts that analyzed the Second Amendment treated all individuals as having the right and construed it as a restraint on state and federal infringement.

Judicial Commentaries:
The Armed Citizen as the
Palladium of Liberty

Although Federalist and Republican differences in interpretation of the Constitution appeared early in judicial thought on subjects as diverse as the general welfare clause and the right of free speech, these points of divergence did not arise with respect to the Second Amendment. In his popular edition of Blackstone's *Commentaries* published in 1803, St. George Tucker, a judge on the Virginia Supreme Court and later on the U.S. District Court for the Eastern District of Virginia,[4] wrote of the Second Amendment: "The right of the people to keep and bear arms shall not be infringed . . . and this without any qualification as to their condition or degree, as is the case in the British government. . . ."[5] In the appendix to the *Commentaries*, Tucker explained in more detail:

> The right of self-defense is the first law of nature; in most governments it has been the study of rulers to confine this right within the narrowest limits possible. Whenever standing armies are kept up, and the right of the people to keep and bear arms is, under any color or pretext whatsoever, prohibited, liberty, if not already annihilated, is on the brink of destruction. In England, the people have been disarmed, generally under the specious pretext of preserving the game; a never-failing lure to bring over the landed aristocracy to support any measure. . . . True it is, their bill of rights seems at first view to counteract this policy; but their right of bearing arms is confined to protestants, and the words 'suitable to their condition or degree' have been intrepreted to authorize the prohibition of keeping a gun or other engine for the destruction of game, by any farmer, or inferior tradesman, or other person not qualified to kill game.[6]

In 1829 appeared William Rawle's second edition of his commentaries on the Constitution, which became a standard text on the subject. The following lengthy analysis of the Second Amendment was prefaced by citing the Tenth:

> *the powers not delegated to congress by the Constitution, nor prohibited by it to the states, are reserved to the states respectively, or to the people.* What we are about to consider are certainly not delegated to congress, nor are they noticed in the prohibitions to states; they are therefore reserved either to the states or to the people. Their high nature, their necessity to the general security and happiness will be distinctly perceived.
>
> In the second article, it is declared, that a *well regulated militia is necessary to the security of a free state;* a proposition from which few will dissent. Although in actual war, the services of regular troops are confessedly more valuable; yet, while peace prevails, and in the commencement of a war before a regular force can be raised, the militia form the palladium of the country. They are ready to repel invasion, to suppress insurrection, and preserve the good order and peace of government. That they should be well regulated, is judiciously added. A disorderly militia is disgraceful to itself, and dangerous not to the enemy, but to its own county. The duty of the state government is, to adopt such regulations as will tend to

make good soldiers with the least interruptions of the ordinary and useful occupations of civil life. In this all the Union has a strong and visible
interest.

The corollary, from the first position, is that *the right of the people to keep
and bear arms shall not be infringed.*

The prohibition is general. No clause in the Constitution could by
any rule of construction be conceived to give to congress a power to disarm the people. Such a flagitious attempt could only be made under some
general pretence by a state legislature. But if in any blind pursuit of inor-
dinate power, either should attempt it, this amendment may be appealed
to as a restaint on both.

In most of the countries of Europe, this right does not seem to be
denied, although it is allowed more or less sparingly, according to circumstances. In England, a country which boasts so much of its freedom,
the right was secured to protestant subjects only, on the revolution of
1688; and it is cautiously described to be that of bearing arms for their
defence, "suitable to their conditions, and as allowed by law." An arbitrary code for the preservation of game in that country has long disgraced
them. A very small proportion of the people being permitted to kill it,
though for their own subsistence; a gun or other instrument, used for
that purpose by an unqualified person, may be seized and forfeited.
Blackstone, in whom we regret that we cannot always trace the expanded
principles of rational liberty, observes however, on this subject, that the
prevention of popular insurrections and resistance to government by disarming the people, is oftener meant than avowed, by the makers of forest and game laws.[7]

Rawle's analysis is cogent in stressing the significance of the first clause of
the Second Amendment as an imperative for a militia system as opposed to a
standing army. The second clause is then treated both in its linkage to the
first clause, inasmuch as the individual right to keep and bear arms encourages
a militia system, and independently as the recognition of a fundamental right
to have arms, unrestrained by state no less than by federal legislation. In his
negative remarks on English policy, Rawle clarifies that the right to have arms
is deemed more absolute in America than in Britian, and he points out that the
Second Amendment protects individual use of arms for nonmilitia purposes,
such as hunting.

Soon after Rawle's work appeared, Henry St. George Tucker, son of St.
George Tucker and president of the Virginia Supreme Court, wrote the following with respect to "the principle absolute rights of individuals":

To secure their enjoyment, however, certain protections or barriers
have been erected which serve to maintain inviolate the three primary

rights of personal security, personal liberty, and private property. These may in America be said to be:

1. The bill of rights and written constitutions. . . .

2. The right of bearing arms—which with us is not limited and restrained by an arbitrary system of game laws as in England; but is particularly enjoyed by every citizen, and is among his most valuable privileges, since it furnishes the means of resisting as a freeman ought, the inroads of usurpation.

3. The right of applying to the courts of justice for the redress of injuries.[8]

In still another treatise on the principles of consitutional liberty that was published at about the same time, Benjamin L. Oliver analyzed the Second Amendment under the chapter heading, "Of the rights reserved to the people of the United States; not being granted either to the general government, or to the state governments."[9] The utility of "the right of the citizens to bear arms" lay in the resulting power of a militia to resist invasion, insurrection, or usurpation. "Another advantage . . . is the assistance which it is always ready to lend the civil arm of the government; in preserving domestic peace and tranquility; in the execution of the process of the law; and in suppressing the tumults and riots and other disorders of the less informed citizens. . . ."[10]

The practice of carrying concealed weapons, Oliver opined, "if it is really unconstitutional to restrain it by law, ought to be discountenanced. . . ."[11] His underlying objection was based upon the unfair advantage of surprise available to the "man, who arms himself with a deadly weapon, . . . and afterwards uses it upon some provocation which does not constitute a legal excuse, and kills his antagonist. . . ."[12] Nevertheless, Oliver firmly believed that "there are without doubt circumstances, which may justify a man for going armed; as, if he has valuable property in his custody; or, if he is travelling in a dangerous part of the country; or, if his life has been threatened."[13] The right to have and to use arms for self-defense, according to Oliver, was also included in the unenumerated rights:

> There are some other rights, which are reserved to the people, though not mentioned in the general constitution. Among these is the right of self-defence, in cases where the danger is so imminent, that the person in jeopardy, may suffer irreparable injury, if he waits for the protection of the laws. . . . [A]s the compact between him and society is mutual, if society is unable to protect him, his natural right revives to protect himself.[14]

Joseph Story, associate justice of the U.S. Supreme Court (1811–1845), interpreted the Second Amendment as providing for an individual right to bear arms that would be sufficient to overcome even the standing army of an oppressive government:

> The militia is the natural defense of a free country against sudden foreign invasions, domestic insurrections, and domestic usurpations of power by rulers. It is against sound policy for a free people to keep up large military establishments and standing armies in time of peace, both from the enormous expenses, with which they are attended, and the facile means, which they afford to ambitious and unprincipled rulers, to subvert the government, or trample upon the rights of the people. The right of the citizens to keep and bear arms has justly been considered, as the palladium of the liberties of the republic; since it offers a strong moral check against usurpation and arbitrary power of the rulers; and will generally, even if these are successful in the first instance, enable the people to resist and triumph over them.[15]

In sum, the antebellum commentators were unanimous in their view of the right to keep and bear arms as an individual liberty which existed for a variety of purposes, from defense against foreign or domestic oppression to personal self-defense. Furthermore, in finding recognition of that right in both common law and in the Bill of Rights, they were equally firm in their understanding of its protection from state and federal infringement alike.

Carrying Weapons Concealed:
The Only Right Questioned in
Early State Cases

A provision of the Kentucky Constitution—"The right of the citizens to bear arms in defense of themselves and the state, shall not be questioned"[16]— provided the occasion for perhaps the first state judicial opinion on the nature and source of the right to bear arms, in the 1822 case of *Bliss* v. *Commonwealth*.[17] The defendant appealed his conviction, for having worn a sword cane concealed as a weapon, by asserting the unconstitutionality of an act prohibiting concealed weapons. The court held, "Whatever restrains the full and complete exercise of that right, though not an entire destruction of it, is forbidden by the explicit language of the constitution."[18] While observing that wearing concealed weapons had been considered a legitimate practice when the constitutional provision was adopted, the court reasoned:

> The right existed at the adoption of the constitution; it had then no limits short of the moral power of the citizens to exercise it, and in fact consisted in nothing else but in the liberty of the citizens to bear arms.

Diminish that liberty, therefore, and you necessarily restrain the right; and such is the diminution and restraint, which the act in question most indisputably imports, by prohibiting the citizens wearing weapons in a manner which was lawful to wear when the constitution was adopted.[19]

Whether carrying and wearing dangerous weapons constituted an affray at common law was the issue in the 1833 Tennessee case of *Simpson* v. *State*,[20] and the court answered in the negative, citing Blackstone's stipulation that violence which terrifies the people must also be present. The prosecutor cited Serjeant Hawkins[21] in maintaining that an affray could exist where one is armed with unusual weapons that would naturally cause terror to the people; the court, however, rejected those "ancient English statutes, enacted in favour of the king, his ministers, and other servants," which provided that "no man . . . except the king's servants, &c. shall go or ride armed by night or by day."[22] The court seemed implicitly resentful of royal privilege in noting that English common-law decisions added a judicial gloss to the statutes: "persons of quality are in no danger of offending against this statute by wearing their common weapons." While rejecting the existence of a common-law abridgment of the right to bear arms,[23] the court held in the alternative that any such abridgment would be abrogated by the state constitution of Tennessee, which then provided "that the freemen of this State have a right to keep and bear arms for their common defense." "By this clause of the constitution, an express power is given and secured to all the free citizens of the State to keep and bear arms for their defense, without any qualification whatever as to their kind or nature. . . ."[24]

Despite this broad language, the subsequent Tennessee case of *Aymette* v. *State*[25] originated the interpretation that the arms which could be possessed were those of ordinary military weapons or weapons that contributed to the common defense. The state constitution of Tennessee guaranteed the people the right to keep and bear arms "for their common defense." These words were defeated in the adoption of the Second Amendment, thus implying that the amendment would not be so limited. Still, other state courts interpreted the phrase "for their common defense" to mean not only combined defense as a militia but individual self-defense. And yet, the *Aymette* case supports the right of each individual to keep and bear any arms used in "civilized warfare," in part to prevent domestic tyranny: "If the citizens have these arms in their hands, they are prepared in the best possible manner to repel any encroachments upon their rights, etc."[26]

Anticipating the three basic lines of disagreement that have characterized twentieth-century analyses of the Second Amendment, the separate opinions rendered in *State* v. *Buzzard*,[27] an 1842 Arkansas case, construed a concealed weapons statute as follows: (1) the individual citizen anytime may bear arms suitable for militia use; (2) the right to bear arms applies exclusively to the militia; and (3) the individual citizen anytime may bear arms of any variety. Since two of the three judges determined that the defendant had borne a concealed weapon unsuitable for militia use, the conviction was upheld. Interestingly, all three judges seemed to assume that the Second Amendment applied to the states. The state provision provided: "That the free white men of this State shall have a right to keep and bear arms in their common defense."[28] The dissenting opinion, which took the third position cited above, argued: "Now, I take the expressions 'a well regulated militia being necessary for the security of a free State,' and the terms 'common defense,' to be the reasons assigned for the granting of the right, and not a restriction or limitation upon the right itself, or the perfect freedom of its exercise."[29]

The classic antebellum opinion—which held that the right of the individual to possess arms is protected from both state and federal infringement, but that the manner in which arms could be borne was a proper subject for regulation—was handed down in *Nunn* v. *State* (1846).[30] An ambiguous Georgia statute apparently proscribed the wearing of concealed breast pistols, but evidently it did not prohibit people from carrying horseman's pistols. While upholding the proscription on the wearing of concealed weapons, the court said that the state constitutions "confer no *new rights* on the people which did not belong to them before," that no legislative body in the Union could deny citizens the privilege of being armed to defend self and country, and that the colonial ancestors had possessed this right, which "is one of the fundamental principles, upon which rests the great fabric of civil liberty. . . ."[31]

In the *Nunn* case the Georgia Supreme Court anticipated the twentieth-century U.S. Supreme Court's selective incorporation doctrine—which holds that various provisions of the Bill of Rights are incorporated in the postbellum Fourteenth Amendment for application against the states—by declaring the First, Fourth, Fifth and Sixth Amendments to be binding on both state and federal governments. The Georgia court reasoned:

> The language of the *second* amendment is broad enough to embrace both Federal and state govenments—nor is there anything in its terms which restricts its meaning. . . . Is this a right reserved to the *State* or to *themselves?* It is not an unalienable right, which lies at the bottom of every free government? We do not believe that, because the people withheld this arbitrary power of disfranchisement from Congress, they ever intended to confer it on the local legislatures. This right is too dear to be confided to a republican legislature.[32]

The Georgia court expounded upon the relation between individual arms possession and the militia: "in order to train properly that militia, the unlimited right of the people to keep and bear arms shall not be impaired."[33] The court added that both constitutional and natural rights were at stake. Contending that the state governments were prohibited from violating the rights to assembly and petition, the right proscribing unreasonable searches and seizures, the right to an impartial jury in criminal prosecutions, and the right to receive assistance of counsel, the court continued:

> Nor is the right involved in this discussion less comprehensive or valuable: "The right of the people to bear arms shall not be infringed." The right of the whole people, old and young, men, women and boys, and not militia only, to keep and bear arms of every description, and not *such* merely as are used by the *militia*, shall not be *infringed*, curtailed or broken in upon, in the smallest degree; and all this for the important end to be attained: the rearing up and qualifying a well-regulated militia, so vitally necessary to the security of a free State. Our opinion is, that any law, State or Federal, is repugnant to the Constitution, and void, which contravenes this *right*. . . .[34]

In 1850, while holding that a statute prohibiting the carrying of concealed weapons was not in violation of the Second Amendment, the Louisiana Supreme Court in *State* v. *Chandler* reasoned that the right to carry arms openly "placed men upon an equality. This is the right guaranteed by the Constitution of the United States, and which is calculated to incite men to a manly and nobel defense of themselves, if necessary, and of their country. . . ."[35]

In 1859, the Texas Supreme Court in *Cockrum* v. *State*[36] upheld the validity of a statute which classified as murder any nonmalicious homicide committed with certain deadly weapons (in this case, a bowie knife), and which classified as manslaughter any homicide committed with other weapons. The court explained that the object of the Second Amendment was to ensure that "the people cannot be effectually oppressed and enslaved, who are not first disarmed."[37] The court continued in reference to the Texas Bill of Rights:

> The right of a citizen to bear arms, in lawful defense of himself or the State, is absolute. He does not derive it from the State government. It is one of the "high powers" delegated directly to the citizen, and "is excepted out of the general powers of government." A law cannot be passed to infringe upon or impair it, because it is above the law, and independent of the law-making power.[38]

The Disarmed Slave and the Dred Scott Dilemma

The general rule in the antebellum courts was that the Second Amendment guaranteed an individual right to keep and bear arms free from both federal and state infringement. In order to disarm blacks, a few courts took the uncharacteristic view that only citizens could have arms and that the Second Amendment did not apply to the states. In some states, free and/or enslaved blacks were disarmed by law in order to maintain their servile condition. State legislation that prohibited blacks from bearing arms was held to be constitutional owing to the lack of status of African Americans as citizens. These statutes ignored the fact that the United States Constitution, as well as most state constitutions, referred to the bearing of arms as a right of "the people" rather than of "the citizen."

In *State* v. *Newsom*[39] the North Carolina Supreme Court upheld a slave-code provision "to prevent free persons of color from carrying fire arms" on the ground that "the free people of color cannot be considered as citizens."[40] By inference, the right to carry firearms was thus considered to be a right that flowed inherently from one's citizenship. The court also stated: "In the second article of the amended Constitution, the States are neither mentioned nor referred to. It is therefore only restrictive of the powers of the Federal Government."[41] In *Cooper* v. *Savannah*,[42] the Georgia Supreme Court similarly stated: "Free persons of color have never been recognized here as citizens; they are not entitled to bear arms, vote for members of the legislature, or to hold any civil office."[43]

The practical hardships suffered by individual blacks because of restrictive legislation are exemplified in two 1859 North Carolina cases. The statutes analyzed by the North Carolina Supreme court in *State* v. *Hannibal*[44] indicate that in the eighteenth century it was not illegal for blacks to carry guns, but they were required to obtain a court certificate to hunt. North Carolina's enactment of 1854 provided tht "no slave shall go armed with a gun, or shall keep such weapons," with a penalty of up to thirty-nine lashes.[45] In this instance, a master had given two slaves guns to guard his store at night, and the slaves were sentenced to twenty lashes each.[46]

In the other 1859 North Carolina case, *State* v. *Harris,* a free person of color had a license to carry a gun on his own land, but he was caught hunting with a shotgun off of his own land with some white companions.[47] The defendant was convicted. Although the court's reasoning demonstrates that some blacks were allowed substantial liberties in possessing firearms, it also shows the danger of arbitrariness in licensing provisions. Thus, under the statute, a court could grant a license

> to a free negro, to enable him to carry a gun, & c., about his person, or keep it in his house. . . . In many cases, the county court might think it a very prudent precaution to limit the carrying of arms to the lands of the free negro. . . . Indeed, the allowance of it will oftentimes operate in favor of the free negroes, who may thus be enabled to keep a gun, & c., for killing game on their own land, or for protecting their own premises. . . .[48]

Just as virtually the only antebellum state cases that limited the right to have arms also functioned to disarm blacks, the ruling of the U.S. Supreme Court in *Dred Scott* v. *Sandford*[49] noted that if African Americans were considered part of the people, they could carry arms anywhere. If members of the African race were "citizens," argued Chief Justice Taney, they would be "entitled to the privileges and immunities of citizens" and would be exempt from the special "police regulations" applicable to them. "It would give to persons of the negro race, who were recognized as citizens in any one State of the Union, the right to enter every other State whenever they pleased, singly or in companies . . .; and it would give them the full liberty of speech . . .; to hold public meetings upon political affairs, and *to keep and carry arms wherever they went.*"[50] Clearly, the Supreme Court thus included among the rights of every citizen the right to have arms wherever he goes. In having been granted citizenship via the Thirteenth and Fourteenth Amendments, blacks were later guaranteed these fundamental rights granted to all citizens. The Court's language also suggests that the right to have and carry arms anywhere is a right and privilege of national citizenship that the states cannot infringe any more than can the federal government—in effect, that the Second Amendment applies to the states.

In explaining further of the citizen that "the Federal Government can exercise no power over his person or property, beyond what that instrument confers, nor lawfully, deny any right which it has reserved," the Chief Justice in *Dred Scott* stated: "Nor can Congress deny the people the right to keep and bear arms, nor the right to trial by jury, nor compel anyone to be a witness against himself in a criminal proceeding."[51] Obviously, "the people" here included all citizens, for the meaning of the term would not reasonably shift from signifying only the active militia, in the case of the right to bear arms, to every individual citizen, in respect to the right to a jury trial.

In a separate passage, Chief Justice Taney did discuss the militia, using as an example the 1815 and 1855 laws of New Hampshire that restricted enrollment in the militia to "free white citizens."[52] Justice Curtis, dissenting, referred to the act of Congress of 17 May 1792, directing the enrollment of "every free, able-bodied, white male citizen" in the militia, to demonstrate that "colored persons . . . have been debarred from the exercise of particular rights or privileges extended by white persons, but . . . always in terms which, by implication, admit they may be citizens."[53] How one could be a citizen without having the citizen's rights is unclear, and dissenting Justice Curtis later, in the same opinion, approved acts of Congress preventing the sale of firearms to Indians.[54]

For the purpose of this study, the truly significant portion of *Dred Scott* is its averment that if African Americans were citizens they would have the right "to keep and carry arms wherever they went."[55] And it was the Reconstruction's Thirteenth and Fourteenth Amendments that were soon to make them citizens.[56]

That "The People" Means All Humans: Abolitionist Origins of the Fourteenth Amendment

Deprivation of arms has always been an elementary feature of the status of slavery. The definition of a slave as one deprived of potential weapons of self-defense or of liberation, and, contrariwise, the definition of a citizen as one who may bear arms, have been basic principles of political philosophy and have formed the basis of legal codes since ancient times.[57] Antebellum slave codes prohibited slaves and, even at the time, free colored persons from having arms. It thus comes as no surprise that those who sought the abolition of slavery and all of its incidents in the United States, and whose efforts led to the adoption of the Thirteenth and Fourteenth Amendments, extensively analyzed the connection between freedom and the right to keep and bear arms.

A great deal of antislavery sentiment existed at the time of the ratification of the Constitution and Bill of Rights. Soon thereafter, one of the most prominent commentators on those documents, St. George Tucker, published *A Dissertation on Slavery: With a Proposal for the Gradual Abolition of it, in the State of Virginia* (1796). Early in his work, Tucker noted that "free Negroes and mulattoes, whose civil incapacities are almost as numerous as the civil rights of our free citizens," were thereby relegated to a state of "civil slavery."[58] Despite their military assistance in the revolution, and their present enrollment "in the lists of those that bear arms," under existing Virginia law

> all but housekeepers, and persons residing upon the frontiers are prohibited from keeping, or carrying any gun, powder, shot, club, or other weapon offensive or defensive. Resistance to a white person . . . is punishable by whipping.[59]

Of course, the same disabilities applied to those subjected to "domestic slavery,"[60] that is, to chattel slaves.

Civil slavery and domestic slavery, Tucker noted, were in blatant contradiction to § 1 of the Virginia Bill of Rights, which held "that *all men* are by nature *equally free* and *independent*. . . ."[61] The "civil rights" of free persons included "the right of personal security,"[62] which Tucker elsewhere pointed out included keeping and bearing arms.[63] These civil rights had been denied to slaves by the Virginia act of 1680, which prohibited slaves from carrying any club, staff, gun, sword, or other weapon, offensive or defensive. This was afterwards extended to all Negroes, mulattoes and Indians whatsoever, with a few exceptions in favor of housekeepers, residents on a frontier plantation, and such as were enlisted in the militia.[64]

> From this melancholy review it will appear that . . . even the right of personal security, has been, at times, either wholly annihilated, or reduced to a shadow. . . .[65]

Of course, the deprivation of arms was one of a bundle of disabilities bolstering the peculiar institution of slavery. "To go abroad without a written permission; to keep or carry a gun, or other weapon; to utter any seditious speech; to be present at any unlawful assembly of slaves; to lift the hand in opposition to a white person, unless wantonly assaulted, are all offences punishable by whipping."[66]

The most perplexing problem for the moderate abolitionist Tucker concerned the mode and consequences of manumission. Under the ancient law of William the Conqueror, English villeins were emancipated as follows: "If any person is willing to enfranchise his slave, let him . . . deliver him *free arms*, to wit, a lance and a sword; thereupon he is a free man."[67] This was not in accord with American practice:

> In England, the presenting the villein with *free arms*, seems to have been the symbol of his restoration to all the rights which a feudatory was entitled to. With us, we have seen that emancipation does not confer the rights of citizenship on the person emancipated. . . .[68]

Specifically, Tucker prescribed that domestic slaves be promoted to a status of what he had earlier defined as "civil slavery." In a detailed plan, he wrote:

> Let no Negroe or mulattoe be capable of taking, holding, or exercising, any public office, freehold, franchise or privilege. . . . Nor of keeping, or bearing arms, unless authorized to do by some act of the general assembly, whose duration shall be limited to three years.[69]

> By denying them the most valuable privileges which civil government affords, I wished to render it their inclination and their interest to seek those privileges in some other climate. . . . [B]y disarming them, we may calm our apprehensions of their resentments arising from past sufferings. . . .[70]

While Tucker's treatise demonstrated the inconsistency of slavery and its incidents with American constitutional ideals, more influential for the framers of the Thirteenth and Fourteenth Amendments were the abolitionists who contended that the existing Constitution already repudiated not only slavery but also deprivation of any rights guaranteed to "the people." William Rawle's *A View of the Constitution* (Second Edition 1829) was cited by Representative John A. Bingham, a Republican from Ohio and the draftsman of the Fourteenth Amendment, to prove that all of "the people," as the phrase is used in the Constituion, are entitled to all rights of citizenship.[71] And in debates on civil rights during the time the Fourteenth Amendment was being considered, Rawle was credited with having "intended a refutation on the position . . . that a negro is neither a citizen nor an alien" but a citizen "entitled to all the rights and privileges appertaining to that capacity."[72] Among these rights and privileges of every person was the right to keep and bear arms, which Rawle held to be protected from both federal and state infringement.[73] In fact, the right of "personal security" as one of the "fundamental civil rights" was demonstrated by reference to Blackstone, Rawle, and Story, all of whom included the right to have arms as a basic right.[74]

The framers of the Fourteenth Amendment were to be influenced by abolitionist theorists of the Constitution who carried the American libertarian ideal to its logical conclusion. "The Fourteenth Amendment is universally presumed to be the outcome of the organized antislavery movement in the United States, yet its modern history continues to be written without reference to the abolitionists."[75] The abolitionists held that "the states were morally bound by the first eight amendments,"[76] and they developed the phraseology incorporated by Bingham, Howard, and other radicals into the Fourteenth Amendment.[77] "The clauses of Section One [of the Fourteenth Amendment] were at the least a shorthand summary of the first eight Amendments for the abolitionist generation whose constitutional climacteric found expression in the Reconstruction Amendments."[78]

The abolitionists considered the right to keep and bear arms as fundamental to the cause of liberation and its guarantee to "the people" in the Bill of Rights as proof of the illegality of slavery. As tenBroek has written:

> The abolitionists saw slavery, the discrimination against free Negroes, and the mistreatment of the abolitionists themselves as a violation of rights and guarantees imposed in the first eight amendments to the United States Constitution . . . They were even at times and to some extent a violation of the right to bear arms, assured in the Second Amendment. . . .[79]

The Fourteenth Amendment's framers were particularly influenced by Lysander Spooner's *Unconstitutionality of Slavery* (1845) and by Joel Tiffany's

Treatise on the Unconstitutionality of Slavery (1849), both of which included "the right to keep and bear arms" as rights of national citizenship.[80] "To this main stream of abolitionist constitutionalism, Bingham added the basic features of the Spooner-Tiffany national citizenship argument."[81]

Since Lysander Spooner was "pre-eminent in the group of abolitionists who developed the constitutional law now incorporated in the Fourteenth Amendment,"[82] his interpretation of the Second Amendment is entitled to great weight. In demonstrating the correct rule of interpretation of the Constitution, Spooner postulates that it should be construed like other legal instruments, with a view to preventing natural injustice. For instance, of the Second Amendment, Spooner says:

> This right "to keep and bear arms," implies the right to use them—as much as a provision securing to the people the right to buy and keep food, would imply their right also to eat it. But this implied right to use arms, is only a right to use them in a manner consistent with natural rights—as, for example, in defence of life, liberty, chastity, &c. . . . If the courts could go beyond the innocent and necessary meaning of the words, and imply or infer from them an authority for anything contrary to natural right, they could imply a constitutional authority in the people to use arms not merely for the just and innocent purposes of defence, but also robbery, or any other acts of wrong to which arms are capable of being applied. The mere verbal implication would as much authorize the people to use arms for unjust, as for just, purposes. But the legal implication gives only an authority for their innocent use.[83]

The above reasoning sought to debunk the interpretation of certain clauses of the Constitution (for example, Article IV, § 2, concerning the delivering up of persons held to service or labor) that allegedly sanctioned slavery. To demonstrate that the Constitution prohibited slavery, Spooner relied on its repeated references to various rights guaranteed to "the people." Under Article I, § 8, granting power to arm the militia, Congress could " *'arm'* those whom the States call slaves and authorize them always to keep their arms by them. . . ."[84] Then there is the right of *"the people"* in the Second Amendment to keep and bear arms.

> These provisions obviously recognize the natural right of all men "to keep and bear arms" for their personal defence: and prohibit both Congress and the State governments from infringing the right of "the people"—that is, of any of the people—to do so; and more especially of any whom Congress have power to include in their militia. This right of man "to keep and bear arms," is a right palpably inconsistent with the idea of his being a slave. Yet the right is secured as effectively to those whom

the States presume to call slaves, as to any whom the States condescend to acknowledge free.

Under this provision any man has a right either to give or sell arms to those persons whom the States call slaves; and there is no *constitutional* power, in either the national or State goverments, that can punish him for so doing; or that can take those arms from the slaves; or that can make it criminal for the slaves to use them, if, from the inefficiency of the laws, it should become necessary for them to do so, in defence of their own lives or liberties; for this constitutional right to keep arms implies the constitutional right to use them, if need be, for the defence of one's liberty or life.[85]

A similar argument was made in 1849, four years after Spooner's first edition, in Joel Tiffany's *Treatise on the Unconstitutionality of Slavery*. Tiffany also included slaves as part of "the people" referred to in the Second Amendment:

Here is another of the immunities of a citizen of the United States, which is guaranteed by the supreme, organic law of the land. This is one of the subordinate rights, mentioned by Blackstone, as belonging to every Englishman. It is called *"subordinate"* in reference to the great, absolute rights of man; and is accorded to every subject for the purpose of *protecting and defending himself*, if need be, in the enjoyment of his absolute rights to life, liberty and property. And this guaranty is to all without any exception; for there is none, either expressed or implied. And our courts have already decided, that in such cases we have no right to make any exceptions. It is hardly necessary to remark that this guaranty is absolutely inconsistent with permitting a portion of our citizens to be enslaved. The colored citizen, under our constitution, has now as full and perfect a right to keep and bear arms as any other; and no State law, or State regulation has authority to deprive him of that right.

But there is another thing implied in this guaranty; and that is the *right of self defence*. For the right to keep and bear arms, also implies the right to use them if necessary in self defence; without this right to use the guaranty would have hardly been worth the paper it consumed.[86]

The right to keep and bear arms was not just a theoretical concept for the abolitionists, who had to keep and use weapons to protect their presses, homes, and even lives. Having employed the instruments for self-defense against his proslavery attackers, Cassius Marcellus Clay, a founder of the Republican Party, wrote that " 'the pistol and the Bowie knife' are to us as sacred as the gown and the pulpit."[87] The right to have and use arms for self-defense against what was conceived of as kidnapping became particularly significant with the passage of the Fugitive Slave Act of 1850. Spooner defended the right of fugitive slaves to resist their potential captors in these terms:

The constitution contemplates no such submission, on the part of the people, to the usurpations of the government, or to the lawless violence of its officers. On the contrary it provides that "The right of the people to keep and bear arms shall not be infringed." This constitutional security for "the right to keep and bear arms," implies the right to use them,—as much as a constitutional security for the right to buy and keep food, would have implied the right to eat it. The constitution, therefore, takes it for granted that, as the people have the right, they will also have the sense, to use arms, whenever the necessity of the case justifies it. . . .

It is no answer to this argument to say, that if an unconstitutional act be passed, the mischief can be remedied by a repeal of it; and that this remedy may be brought about by discussion and the exercise of the right of suffrage; because, if an unconstitutional act be binding until invalidated by repeal, the government may, in the mean time disarm the people, suppress the freedom of speech and the press, prohibit the use of the suffrage, and thus put it beyond the power of the people to reform the government through the exercise of those rights. The government have as much consitutional authority for disarming the people, suppressing the freedom of speech and the press, prohibiting the use of the suffrage and establishing themselves as perpetual and absolute sovereigns, as they have for any other unconstitutional act.[88]

The logic of Spooner and other pro-Constitution abolitionists was compelling for black abolitionist Frederick Douglass, who repeatedly averred that "these gentlemen have, as I think, fully and clearly vindicated the Constitution from any design to support slavery for an hour."[89] To Douglass, when the Constitution and Bill of Rights referred to "the people," it meant exactly what it said. "Then why substitute 'a *part* of the people' for '*the people*.' "[90] The alleged constitutionality of slavery upheld in the *Dred Scott* case disregarded "the plain and commonsense reading of the instrument itself; by showing that the Constitution does not mean what it says, and says what it does not mean. . . ."[91] The rights, privileges, and immunities guaranteed to "the people" could not logically be restricted to a select race or group of orators, petitioners, preachers, or bearers of arms.

Douglass strongly supported the right of fugitive slaves to have and use weapons to resist kidnapping.[92] "When government fails to protect the just rights of any individual man," that man rests on "his original right of self-defense," even if it means, unfortunately, "shooting down his pursuers. . . ."[93] Douglass added: "Slavery is a system of brute force. . . . It must be met with its own weapons."[94] Yet "slaves, without arms" could never attain freedom.[95]

If the antebellum abolitionists articulated the concepts of broad fundamental rights that later found expression in the general phrases of the Fourteenth Amendment, the escalating possession of firearms by both free blacks and

slaves during the Civil War played a key role in emancipation and in protection of their basic rights. The practical necessities of the long and bloody
war, which demanded every human resource, led to the arming of blacks as
soldiers. While originally they had considered it a "white man's war," by 1863
Northern authorities were organizing black regiments on a wide scale. The
Northern government won the war only because of the arming of the slaves,
according to Senator Charles Sumner (Republican of Massachusetts), who
argued that necessity demanded

> first, that the slaves should be declared free; and secondly, that muskets
> should be put into their hands for the common defense. . . . Without
> emancipation, followed by the arming of the slaves, rebel slavery would
> not have been overcome.[96]

At the same time, black civilians were forced to arm themselves privately
against mob violence. During the antidraft riots in New York, according to a
Negro newspaper of the time, "The colored men who had manhood in them
armed themselves, and threw out their pickets every day and night, determined to die defending their homes. . . . Most of the colored men in Brook-
lyn who remained in the city were armed daily for self-defense."[97]

Informally at the beginning of the war, and *de jure* toward the end, Southerners began to support the arming and freeing of slaves who were willing to
fight the invaders.[98] The Virginia legislature, upon passing a bill providing
for the use of black soldiers, repealed its law prohibiting the bearing of arms
by blacks.[99] One opponent of these measures declared: What would be
the character of the returned negro soldiers, made familiar with the use of
fire-arms, and taught by us, that freedom was worth fighting for?"[100] Once it
became evident that slaves plus guns equaled abolition, the Confederates
were divided between those who valued nationhood more than slavery and
those who preferred a restored Union that might not destroy the servile condition of black labor.

The movement for the complete abolition of slavery through the Thirteenth
Amendment began before the end of the war, and members of the U.S. Congress recognized the key role that the bearing of arms had played in the freeing
of the slaves. In debate over the proposed amendment, Representative
George A. Yeaman (a Unionist from Kentucky) contended that regardless of
who won the war, the abolition of slavery was inevitable due to the arming
of blacks:

> Let proclamations be withdrawn, let statutes be repealed, let our armies
> be defeated, let the South achieve its independence, yet come out of
> the war . . . with an army of slaves made freemen for their service, who
> have been contracted with, been armed and drilled, and have seen the

force of combination. Their personal status is enhanced. . . . They will
not be returned to slavery.[101]

At the same time, members of the slavocracy planned to disarm the freedmen. Arguing for speedy adoption of the Thirteenth Amendment, Representative William D. Kelley (Republican of Pennsylvania) expressed shock
at the words of an antisecessionist planter in Mississippi who expected the
Union to restore slavery. Kelley cited a letter from a U.S. brigadier general,
who wrote: " 'What,' said I, 'these men who have had arms in their hands?'
'Yes,' he said, 'we should take the arms away from them, of course.' "[102]

5

Freedmen, Firearms, and
the Fourteenth Amendment

After the conclusion of the War Between the States, judicial commentators continued to interpret the Second Amendment as protection of an individual right from both state and federal infringement. The right to keep and bear arms and other freedoms in the Bill of Rights were viewed as common-law rights explicitly protected by the Constitution.[1] Joel P. Bishop wrote in 1865:

> The constitution of the United States provides, that, "a well-regulated militia being necessary to the security of a free State, the right of the people to keep and bear arms shall not be infringed." This provision is found among the amendments; and, though most of the amendments are restrictions on the General Government alone, not on the States, this one seems to be of a nature to bind both the State and National legislatures.[2]

Yet Bishop's references to "statutes relating to the carrying of arms by negroes and slaves"[3] and to an "act to prevent free people of color from carrying firearms"[4] exemplified the need for further constitutional guarantees to clarify and to protect the rights of all individuals.[5]

The following chapter explores the perceived status of the right to keep and bear arms by the abolitionist-influenced framers of the Fourteenth Amendment through an analysis of the congressional debates on the amendment and on the Civil Rights Act of 1866. The understanding by the public, as seen through newspaper accounts, and by the states as revealed through reports and debates in assemblies which considered ratification, are then surveyed. Next, the impact of the Fourteenth Amendment on the state constitutions, and particularly on those of the Southern states that adopted constitutions consistent with the amendment, is investigated. Congressional debates between 1866 and 1869 on the abolition of the Southern state militias, and during the first half of the 1870s on civil rights acts that sought to enforce the amendment, concludes the analysis. Throughout, the objective is to consider the extent to which the individual right to keep and bear arms was considered fundamental, and to resolve whether the Fourteenth Amendment was intended to protect this right from state infringement.

That No State Shall Disarm a Freedman:
The Proposal of the Fourteenth Amendment

When the war concluded, the slave codes, which limited the access of blacks to land, to arms, and to the courts, began to reappear in the form of the black codes,[6] and legislators in Congress turned their attention to these efforts to reenslave the freedmen. The prototypical 1865 Mississippi statute entitled "Act to Regulate the Relation of Master and Apprentice Relative to Freedmen, Free Negroes, and Mulattoes," provided, in part:

Sec. 1. Be it enacted, . . . That no freedman, free negro or mulatto, not in the military service of the United States government, and not licensed so to do by the board of police of his or her county, shall keep or carry fire-arms of any kind, or any ammunition, dirk or bowie knife, and on conviction thereof in the county court shall be punished by fine, not exceeding ten dollars, and pay the costs of such proceedings and all such arms or ammunition shall be forfeited to the informer; and it shall be the duty of every civil and military officer to arrest any freedman, free negro, or mulatto found with any such arms or ammunition, and cause him or her to be committed to trial in default of bail. . . .

Sec. 3. . . . If any white person shall sell, lend, or give to any freedman, free negro, or mulatto any fire-arms, dirk or bowie knife, or ammunition, or any spirituous or intoxicating liquors, such person or persons so offending, upon conviction thereof in the county court of his or her county, shall be fined not exceeding fifty dollars, and may be imprisoned, at the discretion of the court, not exceeding thirty days.

Sec. 5. . . . If any freedman, free negro, or mulatto, convicted of any of the misdemeanors provided against in this act, shall fail or refuse for the space of five days, after conviction, to pay the fine and costs imposed, such person shall be hired out by the sheriff or other officer, at public outcry, to any white person who will pay said fine and all costs, and take said convict for the shortest time.[7]

The enactment of these black code provisions prompted initiation of civil rights legislation that culminated in the proposal of the Fourteenth Amendment. Among the first legislation proposed, Senate Bill No. 9 declared as void all laws in the rebel states that recognized an inequality of rights based on race. In support of that bill, Senator Henry Wilson (Republican of Massachusetts) explained how the racist gun-control laws of the black codes were being enforced: "In Mississippi rebel State forces, men who were in the rebel armies, are traversing the State, visiting the freedmen, disarming them, perpetrating murders and outrages on them. . . ."[8]

The widely publicized report of Carl Schurz to the president, on which Congress placed great credence,[9] reviewed in detail abuses committed against freedmen, including deprivation of the right to keep and bear arms: "The militia [is] organized for the distinct purpose of enforcing the authority of the whites over the blacks. . . ."[10] In addition to other methods that were meant to restore slavery in fact, planters advocated that "the possession of arms or other dangerous weapons without authority should be punished by fine or imprisonment and the arms forfeited."[11] The report brought to the attention of Congress an ordinance enacted in Opelousas and in other Louisiana towns: "No freedman who is not in the military service shall be allowed to carry firearms, or any kind of weapon, without the special permission of his employer, in writing, and approved by the mayor or president of the board of police." Punishment was forfeiture of the weapon and either five days imprisonment or a fine of five dollars.[12] "This ordinance, if enforced, would be slavery in substance"; it violated the Emancipation Proclamation, held the Freedmen's Bureau.[13]

When Congress took up Senate Bill No. 61, which became the Civil Rights Act of 1866,[14] Senator Lyman Trumbull (Republican of Illinois), chairman of the Senate Judiciary Committee, indicated that the bill would prohibit inequalities embodied in the black codes, including those provisions which "prohibit any negro or mullatto from having fire-arms."[15] In abolishing the badges of slavery, the bill would enforce fundamental rights against racial discrimination in respect of civil rights, the rights to contract, to sue, to engage in commerce, and to be subject to equal criminal penalties. Senator William Saulsbury (Democrat of Delaware) added: "In my State for many years, and I presume there are similar laws in most of the southern States, there has existed a law of the State based upon and founded in its police power, which declares that free negroes shall not have the possession of firearms or ammunition. This bill proposes to take away from the States this police power. . . ." The Delaware Democrat opposed the bill on this basis, anticipating a time when "a numerous body of dangerous persons belonging to any distinct race" would endanger the state, for "the State shall not have the power to disarm them without disarming the whole population."[16] Thus, the bill would have prohibited legislative schemes that, in effect, disarmed blacks but not whites.

Still, supporters of the bill were quick to contend that the bearing of arms was a basic right of citizenship or personhood.

In the meantime, the legislators turned their attention to the Freedmen's Bureau Bill. Representative Thomas D. Eloit (Republican of Massachusetts) attacked the Opelousas, Louisiana, ordinance which deprived blacks of various civil rights, including the race-based prohibition against carrying firearms (quoted above).[17] And Representative Josiah B. Grinnell (Republican of Iowa) complained: "A white man in Kentucky may keep a gun; if a black man buys a gun he forfeits it and pays a fine of five dollars, if presuming to keep in his possession a musket which he has carried through the war."[18] In Kentucky, according to the "Report of the Commissioner of the Freedmen's Bureau," "the civil law prohibits the colored man from bearing arms," and

> their arms are taken from them by the civil authorities. . . . Thus, the right of the people to keep and bear arms as provided in the Constitution is *infringed*. . . .[19]

The abolitionist movement for the right of blacks to have firearms was motivated partly as a self-defense measure against the state militia itself. Senator Trumbull cited a report from Vicksburg, Mississippi, which stated: "Nearly all the dissatisfaction that now exists among the freedmen is caused by the abusive conduct of this militia."[20] Rather than restore order, the militia would typically "hang some freedman or search negro houses for arms."[21] Thus, militia needs were certainly not the only constitutional basis for the right to bear arms.

The first draft of § 1 of the Fourteenth Amendment was introduced in each house of Congress on 13 February 1866. It read simply: "Congress shall have power to make all laws which shall be necessary and proper to secure to citizens of each State all privileges and immunities of citizens in the several States; and to all persons in the several States equal protection in the rights of life, liberty and property."[22] While it was tabled in the Senate, Representative John A. Bingham (Republican of Ohio) argued on its behalf in the House that, previously, "this immortal bill of rights embodied in the Constitution, rested for its execution and enforcement hitherto upon the fidelity of the States."[23] "The proposition pending before the House is simply a proposition to arm the Congress . . . with the power to enforce this bill of rights as it stands in the Constitution today."[24] Representative Frederick E. Woodbridge (Republican of Vermont) characterized the broad rights that sought protection, as follows: "It merely gives the power to Congress to enact those laws which will give to a citizen of the United States the natural rights which necessarily pertain to citizenship."[25]

As debate returned to the Civil Rights bill, Representative Henry J. Raymond (Republican of New York) explained of the rights of citizenship: "Make the colored man a citizen of the United States and he has every right which you or I have as citizens of the United States under the laws and constitution of the United States. . . . He has a defined *status;* he has a country and a home; a right to defend himself and his wife and children; a right to bear arms. . . ."[26] Representative Roswell Hart (Republican of New York) further stated: "The Constitution clearly describes that to be a republican form of government for which it was expressly framed. A government . . . where 'no law shall be made prohibiting a free exercise of religion'; where 'the right of the people to keep and bear arms shall not be infringed';. . ."[27] He rested on the duty of the United States to guarantee that the states have such a form of government.[28]

Representative Sidney Clarke (Republican of Kansas) referred to an 1866 Alabama law providing "that it shall not be lawful for any freedman, mulatto, or free person of color in this State, to own firearms, or carry about his person a pistol or other deadly weapon."[29] This same statute made it unlawful "to sell, give, or lend fire-arms or ammunition of any description whatever, to any freedman, free negro, or mulatto. . . ."[30] Clarke also attacked Mississippi, "whose rebel militia, upon the seizure of the arms of black Union soldiers, appropriated the same to their own use."[31] He continued:

> Sir, I find in the Constitution of the United States an article which declares that "the right of the people to keep and bear arms shall not be infringed." For myself, I shall insist that the reconstructed rebels of Mississippi respect the Constitution in their local laws. . . .[32]

In emotionally referring to the disarmament of former black soldiers, Clarke added:

> Nearly every white man in that State that could bear arms was in the rebel ranks. Nearly all of their able-bodied colored men who could reach our lines enlisted under the old flag. Many of these brave defenders of the nation paid for the arms with which they went to battle. . . . The "reconstructed" State authorities of Mississippi were allowed to rob and disarm our veteran soldiers. . . .[33]

In sum, Clarke presupposed a constitutional right to keep privately held arms for protection against oppressive state militia.

Three months passed after the introduction in each congressional house of the first draft of the Fourteenth Amendment, and during this time numerous debates over the Civil Rights bill took place. The Fourteenth Amendment was then reintroduced in its final form, except for its definition of citizenship. At that time Representative Thaddeus Stevens (Republican of Pennsylvania) remarked that its provisions

> are all asserted, in some form or another, in our DECLARATION or organic law. But the Constitution [that is, the Bill of Rights] limits only the action of Congress, and is not a limitation on the States. This Amendment supplies that defect, and allows Congress to correct the unjust legislation of the States. . . .[34]

This broad character of the amendment prompted this objection by Representative Andrew J. Rogers (Democrat of New Jersey): "What are privileges and immunities? Why, sir, all the rights we have under the laws of the country are embraced under the definition of citizenship."[35] When Representative Bingham added that it would furnish a remedy against state injustices, such as infliction of cruel and unusual punishment,[36] he implied, in the words of H. L. Flack, an authority endorsed by the Supreme Court: "If the section under consideration had this effect as to that Amendment, it necessarily follows that it would apply equally to the other seven Amendments."[37]

When he introduced the Fourteenth Amendment to the House, Senator Jacob M. Howard (Republican of Michigan) referred to "the personal rights guaranteed and secured by the first eight amendments of the Constitution; such as freedom of speech and of the press; . . . *the right to keep and bear arms.* . . ."[38] That state legislation failed to guarantee these rights rendered adoption of the Fourteenth Amendment imperative. "The great object of the first section of this amendment is, therefore, to restrain the power of the States and compel them at all times to respect these great fundamental guarantees."[39] As Irving Brant has observed, "In the entire Senate debate on the Fourteenth Amendment, running from May 23 to June 8, *not a single senator challenged Senator Howard's declaration that Section 1 made the first eight amendments enforceable against the states.*"[40] After all, Howard held a long-established role as a leading political authority in the Republican party. Twelve years before the speech mentioned above, Howard had drafted the first Republican party platform, which had called for the abolition of slavery. Then, he had been instrumental in the passage of the Thirteenth Amendment.[41] Not surprisingly, no one disputed the senator's exposition of the Fourteenth Amendment.

Supporters of what became known as the "Howard Amendment" clearly indicated the broad character of the rights that needed to be protected. Thus, Senator Luke P. Poland (Republican of Vermont) analyzed § 1 as embodying

> the very spirit and inspiration of our system of government, the absolute foundation upon which it was established. It is essentially declared in

the Declaration of Independence and in *all the provisions of the Constitution.* Nothwithstanding this we know that State laws exist, and some of them of very recent enactment, in direct violation of these principles. . . . It certainly seems desirable that no doubt should be left existing as to the power of Congress to enforce principles lying at the foundation of all republican government if they be denied or violated by the States. . . .[42]

The reference to "all the provisions of the Constitution" obviously includes the Bill of Rights,[43] just as the reference to recently enacted state laws included the black code provisions depriving freedmen, *inter alia,* of the rights to free speech and to keep and bear arms. Consistent with this outlook, on a later occasion Senator Poland joined in a report that complained about those who whipped Negroes for having voted the radical ticket "and whenever they had guns, took them from them."[44]

Opponents of the Fourteenth Amendment objected to its adoption precisely because they rejected federal enforcement of the kinds of freedoms made explicit in the Bill of Rights. For instance, Senator Thomas A. Hendricks (Democrat of Indiana) had previously voted against the Thirteenth Amendment[45] as well as against permitting blacks to testify, to act as jurors, to vote, to ride in cars with whites, or even to carry mail.[46] "We do not allow to colored people there [Indiana] many civil rights and immunities which are enjoyed by the white people," he bragged.[47] "It became the policy of the State in 1852 to prohibit the immigration of colored people into that State."[48] Senator Hendricks was undoubtedly aware that his own state's constitution provided that "the people have a right to bear arms for the defence of themselves and the state."[49] Hendricks undoubtedly feared that the Fourteenth Amendment would protect this kind of right without regard to race, for he was present when Howard so stated when introducing the amendment.

Senator Hendricks opposed adoption of the Fourteenth Amendment precisely because "if this amendment be adopted we will then carry the title [of citizenship] and enjoy its advantages in common with the negroes, the coolies, and the Indians."[50] When Hendricks claimed not to understand the meaning of "the word 'abridged,' " Senator Howard simply responded that "it is easy to apply the term 'abridged' to the privilege and immunities of citizens, which necessarily include within themselves a great number of particulars."[51]

Although he joined with Senator Hendricks in voting against the Fourteenth Amendment,[52] Senator Reverdy Johnson more moderately declared:

I am decidedly in favor of the first part of the section which defines what citizenship shall be, and in favor of that part of the section which denies to a State the right to deprive any person of life, liberty, or property without due process of law, but I think it is quite objectionable to provide that "no State shall make or enforce any law which shall abridge the privileges or immunitites of citizens of the United States," simply because I do not understand what will be the effect of that.[53]

If his reservation implied that he thought the privileges and immunities clause to be too broad, Senator Johnson knew that citizenship and protection of life, liberty, and property would include the right of every citizen to keep and bear arms. As counsel for the slave owner in *Dred Scott* v. *Sanford* (1857), Johnson was well aware that citizenship "would give to persons of the negro race". . . the full liberty . . . to keep and carry arms wherever they went."[54] In Senate debate, Johnson reminded his colleagues that the *Dred Scott* case held African descendants not to be citizens.[55] Yet in response to Senator Wilson's complaint about the "disarming" and other abuses of freedmen in Mississippi, Johnson acknowledged as to "these outrages" that "no doubt to a certain extent it is true. . . ."[56]

The Fourteenth Amendment was viewed as necessary to buttress the objectives of the Civil Rights Act of 1866. Rep. George W. Julian (Republican of Indiana) noted that the act

is pronounced void by the jurists and courts of the South. Florida makes it a misdemeanor for colored men to carry weapons without a license to do so from a probate judge, and the punishment of the offense is whipping and the pillory. South Carolina has the same enactments. . . . Cunning legislative devices are being invented in most of the States to restore slavery in fact.[57]

In summary, the framers clearly intended, and opponents clearly recognized, that the Fourteenth Amendment was designed to guarantee the right to keep and bear arms as a right and attribute of citizenship that no state could infringe. The passage of the Fourteenth Amendment accomplished the abolitionist goal that each state recognize the freedoms in the Bill of Rights. Representative Bingham, author of the amendment, "intended," in Flack's words, "to confer power upon the Federal Government, by the first section of the Amendment, to enforce the Federal Bill of Rights in the States. . . ."[58] Flack generalized, as follows:

In conclusion, we may say that Congress, the House, and the Senate, had the following objects and motives in view for submitting the first section of the Fourteenth Amendment to the States for ratification:
1. To make the Bill of Rights (the first eight amendments) binding upon, or applicable to, the States.[59]

Specifically, "it might be said that the following objects and rights were to be secured by the first section . . . the right peaceably to assemble, to bear arms, etc. . . ."[60]

Each clause of § 1 of the Fourteenth Amendment reflects the broad character of the rights for which protection was sought. The final version provided:

> All persons born or naturalized in the United States and subject to the jurisdiction thereof, are citizens of the United States and of the State wherein they reside. No State shall make or enforce any law which shall abridge the privileges or immunities of citizens of the United States; nor shall any State deprive any person of life, liberty, or property, without due process of law; nor deny to any person within its jurisdiction the equal protection of the laws.

Among other freedoms in the Bill of Rights, keeping and bearing arms had been considered part of the definition of "citizen" since the time of Aristotle. Depicted as a "privilege or immunity" in the *Dred Scott* decision and in debates on the Fourteenth Amendment, this liberty interest made possible the defense and practical realization of the guarantee of "life, liberty, or property." This fundamental right under "the laws" (that is, the Bill of Rights) also qualified for "equal protection," but never for deprivation, whether equal or unequal. In short, the language of the Fourteenth Amendment embodied a host of rights recognized by common law, by the Declaration of Independence, by the federal and state bills of rights, and even by natural law. To the framers of the amendment, these universally recognized rights, too numerous to list individually, would be protected by the all-inclusive language which they proposed and which was adopted as part of the Constitution.

The Public Understanding and State Ratifications of the Fourteenth Amendment

That the abolition of slavery and all of its incidents entitled blacks to exercise all fundamental rights, previously restricted to whites, was commonly understood by the public both during and after the adoption of the Thirteenth Amendment. The newly emancipated slaves, encouraged by military decrees prohibiting enforcement of the black codes, took literally the promise of freedom. Gen. D. E. Sickles's General Order No. 1 (1 January 1866) for the Department of South Carolina negated that states's prohibition on possession of firearms by blacks and, at the same time, recognized the right of the conquered to bear arms:

The constitutional rights of all loyal and well disposed inhabitants to bear arms, will not be infringed; nevertheless this shall not be construed to sanction the unlawful practice of carrying concealed weapons; nor to authorize any person to enter with arms on the premise of another without his consent. No one shall bear arms who has borne arms against the United States, unless he shall have taken the Amnesty oath prescribed in the Proclamation of the President of the United States, dated May 19th, 1865, or the Oath of Allegiance, prescribed in the Proclamation of the President, dated December 8th, 1863, within the time prescribed therein.[61]

This "most remarkable order," repeatedly printed in the headlines of the *Loyal Georgian*,[62] a prominent black newspaper of the time, was thought to have been "issued with the knowledge and approbation of the President if not by his direction."[63] The first issue to print the order included the following editorial:

Editor *Loyal Georgian:*
Have colored persons a right to own and carry fire arms?
A Colored Citizen
Almost every day we are asked questions similar to the above. We answer *certainly* you have the *same* right to own and carry arms that other citizens have. You are not only free but citizens of the United States and as such entitled to the same privileges granted to other citizens by the constitution. . . .

Article II, of the amendments to the Constitution of the United States, gives the people the right to bear arms, and states that this right shall not be infringed. Any person, white or black, may be disarmed if convicted of making an improper or dangerous use of weapons, but no military or civil officer has the right or authority to disarm any class of people, thereby placing them at the mercy of others. All men, without distinction of color, have the right to keep and bear arms to defend their homes, families or themselves.[64]

The last paragraph, taken from a Freedmen's Bureau circular, was also printed numerous times in the *Loyal Georgian*.[65] Indeed, "from the first days of freedom, the right to bear arms was defended in black newpapers. . . ."[66] The proposal of the first draft of the Fourteenth Amendment came about the same time as publication of the above issue of the *Loyal Georgian*, which followed the congressional debates carefully.[67] The freedmen readership of such newspapers could only have concluded that the new amendment would further protect their right to keep and bear arms as well as their right to many other liberties.

The general public was well aware of the need to provide safeguards for freedoms in the Bill of Rights that the states had infringed. *Harper's Weekly* informed its readers of Mississippi's prohibition on firearms possession by freedmen, in these words:

> The militia of this country have seized every gun and pistol found in the hands of the (so called) freedmen of this section of the country. They claim that the statute laws of Mississippi do not recognize the negro as having any right to carry arms. They commenced seizing arms in town, and now the plantations are ransacked in the dead hours of night. . . . The colored people intend holding a meeting to petition the Freedman's Bureau to re-establish their courts in the State of Mississippi, as the civil laws of this State do not, and will not protect, but *insist* upon infringing on their liberties.[68]

A continual stream of such reports engendered public demands that Congress accord protection to the right to have arms and to the freedom from unreasonable search and seizure.

During the same weeks as these reports and proclamations were increasing the public's appreciation for the need of further protection for fundamental rights, members of Congress who read the same writings and no doubt heard from their constituents on these matters began laying the appropriate groundwork. Comments by senators and representatives on the need to protect the individual's right to keep and bear arms, made in the course of debate on the Civil Rights bill and the proposed amendment, were published widely.

Of particular note is the front-page press coverage given to Senator Jacob M. Howard's speech introducing the Fourteenth Amendment to the Senate on 23 May 1866. That speech included his explanation that the Fourteenth Amendment would compel the states to respect "these great fundamental guarantees: . . . the personal rights guaranteed by the first eight amendments of the United States Constitution such as . . . the right to keep and bear arms. . . ." On the next day, these words appeared on the first page of the *New York Times*[69] and the *New York Herald*,[70] and were also printed in such papers as the Washington, D.C., *National Intelligencer*[71] and the *Philadelphia Inquirer*.[72] As Flack points out concerning Sen. Howard's speech: "By declarations of this kind, by giving extracts or digests of the principal speeches made in Congress, the people were kept informed as to the objects and purposes of the Amendment."[73]

Numerous editorials appeared on Senator Howard's speech, none of which disputed his explanation that the Fourteenth Amendment would protect freedoms in the Bill of Rights (such as keeping and bearing arms) from state infringement. The *New York Times* editorialized:

With reference to the amendment, as it passed the House of Representatives, the statement of Mr. Howard, upon which the opening task devolved, is frank and satisfactory. His exposition of the consideration which led the Committee to seek the protection, by a Constitutional declaration, of "the privileges and immunities of the citizens of the several states of the Union," was clear and cogent.[74]

The *Chicago Tribune* noted that Howard's explanation "was very forcible and well put, and commanded the close attention of the Senate."[75] "It will be observed," summarized the *Baltimore Gazette*, "that the first section is a general prohibition upon all of the States of abridging the privileges and immunities of the citizens of the United States, and secures for all the equal advantages and protection of the laws."[76] Several papers were impressed with the "length" or "detail" in which Howard explained the amendment.[77]

The Southern Democratic party newspapers generally did not publish any speeches by Republicans, but they reacted to the Howard Amendment in a revealing manner. The Amendment's supporters, complained the *Daily Richmond Examiner*, "are first to make citizens and voters of the negroes."[78] For every Southerner, being a citizen meant keeping and bearing arms. Yet the *Examiner* had a little glee for the senator from Michigan: "Howard, who explained [the Amendment] on the part of the Senate, himself objected to the disenfranchisement feature."[79] The Southern papers never claimed that the amendment was unclear, but they objected to its breadth in conferring on the Negro the kinds of rights to be found in the first eight amendments as well as the privilege of suffrage. Typifying the Southern world view, attacks on Howard, along with prominently displayed advertisements for Remington revolvers, laced the Charleston *Daily Courier*.[80]

When it adopted the Fourteenth Amendment and a joint resolution urging ratification by the states, Congress issued its "Report of the Joint Committee on Reconstruction" (1866). This report, which became highly influential in the state ratification process, further reveals its reasons for adoption. In addition to 150,000 original copies, the report was reprinted widely in the press and figured in the 1866 election campaign.[81] Testimony and documents in the report depicted the deprivation of firearms as a badge of slavery. For instance, after asserting that South Carolina whites sought a "disarmed and defenceless" black population, Gen. Rufus Saxton further testified:

Question. What would be the probable effect of such an effort to disarm the blacks?
Answer. It would subject them to the severest oppression, and leave their condition no better than before they were emancipated, and in many respects worse than it was before.[82]

General Saxton then distributed the following proposed circular to the committee members:

It is reported that in some parts of this State, armed parties are, without proper authority, engaged in seizing all fire-arms found in the hands of the freedmen. Such conduct is in clear and direct violation of their personal rights as guaranteed by the Constitution of the United States, which declares that "the right of the people to keep and bear arms shall not be infringed."[83]

The use by former slaveowners of peonagelike contracts was also of grave concern. "The planters are disposed, in many cases, to insert in their contracts tyrannical provisions to prevent the negroes from leaving the plantation without a written pass from the proprietor; forbidding them . . . to have fire-arms in their possession, even for proper purposes."[84]

The report also included testimony by a subcommissioner of freedmen in Mississippi, in reference to floggings and hangings, that

orders were issued by the governor of the State to disarm the freedmen.
Q. Was that order executed?
A. Yes sir; and mostly by the militia. And it was in the execution, or pretended execution, of that order, that the most of those outrages, were committed.[85]

Other publications of the period in which the states considered the Fourteenth Amendment for ratification further attest to the public's understanding that it would protect the right to keep and bear arms. For instance, Senator Drake of Missouri, in his work *Radicalism Vindicated* (1867), depicted suffrage as necessary as firearms for self-protection:

[The] loyal negro, should have, in the ballot, the means of protecting in himself and securing to his posterity the nation's gift of his freedom. Had it done less, of what value would that freedom have been to him? Of just as much as your money to you, with a robber's pistol at your head and a demand for your money or your life, and you with not so much as a pen-knife for your defence.[86]

By the same token, speeches in Congress appeared in contemporary books. For example, in *History of the Reconstruction Measures* (1868), Representative Raymond's comment of 8 March 1866 appeared: as a citizen, a black would have "a right to defend himself and his wife and children; a right to bear arms. . . ."[87] Again, North Carolina Governor William Holden publicly declared in favor of "the constitutional right of all citizens to the possession of arms for proper purposes. . . ."[88]

Examples of the public understanding of the individual right to keep and bear arms as a fundamental right protected by the Second, Thirteenth, and Fourteenth Amendments—expressed in all kinds of publications—pervade the months during which the Fourteenth Amendment was being considered for ratification and, indeed, during the entire period of Reconstruction.[89] Inescapably, the people in that epoch considered the right to keep and bear arms as a basic right of citizenship.

The records of the states that considered adoption of the Fourteenth Amendment substantiate the perception of the right to keep and bear arms as a human right that no state could infringe. The amendment was submitted to the states in June 1866, less than a month after Senator Howard's widely published speech verifying the incorporation of the Second Amendment in the general language of the proposal. State ratifications began the same month and were two-thirds completed by January 1867. Most of the Southern states initially rejected the amendment, but they ratified it later as a condition for reentry into the Union.

The proponents and opponents of the amendment took their positons on the basis of the broad character of the rights that the amendment guaranteed. This is clear from the messages of governors who submitted the amendment to the state legislatures as well as from the debates (which were recorded in only two states) and committee reports on the amendment. Its meaning was so clear as to receive little rigorous scrutiny in the governors' messages. "The people of this state are thoroughly familiar with its provisions, and with a full understanding of them in all their bearings," the Wisconsin governor said. "I need therefore urge upon you no extended argument in support of it."[90]

The most complete discussion of the meaning of the Fourteenth Amendment and its relation to the Bill of Rights came from the reports of the Committee on Federal Relations in the Massachusetts General Court. That committee split between a majority holding that the Bill of Rights already bound the states, and hence that § 1 of the amendment was unnecessary, and a minority recommending adoption to leave no doubt on the subject. The majority cited the privileges and immunities and republican form of government clauses, as well as four provisions in the Bill of Rights, including the following: "A well-regulated militia being necessary to the security of a free state, the right of the people to keep and bear arms, shall not be infringed." "Nearly every one of the amendments to the constitution grew out of a jealousy for the rights of the people, and is in the direction, more or less direct, of a guarantee of human rights. . . . [T]hese provisions cover the whole ground of section first of the proposed amendment."[91] After noting that all native-born inhabitants were already citizens of the United States and of their own states, the report added:

> *The remainder of the first section,* possibly excepting the last clause, *is covered in terms by the provisions of the Constitution as it now stands, illustrated, as these express provisions are, by the whole tenor and spirit of the amendments.* The last clause, no State shall "deny to any person within its jurisdiction the equal protection of its laws," though not found in these precise words in the Constitution, is inevitably inferable from its whole scope and true interpretation. The denial by any State to any person within its jurisdiction, of the equal protection of the laws, would be a flagrant perversion of the guarantees of *personal rights* which we have quoted.[92]

The committee minority substantially agreed that the proposed amendment expressed preexisting rights, but it urged ratification in a spirit of caution. "As a declaration of the true intent and meaning of American citizenship, it appeals to freemen everywhere. . . . [I]t is an advance in the direction of establishing unrestricted popular rights. . . ."[93] No dispute existed about the nature of the libertarian guarantees sought in both reports, which provided the clearest discussion of § 1 of the Fourteenth Amendment that took place in any ratifying state.[94] No less doubtful in the minds of the Massachusetts legislators was that the meaning of "human rights" guaranteed in the Second Amendment included the personal right of freedmen to keep and bear arms and not the right of the defeated states to maintain militias.

The committee reports issued in Texas, which initially rejected the amendment, present an interesting comparison with the Massachusetts reports. The Republican minority in the Texas legislature, meeting at the state constitutional convention held at the same time that the amendment was working its way through Congress, filed a report supportive of black suffrage, which included the following words:

> These fundamental principles of American liberty constitute the basis of the Bill of Rights, which, under various modifications, pervade all our constitutional charters. . . . [T]he framers of the Federal Constitution were careful to confide all power to the *people,* and to provide for the protection of the *whole* people. To illustrate this, it is only necessary to refer to the constitution itself. . . .

> "ART. 2. A well regulated militia being necessary to the sucess [sic] of a free state, the right of the *people* to keep and bear arms shall not be infringed."[95] . . .

> Those who were lately slaves . . . are now freemen, entitled to all the rights and privileges of American citizens.[96]

When the Texas legislature considered the Fourteenth Amendment, the report of the Senate Committee on Federal Relations admitted that the Negro had no right of suffrage. "But our Constitution guarantees to the negro *every other right of citizenship.*"[97] Indeed, the Texas Constitution provided: "Every citizen shall have the right to keep and bear arms in the lawful defence of himself or the State."[98] On the other hand, the House report suggested that § 1 of the Fourteenth Amendment would make Negroes "entitled to all 'the privileges and immunities' of white citizens; in these privileges would be embraced the exercise of suffrage at the polls, participation in jury duty in all cases, bearing arms in the militia. . . ."[99] The "ancient militia laws" in Texas at that time, according to a congressman, "authorize anybody and everybody . . . to organize a militia hostile to the Government. . . ."[100] Thus, while the Senate committee did not object to blacks keeping and bearing arms and exercising other rights of citizenship aside from voting, the House committee rejected the Fourteenth Amendment because it was perceived as protecting from state infringement privileges including bearing arms and associating voluntarily into militia companies.

A comprehensive survey of the committee reports of all states reveals not the slightest suggestion that the Fourteenth Amendment failed to protect the individual right to keep and bear arms from state infringement. The typical objection to the amendment was that the federal government would become protector of the fundamental rights of citizens, thereby swallowing up the functions of the state governments. For instance, in Wisconsin the Senate minority report averred:

> The absolute rights of *personal security*, personal liberty and the right to acquire and enjoy private property, descended to the people of this government as a part of the common law of England. . . . They were a part of the Magna Charta, the great charter of England, and form a part of the bill of rights in nearly all the constitutions of the states of this union, as well as of the federal constitution. Why, then, is it necessary to engraft into the federal constitution that part of section one [of] the amendments which says: "Nor shall any state deprive any person of life, liberty or property, without due process of law?"[101]

As is well known, Blackstone included the right of the subject to have arms as an auxiliary right to the absolute right of personal security.

Debates on the Fourteenth Amendment, while they were recorded only in Pennsylvania and Indiana, reiterate the common understanding that it incorporated the broad freedoms confirmed in the Bill of Rights. Thus, supporters of the Fourteenth Amendment in the Pennsylvania General Assembly agreed of § 1 that "the spirit of this section is already in the Constitution, and that we are only reenacting it in plainer terms. . . ."[102] It protected "the rights to life, liberty and property; in short the inalienable rights enunciated in the Declaration of Independence. . . ."[103] The proposed amendment embodied the same safeguards as the provision in the Pennsylvania Declaration of Rights that "all men . . . have certain inherent and indefeasible rights, among which are those of . . . defending life and liberty, of . . . protecting property. . . ." The legislators were urged to confer on blacks "all the rights which the constitution provides for men—all the rights which this amendment indicated—in full."[104]

Opponents of the amendment objected on the basis of the argument that all of the rights of citizenship other than suffrage were already protected. "The object of the first clause was to meet the doctrine enunciated in the somewhat celebrated Dred Scott decision." This was said to be already covered in the Civil Rights Act.[105] The same speaker also objected to Negro suffrage, as did a colleague who contended that unless the section meant to establish that right "the whole section is mere surplusage, conveying no additional right or safeguard not already conveyed in better form. . . ."[106] In short, opponents urged, blacks were already protected in all rights of citizenship (which the Dred Scott decision had ruled included the private keeping and bearing of arms) other than suffrage, which was apparently the only right that the Pennsylvania delegates opposed conferring on the freedmen.

In Indiana, one opponent "considered what privileges and immunities the negro would acquire under this amendment. They were the same as those enuring to the white men."[107] These rights clearly included the rights guaranteed under the U.S. and Indiana constitutions, both of which included the right to keep and bear arms. These perceived rights of citizens prompted the assertion that "the first section assumed too much for the United States—to say who shall be citizens of a particular state. . . ."[108] That speaker "objected to the exaltation of the negro to citizenship, . . . because it strikes down the definition of citizenship in the Constitution of the State of Indiana."[109] These arguments were defeated by distinguishing Bill of Rights–type freedoms from suffrage: "Civil rights were inherent—were of God; political rights were conferred by constitutions."[110]

The Fourteenth Amendment was promulgated as having been adopted as part of the Constitution on 28 July 1868, following ratification by several Southern states within the prior two months. The state records on the amendment contain not one shred of evidence that the right to have arms was neither individual in character nor protected from state infringement. To the contrary, the records of the states that ratified or rejected the Fourteenth Amendment confirm that the right to keep and bear arms was considred a fundamental human right fully protected from federal or state infringement.

The Impact of the Fourteenth Amendment
upon State Constitutions

In 1867, Congress required by law that the constitutions of the reconstructed states conform to the U.S. Constitution, and it included in this mandate the Fourteenth Amendment, even though it was then not yet fully ratified.[111] Ten of the Southern states held conventions in 1867–1868 that produced new state constitutions, and thereby these ex-Confederate states won the approval of Congress for reentry into the Union. In 1870, Tennessee, the only ex-Confederate state not included in the act, adopted a constitution consistent with the Fourteenth Amendment.

The antebellum constitutions and common law of these states guaranteed the right to keep and bear arms to the people, the citizens, or the free white men. Blacks, not considered to be encompassed in these classifications, were denied the right to keep and bear arms. The following analysis demonstrates the impact of the Fourteenth Amendment upon these constitutions and laws, and thus the extent to which that amendment was perceived as incorporating the Second Amendment. It concludes with a summary of the status of the right to have arms under the constitutions of all the states during Reconstruction.

Alabama. The constitutional convention of Alabama in 1867 reenacted its antebellum provision: "Every citizen has a right to bear arms in defense of himself and the State."[112] Alabama's high court had held of this right: "A statute which, under the pretence of regulating, amounts to a destruction of the right, or which requires arms to be borne as to render them wholly useless for the purpose of defence, would be clearly unconstitutional."[113] A recommendation in the convention that would have limited this right to "the common defense" failed.[114] Since the new constitution made citizens of all residents, pursuant to the requirement that it be consistent with the Fourteenth Amendment, the change was hardly nominal because now blacks, as citizens, were protected by the Alabama Constitution in keeping and bearing arms.

Arkansas. The antebellum constitution of Arkansas provided: "That the free white men of this State shall have a right to keep and bear arms for their common defence."[115] The three judges who construed this provision before the war seemed to assume that the Second Amendment applied to the states, but they divided, in dictum, over whether the right to have arms for "common defence" was held by all individuals or only by the militia and whether all or only militia arms were protected.[116] The court actually held only that neither constitution protected the carrying of concealed weapons.

When Arkansas seceded in 1861, the provision was amended to broaden the holders and purposes of the right: "That the free white men, and Indians, of this state shall have the right to keep and bear arms for their individual or

common defence."[117] In 1864, the pro-Union state convention changed the
guarantee back to its earlier and more narrow version.[118] Two years later,
Arkansas Senator William D. Snow explained the convention's action to the
Joint Committee on Reconstruction:

> The old constitution declares, "that the free white men of the State
> shall have a right to keep and to bear arms for their common defence."
> The new constitution retains the words "free white" before the word
> "men." I think I understand something of the reasoning of the conven-
> tion on that score. At the time this new constitution was adopted we
> were yet in the midst of a war, and, to some southern eyes, there was
> yet an apparent chance as to which way the war might terminate; in other
> words, the rebellion was not entirely crushed. Two years ago in January,
> there was also some uncertainty in the minds of timid men as to what
> the negro might do, if given arms, in a turbulent state of society, and in
> his then uneducated condition; and to allay what I was confident was an
> unnecessary alarm, that clause was retained. In discussing the subject,
> the idea prevailed that that clause, being simply permissive, would not
> prevent the legislature, if at a future time it should be deemed advisable,
> from allowing the same rights to the colored man.[119]

Senator Snow's explanation demonstrates the understanding of the convention that having arms was the individual's and not just the militiaman's
right. Otherwise the issue of whether this right should be granted to "the
negro" would never have arisen. Since the provision clearly violated the Fourteenth Amendment, the ratification of which Congress mandated, the convention of 1868 reworded it thus: "The citizens of this State shall have the
right to keep and bear arms for their common defense."[120] The debates in
that convention indicated the deep awareness by the delegates of their obligation to adopt a constitution fully consistent with the Fourteenth Amendment.[121] As in other conventions, black suffrage, and not freedoms in the
Bill of Rights, was the most debated topic.

Recognized as citizens under both state and federal constitutions, blacks
were now protected in their right to keep and bear arms. Furthermore, in a
decision rendered eight years later, the Arkansas Supreme Court apparently
assumed that the Fourteenth Amendment protects the right to have arms from
state infringement. That court declared invalid a state prohibition on carrying pistols by holding that the Second Amendment protected "the army and
navy repeaters."[122] Significantly, the court added: "The arms which it [the
amendment] guarantees American citizens the right to keep and bear, are
such as are needful to, and ordinarily used by a well regulated militia, and
such as are necessary and suitable to a free people, to enable them to resist
oppression, prevent usurpation, repel invasion, etc., etc."[123]

Florida. The right-to-arms provision of Florida's antebellum constitution was identical with that of Arkansas: "That the free white men of this State shall have a right to keep and bear arms for their common defence."[124] The convention of 1865, while adopting a declaration of rights which included that of "defending life and liberty [and of] protecting property,"[125] completely eliminated an arms provision. Since the proposed Bill of Rights passed the convention unanimously,[126] the deletion must have been intended to preclude recognition of the right of blacks to have arms. While federal authorities allowed Arkansas to restrict this right to "free white man" in early 1864, it must have appeared highly unlikely that they would do so after the completion of their victory.

Lack of a right-to-arms provision cleared the way for the Florida legislature in 1865 to make it "unlawful for any Negro, mulatto, or person of color to own, use, or keep in possession or under control any bowie-knife, dirk, sword, firearms or ammunition of any kind, unless by license of the county judge or probate, under a penalty of forfeiting them to the informer, and of standing in the pillory one hour, or be whipped not exceeding thirty-nine stripes, or both, at the discretion of the jury."[127] Characterized in a speech advocating congressional adoption of the Fourteenth Amendment as an act designed "to restore slavery in fact,"[128] the act was considered a violation of the U.S. Constitution. Thus, in his message to the Florida legislature, Governor David S. Walker stated: "I recommend a revision of the laws you passed at your last session in regard to freedmen. The one in regard to freedmen carrying firearms does not accord with our Constitution, has not been enforced and should be repealed."[129] The governor must have assumed that the Second Amendment applied to the states, and/or that the prohibition of slavery in the Thirteenth Amendment[130] served to render the Florida statute invalid.

Among other objectives, the Fourteenth Amendment was proposed and adopted to cause the states to recognize in their own legislation the norms set by the Second and Thirteenth Amendments. Consistent with the mandates of those three amendments, the Florida convention of 1868 adopted in the new Declaration of Rights the following: "The people shall have the right to bear arms in defence of themselves and the lawful authority of the State."[131]

Georgia. Although the Georgia Constitution had no right-to-bear-arms provision prior to 1861, the classic case of *Nunn* v. *State* in 1846 had held that "the language of the *second* amendment is broad enough to embrace both Federal and State governments—nor is there anything in its terms which restricts its meaning."[132] The Georgia high court declared invalid a statutory prohibition on breast pistols on the basis of the guarantees of the U.S. Constitution: "The right of the whole people, old and young, men, women and boys, and not militia only, to keep and bear *arms* of every description, and not *such* merely as are used by the *militia,* shall not be infringed. . . ."[133] However, the same court narrowed this language two years later in stating that "free persons of color have never been recognized as citizens of Georgia; they are not entitled to bear arms. . . ."[134]

The postwar Georgia Constitution of 1865 adopted a right-to-have-arms provision identical with that of the U.S. Constitution.[135] This indicated the common understanding that the Second Amendment protected the individual right to keep and bear arms rather than a state right to maintain militias. After all, it would have been incomprehensible for a state constitution to declare the same state's right to maintain its militia free from infringement by itself.

As amended by the convention of 1868, the guarantee read: "A well regulated militia being necessary to the security of a free people, the right of the people to keep and bear arms shall not be infringed, but the General Assembly shall have the power to prescribe by law the manner in which arms may be borne."[136] When proposed in convention, the last part read, "borne *by private persons.*"[137] This again demonstrates the individual character of the right, for no need existed to mention "private persons" in the latter part unless the former part protected this same class. This phrase was deleted in the final draft to eliminate surplusage, apparently because everyone knew the prohibition on concealed carrying of weapons applied to private persons, and to prevent a "public persons" defense to that prohibition.

The antebellum Georgia Supreme Court had held that the Second Amendment applied to the states. Georgia's adoption of the same provision for its postwar constitutions did not stem simply from the mandate of Congress that the Southern state constitutions reflect the Thirteenth and Fourteenth Amendments. It was also rooted in the fundamental character of the right to keep and bear arms as viewed in that state's tradition. Thus, Georgia's 1868 constitution amounted to reenactment of the *Nunn* v. *State* view that the federal Constitution prohibits states from infringing on the fundamental right to possess either pistols or long guns.[138]

Louisiana. Since its antebellum courts had held that the Second Amendment applied to the states, the prewar and postwar constitutions of Louisiana included no right-to-have-arms guarantees.[139] Thus, in *State* v. *Chandler* (1850), the high court of Louisiana had held that the right to carry arms openly "places men upon an equality. This is the right guaranteed by the Constitution of the United States, and which is calculated to incite men to a manly and noble defence of themselves, if necessary, and of their country. . . ."[140]

In the constitutional convention of 1867–1868, a bill of rights was proposed and referred to committee. It included a provision that the military should be subordinate to the civil power and that "every citizen has the right to keep and bear arms for the common defense, and this right shall never be questioned."[141] The committee reporting the bill of rights deleted the arms provision.[142] As neither the majority nor the minority reports on a bill of rights included the provision, presumably no significance can be attributed to its deletion, and the right to have arms was apparently intended to be included in the unenumerated rights guarantee.[143] When the convention debated the proposed bill of rights, racial equality was the main subject of contention, and again no one objected to lack of a right-to-arms provision or moved to insert one.[144]

In conclusion, since Louisiana jurisprudence held that the Second Amendment protected the right to keep and bear arms from state infringement, a view which would undoubtedly be strengthened by the Fourteenth Amendment, the Louisiana convention apparently deemed a specific right to arms provision unnecessary. Subsequently, the high court of that state continued to recognize "the constitutional right to keep and bear arms."[145]

Mississippi. The antebellum Mississippi constitution provided: "Every citizen has a right to bear arms, in defence of himself and the State."[146] After the war, because blacks were not considered citizens, the legislature enacted a statute "that no freedman, free negro or mulatto, . . . not licensed so to do so by the board of police of his or her county, shall keep or carry firearms of any kind. . . ."[147] As seen previously in this study, this was among the black code provisions cited in Congress in support of the need for the Civil Rights Act of 1866 and the Fourteenth Amendment.

When the convention met in 1868, the Bill of Rights committee proposed: "Every person shall have a right to keep and bear arms for their common defense."[148] While a motion to change "person" back to "citizen" failed, the word "common" was striken from the clause.[149] As adopted, the provision read: "All persons shall have a right to keep and bear arms for their defense."[150] Thus, the Fourteenth Amendment, and the state provision adopted to be consistent therewith, served to invalidate Mississippi's prohibition against unlicensed firearms.

North Carolina. The Declaration of Rights of North Carolina, which dates to 1776, included the guarantee "that the people have a right to bear arms, for the defense of the State. . . ."[151] Accordingly, the high court of that state held: "A man may carry a gun for any lawful purpose of business or amusement. . . ."[152] To uphold an act to prevent free persons of color from carrying firearms, the North Carolina Supreme Court in *State* v. *Newsom* (1844) denied citizenship to them.[153] It also originated the interpretation that the Second Amendment did not apply to the states: "In the second article of the amended Constitution, the States are neither mentioned nor referred to. It is therefore only restrictive of the powers of the Federal Government."[154]

The original 1776 provision was proposed in the 1868 convention,[155] which substituted instead language identical with the Second Amendment.[156] As in the case of Georgia, the North Carolina delegates responded to the requirement that they amend their constitution strictly in conformity with the Fourteenth Amendment by adopting the Second Amendment verbatim. This served to overrule the *Newsom* precedent, which had circumvented the federal Bill of Rights by holding that it did not apply to the states.

Incorporation of the language of the federal Second Amendment into a state constitution again clarifies the common understanding that the federal amendment protected the individual right to have arms, for there was no need in a state constitution to protect a right of the state to form militias from infringement by that same state. Militia issues and provisions were treated separately by that convention.[157] Another convention, held before the end of Reconstruction, added to the right-to-arms guarantee: "Nothing herein contained shall justify the practice of carrying concealed weapons, or prevent the Legislature from enacting penal statutes against said practice."[158] The new latter clause clearly indicated the individual nature of the main guarantee.[159]

South Carolina. The antebellum constitution of South Carolina contained no bill of rights.[160] The provisions of the slave codes on arms control were the only serious interference with keeping and bearing arms, and these provisions were reenacted at the end of the war and were cited in debates in Congress in support of adoption of the Fourteenth Amendment.

Pursuant to congressional mandate that South Carolina adopt a constitution consistent with the Fourteenth Amendment, the 1868 convention proposed a Declaration of Rights which included the following: "Every citizen has a right to keep and bear arms in defence of himself and the State, and this right shall never be questioned."[161] As reported from committee and as finally adopted, this was changed to read, "the people have a right to keep and bear arms for the common defence."[162] No substantive change was intended, for the rights of "defending their lives and liberties . . . and protecting property," as well as all unenumerated rights, were retained.[163] Indeed, apparently no one objected to the alteration, and the extensive debate on the provision centered on the additional clause providing that the military power shall always be subject to the civil authority.[164] The latter clause was controversial since, after all, the state was under military occupation at the time. C. C. Bowen, who had proposed the right-to-arms provision in its original form, linked the arms guarantee with subordination of military to civil power:

I find men very zealous of the liberties of the people, now willing to put those liberties in the hands of the military. . . . [I]f a military officer

has a sufficient number of bayonets to carry out his edict [declaring martial law], he may enforce it by simple force of arms, and yet have no
right to do so.[165]

That the arms provision as adopted did not provide only a militia-related
right is clear in that debate and provisions on the militia were covered elsewhere.[166] Indeed, B. O. Duncan, who unsuccessfully opposed the clause sub-
ordinating the military to the civil authority,[167] moved that "the Legislature
shall enact such laws as it may deem proper and necessary to punish the carrying of concealed deadly weapons."[168] This indicates an understanding of the
arms guarantee as a private right, for otherwise authority to prohibit the carrying of concealed weapons would have been unnecessary.[169]

Tennessee. Like the constitutional provisions of Arkansas and Florida, Tennessee's antebellum constitution provided: "That the free white men of this
State have a right to keep and bear arms for their common defence."[170] The
Tennessee Supreme Court in 1833 quashed an indictment for carrying arms
on the following grounds: "By this clause of the constitution, an express power
is given and secured to all the free citizens of the State to keep and bear arms
for their defence, without any qualification whatever as to their kind or
nature."[171] Seven years later the same court stated: "If the citizens have these
[military] arms in their hands, they are prepared in the best possible manner
to repel any encroachments upon their rights, etc."[172]

So thorough had been the Northern conquest there that Tennessee was
the only Southern state not required to adopt a constitution consistent with
the Fourteenth Amendment as a precondition to reentry into the Union. The
state therefore was not required to hold a convention in 1868. Nonetheless,
when a convention was called in 1870, provisions inconsistent with that
amendment were struck. Thus, it was moved that the arms guarantee "be so
amended as to strike out the words 'the free white men' and insert the words
'all persons.' "[173] Earlier drafts sought to substitute "all citizens" or "the
citizens."[174] An allowance for legislative regulation of the manner of carrying
weapons was moved,[175] again recognizing the individual character of the right
to carry arms and the unqualified right to *keep* arms. As adopted, the provision
read: "That the citizens of this State have a right to keep and bear arms for
their common defense. But the Legislature shall have the power, by law, to
regulate the wearing of arms with a view to prevent crime."[176]

In response to the guarantee that all citizens, not just free white men, could
keep and bear arms, the Tennessee legislature promptly declared that it was
unlawful, *inter alia,* "for any person to publicly or privately carry a . . . revolver."[177] In the following year the state supreme court declared this unconstitutional. "We find that, necessarily, the same rights, and for similar reasons,
were being provided for and protected in both the federal and State constitu-

tions,"[178] the court stated, after quoting the Second Amendment and the pertinent Tennessee provision. The court held that the right of the people to keep arms includes the rights to purchase arms and ammunition, to practice with them, and "to use such arms for all the ordinary purposes, and in all the ordinary modes usual in the country. . . ."[179] Referring to the clause of the state guarantee added by the recent convention, the court pointed out that "the power to regulate does not fairly mean the power to prohibit. . . ."[180]

Texas. The prewar constitution of Texas provided: "Every citizen shall have the right to keep and bear arms in the lawful defence of himself or the State."[181] The high court of Texas construed this provision as follows:

> The right of a citizen to bear arms, in lawful defence of himself or the State, is absolute. . . . A law cannot be passed to infringe upon or impair it, because it is above the law, and independent of the law making power.[182]

Although the 1868 convention did not alter the provision, existing records of that convention reveal the understanding that the state constitution was required to be consistent with the Fourteenth Amendment and that the Fourteenth Amendment incorporated the Bill of Rights. The "Report of the Attorney General of Texas for 1867," appended to the convention journal, contains an analysis of what it called "Pretended Laws of 1866 against the Freedmen":

> The main object kept in view by . . . those who devised the pretended laws . . . was the restoration of African slavery, in the modified form of peonage. . . .
>
> Ch. 80, p. 76—The so-called labor law.—It provides expressly for a system of peonage, without using that term. . . . It is directly opposed to the Thirteenth Amendment of the Constitution of the United States, and of the Civil Rights Act. . . .
>
> Ch. 92, p. 90—Makes the carrying of fire-arms on enclosed land, without consent of the land-owner, an offence. It was meant to operate against freedmen alone, and hence is subject to the same objections. . . .
>
> Joint Resolution No. 13, p. 166—The refusal to ratify the fourteenth proposed amendment to the constitution of the United States. As the first section of this amendment guarantees freedmen their civil rights as citizens of the United States and of the States in which they reside, the rejection of the amendment . . . is subject to the further objection of being a rejection of a condition precedent since imposed by the military reconstruction act.[183]

The usual complaints of freedmen being disarmed are found in convention

records. A committee report noted that Union men "can hold public meetings only when supported by troops or armed men. . . ." Even though the
freedmen were "generally as well armed as the whites,"[184] "bands of armed
whites are traversing the country, forcibly robbing the freedmen of their arms,
and committing other outrages upon them."[185] Gen. J. J. Reynolds reported
to Washington that Ku Klux Klan organizations sought "to disarm, rob, and
in many cases murder Union men and negroes. . . ."[186]

Talk in the convention about adopting "every safeguard contemplated by
the Fourteenth Amendment to the Constitution of the United States"[187] led
to suggestions for amendments modeled after the U.S. Bill of Rights. One
delegate introduced the following:

> A well regulated militia being necessary to the safety of a free State,
> every citizen shall have the right to keep and bear arms for the common
> defence. Nevertheless this article shall not be construed as giving any
> countenance to the evil practice of carrying private or concealed weap-
> ons about the person. . . .[188]

Precisely adhering to the theme that the state constitution must be in accord
with the Fourteenth Amendment, which in turn incorporated the Bill of
Rights, the Committee on General Provisions proposed: "The inhibitions of
power enunciated in articles from one to eight inclusive, and thirteen, of the
amendments to the Constitution of the United States, deny to the States, as
well as to the General Government, the exercise of the powers therein reserved to the people, and shall never be exercised by the government of this
State."[189] M. C. Hamilton, the committee chairman, explained this provision as follows: "It will be observed that section 3 embodies the substance of
ten of the sections in the Bill of Rights in the Constitution of 1845, it being
the opinion of your Committee that the inhibitions enumerated in the said
ten sections are fully covered by the nine articles mentioned as amendments
to the Constitution of the United States, thus dispensing with a long string of
sections which are deemed useless."[190]

The committee's report is highly significant in several respects. First, it
reaffirms the understanding that the Second Amendment protected individual rights, for it "embodies the substance" of the guarantee in the 1845 constitution that "every citizen shall have the right to keep and bear arms in the
lawful defence of himself or the State." Secondly, it clearly recognizes that
the Fourteenth Amendment, which the proposed state bill of rights was precisely fashioned to emulate, made "articles from one to eight inclusive . . .
of the amendments to the Constitution of the United States" applicable to
the states. Thirdly, failure to adopt the proposed new bill of rights signified
no rejection of its principles because the 1845 provisions guaranteed the same
protections as the U.S. Bill of Rights.

Four years after the 1868 convention, the Texas Supreme Court reiterated the view that the federal Constitution protects the right to keep and bear arms—a "personal right" which is "inherent and inalienable to man"—from state deprivation.[191] Citing the Second Amendment, the court agreed with Joel P. Bishop that " 'though most of the amendments are restrictions on the general government alone, not on the States, this one seems to be of a nature to bind both the State and National legislatures,' and doubtless it does."[192]

Virginia. The Virginia Declaration of Rights of 1776 provided: "That a well regulated militia, composed of the body of the people, trained to arms, is the proper, natural and safe defense of a free state. . . ."[193] The common law in effect in Virginia also protected "the right of bearing arms—which with us is not limited and restrained by an arbitrary system of game laws as in England; but is practically enjoyed by every citizen, and is among his most valuable privileges, since it furnishes the means of resisting as a freeman ought, the inroads of usurpation."[194]

That the provision of the Declaration of Rights recognized private rights and not simply militia duties is evidenced by the fact that the convention of 1867–1868 readopted it under the label "RIGHT TO BEAR ARMS,"[195] and provided for the militia in a separate article.[196] In the words of convention delegate John Hawnhurst: "The Bill of Rights . . . is a declaration of individual rights, as against the Government. It is an assertion of certain rights that the Government shall not take away from the individual."[197]

Discussion centered on the fact that the Fourteenth Amendment would confer citizenship on freedmen, and the delegates were well aware from the authorities upon which they relied that "citizenship" carried with it broad rights, including keeping and bearing arms.[198] The utility of being armed to resist oppression was suggested in the following analogy by Thomas Bayne in support of the Freedmen's Bureau:

> Now, as on former occasions, in every age and country of the world, the weak must always suffer when the strong oppress them. If the highway robber meets the unarmed man in the road he takes his purse away from him simply because he wants it and is able to take it.[199]

In conclusion, the Virginia convention reaffirmed that state's traditional concept of the value of an armed populace, and recognized that the Fourteenth Amendment would confer upon the freedmen the basic rights of citizenship.

In sum, the antebellum Southern states considered the right to keep and bear arms as a fundamental one, although they denied the right to blacks. The Fourteenth Amendment's protection of the right of all persons to have arms caused amendment of the constitutions of Arkansas, Florida, and Tennessee, which had only recognized this right for free white men. It also invalidated the prohibition of unlicensed firearms or similar gun control laws applied to freedmen in Mississippi, Louisiana, Alabama, and South Carolina.

It should be added that the constitutions of all other states were consistent with the Fourteenth Amendment's incorporation of the right to keep and bear arms both before and after its adoption.[200] An analysis of state constitutions through the end of Reconstruction reveals that twenty-three state constitutions had specific right-to-bear-arms provisions, while twelve states either had no bill of rights or, if so, no arms provision.[201] Of the twenty-three, the right is described as being held by one of the following entities: "every citizen," "the citizen," "every person," "the people," or "all persons." The following are stated as objectives of the right:

Stated Objective	Number of States
1. "defense of himself [or themselves] and the State"[202]	10
2. "common defence"[203]	5
3. "their defense [and security]"[204]	3
4. "[defense of his] home, person, or property"[205]	2
5. [language equivalent to the Second Amendment][206]	2
6. [no specific purpose stated][207]	1

The state bills of rights that did not specifically mention a right to have arms invariably included unenumerated rights; a right to defend and protect life, liberty, and property; and/or citizen's militia clauses. The idea that the federal Constitution protected the right to keep and bear arms led to the belief that an equivalent state guarantee was unnecessary. For instance, a proposal in the Maryland convention of 1867 would have added to its bill of rights the following: "every citizen has the right to bear arms in defense of himself and the State." The following debate took place in response:

> Mr. Garey read from the constitution of the United States: "The right of the people to keep and bear arms shall not be infringed." He considered the proposed amendment entirely in accordance with the constitution of the United States, and that it should be adopted.
> Mr. Jones said that for the very reason that it was in the constitution of the United States, he hoped it would not be inserted here. That was amply sufficient.[208]

In conclusion, on the adoption of the Fourteenth Amendment, most state constitutions already protected, and three were amended to protect, the right of all private citizens or persons to keep and bear arms. The common law of all states and the federal Constitution were universally viewed as protecting this same private right.

That No Militia Shall Disarm a Freedman: The Abolition of the Southern Militia Organizations, 1866–1869

While not directly related to the debates over the Fourteenth Amendment, abuses committed by militias in the South gave rise to further analysis of the Second Amendment and to congressional deliberation between 1866 and 1869 over whether the federal government could constitutionally abolish these militias. In early 1866, Senator Henry Wilson (Republican of Massachusetts) introduced the joint resolution S. Res. No. 32 to disband the militias in most Southern states, citing reports from the Freedmen's Bureau that militias were disarming blacks: "Nearly all the dissatisfaction that now exists among the freedmen [in Mississippi] is caused by the abusive conduct of the militia. . . . [T]he militia organizations of . . . South Carolina (Edgefield) were engaged in disarming the negroes."[209]

In opposition to referring the joint resolution to committee, Senator Willard Saulsbury (Democrat of Delaware) argued that the power of Congress under Article I, § 8 to organize, arm, and discipline the militia

does not give power to Congress to disarm the militia of a State, or to destroy the militia of a State, because in another provision of the Constitution, the second amendment, we have these words:

"A well-regulated militia being necessary to the security of a free State, the right of the people to keep and bear arms shall not be infringed."

The proposition here . . . is an application to Congress to do that which Congress has no right to do under the second amendment of the Constitution. . . . [U]nless the power is lodged in Congress to disarm the militia of Massachusetts, it cannot be pretended that any such power is lodged in Congress in reference to the State of Mississippi.

We hear a great deal about the oppressions of the negroes down South, and a complaint here comes from somebody connected with the Freedmen's Bureau. Only the other day I saw a statement in the papers that a negro, in violation of the law of Kentucky, was found with concealed weapons upon his person. The law of Kentucky, I believe, is applicable to whites and blacks alike. An officer of the Freedmen's Bureau, however, summoned the judge of the court before him, ordered him to deliver up the pistol to that negro, and to refund the fine to which the negro was subject by the law of Kentucky. The other day your papers stated that one of these negroes shot down a Federal officer in the State of Ten-

nessee. Yet, sir, no petitions are here to protect the white people against
the outrages committed by the negro population; but if a few letters are
written to members here that oppression has been practiced against negroes, then the whole white population of a State are to be disarmed.[210]

Senator Wilson responded that ex-Confederates went "up and down the
country searching houses, disarming people, committing outrages of every
kind and description." He concluded: "Congress has power to disarm ruffi-
ans or traitors, or men who are committing outrages against law or the rights
of men on our common humanity."[211] The resolution was then referred to
committee.

Both senators upheld the peaceful citizen's right to keep and bear arms,
but they disagreed over who in the South were aggressors and consequently
lost this and other rights. Wilson had complained two months before about
the deprivation of arms of freedmen in Mississippi, pursuant to that state's
firearms prohibition law which applied to blacks.[212] And while Saulsbury had
just three weeks before opposed the Civil Rights bill because it would prohibit states from disarming free Negroes,[213] he now invoked the Second
Amendment to protect the right of "the whole white population" not only to
be armed but also to organize and operate as militia.

A few days later, Wilson reported his bill to disband the Southern militias,[214]
but it was not taken up until the next session. The bill read:

> And be it further enacted, That all militia forces now organized or in
> service in either of the States of Virginia, North Carolina, South Carolina,
> Georgia, Florida, Alabama, Louisiana, Mississippi, and Texas, be forth-
> with disarmed and disbanded, and that the further organization, arming,
> or calling into service of the said militia forces, or any part thereof, is
> hereby prohibited under any circumstances whatever until the same shall
> be authorized by Congress.[215]

In response to a request for an explanation of the bill by Senator Charles
R. Buckalew (Democrat of Pennsylvania), Senator Wilson pointed out that
"we have evidence of great wrongs perpetrated" by the "local State militia"
in those states.[216] Buckalew responded: "The organization of local forces for
the preservation of order and for defense is one of those ordinary and common rights and privileges, which ought not to be curtailed. . . ."[217] Senator
Henry S. Lane (Republican of Indiana) justified "dissolving these local militia organizations" because they were not "in harmony with Government or
with the Union sentiment of the country. . . ."[218] After Senator Thomas A.
Hendricks (Democrat of Indiana) objected that it would amount to "repealing
a clause of the Constitution,"[219] consideration of the bill was postponed.

When the bill was taken up again a week later, Senator Wilson urged abolition of the organized militias on the grounds that "in some localities they
have been used to disarm portions of the people. . . ."[220] Abolition of the
militia was vigorously opposed by Senator Waitman T. Willey (Republican
of West Virginia) on the grounds that "the militia should at least carry arms to
a limited extent. . . . [T]here may be some constitutional objection against
depriving men of the right to bear arms and the total disarming of men in
time of peace."[221] Senator Wilson, a strong supporter of the Fourteenth
Amendment, explained that the militia organizations "go up and down the
country taking arms away from men who own arms, and committing outrages
of various kinds. . . ."[222] But Willey was still unsatisfied because the bill

> takes the right to bear arms away from every citizen of the southern
> States. . . . I should be very willing to favor discriminating legislation
> that would regulate the *use* of arms by the militia in the South; but a
> sweeping enactment of the character that I understand this to be does
> not meet my approbation as at present advised.[223]

It was the argument of Senator Hendricks that the bill would violate the
Second Amendment by disarming not only state militias, but also individuals,
that carried the most weight in the fate of the bill:

> I am not able to see how the proposition can be adopted by the Senate,
> in view of the second article of the Amendments to the Constitution,
> which declares, "a well-regulated militia being necessary to the security
> of a free State, the right of the people to keep and bear arms shall not be
> infringed." If this infringes the right of the people to bear arms we have
> no authority to adopt it. *This provision does not relate to States alone; it relates
> to people wherever they may be under the jurisdiction of the United States.* Of
> course in time of war people bearing arms in hostility to the Govern-
> ment would not be protected by this provision of the Constitution; but
> when there is no war, in a time of peace, certainly the provision of the
> Constitution applies now, if it ever does.[224]

Hendrick's argument was persuasive even for Wilson, who then conceded:
"I am willing, however to modify the amendment by striking out the word
'disarmed.' Then it will provide simply for disbanding these organizations."[225]
This made the bill "very much more acceptable to me than it was originally,"
replied Wilson's fellow Republican, Senator Willey. "The idea, by a sweeping enactment . . . , of disarming the whole people of the South seemed to
me to be so directly in the face of the Constitution itself, as to strike me as
somewhat strange."[226] The bill then passed the Senate,[227] and subsequently
the House,[228] and became law.

These debates demonstrate that, in the understanding of the same legislators who, less than a year before, had either supported or opposed the Fourteenth Amendment as it had made its way through the Senate, the Second
Amendment guaranteed primarily the individual right to keep and bear arms,
and only secondarily the right of a state to maintain a militia. Wilson proposed the militia-disbanding bill because the state militia organizations were
disarming individuals. Hendricks objected that such a bill "does not relate to
the States alone; it relates to people," and therefore it violated the Second
Amendment. And Willey thought that Congress could "regulate the use of
arms by the militia" but could not disarm individuals because the Constitution guaranteed "the right to bear arms . . . [to] every citizen." In sum, both
proponents and opponents of the Fourteenth Amendment in the Senate unanimously viewed the Second Amendment as guaranteeing an individual right
to keep and bear arms to every person, but the anti-Southern majority were
unpersuaded that it guaranteed a state right to maintain militias.[229]

House action on the bill to disband the Southern militias presents an interesting contrast with its action on H. R. No. 1145, the bill to provide for
organizing a national militia. Reported by Representative Halbert E. Paine
(Republican of Wisconsin), the bill provided that all able-bodied males of
ages 18 through 45 were "liable to enrollment in the enrolled militia," from
which would be composed "the national guard of active militias. . . ."[230] In
debate a few days later, Representative Harding (Republican of Illinois),
rejecting the objection "that the bill infringes on the constitutional powers of
the States," stated:

> The people of the free States are without arms. . . . They have sur-
> rendered their arms up to the Government, and those arms are now
> deposited in large quantities in the various United States arsenals. This
> proposition is to return them to *a small portion of the people* selected by
> enlistment from the militia body. . . . [T]he regiments of infantry being
> fully armed and equipped . . . shall be constituted and called the "Na-
> tional Guard."[231]

To Representative Charles A. Eldridge (Democrat of Wisconsin), the bill
was "designed to establish a standing army" and thus "the same despotic
rule that you have endeavored to fasten upon the southern States."[232] Representative Lewis W. Ross (Democrat of Illinois) agreed that it would "create a
great standing army to eat out the substance of the people and overturn their
liberties." Representative Francis C. LeBlond (Democrat of Ohio) argued:
"This bill proposes very radical changes in the laws of the States in regard to
the militia."[233] Later the same day, in debate on the army appropriation bill
(H. R. No. 1126), Representative Ross reiterated his objection to "a large

military establishment" and "a militia bill providing for the military enrollment of the entire community."[234]

On the next day, the bill was amended to encompass in the Southern states
"companies of the national guard herein provided for, composed exclusively
of loyal persons, without respect of color. . . ."[235] To the standing army
argument, Representative Paine responded that "it is a militia system which
is proposed by this bill, the entire control of which will be in the hands of the
local authorities, and none of it in the hands of the Federal Government."[236]

As the session hurried to a close, the Senate joined its bill to disband the
Southern militias to the House's army appropriations bill, and sought House
concurrence.[237] The appropriations bill was then pushed through the House
without further debate and approved on the second of March.[238]

Characteristically, proponents of the bill to organize the National Guard
never relied on the Second Amendment, and in fact they never sought to
equate "the people" with the "National Guard," described by Representative Harding as only "a small portion of the people." Further, those who
opposed the "National Guard" as a standing military establishment did not
bother to raise Second Amendment objections (or any other criticisms, for
that matter) against the bill to disband the Southern militias. After all, in the
bill that it sent to the House, the Senate had already deleted the proposal to
"disarm" those militias (which were interpreted as including all the people
of the South) and only sought to disband the state militia organizations. Thus,
this early mention of a "National Guard" was not associated with the militia
of the people described in the Second Amendment.

At the end of 1868, S. Res. No. 665 was reported to repeal the portion of
the act, approved 2 March 1867, "as prohibits the organization, arming, or
calling into service of the militia forces in the States lately in rebellion. . . ."[239]
Senator Wilson began by noting that the president had recommended the
repeal of that act and that nobody had opposed repeal in the last session.
Senator George F. Edmunds (Republican of Vermont) asked why they should
permit Virginia, Texas, and Mississippi, which had not been readmitted to
the Union, "which are yet in a state of rebellion and who are held under the
authority of military law, to set up a local militia of their own."[240] Senator
Thomas A. Hendricks (Democrat of Indiana) contended: "At the time the
bill passed there had been no serious outrages by local military power," but
"great wrongs and outrages are perpetrated by the local militia" in Arkansas
and Tennessee.[241]

Senator William P. Fessenden (Republican of Maine) replied that the act
had passed originally because of "a general distrust of the loyal character of
the provisional governments formerly existing in those States, and that it would
be dangerous to put an armed militia within their control."[242] As to Texas,
"the militia of that State, if you call it a State, should be organized in order

that there may be some force adequate to the suppression of these outrages."[243] Senator Edmunds was willing to allow a militia force of "loyal men"
(that is, Republicans) in Texas, but not a militia of the general populace.
"But the difficulty of repealing this general prohibitory clause will be . . .
that it will authorize anybody and everybody in the State of Texas, under
what they call its ancient militia laws . . . to organize a militia hostile to the
Government that we are undertaking to administer there. . . ."[244] Thus,
Edmunds advocated "a selected militia" approved by the Texas government
and by Congress.

After further debate, Senator Charles R. Buchalew (Democrat of Pennsylvania) reiterated that the president, in his annual message, had denounced
the militia disbanding law

> because at all times, both when it was placed upon the statute-book and
> every moment since, it was and is in his judgment a violation of the Con-
> stitution of the United States. One of the amendments to our fundamen-
> tal law expressly provides that "the right of the people to keep and bear
> arms shall not be infringed"—of course by this Government; and it gives
> the reason that a well-regulated militia in the several divisions of the
> country is necessary for the protection and for the interests of the people.
>
>   . . . The party in power in Congress [the Republicans] passed this
> law in order to weaken the then existing political governments in the
> South which were not in accord with them . . . in a political sense—and
> they now propose to restore to that section of the country all power over
> local militia and to furnish arms for their organizations, because the politi-
> cal power which now exists is politically friendly to them. . . . It will
> influence elections. . . .[245]

Senator Wilson rejoined the fray with an explanation of why the act was
originally passed: "This militia went up and down the country disarming
Union men, black and white, and committing outrages upon the people."[246]
But Senator Garrett Davis (Democrat of Kentucky) countered that only the
people of a state could organize a state government:

> Whenever a State organizes a government it has of its own inherent right
> and power authority to organize a militia for it. Congress has no right to
> abolish that militia after it is organized. Congress has no authority to invest
> that State with power to organize a militia. It has no right to prohibit that
> State from the organization of its militia.
>
>   . . . [Republicans] ask for a repeal of this law that they may have the
> formal sanction of Congress to authorize a militia exclusively under the
> leaders of their own faction, and place the arms which they get from the
> Government of the United States in their hands. . . .[247]

As the debate came to an end, and the Senate neared passage of the bill,[248] Senator Willard Warner (Republican of Alabama) stressed the first clause of the Second Amendment as having invalidated the act in the first place:

> we have the right now, being restored to our full relation to the Federal Government, to organize a militia of our own, and that we could have done so at any time in the past, this law to the contrary notwithstanding. Article two of the amendments of the Constitution provides that—
> "A well regulated militia being necessary to the security of a free State, the right of the people to keep and bear arms shall not be infringed."[249]

In this debate, Senators Wilson and Fessenden both complained about militia abuses, but each had in mind different militias, that is, Democratic and Republican militias, respectively. Senator Edmunds feared the ancient militia tradition that "anybody and everybody" could form a militia, while Buchalew favored that tradition, holding that the people's right to keep and bear arms, part of "our fundamental law," encourages a well-regulated militia. The right of states to maintain militias was supported by Senator Davis, on a reserved powers theory akin to the Tenth Amendment, and by Senator Warner, on the authority of the Second Amendment, which, after all, declares that a well regulated militia is necessary for a free state's security.

When the House debated the proposal to allow Southern states to maintain militias, its proponents relied on state's rights arguments and did not mention the Second Amendment. Having reported the bill back from the Committee on Reconstruction, Representative Halbert E. Paine (Republican of Wisconsin) pointed out that "several of those States have been restored to their relations to the Federal Government. The repeal of the provision becomes necessary to the organization and maintenance of the State militia in those States as the State militia is maintained in other States of the Union."[250] After a complaint from Representative Charles A. Eldridge (Democrat of Wisconsin) on the exclusion of Georgia from the bill, information that the Senate had passed a similar bill the day before short-circuited further debate.[251] Even so, the following exchange took place between Representative John F. Farnsworth (Republican of Illinois) and Representative Paine:

> Mr. Farnsworth. I will vote for this bill, but at the same time I do not want to be put upon the record as agreeing to the doctrine that Congress may prevent States from organizing militia.
> Mr. Paine. Of course, then, the gentleman will vote for this bill, which repeals a provision involving that doctrine.[252]

The Senate approved the House bill the following day. Senator Howard requested an explanation of the bill from Senator Wilson, who pointed out that the Senate had already passed a similar bill at a time when Howard had been absent.[253] Unfortunately, Howard, a leading exponent of the Fourteenth Amendment, had not been present when the Second Amendment had been commented on several times by his colleagues. In any case, the House bill became law in early 1869.[254] When the Senate bill was finally considered in the House, Representative Glenn W. Scofield (Republican of Pennsylvania) commented: "I think it is right. We had a law which prohibited them from organizing their militia."[255] The bill was then approved.[256]

Analysis of the debates on the militia controversy during the years 1866 to 1869 significantly contribute to the understanding of the intention of the Congress which proposed the Fourteenth Amendment to the states. Supporters of the Fourteenth Amendment considered the individual right to keep and bear arms so fundamental that they were ready to abolish the state militias to protect freedmen from deprivation of this right. Opponents of the Fourteenth Amendment had an equally strong commitment, based on a wholly different factual world view, to the citizen's right to keep and bear arms, which they deemed even more fundamental than the power of a state to maintain a militia. In the view that predominated, the state power to raise militia organizations might be temporarily abated by Congress, which simultaneously would take care not to infringe on the right of the people to keep and bear arms, in order to protect against state infringement of that very same right of freedmen and all other persons to keep and bear arms. In short, the same Congress that passed the Fourteenth Amendment was willing to dissolve the state militias, and even to disenfranchise most Southern whites; it took care not to infringe upon the right of the disenfranchised Southern whites to have weapons, while safeguarding the same right for newly emancipated slaves.

Against Deprivation under Color of State Law of the Right to Keep and Bear Arms: The Civil Rights Acts of 1871 and 1875

The Fourteenth Amendment having been declared in effect in 1868, Congress soon afterward began to consider enforcement legislation both to remedy infringement of rights under color of state law and to suppress the Ku Klux Klan. The entitlement of freedmen to all the rights of citizenship, including the right to keep and bear arms, was clear enough; the question became how these rights might be protected by statute and in the courts. That no state could officially deprive a citizen of the right to have arms was exemplified clearly enough in a report by Rep. William Loughridge (Republican of Iowa) in early 1871:

The case of Cooper *vs.* the Mayor of Savannah, (4 Ga. 72 [1848],) involved the question whether a free negro was a citizen of the United States. The court, in the opinion, says:

"Free persons of color have never been recognized as citizens of Georgia; they are not entitled to bear arms, vote for members of the legislature, or hold any civil office. . . ."

That they could not vote, hold office, & c., was held evidence that they were not regarded as citizens. . . .

But all such fallacious theories as this are swept away by the fourteenth amendment, which abolishes the theory of different grades of citizenship, . . . guaranteeing to all citizens the rights and privileges of citizens of the republic.[257]

Concurring in this analysis was Representative Benjamin F. Butler (Republican of Massachusetts), whose report on violence in the South appeared a few days later. Noting instances of terrorism against the freedmen by "armed confederates" who doubled as militiamen, the report stated that "in many counties they have preceded their outrages upon him by disarming him, in violation of his right as a citizen to 'keep and bear arms,' which the Constitution expressly says shall never be infringed."[258] The congressional power, based on Section 5 of the Fourteenth Amendment, to legislate to prevent states from depriving any U.S. citizen of life, liberty, or property justified the following provision of the committee's anti-KKK bill:

That whoever shall, without due process of law, by violence, intimidation, or threats, take away or deprive any citizen of the United States of any arms or weapons he may have in his house or possession for the defense of his person, family, or property, shall be deemed guilty of a larceny thereof, and be punished as provided in this act for a felony.[259]

Representative Butler explained the purpose of this provision in these words:

Section eight is intended to enforce the well-known constitutional provision guaranteeing the right in the citizen to 'keep and bear arms,' and provides that whoever shall take away, by force or violence, or by threats and intimidation, the arms and weapons which any person may have for his defense, shall be deemed guilty of larceny of the same. This provision seemed to your committee to be necessary, because they had observed that, before these midnight marauders made attacks upon peaceful citizens, there were very many instances in the South where the sheriff of the county had preceded them and taken away the arms of their victims. This was specially noticeable in Union County, where all

the negro population were disarmed by the sheriff only a few months
ago under the order of the judge . . .; and then, the sheriff having disarmed the citizens, the five hundred masked men rode at night and murdered and otherwise maltreated the ten persons who were in jail in that
county.[260]

Referred to the Judiciary Committee, the bill was later reported as H. R.
No. 320 without the section quoted above. After all, that section's proscription extended to simple individual larceny over which Congress had no constitutional authority, and state or conspiratorial action involving the disarming
of blacks was covered by more general provisions of the bill. Supporters of
the rewritten anti-KKK bill continued to show the same concern over the
deprivation of arms of freedmen. Senator John Sherman (Republican of Ohio)
stated the Republican position: "Wherever the negro population prepon-
derates, there they [the KKK] hold their sway, for a few determined men . . .
can carry terror among ignorant negroes . . . without arms, equipment, or
discipline."[261]

Further comments clarified that the right to arms was a necessary condition
for the right of free speech. Senator Adelbert Ames (Republican of Mississippi)
averred: "In some counties it was impossible to advocate Republican principles, those attempting it being hunted like wild beasts; in others, the speakers had to be armed and supported by not a few friends."[262] Representative
William L. Stoughton (Republican of Michigan) exclaimed: "If political opponents can be marked for slaughter by secret bands of cowardly assassins who
ride forth with impunity to execute the decrees upon the unarmed and defenseless, it will be fatal alike to the Republican party and civil liberty."[263]

Section 1 of the bill, taken partly from Section 2 of the Civil Rights Act of
1866, survives today as 42 U.S.C. § 1983. It meant to enforce Section 1 of
the Fourteenth Amendment by establishing a remedy for deprivation under
color of state law of federal constitutional rights of all people and not only of
former slaves. This portion of the bill provided:

> That any person who, under color of any law, statute, ordinance,
> regulation, custom, or usage of any State, shall subject, or cause to be
> subjected, any person within the jurisdiction of the United States to the
> deprivation of any rights, privileges, or immunities to which . . . he is
> entitled under the Constitution or laws of the United States, shall . . .
> be liable to the party injured in an action at law, suit in equity, or other
> proper proceeding for redress. . . .[264]

Representative Washington C. Whitthorne (Democrat of Tennessee) complained that "in having organized a negro militia, in having disarmed the white
man," the Republicans had "plundered and robbed" the whites of South Car-

olina through "unequal laws." He objected to Section 1 of the anti-KKK bill on these grounds:

> It will be noted that by the first section suits may be instituted with-out regard to amount or character of claim by any person within the lim-its of the United States who conceives that he has been deprived of any right, privilege, or immunity secured him by the Constitution of the United States, under color of any law, statute, ordinance, regulation, custom, or usage of any State. This is to say, that if a police officer of the city of Richmond or New York should find a drunken negro or white man upon the streets with a loaded pistol flourishing it, & c., and by virtue of any ordinance, law, or usage, either of city or State, he takes it away, the officer may be sued, because the right to bear arms is secured by the Constitution, and such suit brought in distant and expensive tribunals.[265]

The Tennessee Democrat assumed that the right to bear arms was abso-lute and that deprivation of such right would create a cause of action against state agents under Section 1 of the anti-KKK bill. In the minds of the bill's supporters, however, the Second Amendment as incorporated in the Four-teenth Amendment recognized a right to keep and bear pistols and other arms safe from state infringement, not a right to commit assault or otherwise engage in criminal conduct with arms by pointing them at people or wantonly bran-dishing them about so as to endanger others. Contrary to the congressman's exaggerations, the proponents of the bill had the justified fear of the oppo-site development, that is, that a black or white person of the wrong political party would legitimately have or possess arms and a police officer of Rich-mond or New York, drunken with racial prejudice or partisan politics, would take it away, perhaps to ensure the success of an extremist group's attack. Significantly, none of the representatives's colleagues disputed his assump-tion that state agents could be sued under the predecessor to § 1983 for depri-vation of the right to keep arms.

Representative William D. Kelley (Republican of Pennsylvania), speaking in reply to Representative Whitthorne, did not deny the argument that Sec-tion 1 allowed suit for deprivation of the right to possess arms, but he empha-sized the arming of the KKK. He referred to "great numbers of Winchester rifles, and a particular species of revolving pistol" coming into Charleston's ports. "Poor men, without visible means of support, whose clothes are rag-ged and whose lives are almost or absolutely those of vagrants, are thus armed with new and costly rifles, and wear in their belts a brace of expensive pis-tols."[266] These weapons were used against Southern Republicans, whose con-stitutional rights must thereby be guaranteed by law and arms.

However, like Congressman Whitthorne, Representative Barbour Lewis

(Republican of Tennessee) also decried the loss of state agent's immunity should the bill pass: "By the first section, in certain cases, the judge of a State court, though acting under oath of office, is made liable to a suit in the Federal court and subject to damages for his decision against a suitor, however honest and conscientious that decision may be; and a ministerial officer is subject to the same pains and penalties. . . ."[267] Tennessee Republicans and Democrats alike thus agreed that what is today § 1983 provided an action for damages against state agents, in general, for deprivation of constitutional rights.

Debate over the anti-KKK bill naturally required exposition of Section 1 of the Fourteenth Amendment, and none was better qualified to explain that section than its draftsman, Representative John A. Bingham (Republican of Ohio):

> Mr. Speaker, that the scope and meaning of the limitations imposed by the first section, fourteenth amendment of the Constitution may be more fully understood, permit me to say that the privileges and immunities of citizens of a State, are chiefly defined in the first eight amendments to the Constitution of the United States. Those eight amendments are as follows:
>
> ARTICLE I
> Congress shall make no law respecting an establishment of religion, or prohibiting the free exercise thereof, or abridging the freedom of speech, or of the press, or the right of the people peaceably to assemble, and to petition the Government for a redress of grievances.
>
> ARTICLE II
> A well-regulated militia being necessary to the security of a free State, the right of the people to keep and bear arms shall not be infringed. . . .
> [The Third through the Eighth Amendments, also listed by Bingham, are here omitted.]
> These eight articles I have shown never were limitations upon the power of the States, until made so by the fourteenth amendment. The words of that amendment, "no State shall make or enforce any law which shall abridge the privileges or immunities of citizens of the United States," are an express prohibiton upon every State of the Union. . . .[268]

This is a most explicit statement of the incorporation thesis by the architect of the Fourteenth Amendment. Although he based the incorporation on the privileges and immunities clause and not on the due process clause, as had subsequent courts of selective incorporation, Representative Bingham could hardly have anticipated the judicial transformation of the late nineteenth century in this respect. In any case, whether based on the citizenship, due process, privileges and immunities, and/or equal protection of the law clauses, the legislative history supports the view that the incorporation of the First through the Eighth Amendments was clear and unmistakable in the minds of the framers of the Fourteenth Amendment.

In contrast with the above legal analysis by Bingham, some congressmen's further comments on the enforcement of the Fourteenth Amendment returned to discussion of the power struggle between Republicans and unreconstructed Confederates. While Republicans deplored the armed condition of white Southerners and the unarmed state of black Southerners, Democrats argued that the South's whites were disarmed and endangered by armed carpetbaggers and Negro militia. Thus, Representative Ellis H. Roberts (Republican of New York) lamented the partisan character of KKK violence: "The victims whose property is destroyed, whose persons are mutilated, whose lives are sacrificed, are always Republicans. They may be black or white. . . ." Of the still rebellious whites, Roberts said: "Their weapons are often new and of improved patterns; and however poor may be the individual member he never lacks for arms or ammunition. . . . In many respects the Ku Klux Klan is an army, organized and officered, and armed for deadly strife."[269]

Representative Boyd Winchester (Democrat of Kentucky) set forth the contrary position, favorably citing a letter from an ex-governor of South Carolina to the Reconstruction governor regretting the latter's "Winchester-rifle speech" that "fiendishly proclaimed that this instrument of death, in the hands of the negroes of South Carolina, was the most effective means of maintaining order and quiet in the State."[270] While calling on the governor to "disarm your militia," the letter referred to the disaster that resulted "when you organized colored troops throughout the State, and put arms into their hands, with powder and ball, and denied the same to the white people."[271] The letter proceeded to cite numerous instances where the "colored militia" murdered white people. According to Representative Winchester, the arming of blacks and the disarming of whites resulted in white resistance. "It would seem that wherever military and carpetbagger domination in the South has been marked by the greatest contempt for law and right, and practiced the greatest cruelty toward the people, Ku Klux operations have multiplied."[272]

The utility of the right to keep and bear arms for protection against violence initiated by state agents who were members of secret extremist organizations was exemplified in a letter cited by Representative Benjamin F. Butler:

> Then the Ku Klux fired on them through the window one of the bullets striking a colored woman . . . and wounding her through the knee badly. The colored men then fired on the Ku Klux, and killed their leader or captain right there on the steps of the colored men's house. . . . There he remained until morning when he was identified, and proved to be "Pat Inman," a constable and deputy sheriff. . . .[273]

By contrast, Representative Samuel S. Cox (Democrat of Ohio) assailed those who "arm negro militia and create a situation of terror," exclaimed that South Carolinians "actually clamored for United States troops to save them from the rapacity and murder of the negro bands and their white allies," and saw the Klan as their only defense: "Is not repression the father of revolution?" The congressman compared the Klan with French Jacobins, Italian Carbonari, and Irish Fenians.[274] Representative John Coburn (Republican of Indiana), deploring both state and private disarming of blacks, saw the situation in an opposite empirical light: "How much more oppressive is the passage of a law that they shall not bear arms than the practical seizure of all arms from the hands of the colored men?"[275]

On the next day Representative Henry L. Dawes (Republican of Massachusetts) returned to a legal analysis, which again asserted the incorporation thesis. Of the anti-Klan bill he argued:

> The rights, privileges, and immunities of the American citizen, secured to him under the Constitution of the United States, are the subject-matter of this bill. . . .
> . . . In addition to the original rights secured to him in the first article of amendments he had secured the free exercise of his religious belief, and freedom of speech and of the press. Then again he has secured to him the *right to keep and bear arms in his defense*. [Dawes then summarizes the remainder of the first eight amendments.] . . .
> . . . And still later, sir, after the bloody sacrifice of our four years' war, we gave the most grand of all these rights, privileges, and immunities, by one single amendment to the Constitution, to four millions of American citizens. . . .
> . . . [I]t is to protect and secure to him in these rights, privileges, and immunities this bill is before the House.[276]

Representative Horatio C. Burchard (Republican of Illinois), while generally favoring the bill insofar as it provided against oppressive state action, rejected the interpretation by Dawes and Bingham regarding the definition of "privileges and immunities," which Burchard felt were contained only in Articles IV, V, and VI rather than in I through VIII. However, Burchard still spoke in terms of "the application of their eight amendments to the States,"[277] and in any case Dawes had used the terms "*rights*, privileges and immunities." Thus, Burchard apparently viewed the first eight amendments as involving "rights" and only three of those amendments as containing "privileges and immunities." The anti-Klan bill finally was passed along partisan lines as An Act to Enforce the Provisions of the Fourteenth Amendment.[278]

With the passage of the Civil Rights Act of 1871, Congress created the Joint Select Committee on the Condition of Affairs in the Late Insurrectionary States. In deliberating and holding for almost a year what came to be known as the "KKK hearings", the committee issued its thirteen-volume report of proceedings in early 1872. The majority report, joined in by Senate Chairman John Scott (Republican of Pennsylvania) and House Chairman Luke P. Poland (Republican of Vermont), urged the need for further enforcement legislation: "negroes who were whipped testified that those who beat them told them that they did so because they had voted the radical ticket, . . . and wherever they had guns took them from them."[279] The subcommittee report which followed analyzed "the spirit of the constitutions and laws passed by the old rulers of the South in 1865–66," for instance, the continuation of the old codes whereby "before the law of South Carolina a free person of color was only a little lower than a slave. . . . They were forbidden to carry or have arms."[280] General Howard's 1866 letter criticizing the disarming of freedmen under Kentucky law was restated, including his words: "Thus the right of the people to keep and bear arms as provided in the Constitution is *infringed*. . . ."[281]

The minority on the committee also complained of infringements on the right to keep and bear arms. The following situation allegedly existed in Texas:

> The people have been disarmed throughout the State, notwithstanding their constitutional right "to keep and bear arms.". . .
>
> The police and State guards are armed, and lord it over the land, while the citizen dare not, under heavy pain and penalties, bear arms to defend himself, unless he has reasonable grounds for fearing an unlawful attack on his person, and that such grounds of attack shall be immediate and pressing. The citizen is at the mercy of the policeman and the men of the State Guard. . . .
>
> By orders executed through his armed bodies of police, the executive has taken control of peaceable assemblies of the people . . . and there suppressed free speech. . . .[282]

Testimony of the disarmament of blacks by white militia or by Klansmen, and of whites by black Republican militias, saturate the KKK hearings. Some expressed resentment that blacks had acquired all the rights of the citizen. For instance, a North Carolina law officer testified that the famous "Lowry gang" had resisted capture because "the use of fire-arms has been allowed to that class of people; their right to use fire-arms did not exist before the war." The congressman responded rhetorically, "Does the fact that colored men have been permitted, since the war, to testify in the courts, affect your ability to have this gang of men arrested?"[283] A South Carolinian "disapproved entirely of the manner of organizing the colored people and arming them, without doing it generally in regard to all the people, white and black."[284]

The index to volumes eight and nine of the hearings refers to over twenty pages under the topic "Arms, colored people deprived of." One witness reckoned that "most every white man keeps a gun about his house, as also do a great many colored men . . . almost every head of a family has a gun about his house."[285] The following exchanges were typical:

Q: Did you ever hear of the Ku-Klux visiting the colored people's houses for the purpose of taking their arms of defense?
A: . . . They took the weapons from mighty near all the colored people in the neighborhood. . . .
Q: They just came in and got their guns and pistols, and took them and left?
A: Yes, sir.[286]

A: Well, they took a great many arms from the colored people; pistols, and guns. . . .[287]
Q: What do you know of the negroes being visited and their arms taken away by these bands in disguise?
A: . . . They have taken their arms from them—guns and pistols.
Q: Were they taken away from the blacks generally?
A: Yes, sir.[288]

Q: Is that the general understanding there, that the Ku Klux took their guns from them?
A: Yes, sir; and any other man, white or black, that didn't walk as they wished him to walk, they took his arms.[289]

A: . . . I had a pistol, and it was hung up by the door, and they took it and my gun too. . . . They killed an old man there. . . .
Q: Did they search all the houses for guns?
A: Yes, sir. . . .[290]

Q: Did you understand that there was a systematic effort to disarm the negroes previous to the election?
A: . . . it was done. . . .
Q: Was there, in your opinion, any well-founded ground of apprehension that the negroes would use their arms except in self-defense?
A: No, sir. . . .
Q: I would like to inquire of you general, whether . . . these negroes who were thus deprived of their arms ever obtained any legal redress in the courts . . . ?
A: No, sir.[291]

A: They then asked me if I had a pistol. . . . One of the other men said, "where is the rope? Hang him."[292]

Extensive records were kept and read in the hearings concerning blacks who had been whipped, killed, deprived of firearms, and otherwise mistreated.[293] On the other side, Southern whites testified that the Klan originated for defense against carpetbagger militia abuses, as well as against black violence and crimes against whites, but that the Klan subsequently degenerated into offensive terrorism.[294]

The Joint Report also included transcripts of KKK trials in South Carolina in 1871, which are significant both as an interpretation of the Fourteenth Amendment in that epoch and also because they increased public awareness of the systematic effort to disarm blacks. In those trials, a number of indictments charged defendants with violation of the First Enforcement Act (1870) by conspiring "to deprive citizens of the right to have and bear arms, and to deprive them of the possession of arms as well as to prevent them from voting."[295] While the court dismissed search and seizure counts and never ruled on the right to have arms counts (because no action by the state or by its agents was alleged in the indictments, and because the Fourteenth Amendment applies only to acts committed by a "state"), counsels' argument is revealing:

> [U.S. Attorney] Corbin: If the Court please, if there is any right that is dear to the citizen, it is the right to keep and bear arms, and it was secured to the citizen of the United States on the adoption of the amendments to the Constitution. . . . That as Congress heretofore could not interfere with the right of the citizen to keep and bear arms, now, after the adoption of the fourteenth amendment, the State cannot interfere with the right of the citizen to keep and bear arms. That is included in the fourteenth amendment among the privileges and immunities of the citizens that were not referred to. . . .
>
> But this right is a distinctive right secured by the Constitution of the United States, and for the first time in the history of the world, except in the case of the Protestants of England, has it been secured to the citizen.[296]
>
> [Defense counsel] Johnson: . . . Has he a right to bear arms? He has. It is an absolute right, secured by the Constitution. . . . [T]o permit one class of citizens to bear arms, and to practically deny it to the other, is to place that other in subjection to the former.[297]

The hearings and conclusions of the Joint Select Committee on the Condition of Affairs in the Late Insurrectionary States suggested the need for further enforcement legislation. Accordingly, Congress enacted the Civil Rights Act of 1875.[298] With the introduction of the bill which became that civil rights act, the exposition of the meaning of § 1 of the Fourteenth Amendment continued on the floors of congress. Senator Matthew H. Carpenter (Republican of Wisconsin) relied on *Cummings* v. *Missouri* (1866),[299] where the U.S. Supreme Court contrasted the French legal system, which allowed deprivation of civil rights, "and among these of the right of voting, . . . of bearing arms," with the American legal system—in support of the proposition that the Fourteenth Amendment prevented states from taking away these privileges of the American citizen.[300]

Senator Allen G. Thurman (Democrat of Ohio) argued that the "rights, privileges, and immunities of a citizen of the United States" were included in the First through the Eighth Amendments. Reading and commenting on each of these amendments, he said of the Second Amendment: "Here is another right of a citizen of the United States, expressly declared to be his right—the right to bear arms; and this right, says the Constitution, shall not be infringed." After prodding from John A. Sherman (Republican of Ohio), Thurman added the Ninth Amendment to the list.[301]

The incorporationist thesis was stated succinctly by Senator Thomas M. Norwood (Democrat of Georgia) in one of the final debates over the civil rights bill. Referring to a U.S. citizen residing in a territory, Senator Norwood stated:

> His right to bear arms, to freedom of religious opinion, freedom of speech, and all others enumerated in the Constitution would still remain indefeasibly his, whether he remained in the Territory or removed to a State.
>
> And those and certain others are the privileges and immunities which belong to him in common with every citizen of the United States, and which no State can take away or abridge, and they are given and protected by the Constitution. . . .
>
> The following are most, if not all the privileges and immunities of a citizen of the *United States:*
>
> The right to the writ of *habeas corpus;* of peaceable assembly and of petition; . . . *to keep and bear arms* [emphasis added]; . . . from being deprived of the right to vote on account of race, color or previous condition of servitude.[302]

Arguing that the Fourteenth Amendment created no new rights but declared that "certain existing rights should not be abridged by States," the Georgia Democrat explained:

> Before its [Fourteenth Amendment] adoption any State might have established a particular religion, or restricted freedom of speech and of the press, or *the right to bear arms* [emphasis added]. . . . A State could have deprived its citizens of any of the privileges and immunities contained in those eight articles, but the *Federal Government* could not. . . .
>
> . . . And the instant the fourteenth amendment became a part of the Constitution, every State was at that moment disabled from making or

enforcing any law which would deprive any citizen of a State of the bene-
fits enjoyed by citizens of the United States under the first eight amendments to the Federal Constitution.[303]

In sum, in the understanding of Democrats and Republicans alike, the
Fourteenth Amendment made the right to keep and bear arms, like other
Bill of Rights freedoms, applicable to the states. Rather than predicating the
right to keep and bear arms on the needs or existence of an organized state
militia, the framers of the Fourteenth Amendment and of the civil rights acts
of Reconstruction based it on the right of the people individually to possess
arms for protection against any oppressive force—including racist or political
violence by the militia itself or by other state agents, such as sheriffs. At the
same time, the militia was understood to be the whole body of the people,
including blacks.[304] With the passage of the Fourteenth Amendment, the
individual right and privilege to keep and bear arms was protected from both
state and federal infringement, and passage of the Civil Rights Act of 1871
gave access to federal courts for all victims of state infringement.

6

The Supreme Court Speaks

In *Cummings* v. *Missouri* (1867)[1] the Supreme Court held that a state's test oath was unconstitutional as a bill of attainder and ex post facto law. Analyzing civil rights protected by the Constitution, the Court stated:

> In France, deprivation or suspension of *civil rights* or of some of them, and among these of the right of voting, of eligibility of office, of taking part in family councils, of being guardian or trustee, *of bearing arms*, and of teaching or being employed in a school or seminary of learning, are punishments prescribed by her Code.
>
> The theory upon which our political institutions rest is, that all men have certain inalienable rights—that among these are life, liberty and the pursuit of happiness; and that in the pursuit of happiness all avocations, all honors, all positions, are alike open to everyone and that in the protection of these rights all are equal before the law. *Any deprivation or suspension of any of these rights for past conduct is punishment*, and can be in no otherwise defined.
>
> Punishment not being, therefore, restricted as contended by counsel, to the deprivation of life, liberty or property, but also embracing deprivation or suspension of political or *civil rights*, and the disabilities prescribed by the provisions of the Missouri Constitution being, in effect, punishment, we proceed to consider whether there is any inhibition in the Constitution of the United States against their enforcement.[2]

Ironically, prior to the adoption of the Fourteenth Amendment, the bearing of arms and other civil rights were thus deemed as protected by the Constitution; the above language from *Cummings* was cited on the floor of Congress as a norm that the Fourteenth Amendment meant to attain.[3] But after the adoption of the Fourteenth Amendment and with the end of Reconstruction the Court took a restrictive view of the extent to which the federal government could protect civil rights. Nonetheless, the Court continued to treat the right to have arms as a fundamental right and vindicated the right to use deadly force in self-defense. Then, in *United States* v. *Miller* (1939)[4] the Supreme Court held that the Second Amendment protected the right to keep and bear militia-type arms and relied on case law holding that all citizens were members of the militia. In more recent times, the Court has also alluded to the right to have arms as a specific guarantee provided in the Constitution.

Post-Reconstruction Decisions

The Fourteenth Amendment did not exist when Chief Justice Marshall wrote the opinion in *Barron* v. *Mayor and City Council of Baltimore* (1833),[5] which held that the Bill of Rights was inapplicable to the states. That precedent's influence remained long after 1868, to the extent that selective incorporation by the Supreme Court did not begin until the turn of the century and became more fully developed only in the 1960s. Yet far more progressive antebellum state courts held fundamental rights guaranteed in the Bill of Rights to be protected from state deprivation. Even the notion of selective incorporation, which applies some freedoms in the Bill of Rights to the states and does not apply others, was articulated by state courts. The opinion of the Texas State Supreme Court in *English* v. *State* (1872)[6] assumed that the Second Amendment applies to the state and referred to the right to keep and bear arms as a "personal right" that is "inherent and inalienable to man."[7] Owing to the fundamental character of the right, the Court approvingly cited Bishop's treatise on criminal law that "though most of the amendments are restrictions on the general government alone, not on the States, this one seems to be of a nature to bind both the State and National Legislatures, and doubtless it does."[8]

Implicit rejection of the applicability to the states of the Bill of Rights via the Fourteenth Amendment was initiated in the *Slaughter-House Cases* (1873),[9] the first Supreme Court opinion to construe the Reconstruction amendment. This now discredited opinion was soon followed by *United States* v. *Cruikshank* (1876),[10] which has been cited by modern gun prohibitionists as a precedent for the proposition that the Fourteenth Amendment implies no individual right to keep and bear arms. Actually, the Court decided nothing of the kind, and *Cruikshank* asserts the fundamental character of the right to bear arms.

As it had done in the KKK prosecutions in South Carolina,[11] elsewhere the U.S. government obtained indictments under the Enforcement Act of 31 May 1870,[12] for depriving citizens of the right to keep and bear arms. In Louisiana, nearly one hundred persons were indicted for violating the rights of Levi Nelson and Alexander Tillman, citizens "of African descent and persons of color." One set of counts charged a conspiracy to deprive them of "the right peaceably to assemble together" and of "the right to keep and bear arms," while another set of counts charged a murder of the two men while carrying out the conspiracy. Three of the defendants, including William J. Cruikshank, were convicted under the first set of counts and appealed.

Sitting as a circuit justice, Supreme Court Justice Bradley delivered an opinion that granted arrest of judgment (which effectively meant dismissal of the case) because *(a)* a private conspiracy alleging deprivation of the rights to assemble and bear arms must be, but was not, alleged to be committed by reason of the race, color, or previous condition of servitude of the person conspired against; and *(b)* no action by the state or its agents acting for it existed.[13] Justice Bradley reasoned:

> The first count is for a conspiracy to interfere with the right "to peaceably assemble together. . . ." This right is guaranteed in the first amendment to the constitution. . . . The 14th amendment declares that no state shall by law abridge the privileges or immunities of citizens of the United States. *Grant that this prohibition now prevents the states from interfering with the right to assemble,* as being one of such privileges and immunities, still, does it give congress power to legislate over the subject? . . . If the amendment is not violated, it has no power over the subject.
>
> The second count, which is for a conspiracy to interfere with certain citizens in *their right to bear arms,* is open to the same criticism as the first. . . .
>
> . . . In none of these counts is there any averment that the state had, by its laws interfered with any of the rights referred to. . . .[14]

Thus, Justice Bradley, sitting on the circuit court, upheld incorporation of the Second with the Fourteenth Amendment but not its application to purely private acts of deprivation of rights guaranteed therein. While the government appealed to the U.S. Supreme Court, it failed to mention the Second Amendment or to argue for its incorporation into the Fourteenth Amendment.[15] Nor did the two briefs filed for the defendants mention the incorporation issue; instead, they relied on the fact that only private, not state, action existed in the case. There was no federal jurisdiction over private action, so that Cruikshank's attorney could concede: "The right of self-defense is a natural right; and the right to keep and bear arms for that purpose cannot be questioned."[16]

In assessing the Supreme Court's opinion in *Cruikshank,* it is significant that Justice Bradley again wrote the opinion. His lower court opinion, which had granted that the Fourteenth Amendment incorporated the Second, has been cited as authority by the High Court in later cases.[17] The incorporation issue was not briefed by the government or the defendants, undoubtedly because only a private conspiracy was shown. The circumstance of lack of state action perhaps made it appropriate that on appeal "it does not seem to have been argued that the Fourteenth Amendment made the Bill of Rights applicable to the states."[18]

Early in its opinion, the Supreme Court decided that the First Amendment "was not intended to limit the powers of the State governments in respect to their own citizens, but to operate upon the National government alone."[19] Regarding the seizure of arms by the alleged conspirators, the Court opined:

> The second and tenth counts are equally defective. The right there specified is that of bearing arms for a lawful purpose. This is not a right granted by the Constitution. Neither is it in any manner dependent upon that instrument for its existence. The second amendment declares that it shall not be infringed; but this . . . means no more than that it shall not be infringed by Congress. This is one of the Amendments that has no other effect than to restrict the powers of the national government, leaving the people to look for their protection against any violation by their fellow-citizens of the rights it recognizes to . . . the "powers which relate to merely municiple legislation, or what was, perhaps, more properly called internal police. . . ."[20]

This passage may be reduced to two propositions. First, bearing arms was not a right granted by the Constitution but existed independently of that charter since the right long antedated the Constitution. Using similar language, the Court only two pages previously had explained more fully its meaning in reference to the First Amendment:

> The right of the people peaceably to assemble for lawful purposes existed long before the adoption of the Constitution of the United States. In fact, it is and always has been, one of the attributes of citizenship under a free government. It "derives its source . . . from those laws whose authority is acknowledged by civilized man throughout the world." It is found wherever civilization exists. It was not, therefore, a right granted to the people by the Constitution. The government of the United States when established found it in existence, with the *obligation on the part of the States to afford it protection*.[21]

Thus, while the First and Second Amendments only applied to the federal government, the rights of the people to assemble publicly and to bear arms were basic to the kind of free civilization that the states were bound to protect.

The second proposition embodied in the Court's language on the Second Amendment is that the Second Amendment (like the First) only restricted the powers of the national government in the sense that private infringement of the right could be remedied only in the state courts. Far from denying that the states need not respect any right to keep and bear arms, the Court averred that municipal legislation and internal police rather than federal authority must protect the right. "It is no more the duty or within the power of the United States to punish for a conspiracy to falsely imprison or murder within a State, than it would be to punish for false imprisonment or murder itself,"[22] the justices reasoned by analogy. The federal courts therefore could not offer relief against defendants accused of conspiracy to deprive complainants of their freedom of action and their firearms, for these violations were common-law crimes actionable only at the local level.

Lastly, the *Cruikshank* Court could not offer relief on the basis of the Fourteenth Amendment because private conspiracy rather than state action was involved: "The Fourteenth Amendment prohibits a State from depriving any person of life, liberty, or property, without due process of law; but this adds nothing to the rights of one citizen as against another. It simply furnishes an additional guaranty against any encroachment by the State upon the fundamental rights which belong to every citizen as a member of society."[23] The rights to free assembly and to the possession of arms were considered fundamental rights of the citizen, but the encroachment by the state on these rights were not issues in *Cruikshank*. Thus, complainants were denied relief.

Whatever its constitutional grounds, the Supreme Court chose not to protect the blacks' rights to free speech and its armed protection. *Cruikshank* came to symbolize, and perhaps to hasten, the end of Reconstruction. As noted by present-day historians Lee Kennet and James Anderson, "Firearms in the Reconstruction South provided a means of political power for many. They were the symbol of the new freedom for blacks. . . . In the end . . . the blacks were effectually disarmed."[24] And black historian W.E.B. DuBois contended that arms in the hands of blacks, and hence possible economic reform, aroused fear in the North and the South alike, resulting in such decisions as *Cruikshank*, which made the Fourteenth Amendment an instrument of protection for corporations rather than for freedmen.[25] Current Supreme Court Justice Marshall has recently referred to *Cruikshank* and similar cases in these terms: "The Court began by interpreting the Civil War Amendments in a manner that sharply curtailed their substantive provisions."[26]

Unlike the fact pattern in *Cruikshank*, state action was involved in *Presser* v. *Illinois* (1886),[27] the second Supreme Court decision to treat the issue regarding the relation between the Second Amendment and the states. Presser was indicted under an Illinois act for parading a body of four hundred men with rifles through the streets of Chicago without having a license from the governor. The participants were members of *Lehr und Wehr Verein*, a corporation of German immigrants whose stated objectives included education and military exercise to promote good citizenship. The Court upheld the guilty

verdict against the defendant's claim that the state legislation violated the
Second Amendment:

> We think that the sections under consideration, which only forbid bod-
> ies of men to associate together as military organizations, or to drill or
> parade with arms in cities and towns unless authorized by law, do not
> infringe the right of the people to keep and bear arms. But a conclusive
> answer to the contention that this amendment prohibits the legislation
> in question lies in the fact that the amendment is a limitation only upon
> the power of Congress and the National government, and not upon that
> of the States. It was so held by this court in the case of *United States* v.
> *Cruikshank.* . . .[28]

In short, the court held that the armed paraders went beyond the individual right of keeping and bearing weapons and that in the alternative and more
generally, the Second Amendment does not apply to the states. The former
proposition was explained further in the Court's rejection of a First Amendment right of assembly applicable to Presser's band:

> The right voluntarily to associate together as a military company, or to
> drill or parade with arms, without, and independent of, an act of Con-
> gress or law of the State authorizing the same, is not an attribute of
> national citizenship. Military organization and military drill and parade
> under arms are subjects especially under the control of the government
> of every country. They cannot be claimed as a right independent of law.[29]

Thus, *Presser* fails to apply to the issue of the right of individuals to keep and
bear arms, but it is directly applicable to situations involving essentially private armies.[30]

The above proposition to the effect that *Cruikshank* "held" that the Second Amendment is not a limitation on the states ignored that *Cruikshank* did
not involve state infringement of rights. While *Presser* was thereby really the
first Supreme Court decision to hold that the Second Amendment was inapplicable to the states in the case of banning private armed marches, it made
no mention of whether the Second or the Fourteenth Amendments might
guarantee a right to keep and bear arms as at common law. Indeed *Presser*
upheld the concept of an arms-bearing population on the following grounds:

> It is undoubtedly true that all citizens capable of bearing arms consti-
> tute the reserved military force or reserve militia of the United States
> as well as of the States, and, in view of this prerogative of the general
> government . . . the States cannot, even laying the constitutional provi-
> sion in question out of view, prohibit the people from keeping and bear-

ing arms, so as to deprive the United States of their rightful resource for maintaining the public security, and disable the people from performing their duty to the general government. But, *as already stated*, we think it clear that the sections under consideration do not have this effect.[31]

What "effect"? Earlier in the opinion, the Court stated that the statute's provisions simply "do not infringe the *right of people to keep and bear arms.*" This "right of the people" stemmed from common law. At common law, private armed marches were dubiously protected. Thus, it follows here from *Presser* that any infringement of the *common-law* right of the people to keep and bear arms indeed would have the "effect" of depriving the U.S. of its rightful resource for "maintaining the public security" as at common law. The "public security" concept at common law included justifiable homicide of violent felons and citizens' arrests of fleeing felons who could not otherwise be apprehended.[32]

In short, even if the Second Amendment was not infringed by a state requirement of a license for private armed marches or even if it did not apply to the states, nevertheless, a right to keep and bear arms existed for "all citizens capable of bearing arms," and this right could not be infringed by the states. However, this principle did not prevent the Court from affirming the conviction of the German leader, just as in the earlier precedent the court found reasons not to protect the freedmen's rights. The legal realist might reach the sociological conclusion that at worst *Cruikshank* and *Presser* reflected the fear of established American power elites toward the challenges of blacks, foreigners, and the laboring class.[33]

Sociology aside, it is important to distinguish what *Presser* did *not* hold. Specifically, it never suggested that the Second Amendment guaranteed a state right to maintain militias rather than an individual right to keep and bear arms. While the decision is silent on state's rights, the Attorney General's Brief in *Presser* summarized U.S. Supreme Court precedent, at that time, as follows:

> But the power of the State to provide the organization of its own militia is not derived from the constitution of the United States. That power existed before the adoption of the constitution of the United States, and its exercise by the States is not prohibited by that instrument.[34]

In a further distinction, fully recognized in the Supreme Court's opinion, the attorney general had argued that "the right to keep and bear arms by no means includes the right to assemble and publicly parade in the manner forbidden by the law under which the conviction in this case was had."[35] Since individual rights were not really at issue in *Presser*, a commentator has written, "The question does not seem to have been raised whether the Second Amendment has been made applicable to the states through the incorporation of the Bill of Rights into the Fourteenth Amendment."[36]

Miller v. *Texas* (1894),[37] the final opinion of the U.S. Supreme Court to rule on the direct applicability of the Second Amendment to the states, clarified that its predecessor cases had refrained from deciding whether the Fourteenth Amendment included or incorporated a prohibition of state infringement on the right to keep and bear arms. Convicted of murder and sentenced to die, defendant Miller "claimed that the law of the State of Texas forbidding the carrying of weapons, and authorizing the arrest without warrant of any person violating such law . . . was in conflict with the Second and Fourth Amendments to the Constitution."[38] While assuming that "the restrictions of these amendments operate only upon the Federal power," the Court left open the possibility that the rights to keep and bear arms and freedom from warrantless arrests or unreasonable seizures would apply to the states through the Fourteenth Amendment: "If the Fourteenth Amendment limited the power of the States as to such rights, as pertaining to citizens of the United States, we think it was fatal to this claim that it was not set up in the trial court."[39] Rather than reject incorporation of the Second and Fourth Amendments into the Fourteenth, the Supreme Court merely refused to decide the defendant's claim because its powers of adjudication were limited to the review of errors timely objected to in the trial court. In short, the Court was precluded from hearing novel arguments. In sum, the careful distinction drawn by the *Miller* (1894) Court between rights based solely on provisions in the Bill of Rights and those based on the Fourteenth Amendment, and the Court's reliance on *Cruikshank* and *Presser*, demonstrate that none of the three cases dealt with the issue of whether the Fourteenth Amendment prohibits the states from infringing on the right to keep and bear arms.[40] Indeed, dictum in *Cruikshank* suggests that this right, like the right to free speech, is a fundamental right which existed prior to the Constitution and which every free civilization must respect, and dictum in *Presser* suggests strongly that the States may not "infringe the right of the people to keep and bear arms."

Cruikshank (1876), *Presser* (1886), and *Miller* (1894) were the only nineteenth century Supreme Court cases where the nature of the right to have arms was the issue. However, the case of *Robertson* v. *Baldwin* (1897),[41] which dealt with the question of whether compulsory service of deserting seamen constituted involuntary servitude, treated the bearing of arms as a fundamental and centuries-old right that could not be infringed. Referring to the seaman's contract as an exception to the Thirteenth Amendment, Justice Brown, who delivered the opinion of the Court, analogized:

The law is perfectly well settled that the first ten Amendments to the constitution, commonly known as the Bill of Rights, were not intended to lay down any novel principles of government, but simply to embody certain guaranties and immunities which we had inherited from our English ancestors, and which had from time immemorial been subject to certain well-recognized exceptions arising from the necessities of the case. In incorporating these principles into the fundamental law there was no intention of disregarding the exceptions, which continued to be recognized as if they had been formally expressed. Thus, the freedom of speech and of the press (article 1) does not permit the publication of libels, blasphemous or indecent articles or other publications injurious to public morals or private reputation; the right of the people to keep and bear arms (article 2) is not infringed by laws prohibiting the carrying of concealed weapons. . . .[42]

In this striking passage, the U.S. Supreme Court recognized the right to bear arms as having existed "from time immemorial," as having been handed down as a guarantee of Englishmen long predating its formal expression in the Second Amendment, and as being part of "the fundamental law." That the prohibition of carrying concealed weapons did not infringe this right indicates that the Court viewed the right as belonging to individuals, independently of any organized militia. The Court's reference to legislation on concealed weapons referred to state statutes concerning the manner in which private persons carried handguns and other small weapons in public. There certainly were no statutes prohibiting organized militiamen from carrying concealed weapons. The Court's pronouncement further indicates strongly that the individual right to carry weapons openly, by being basic to our system of government, was protected from both federal and state infringement. Otherwise, it would be ludicrous to speak of state statutes prohibiting the carrying of concealed weapons as not infringing on the right to bear arms, for by definition *no* state statute could infringe on this right if it was protected only from federal infringement and was not part of the fundamental law.[43]

In two further cases near the turn of the century, the Supreme Court, without specifically referring to the Second Amendment, upheld the right of individuals to have and to use firearms in self-defense. In the first of these cases, *Beard* v. *United States* (1894),[44] the Court reversed a judgment of conviction for manslaughter because the judge had improperly instructed the jury that the defendant had a duty to retreat before using deadly force. Delivering the opinion of the Court, Justice Harlan found nothing improper in the fact that before the incident the defendant had "with him a shot-gun that he was in the habit of carrying, when absent from home. . . ."[45] In reasonably anticipating armed attack from his assailants but seeking to disarm rather than to kill them, he crushed the skull of the deceased with the shotgun.

Stating that the defendant had legally armed himself and commanded the trespassers to leave his premises,[46] the court held that his reasonable anticipation of deadly attack gave him the further right to "strike the deceased with his gun, and thus prevent his further advance upon him."[47] In approving the common-law rule that "a man may repel force by force in defense of his person, habitation, or property,"[48] the Court concluded that the defendant "was entitled to stand his ground and meet any attack made upon him with a deadly weapon, in such way and with such force" as was reasonably necessary to protect himself "from great bodily injury or death."[49]

In *Patsone* v. *Pennsylvania* (1914),[50] the Court considered whether a statute making it unlawful for any unnaturalized foreign-born resident to own or possess a shotgun or rifle violated the Fourteenth Amendment. While curiously classifying the Italian defendant as a member of a group the legislature could reasonably identify as "the peculiar source of the evil that it desired to prevent" (that is, violation of the game laws),[51] Justice Holmes also wrote:

> The possession of rifles and shotguns is not necessary for other purposes not within the statute. It is so peculiarly appropriated to the forbidden use that if such a use may be denied to this class, the possession of the instruments desired chiefly for that end also may be. The prohibition does not extend to weapons such as pistols that may be supposed to be needed occasionally for self-defense.[52]

Justice Holmes thus assumed that even a foreigner had the right to self-defense and thus to possess the instrument regarded as commonly used and appropriate therefor (that is, the pistol). But a foreigner had no right to hunt game and therefore could be denied the right to have a shotgun or a rifle. In short, Holmes found the statute valid in part because it failed to deprive an alien of the right to have pistols for self-defense. In the Court's words, "weapons such as pistols" (which implies that weapons other than pistols are appropriate for self-defense) would be instruments "necessary for other purposes not within the statute," that is, for self-defense.[53] *Patsone*, in essence, assumed that citizens and foreign-born residents alike could not be deprived of the right to possess pistols for self-defense.[54]

The Right to Keep and Bear Militia Arms:
United States v. *Miller* (1939)

The nearest the U.S. Supreme Court has come to a direct construction of the Second Amendment is the case of *United States* v. *Miller* (1939),[55] which reversed the district court's invalidation of the National Firearms Act of 1934[56] as in violation of the Second Amendment.[57] Defendants were convicted of transporting through interstate commerce a shotgun having a barrel less than eighteen inches without having in their possession the stamp-affixed written order required under the act. The National Firearms Act of 1934 was the first federal statute ever passed that restricted the keeping and bearing of arms, and the statute taxed and required the registration of certain types of firearms.

Since the defendants made no appearance on appeal, the Supreme Court was only apprised of the cases and arguments that the U.S. attorneys brought to its attention; thereby, the Court failed to benefit from hearing the adverse views which would have rendered balanced opinions more likely.[58] Even so, the opinion of the Court in *Miller* (1939), as delivered by Mr. Justice McReynolds (with Mr. Justice Douglas taking no part in the decision), stands for the proposition that the U.S. government cannot regulate the right to keep and bear arms suitable for militia use but can regulate possession of only those arms that are unsuitable for militia use. The Court began the opening of its brief analysis of the Second Amendment in these terms:

In the *absence of any evidence* tending to show that possession or use of a "shotgun having a barrel of less than eighteen inches in length" at this time has some reasonable relationship to the preservation or efficiency of a well regulated militia, we cannot say that the Second Amendment guarantees the right to keep and bear such an instrument. Certainly it is *not within judicial notice* that this weapon is any part of the ordinary military equipment or that its use could contribute to the common defense. *Aymette* v. *State*, 2 Hump. 154, 158.[59]

The italicized portions in the above quotation do not suggest that "sawed-off" shotguns fail the test of the Second Amendment, but they do confirm that no evidence was presented on a matter of dispute and not of such common knowledge as to be cognizable judicially without the aid of factual testimony in the trial court.[60] The Court in *Miller* (1939) assumed that the weapon had not been shown to be "ordinary military equipment" that "could contribute to the common defense"; had this been shown, the Court's wording clearly implies that the weapon's possession by an individual would be constitutionally protected.

The Court clarified all this by referring to the *Aymette* case,[61] which had stated a hundred years earlier (on the page cited by *Miller* [1939]) on the right of each individual to bear arms: "If the citizens have these arms in their hands, they are prepared in the best possible manner to repel any encroachments upon their rights, etc."[62] Even so, the Tennessee Constitution's guarantee of the people's right "to keep and bear arms for their common defense" contains the very qualification explicitly rejected when the Second Amendment was ratified. Thus, the Supreme Court was misguided in its restriction of the arms each individual may possess to military or militia arms.

The Court proceeded to cite the militia clause of the Constitution[63] and stated that "to assure the continuation and render possible the effectiveness of such forces the declaration and guarantee of the Second Amendment were made."[64] The Court clearly perceived this militia as the armed people: "The sentiment of the time strongly disfavored standing armies; the common view was that adequate defense of Country and laws could be secured through the Militia—civilians primarily, soldiers on occasion."[65] In more detail, the Court declared:

> The signification attributed to the term Militia appears from the debates in the Convention, the history and legislation of Colonies and States, and the writings of approved commentators. These show plainly enough that *the Militia comprised all males physically capable of acting in concert for the common defense.* "A body of citizens enrolled for military discipline." And further, that ordinarily when called for service *these men were expected to appear bearing arms supplied by themselves* and of the kind in common use at the time.[66]

Having quoted Blackstone[67] to the effect that King Alfred "first settled a national militia," Adam Smith was then cited: "Men of republican principles have been jealous of a standing army as dangerous to liberty . . . In a militia, the character of the labourer, artificer, or tradesman, predominates over that of the soldier. . . ."[68] The Court then reviewed the militia acts of the American colonies, beginning with these generalizations from the historian H.L. Osgood:

> In all the colonies, as in England, the militia system was based on the principle of the assize of arms. This implied the *general obligation of all adult male inhabitants to possess arms.* . . . The possession of arms also implied the possession of ammunition. . . .[69]

The General Court of Massachusetts directed in 1784 that "all able bodied men" under sixty years of age be available for the Train Band or Alarm List, and that each individual "shall equip himself, and be constantly provided with a good fire arm. . . ."[70] Defining a "militiaman" as "every able-bodied Male Person" who resided in the state between the ages of sixteen and forty-five, the New York legislature directed each man to "provide himself, at his own Expense, with a good Musket or Firelock" and ammunition.[71] Finally, in 1785 the General Assembly of Virginia declared, "the defense and safety of the commonwealth depend upon having its citizens properly armed," and it directed that "all free male persons" between the ages of eighteen and fifty be considered members of the militia, who were obliged to be armed on muster day with a clean musket or rifle, cartridges, a pound of powder, lead, and other equipment, and to "constantly keep the aforesaid arms, accoutrements, and ammunition. . . ."[72]

The Supreme Court's historical review demonstrates that the "well regulated militia" referred to in the Second Amendment meant the whole people armed and not a select group, that each private individual had the right and duty to keep and bear arms, and that the people were to provide their own armed protection rather than depend upon a militarist and oppressive standing army. The Supreme Court thus sanctioned the view that the entire armed population—not simply the organized armed minorities on the payroll of the U.S. or state governments (that is, the four branches of the national "armed forces" and the "National Guard")—was responsible for protecting the people's freedom. It also implied that a standing army is contrary to "the security of a free state" and unconstitutional.

Next, the Court pointed out: "Most if not all of the States have adopted provisions touching the right to keep and bear arms. Differences in the language employed in these have naturally led to somewhat variant conclusions concerning the scope of the right guaranteed."[73] While asserting that these provisions failed to support the defendants in this case, this statement reaffirmed the right to keep and bear arms as clearly "guaranteed."

Perhaps the most significant portion of the relatively short opinion in *Miller* (1939) was the collection of authorities in a footnote, which the Court labelled "some of the more important opinions and comments by writers. . . ."[74] Although reviewed elsewhere in this work, as authorities approved by the U.S. Supreme Court they merit summarization here to clarify further the Court's intent and meaning in 1939.

The note begins by citing *Presser* v. *Illinois* (1886)[75] and *Robertson* v. *Baldwin* (1897).[76] As seen previously, *Presser* only held that the Second Amendment did not protect private armies marching through a city without a permit, and it asserted that the states could not deprive the people of their right to keep and bear arms or prevent the armed people from doing their duty as militia under the U.S. Constitution.[77] *Robertson*, in dictum, viewed the right to keep and bear arms (which it did not restrict to arms appropriate to a militia) as a fundamental privilege and immunity that antedated the adoption of the Constitution. The *Robertson* Court further implied that an individual right to keep and bear arms was protected from state and federal infringement, since the Court sanctioned regulation only of concealed weapons, an issue hardly relevant to the organized militia[78] and demonstrative of the existence of a right to carry arms openly.

Aside from the two Supreme Court cases cited above, the *Miller* (1939)

Court largely refers in the aforementioned note to several state cases. In the order of their appearance, the following are cited.

The Arkansas case of *Fife* v. *State* (1876)[79] upheld the right of individuals to bear large, but not pocket, pistols in part to enable the people to resist domestic oppression. It should be noted that the state constitutional provision in question qualified the right to keep and bear arms for the "common defense," a qualification that was defeated in the Second Amendment. Arguably, possession of pocket pistols are thereby protected by this amendment.

The Georgia case of *Jeffers* v. *Fair* (1862)[80] upheld the right of the Confederate States of America to conscript men to combat the invasion of their soil by a domestic tyranny transformed into a foreign aggressor. The case discusses the value of the militia in a general manner without expounding directly on the Second Amendment or its equivalent in the Confederate constitution, which adopted identical wording.[81]

The Kansas case of *Salina* v. *Blaksely* (1905),[82] which in dictum stated that the right to bear arms applied to members of the militia, also assumed that the masses were the militia in concluding that weapons ordinarily used in civil warfare were protected by the amendment. In addition, this presupposed the applicability to the states of the Second Amendment.

The Michigan case of *People* v. *Brown* (1931)[83] not only defined the militia as "all able-bodied men" but went further and determined that each private individual may bear any commonly used arms, even those which may have no militia purpose. *Brown*, in turn, was partly based on *People* v. *Zerillo* (1922),[84] which held that the state could not make it criminal for anyone, even an alien, to possess a revolver for self-defense.

The Tennessee case of *Aymette* v. *State* (1840)[85] upheld the possession by "the citizens" of arms appropriate for militia use under a state constitution that referred to arms kept "for their common defense"—a restriction nonexistent in the Second Amendment.

The Texas case of *State* v. *Duke* (1875),[86] while averring that the Second Amendment did not apply to the states, held that large pistols could be carried legitimately and that the term "arms" is more comprehensive than the phrase the "arms of militiaman or soldier." The types of arms commonly and customarily kept were protected by the state's constitutional provision.

The West Virginia case of *State* v. *Workman* (1891)[87] upheld protection under the Second Amendment of individual possession of swords, guns, rifles, and muskets to protect civil liberty, but it also upheld a statute forbidding the carrying of pistols except by those of good repute.

All of the above cases, defining the militia as the whole people, asserted the right of each individual to keep and bear arms with a militia use. The same precedents are split on whether Second Amendment protection extends to weapons not ordinarily used for militia purposes and on whether the amendment applied to the states apart from the Fourteenth Amendment.

Lastly, the *Miller* Court's note sanctioned Justice Story's exposition of the amendment, which stressed that "the right of the citizens to keep and bear arms has justly been considered, as the palladium of the liberties of the republic," in part to resist the usurpations of rulers. Those who argue that the U.S. armed forces and National Guard—both standing armies, whose weapons are owned by the federal government and not by the soldier—now take the place of the militia have a sense of confidence in standing armies and in the rulers that Justice Story would have considered naive. Furthermore, the faith presupposed by such advocates in the armed state, and their concomitant lack of faith in the armed people, appears curious alongside their stress on the militia concept as a limitation on the right to bear arms and their constant reiteration that the Constitution's framers rejected the standing army, an institution such advocates find laudable. Justice Story's comments, endorsed by the U.S. Supreme Court, remain valid political philosophy today as much as ever.

The comparable exposition of the Second Amendment by Judge Thomas M. Cooley, also a commentator approved by the Court in the same note, stated:

> The right declared was meant to be a strong moral check against the usurpation and arbitrary power of rulers, and as a necessary and efficient means of regaining rights when temporarily overturned by usurpation.
>
> The Right is General—It may be supposed from the phraseology of this provision that the right to keep and bear arms was only guaranteed to the militia; but this would be an interpretation not warranted by the intent. . . . But the law may make provision for the enrollment of all who are fit to perform military duty, or of a small number only, or it may wholly omit to make any provision at all; and if the right were limited to those enrolled, the purpose of this guaranty might be defeated altogether by the action or neglect to act of the government it was meant to hold in check. The meaning of the provision undoubtedly is that the people from whom the militia must be taken, shall have the right to keep and bear arms, and they need no permission or regulation of law for the purpose. . . .[88]

Despite Judge Cooley's entreaty, the Supreme Court reversed the judgment of the district court and remanded the cause for further proceedings. The defendants then had an opportunity, which they failed to take, to demonstrate that short-barrelled shotguns have utility for militia use. In sum, *Miller* stands for the proposition that the people, in their capacity as individuals, could keep and bear any arms appropriate to militia use.

The Logic of Incorporation and the Fundamental Character of the Right to Keep and Bear Arms

The Supreme Court's analytical treatment in *Miller* v. *Texas* (1894)[89] indicated a growing tendency of the justices toward incorporation of the Bill of Rights in the Fourteenth Amendment. The first incorporationist opinion, handed down only three years later, recognized a right to compensation for property taken by the state.[90] In the early 1920s the Court persisted in its refusal to apply the First Amendment to the states,[91] but by mid-decade it had guaranteed freedom of speech from state deprivation.[92] Still, the Court continued to hand down some of its classic anti-incorporationist opinions.[93] Then *Mapp* v. *Ohio* (1961)[94] applied the Fourth Amendment to the states through the Fourteenth Amendment, thereby prohibiting illegally obtained evidence in state trials. The dominoes began to fall as most other provisions of the Bill of Rights were also subsequently made applicable to the states through the Fourteenth Amendment—right to counsel,[95] self-incrimination,[96] right to warnings before confession, [97] speedy trial,[98] compulsory process,[99] jury trial,[100] double jeopardy,[101] and so on. A few rights remain in unincorporated, including keeping and bearing arms, freedom from unconsented quartering of soldiers in houses except during war, indictment by a grand jury,[102] a jury in civil cases, and reasonable bail. Nevertheless, presumably the same principles of construction would apply to both incorporated and unincorporated rights, should appropriate cases arise concerning the latter.

Following the logic of previous cases, the Supreme Court could apply the Second Amendment to the states directly through the due process or the privileges and immunities clauses of the Fourteenth Amendment. It could also adopt a broader "penumbra" theory to guard the right to keep and bear arms from state infringement.[103] Under this theory, unenumerated rights protected by the Ninth Amendment could be defined, in part, by reference to the objectives of the other amendments—the First (privacy), the Second (security and self-defense), the Third (protection of home), the Fourth (protection of house and person), the Fifth (protection of of life, liberty, and property), and the Tenth ("powers" reserved to the people).

In view of the debatable proposition that the Second Amendment guarantees the right to keep and bear arms only if they are militia arms—a view which is question-begging in that the militia is legally the whole arms-bearing people[104] and because all small arms have conceivable militia uses[105]—the penumbra theory would offer the broadest recognition of the right.

Several commentators have argued that the Second Amendment should be construed as an absolute right protected from state and federal infringement[106] and that the right to keep and bear arms might be considered a fundamental right which should be recognized as part of the Fourteenth Amendment through selective incorporation.[107] Others have opposed the view that the Supreme Court's analytical framework for incorporation of Bill of Rights provisions in the Fourteenth Amendment logically encompasses the right to keep and bear arms.[108]

Recent dictum suggests that the right to keep and bear arms could be considered constitutionally protected from state infringement. In *Poe* v. *Ullman* (1961),[109] decided before the Supreme Court majority held Connecticut's anti-contraceptive statute to be unconstitutional, Justice Harlan dissented, declaring that the first eight amendments do not limit the full scope of due process. Harlan also mentioned the right to keep and bear arms as one of the *specific* guarantees of these first eight amendments provided in the Constitution. The Connecticut statute was soon overturned in *Griswold* v. *Connecticut* (1965),[110] which resorted to the penumbra theory to protect zones of privacy from state infringement. Then in *Moore* v. *East Cleveland* (1977),[111] which invalidated a zoning ordinance as overly restrictive in its definition of "family," Justice Powell delivered an opinion, in which four other justices joined. This opinion favorably recalled Harlan's dissent in *Poe*, which had described the Court's function under the due process clause of the Fourteenth Amendment, as follows:

> The full scope of the Due Process Clause cannot be found in or limited by the precise terms of the *specific guarantees* elsewhere *provided in the Constitution*. This "liberty" is not a series of isolated points pricked out in terms of the taking of property; the freedom of speech, press, and religion; *the right to keep and bear arms;* the freedom from unreasonable searches and seizures; and so on. It is a rational continuum which, broadly speaking, includes a freedom from all substantial arbitrary impositions and purposeless restraints. . . .[112]

Thus, according to Harlan, the *specific* guarantees of the Constitution constituted a minimum, but not maximum, set of federally protected rights. The same passage was cited in Justice White's dissenting opinion, which termed Harlan's view "consistent" and "the preferred approach."[113] Should the Supreme Court in a future case adopt as its legal standard the applicability to the states of the right to keep and bear arms as a specific constitutional guarantee, it would be fully supported by the principles it had previously laid down in several nineteenth-century precedents and in the twentieth-century avalanche of incorporationist decisions mentioned above.

Discussion of the fundamental character of the right to keep and bear arms has arisen more recently in *Lewis* v. *United States* (1980),[114] where the Supreme Court held that Title VII of the Omnibus Crime Control and Safe Streets

Act of 1968 prohibits a felon from possessing a firearm even though the felony may be subject to collateral attack based on lack of counsel. "The firearms regulatory scheme at issue here is consonant with the concept of equal protection embodied in the Due Process Clause of the Fifth Amendment if there is 'some "rational basis" for the statutory distinctions made . . . or . . . they "have some relevance to the purpose for which the classification is made." ' "[115] Holding that the section meets the rational relation test, the Court stated: "These legislative restrictions on the use of firearms are neither based upon constitutionally suspect criteria, nor do they trench upon any constitutionally protected liberties. See *United States* v. *Miller*, 307 U.S. 174, 178 (1939) (the Second Amendment guarantees no right to keep and bear a firearm that does not have 'some reasonable relationship to the preservation or efficiency of a well regulated militia'). . . ."[116]

Since felons were always excluded from the militia, the Court's wording of the holding in *Miller* clearly indicates its acceptance of a Second Amendment right of law-abiding individuals to possess any firearms with any militia uses. To date, then, the Supreme Court has never held or even suggested that the Second Amendment guarantees merely a "collective" right for members of the National Guard to have governmentally owned arms while on duty. In dictum, the *Lewis* Court added that "a legislature constitutionally may prohibit a convicted felon from engaging in activities far more fundamental than the possession of a firearm."[117] The Court's mention of prohibitions against voting, holding union office, and the practice of medicine as examples of activities presumably "more fundamental" than possession of a firearm indicates no criteria by which degrees of fundamentalness may be calculated for law-abiding citizens as opposed to felons. The Court's language clearly implies that it considers possession of a firearm in the hand of a law-abiding citizen as a "fundamental" right.

Depiction of the right to keep and bear arms as a "specific guarantee" in *Moore* and a "fundamental" right in *Lewis* would seem likely to affect the existing contours of Second Amendment litigation and to create the need for further and precise treatment by the Supreme Court of the subject. State agents, but not federal agents, can be sued in federal courts under the Civil Rights Act for violating federally protected constitutional rights. Thus, there would be no legal remedy for violations of the Second Amendment committed by federal officers. However, a further recent development may conceivably prompt more extensive clarification of the Second Amendment by the courts, namely, the extension of the *Bivens* action to the Fifth and Eighth Amendments. In *Bivens* v. *Six Unknown Named Agents of the Federal Bureau of Narcotics* (1971)[118] the Supreme Court held that a cause of action for damages, cognizable by the federal courts, arises under the Constitution where Fourth Amendment rights are violated by federal agents while acting for the federal government. "Historically, damages have been regarded as the ordinary remedy for an invasion of personal interests in liberty."[119] Concurring with the majority, Justice Harlan added that "federal courts do have the power to award damages for violations of 'constitutionally protected interests,' "[120] a principle which presumably would apply to all interests protected in the Bill of Rights.

During the 1970s, most federal courts that treated the question extended the *Bivens* rationale to the First, Fifth, Sixth, Eighth, and Fourteenth Amendments. There have apparently been no reported decisions that pertain to any *Bivens* actions based on the Second Amendment.[121] The Supreme Court finally itself extended the *Bivens*-type action to causes arising under the due process clause of the Fifth Amendment in *Davis* v. *Passman* (1979)[122] and under the Eighth Amendment (cruel and unusual punishment) in *Carlson* v. *Green* (1980).[123] The latter case states: "Bivens established that the victims of a constitutional violation by a federal agent have a right to recover damages against the official in federal court. . . ."[124] The general use of the term "constitutional violation" would presumably include a Second Amendment violation.

Just as more rights guaranteed in the Bill of Rights are increasingly being deemed as incorporated in the Fourteenth Amendment, the *Bivens*-type action is also being applied to more of the rights guaranteed in the Bill of Rights. Both of these developments make it all the more appropriate that the Supreme Court should rule sometime on the status of the Second Amendment in regard to its applicability to the states and on whether its deprivation gives rise to an action in federal court for monetary damages.

Even though the Supreme Court has not ruled comprehensively on whether the Fourteenth Amendment incorporates the Second Amendment, it has adopted a methodology of constitutional interpretation that provides the decisive answer to this query. The Court formulated this methodology a century ago in this language: "Is is never to be forgotten that, in the construction of the language of the Constitution . . . we are to place ourselves as nearly as possible in the condition of the men who framed the instrument."[125] Moreover, in *Shelly* v. *Kramer* (1947) the Court relied on "the civil rights intended to be protected from discriminatory state action by the Fourteenth Amendment," that is, such equality in rights as "was regarded by the framers of that Amendment as an essential pre-condition to the realization of other basic civil rights and liberties which the Amendment was intended to guarantee."[126]

The Court has specifically relied on the intent of the framers to support incorporation of Bill of Rights freedoms into the Fourteenth Amendment. *Malloy* v. *Hogan* (1964) cited several past decisions that rejected application of the first eight amendments to the states—including "United States v. Cruikshank . . . (First Amendment); Presser v. Illinois . . . (Second Amendment); Weeks v. United States . . . (Fourth Amendment)"; and cases involving the Fifth, Sixth, Seventh, and Eighth Amendments.[127] The opinion added: "The Court has not hesitated to re-examine past decisions according the Fourteenth Amendment a less central role in the preservation of basic liberties than that which was comtemplated by its Framers when they added the Amendment to our constitutional scheme."[128]

In the course of reexamining those past decisions, the Court has endorsed specific speeches of the framers that clearly stated their intent to incorporate Bill of Rights provisions, including the right to keep and bear arms, into the Fourteenth Amendment. Thus, in his concurring opinion in *Duncan* v. *Louisiana* (1968), Justice Black recalled the following words of Senator Jacob M. Howard in introducing the amendment to the Senate in 1866: "The personal rights guaranteed and secured by the first eight amendments of the Constitution; such as . . . the right to keep and bear arms. . . . The great object of the first section of this amendment is, therefore, to restrain the power of the States and compel them at all times to respect these great fundamental guarantees."[129]

The intent of the framers of the Fourteenth Amendment is also known through analysis of debates on the subsequent enforcement legislation they passed. "The broad concept of civil rights embodied in the 1866 Act and in the Fourteenth Amendment is unmistakably evident in the legislative history of § 1 of the Civil Rights Act of 1871, 17 Stat 13, the direct lineal ancestor of §§ 1983 and 1343(3)."[130]

A lengthy "fresh analysis of debate on the Civil Rights Act of 1871," held *Monell* v. *Dept. of Social Services of City of New York* (1978),[131] justified overruling prior precedent[132] on the subject of municipal liability. *Monell* relies heavily on a speech the Representative John Bingham delivered on 31 March 1871:

> Representative Bingham, for example, in discussing § 1 of the bill, explained that he had drafted § 1 of the Fourteenth Amendment with the case of *Barron* v. *Mayor of Baltimore*, 7 Pet. 243 (1833), especially in mind. . . . Bingham's further remarks clearly indicate his view that such taking [of private property] by cities, as had occurred in *Barron*, would be redressable under § 1 of the bill.[133]

Had it been pertinent to the case, the Court might have noted that, on the same page of the speech where he mentioned *Barron*, Representative Bingham characterized "the right of the people to keep and bear arms" as one of the "limitations upon the power of the States . . . made so by the Fourteenth Amendment."[134] The Court did point out, however, that "Representative Bingham, the author of § 1 of the Fourteenth Amendment, for example, declared the bill's purpose to be 'the enforcement . . . of the Constitution on behalf of every individual citizen of the Republic . . . to the extent of the rights guaranteed to him by the Constitution.' "[135]

Another authority relied on in *Monell* was Representative Henry L. Dawes,[136] whose speech a few days after Bingham's included the remark that the Fourteenth Amendment "has secured to [the citizen] the right to keep and bear arms in his defense."[137] It is noteworthy that nobody in Congress ever disputed the interpretation by Senator Howard and Congressmen Bingham and Dawes that the amendment protected the right to keep and bear arms, the kind of circumstance that was deemed decisive in *Jones* v. *Mayer* (1968):

> When Congressman Bingham of Ohio spoke of the Civil Rights Act, he charged . . . that it would extend the territorial reach of that bill throughout the United States. . . . *[N]obody who rose to answer the Congressman disputed his basic premise.* . . .[138]

In addition to the intent of the framers, the understanding of the amendment by the states has been seen by the Supreme Court as decisive. In his dissenting opinion in the *Civil Rights Cases* (1883), an opinion which ultimately prevailed in the twentieth century, Justice Harlan stated that the privileges and immunities protected by the Fourteenth Amendment "are those which are fundamental in citizenship in a free republican government, such as are 'common to the citizens in the latter States under their constitutions and laws by virtue of their being citizens.' "[139]

In *Bartkus* v. *Illinois* (1959),[140] the Supreme Court held that those provisions in the Bill of Rights also guaranteed in or consistent with the state constitutions, but not necessarily those provisions which were inconsistent therewith, were deemed to be "fundamental" and hence federally protected. "Evidencing the interpretation by both Congress and the States of the Fourteenth Amendment is a comparison of the constitutions of the ratifying States with the Federal Constitution."[141] The Court noted that "only one-half, or fifteen, or the ratifying States had constitutions in explicit accord" with certain provisions of the Fifth, Sixth, and Seventh Amendments; "of these fifteen," the Court continued "four made alterations in their constitutions by 1875 which brought them into important conflict" with the federal Constitution.[142] While the Court's refusal to incorporate the double jeopardy clause under this reasoning has been overruled,[143] presumably a Bill of Rights provision which passes the overly stringent *Bartkus* test (as does the right to keep and bear arms) should be deemed incorporated into the Fourteenth Amendment. After all, 60 percent or twenty-one of the ratifying states had constitutions which explicitly guaranteed the right to bear arms,[144] and not one state to date has adopted any constitutional provision in conflict with the Second Amendment.

Does the Fourteenth Amendment protect the right of the people to keep and bear arms from state infringement? This may be answered by use of the methodology adopted by the Supreme Court to determine the framers' and people's original understanding. Debates in Congress in 1866 on the Civil Rights Act and on the amendment itself were examined. Previous portions of this study analyzed the abolitionist origins of the Fourteenth Amendment, based in part on sources subsequently approved by the Supreme Court. Also scrutinized were the understanding of the public at large, the state conventions called to ratify the amendment, and the Southern state conventions required to adopt constitutions consistent with the amendment. Finally, congressional debates between 1866 and 1869 on the abolition of the Southern militia organizations and debates on the Civil Rights Acts of 1871 and 1875, which sought to enforce the Fourteenth Amendment, were analyzed as further expressions of the intent of the framers.

A review of these original sources leads to the inescapable conclusion that in the minds of its framers and of the people who adopted it, the Fourteenth Amendment protected the fundamental, individual right to own and possess firearms from state deprivation. If the Supreme Court adheres to its historical methodology, set out above, it will some day be compelled to recognize the full worth of this constitutional right.

The most recent U.S. Supreme Court decision to analyze the intent of the framers of the Civil Rights Act of 1871, now 42 U.S.C. § 1983, is *Patsy* v. *Flordia Board of Regents* (1982).[145] That case dealt with the issue of whether a person who brought suit in federal court under the Civil Rights Act could first be required to exhaust all available state or federal administrative procedures before bringing suit. Delivering the opinion of the Court, Justice Thurgood Marshall said, "Although we recognize that the 1871 Congress did not expressly comtemplate the exhaustion question, we believe that the tenor of the debates . . . supports our conclusion that exhaustion of administrative remedies in § 1983 actions should not be judicially imposed."[146] Significantly, the very sources Marshall proceeds to rely upon show that the 1871 Congress *did* "expressly comtemplate" the right-to-have-arms question, and that not only "the tenor of the debates" but also the proponents and opponents of the civil rights bill explicitly understood the right to keep and bear arms to be protected under what is now § 1983.

The *Patsy* opinion begins its analysis by pointing out that, in passing the Civil Rights Act,

Congress assigned to the federal courts a paramount role in protecting constitutional rights. Representative Dawes expressed this view as follows:
  "The first remedy proposed by this bill is a resort to the courts of the United States. . . . If there be power to call into courts of the United

States an offender against *these rights, privileges, and immunities,* and hold him to an account there, either civilly or criminally, for *their* infringement, . . . there is no tribunal so fitted . . . as that great tribunal of the Constitution."[147]

"These rights, privileges, and immunities," which the Supreme Court noted are "constitutional rights" that the federal courts are bound to protect, were identified in detail by Representative Dawes just before he uttered the words quoted above by the Court. Dawes stated, in part:

The rights, privileges, and immunities of the American citizen, secured to him under the Constitution of the United States, are the subject matter of this bill. . . .
. . . Then again *he has secured to him the right to keep and bear arms in his defense.* . . .
It is all these, Mr. Speaker, which are comprehended in the words, "American citizen," and it is to protect and to secure him in *these rights, privileges and immunities* this bill is before the House.[148]

After quoting Representative Dawes, the Supreme Court significantly buttresses its conclusion further by asking the reader to "see also . . . remarks of" Representatives Hoar, Lowe, Butler, and Coburn.[149] The page reference to Hoar indicates that he was seeking protection of "the fundamental rights of citizens"; two pages later, he accorded Fourteenth Amendment protection for "all the privileges and immunities declared to belong to the citizen by the Constitution itself."[150] Lowe sought protection for the "civil rights and personal security" guaranteed in the Fourteenth Amendment.[151] On the pages referred to by the Court, Butler argued for protection of "rights, immunities, and privileges" guaranteed in the Constitution.[152] In a report introducing the civil rights bill just a month and a half before, Butler had advocated protection for "the well-known constitutional provision guaranteeing the right in the citizen to 'keep and bear arms'. . . ."[153] Finally, the page reference to Coburn finds him supporting the bill to prevent state and private disarmament of blacks: "How much more oppressive is the passage of a law that they shall not bear arms than the practical seizure of all arms from the hands of the colored men?"[154]

In the *Patsy* case, the Supreme Court continues, in a note: *"Opponents of the bill also recognized this purpose* and complained that the bill would usurp the State's power. . . . See, e.g., . . . remarks of Representative Whitthorne. . . ."[155] On the page referred to by the Court, Whitthorne noted that the proposed Civil Rights Act, today's § 1983, would allow suits by any person "who conceives that he has been deprived" by any form of state action "of any right, privilege, or immunity secured to him by the Constitution of the United States." Whitthorne added that if a police officer seized a pistol from a "drunken negro," "the officer may be sued, because the right to bear arms is secured by the Constitution. . . ."[156]

In the same note, *Patsy* refers to three congressmen who opposed the bill because of its wide protections. Even so, one of them, Representative Kerr, called his colleagues' attention "to the first eleven amendments of the Constitution of the United States, and I say that in them, as against the United States and the States and all the world, the Constitution guarantees to the people certain great personal rights. . . . [T]hey are fundamental guarantees to the people."[157] A page later, Kerr argued that the privileges and immunities clause of the Fourteenth Amendment "constitute a limitation on the power of the States as against any infringement of the rights of citizens of the United States."[158] The other two congressmen, Senators Thurman and Bayard, feared that the phrase "any right, privilege, or immunity" would be unduly extended far beyond the rights traditionally recognized as such.[159]

The Supreme Court cites Senator Thurman four times as a representative opponent of the civil rights bill.[160] The Court depicts such opponents as correctly recognizing the bill's deep and widespread purpose and scope, to which they objected.[161] On a later occasion Senator Thurman included the Second Amendment among the "rights, privileges, and immunities of a citizen of the United States." "Here is another right of a citizen of the United States, expressly declared to be his right—the right to bear arms; and this right, says the Constitution, shall not be infringed."[162] Senator Sherman—whom *Patsy* relied upon as a proponent of the bill[163]—agreed with Thurman's assessment as far as it went.[164]

The *Patsy* Court did not ignore Representative Bingham, the draftsman of the Fourteenth Amendment, and approvingly cites the same page of his well-known speech: "that the scope and meaning of the limitations imposed by the first section, fourteenth amendment of the Constitution may be more fully understood, permit me to say that the privileges and immunities of citizens of a State, are chiefly defined in the first eight amendments to the Constitution of the United States."[165] Bingham proceeded to read each of those amendments, including the Second Amendment.

The U.S. Supreme Court in *Patsy* (1982) favorably recalled a further quotation from Bingham: "admitting that the States have concurrent power to enforce the Constitution of the United States within their respective limits, must we wait for their action?"[166] Presumably, the same rhetorical query must meet with the same negative response today.

7

State and Federal
Judicial Decisions

The Pistol as a Protected Arm

For over a century now since Reconstruction, state courts have rendered comprehensive analyses and a large number of opinions involving the nature of the right to keep and bear arms, more so than have the U.S. Supreme Court and the lower federal courts combined. The Texas Supreme Court, after its progressive holding in *English* v. *State* (1872)[1] that the Second Amendment involved fundamental rights and applied to both state and federal legislatures, reversed itself in *State* v. *Duke* (1875)[2] by reverting to the view[3] that the Bill of Rights was inapplicable to the states. Even so, the Texas court held that the defendant could not constitutionally be convicted for carrying a six-shooter pistol. The Texas Supreme Court in *Duke* held that under the Texas Constitution the term "arms" is more comprehensive than merely "arms of the militiaman or soldier": "The arms which every person is secured the right to keep and bear . . . must be such arms as are commonly kept, according to the customs of the people, and are appropriate for open and manly use in self-defense. . . ."[4]

The Arkansas case of *Fife* v. *State* (1876)[5] concerned the constitutionality of an act prohibiting the carrying of easily concealable pocket pistols but not of larger handguns. While holding the act to be valid under a state constituion that guaranteed the right to bear arms for the "common defense," the court added that the Second Amendment protects the individual right to possess "the army and navy repeaters, which, in recent warfare, have very generally superseded the old-fashioned holster, used as a weapon in the battles of our forefathers."[6] The court restricted protected arms to those useful for militia purposes, indicating that one function of the Second Amendment was to provide such arms to all citizens to overthrow a domestic tyranny. The court further clarified that all citizens were militiamen: "The arms which it guarantees American citizens the right to keep and bear, are such as are needful to, and ordinarily used by a well regulated militia, and such as are necessary

179

and suitable to a free people, to enable them to resist oppression, prevent usurpation, repel invasion, etc., etc."[7]

The West Virginia case of *State* v. *Workman* (1891)[8] also upheld an act designed to prevent the carrying of certain concealed weapons, such as brass knuckles, small pistols, and billies that were commonly used in brawls and street fights. Yet the court declared Second Amendment protection for individual arms possession such as would aid the people to revolt to protect the public liberty, asserting that "the weapons of warfare to be used by the militia, such as swords, guns, rifles, and muskets,—arms to be used in defending the state and civil liberty"—were constitutionally protected in the hands of the people.[9]

The West Virginia high court assumed in the above analysis, without explicitly so holding, that the Second Amendment applied to the states. The Supreme Court of Idaho in *In Re Brickey* (1902)[10] held that the carrying of firearms was protected from state interference by the federal Constitution as well as by the Idaho state provision that ensured the right to bear arms for security and defense.

> Under these constitutional provisions, the legislature has no power to prohibit a citizen from bearing arms in any portion of the state of Idaho, whether within or without the corporate limits of cities, towns, and villages. The legislature may, as expressly provided in our State constitution, regulate the exercise of this right, but may not prohibit it. . . . But the statute in question does not prohibit the carrying of weapons concealed, which is of itself a pernicious practice, but prohibits the carrying of them in any manner in cities, towns and villages. We are compelled to hold this statute void.[11]

The Supreme Court of Vermont went even further in *State* v. *Rosenthal* (1903)[12] by declaring an ordinance prohibiting the carrying of concealed weapons without a permit to be contrary to Vermont's constitutional provision: "The people of the state have a right to bear arms for the defense of themselves and the state."[13] The court reasoned:

> under the general laws, therefore, a person not a member of a school may carry a dangerous or deadly weapon, openly or concealed, unless he does it with the intent or avowed purpose of injuring another. . . . By the ordinance in question, no person can carry such weapon concealed on his person within the city of Rutland in any circumstances, nor for any purpose, without the permission of the mayor or chief of police in writing. Therein neither the intent nor purpose of carrying them enters into the essential elements of the offense.[14]

Yet in *Salina* v. *Blaksley* (1905),[15] the Supreme Court of Kansas, in upholding a conviction for carrying a revolver while intoxicated, took a restrictive view both of the relevant state constitutional provision, guaranteeing arms possession for defense and security, and of the federal Second Amendment: the court declared that only "the right to bear arms as a member of the state militia" was intended.[16] Contrariwise, the court treated the federal provision as applicable to the states and agreed that "the legislature can regulate the mode of carrying deadly weapons, provided they are not such as are ordinarily used in civilized warfare."[17] The collectivist approach taken in *Salina*, that the relevant constitutional provisions only referred to the right to bear arms in a military organization provided by law, "went further than any other case"[18] except for the opinion of one concurring judge in the early Arkansas case of *State* v. *Buzzard*.[19] This approach appears illogical on its face: the members of a military organization constitutionally provided for by state law could hardly need any state constitutional right to bear arms.

In still another approach, the New York case of *People* v. *Warden of City Prison* (1913)[20] upheld a conviction for possession of a pistol without a license in the defendant's home because the statute regulated rather than prohibited arms. Yet the court forcibly contended:

> Nevertheless we fully recognize the proposition that the rights enumerated in the [New York] Bill of Rights were not created by such declaration. They are of such character as necessarily pertain to free men in a free state. . . .
>
> The right to bear arms is coupled with the statement why the right is preserved and protected, viz., that "a well-regulated militia is necessary to the security of a free state." If the Legislature had prohibited the keeping of arms, it would have been clearly beyond its power.[21]

Note the court's distinction between keeping and carrying arms: the legislature has far less power over keeping arms. In any event, the court failed to examine whether the licensing requirement could be any more effective than the law it had approved against carrying concealed weapons, which in its own words "did not seem effective in preventing crimes of violence in this state."[22]

In 1921, the North Carolina Supreme Court affirmed a directed verdict for a defendant who was prosecuted for carrying a pistol after having been threatened with violence. More specifically, the Supreme Court of North Carolina in *State* v. *Kerner* (1921)[23] forcefully declared that the right to keep and bear arms was "a sacred right based upon the experience of the ages in order that the people may be accustomed to bear arms and ready to use them for protection of their liberties or their country when occasion serves."[24] Historically,

" 'pistol' ex vi termini is properly included within the word 'arms,' and . . .
the right to bear such arms cannot be infringed."[25] The constitutional guarantee extended to arms that the individual could keep and bear, and not to war
planes or cannons:

> It is true that the invention of guns with a carrying range of probably
> 100 miles, submarines, deadly gases, and of airplanes carrying bombs
> and other devices, have much reduced the importance of the pistol in
> warfare except at close range. But the ordinary private citizen, whose
> right to carry arms cannot be infringed upon, is not likely to purchase
> these expensive and most modern devices just named. To him the rifle,
> the musket, the shotgun, and the pistol are about the only arms which
> he could be expected to "bear," and his right to do this is that which is
> guaranteed by the Constitution.[26]

In short, the arms that the individual is guaranteed the right to have are
those which ordinarily are and can be purchased, kept, and borne by a private individual. Furthermore, this individual right "was guaranteed for the
sacred purpose of enabling the people to protect themselves against invasions
of their liberties." The "common people," who were "accustomed to the
use of arms," won the American Revolution, the court further declared. Not
dependent on the select militia at all, the right was held by the court to exist,
in fundamental part, for defense against the militia: "In our own state, in
1870, when Kirk's militia was turned loose and the writ of habeas corpus was
suspended, it would have been fatal if our people had been deprived of the
right to bear arms and had been unable to oppose an effective front to the
usurpation."[27]

The *Kerner* court also expressed the opinion that the right to bear arms
"should be construed to include all 'arms' as were in common use, and borne
by the people as such when this provision was adopted."[28] "The intention
was to embrace the 'arms,' an acquaintance with whose use was necessary for
their protection against the usurpation of illegal power—such as rifles, muskets, shotguns, swords, and pistols."[29]

Conscious of the need of the poor and the unpopular "to acquire and retain
a practical knowledge of the use of fire arms," the court stated:

> This is not an idle or an obsolete guaranty, for there are still localities,
> not necessary to mention, where great corporations, under the guise of
> detective agents or police forces, terrorize their employees by armed
> force. If the people are forbidden to carry the only arms within their
> means, among them pistols, they will be completely at the mercy of these
> plutocratic organizations. Should there be a mob, is it possible the law-
> abiding citizens could not assemble with their pistols carried openly and

protect their persons and their property from unlawful violence without going before an official and obtaining license and giving bond?[30]

A classic opinion, *Kerner* analytically treats the term "arms" as including pistols but excluding war planes. Its progressive pragmatism evaluates the right as providing protection from oppression whatever its source—whether colonialism, lawless militia, or corporate or mob violence. It broadly construes individual rights provided in constitutional guarantees. An interesting contrast to *Kerner's* anticorporate stance is the Michigan case of *People* v. *Gogak* (1919),[31] which upheld special privileges of corporation employees to carry concealed weapons.

The Michigan Supreme Court in *People* v. *Zerillo* (1922)[32] held that not only individual citizens but also unnaturalized foreign-born residents receive protection under the state constitutional provision: "Every person has a right to bear arms for the defense of himself and the state."[33] The court viewed the policy issue as follows: "Firearms serve the people of this country a useful purpose wholly aside from hunting, and under a constitution like ours, granting . . . to every person the right to bear arms for the defense of himself and the state, . . . the Legislature has no power to constitute it a crime for a person, alien, or citizen, to possess a revolver for the legitimate defense of himself and his property."[34]

By contrast, in *Ex Parte Rameriz* (1924),[35] the California Supreme Court upheld a statute, perhaps aimed at Mexican Americans, which prohibited aliens from possessing concealable weapons. Even so, the court added that "an absolute prohibition of such right might be held to infringe a fundamental right."[36] In the same year, *People* v. *Camperlingo*[37] characterized arms bearing as a "natural right" that could be taken away from convicted felons: "It therefore becomes apparent that the right of the citizen to bear arms is not acquired from any constitutional provision, and . . . it may be said that, by the operation of the statute under consideration, a citizen is deprived of one of his natural rights, in that his ability to better defend himself from personal violence, if offered, will be somewhat lessened. . . ."[38]

Similarly, the Michigan Supreme Court in *People* v. *Brown* (1931)[39] upheld the sentence of life imprisonment of a recidivist felon convicted of possessing a blackjack. Reviewing the nature of the historical militia as being "composed of all able-bodied men," the Michigan Supreme Court rejected *(a)* the view that individuals may bear only such arms as are customary in the militia and *(b)* the extreme view, taken in *Salina,* that the Constitution only protects military organizations. The court reasoned:

When the bulwark of state defense was the militia, privately armed, there may have been good reason for the historical and military test of the right to bear arms. But in this state the militia, although legally existent and composed of all able-bodied male citizens . . . , is practically extinct and has been superseded by the National Guard and reserve organizations. . . . The historical test would render the constitutional provision lifeless.

The protection of the Constitution is not limited to militiamen nor military purposes, in terms, but extends to "every person" to bear arms for the "defense of himself" as well as , f the state.[40]

State Court Decisions since World War II

Not surprisingly, it was the courts of New York, home of the Sullivan Law, which provided the occasion for further exposition of the amendment. In *Moore* v. *Gallup* (1943)[41] an admittedly law-abiding citizen was denied a license to carry a concealed weapon. The court upheld the denial despite the Second Amendment (which the court held was inapplicable to the states) and § 4 of the Civil Rights Law of the State of New York, which was identical to the amendment except for the substitution of "cannot" for "shall not." In a statement which would have seemed to have strengthened the applicant's position, the court observed that "the Second Amendment created no right to bear arms, a right which long antedated the adoption of the Federal Constitution, having originated in a design to strengthen the national militia, an institution first established by King Alfred."[42] The long-standing character of the right would seem to have caused the court to deem it of more importance to individuals, as would the court's reference to Judge Cooley's point that the right existed partly to resist oppression.[43] The dissenting opinion emphasized that the Sullivan Law was enacted to make it difficult for criminals to possess arms, and not to harass peaceful citizens who, for the sake of "home defense," should "become proficient in the use of firearms."[44]

Similarly, the New York case of *Application of Cassidy* (1944)[45] declared that the Second Amendment "does not grant a license to carry arms";[46] this decision upheld the rejection of an application to the bar of an applicant who advocated a right-wing private militia to defeat a communist insurrection.

In sharp contrast, the Municipal Court of the City of New York, Borough of Queens, in *Hutchinson* v. *Rosetti* (1960)[47] ordered the police to return a hunting rifle to one who had used it to defend himself against an angry and prejudiced mob. "Passing for the moment that the law, as a matter of broad policy, frowns on forfeiture, there is the constitutional guarantee of the right of the individual to bear arms. Amendments Art. II."[48] Clearly interpreting the amendment as guaranteeing an individual right against state or federal infringement, the court added that the presumption of innocence and "the elemental right of self-defense" were both basic and long recognized in Anglo-

American jurisprudence.[49] "The Constitution permits citizens the right to bear arms."[50]

It was the civil unrest of the sixties, and the legislation which sought to control such unrest, that led to a great increase in the number of judicial opinions in the third quarter of the decade. The North Carolina case of *State* v. *Dawson* (1968)[51] returned to the old issue of whether it was a common-law crime to go armed with unusual and dangerous weapons to the terror of the people. The defendant had been convicted of breaking and entering and unlawfully shooting into a dwelling. Still, the court said that "the carrying of a gun, *per se*, constitutes no offense," whether for business or amusement.[52] The North Carolina court also stated: "While the purpose of the constitutional guaranty of the right to keep and bear arms was to secure a well regulated militia and not an individual's right to have a weapon in order to exercise his common-law right of self-defense, this latter right was assumed."[53] Although explicitly upholding the individual's right to keep and bear arms, the court grounded its holding on its fear of "social upheaval," as represented by "night riders or day-time demonstrators" who armed themselves to the terror of the people.[54]

A concurring and dissenting opinion averred that, without a constitutional amendment to allow legislation to prohibit carrying concealed weapons, under the language of the state constitution (which repeated the language of the Second Amendment) even this practice could not be lawfully interdicted, for the right was absolute. Referring to Edward III's proscription of being armed to the people's terror, the judge reflected: "It was the very fact that the right to bear arms had been infringed in England, and that this is a step frequently taken by a despotic government, which caused the adoption of the provision in the North Carolina Declaration of Rights of 1776 and the insertion in the Federal Bill of Rights of the Second Amendment."[55] The nondependence of the right on formal militia use, and its existence in part to resist an oppressive militia, was indicated in earlier North Carolina precedent.[56] Finally, the Fourteenth Amendment mandated Bill of Rights provisions necessary to preserve liberty on the states.[57]

A more striking erosion of the right to possess arms was exemplified in the New Jersey case of *Burton* v. *Sills* (1968).[58] It originated when members of sportsman clubs and gun dealers brought an action to declare unconstitutional the state's gun-control law, which imposed restrictive requirements. Conjuring up an image of "political assassinations, killings of enforcement officers, and snipings during riots,"[59] the court expressed exaggerated fears of a revolution. The New Jersey Supreme Court restricted the definition of militia to "the active, organized militias of the states," that is, the National Guard.[60] The court's very use of these adjectives to modify the word "militia" ignores the constitutional militia comprised of all persons capable of bearing arms.[61]

The *Burton* opinion simply fails to provide a scholarly, historical, and analytical treatment of the subject, as indeed primarily only the antebellum state opinions do provide.

Some opinions of state courts in the decade since 1968 have, by and large, depended on the following arguments in the alternative: The Second Amendment applies to Congress alone, and thus state firearms regulation cannot infringe on the right; if the Second Amendment applies to the states through the Fourteenth Amendment, then *(a)* only militia-type arms are protected or *(b)* only the National Guard is protected; and finally, if the Second and Fourteenth Amendments prevent the states from infringing on an individual right to possess arms, then existing regulatory schemes are within the police power and do not so infringe on any right (including due process or equal protection)[62] as long as they are not applied arbitrarily.[63] Some of these opinions, that is, the ones which burden law-abiding citizens in the exercise of their right to keep and bear arms, appear to be based on misreadings of nineteenth-century U.S. Supreme Court cases as well as of *Miller;* they ignore the scholarly and extensive treatments given the topic by state courts from earliest times until the *Miller* era, and they seem totally unaware that the framers of the Fourteenth Amendment agreed on the incorporation of the Second Amendment. Even so, negative treatment of the right to keep and bear arms by state courts has been of relatively short duration, while positive treatment has existed for one hundred and fifty years and thereby constitutes a more enduring body of common law and constitutional interpretation.

The swing back toward a favorable judicial treatment of the right to keep and bear arms is already discernible since the close of the turbulent sixties and seventies. Two decisions rendered by state courts during 1980 exhibit an increasing concern to protect the constitutional right to have arms. In *Schubert* v. *DeBard,*[64] the intermediate Court of Appeals of Indiana held that the state police superintendent's denial of an application for a license to carry a handgun was wrongful. Self-protection is guaranteed under the following provision of the Indiana Constitution: "The people have a right to bear arms, for the defense of themselves and the State."[65] Since "constitutional language was carefully chosen to express the framer's intention," the court concluded that "our constitution provides our citizenry the right to bear arms for their self-defense." The constitutional guarantee precluded police discretion on whether an applicant "needed" to carry a handgun for self-defense, for such discretion "would supplant a right with a mere administrative privilege which might be withheld simply on the basis that such matters as the use of firearms are better left to the organized military and police forces even where defense of the individual is involved."[66]

The identical provision in the Oregon Constitution led the supreme court of that state, in *State* v. *Kessler,*[67] to invalidate a statute prohibiting possession of a billy club. Rather than imposing its own value judgments regarding "the current controversy over the wisdom of a right to bear arms," the court determined that its task "in construing a constitutional provision is to respect the principles given the status of constitutional guarantees and limitations by the drafters; it is not to abandon these principles when this fits the needs of the moment."[68] The court thereby employed the historical methodology of tracing the right to bear arms from its usage by early mankind to the English Bill of Rights of 1689 and the American Revolution.

Besides "the deterrence of government from oppressing unarmed segments of the population,"[69] the purpose of the right to bear arms included individual self-defense, which the common law recognized as early as 1400.[70] Protected arms therefore included those commonly used and suitable for personal and military defense.

> The term "arms" was not limited to firearms, but included several hand-carried weapons commonly used for defense. The term "arms" would not have included cannon or other heavy ordnance not kept by militiamen or private citizens.[71]

The strong historical analysis employed by the *Kessler* court to demonstrate the continuing constitutional and utilitarian viability of the right to bear arms represents a return to traditional American and English constitutional common-law principles.[72]

To Disarm Felons or to Disarm Citizens?
Federal Court Decisions from 1940

The first lower federal court to exposit *Miller* involved, rather than firearms regulation, the validity of the federal conscription act passed in 1940.[73] Rejecting the defendant's argument that the draft constituted involuntary servitude, the district court in *Stone* v. *Christenson* (1940)[74] relied on *Miller* as authority that the whole people constituted the militia:

> Stone, ever since he became of a suitable age, has been by Federal law a member of the unorganized militia.[75] By a series of laws, the first of which was adopted soon after the organization of government under the federal constitution, the liability of able-bodied citizens to military service and training under federal authority has been continuously declared.[76]

The court proceeded to cite the act of 8 May 1792, which provided for the inclusion in the militia of "each and every free able-abodied white male citizen" between the ages of eighteen and forty-five.[77] The "unorganized militia" included all able-bodied men, not just those who registered: Congress in the act of 1917[78] "ordered part of the organized militia, the National Guard, into service and the registration of a portion of the unorganized militia."[79]

The First Circuit Court of Appeals, in deciding *Cases* v. *United States* (1942),[80] began what can only be described as a rebellion against the holding in *Miller* that the Second Amendment guarantees the right of every individual to keep and bear any arms suitable for militia use. The defendant in *Cases,* a Puerto Rican who had earlier been convicted of a crime of violence, received into his possession a firearm and ammunition in violation of the 1938 Federal Firearms Act.[81] The court began its analysis in relation to the Second Amendment with the observation that the act "undoubtedly curtails to some extent the right of individuals to keep and bear arms," which, in itself, does not render it invalid under the Second Amendment. The court proceeded to state: "The right to keep and bear arms is not a right conferred upon the people by the federal constitution."[82] It then suggested that only local legislation grants this right and that the Second Amendment prevents "the federal government only from infringing that right." Despite its reference to the Supreme Court case of *Robertson* v. *Baldwin,*[83] it ignored the fact that the federal Constitution failed to confer the right to keep and bear arms only because the right had long antedated the Constitution.

The circuit court's analysis of *Miller* is worth quoting at length:

> Apparently, then, under the Second Amendment, the federal government . . . cannot prohibit the possession or use of any weapon which has any reasonable relationship to the preservation or efficiency of a well regulated militia. . . . At any rate the rule of the Miller case, if intended to be comprehensive and complete would seem to be already outdated, in spite of the fact that it was formulated only three and a half years ago, because of the well known fact that in the so-called "Commando Units" some sort of military use seems to have been found for almost any modern lethal weapon. In view of this, if the rule of the Miller case is general and complete, the result would follow that, under present day conditions, the federal government would be empowered only to regulate the possession or use of weapons such as a flintlock musket or a matchlock harquebus. But to hold that the Second Amendment limits the federal government to regulations concerning only weapons which can be classed as antiques or curiosities,—almost any other might bear some reasonable relationship to the preservation or efficiency of a well regulated militia unit of the present day,—is in effect to hold that the limitation of the Second Amendment is absolute.[84]

The lower court ended its rejection of the authority of the U.S. Supreme

Court by complaining that "another objection to the rule of the Miller case" includes its failure to prevent the possession by individuals, who are not members of "any military unit," of such weapons as machine guns and mortars.[85] Interestingly, most of *Cases* may be considered mere *dictum* because its narrow holding was that convicted violent felons (a class which traditionally had forfeited various civil rights, including militia membership) could be constitutionally disarmed.

The Third Circuit Court of Appeals, the next lower federal court to construe the Second Amendment, which decided *Tot* v. *United States* (1942),[86] is the only federal district court or court of appeals to cite, to date, any significant original sources to buttress its claim that the amendment protects the rights of states but not those of individuals.[87] In fact, those federal cases which adopted this view in reaction to challenges (usually by felons) to the 1968 gun-control legislation almost invariably seek support not in any historical document, but in similarly nonsupported previous cases, traceable to the *Cases* and *Tot* precedents.[88] Thus, those lower federal courts to have adopted a collectivist view of the Second Amendment comply with the intent of its framers only if *Tot* is consistent with that intent.

For its allegation that the Second Amendment "was not adopted with individual rights in mind," *Tot*[89] cites "the discussions of this amendment": *a)* "contemporaneous with its proposal and adoption" and *b)* "those of learned writers since." Yet a thorough review of each of these references, not one of which gives any historical support to the claimed denial of individual rights, produces the impression that the writer of the *Tot* opinion falls below the undergraduate level in scholarly standards.

Ignoring the numerous explicit expositions of the Second Amendment, which were truly "contemporaneous with its proposal and adoption," and detailed earlier in the present study, *Tot* refers to three statements made several months and even years before the Second Amendment was even proposed in 1789. The Court relies on Roger Sherman of Connecticut at the federal convention of 1787. Yet the page cited by the Court reveals merely that "Mr. Sherman took notice that the states might want their militia for defence against invasions and insurrections, and for enforcing obedience to their laws."[90] Indeed, on the page before, Oliver Ellsworth opposed "a select militia" and favored "the great body of the militia."[91]

The Court also refers to two pages from Luther Martin's letter of 1787 to the Maryland legislature. Martin complained that the militia clauses of Art. I, § 8, cl. 15 and 16 of the proposed Constitution would enable Congress to force militias out of their own states and would deprive the states of "the security of their rights against arbitrary encroachments of the general government. . . ."[92] He warned that a standing army could "leave the militia totally unorganized, undisciplined, and even to disarm them. . . ."[93]

The argument of William Lenoir at the North Carolina convention in mid-1788 is the only other original source relied on by *Tot* for its proposition that the Second Amendment fails to protect individual rights. The page cited finds Lenoir expressing alarm at the powers of Congress: "They can disarm the militia. If they are armed, they would be a resource against oppressions. . . . If the laws of the Union were oppressive, they could not carry them into effect, if the people were possessed of proper means of defense."[94] It should be added that Lenoir voted for a Declaration of Rights,[95] in which the people's right to have arms is stated in a proposition independent of the militia clause: "That the people have a right to keep and bear arms; that a well regulated militia, composed of the body of the people, trained to arms, is the proper, natural and safe defense of a free state. . . ."[96]

The "learned writers" relied on by *Tot* for its claim that the Second Amendment "was not adopted with individual rights in mind" were nothing more than three obscure law review writers who published brief articles on the subject during this century. The Court ignored the legal giants, such as St. George Tucker, Justice Story, William Rawle, and Judge Cooley, all of whom recognized that the Second Amendment guarantees individual rights. Further, not one of the three law review articles relied on by the Court contains a single source from the period in which the Bill of Rights was debated.

At least two of these three articles directly contradict the *Tot* thesis. The article published in *Harvard Law Review* in 1915 states that the purpose of the right to keep and bear arms is "for preserving to the people the right and power of organized military defense of themselves and the state and of organized military resistance to unlawful acts of the government itself, as in the case of the American Revolution."[97] The legislature may regulate the carrying of weapons, "however powerless it may be as to the simple possessing or keeping weapons."[98]

A second article, published in the *Marquette Law Review* in 1928, stated: "A number of the constitutional provisions say that the guarantee of the right to keep and bear arms is to enable a man to defend his person, property, etc. Under American legal theory clearly such a right of defense exists."[99] "[I]ts origin may be found in man's very nature."[100] "Arms" include "horseman's pistols" and "the customary weapons which people had possessed when the constitution had been adopted."[101]

Only the article published in the *Bill of Rights Review* in 1941 seems to support *Tot* when it concluded that the right to have arms exists for "common defense" and not "private brawls."[102] This false dilemma fails to take account of individual possession of arms for purely defensive purposes. Thus, out of three original sources and three law review articles relied on by *Tot* to deny that the Second Amendment protects individual rights, only one of the articles, itself based on no original sources, lends support to that doctrine.

Tot then cites *The Federalist* Nos. 24 through 29 and No. 46 in support of its view that the Second Amendment provides "protection for the States in the maintenance of their militia organizations against possible encroachments by the federal power."[103] While these numbers of the *Federalist* undoubtedly assert that the state governments should protect their citizens from oppressive federal usurpation, none characterize the right to keep and bear arms as subject to legislative deprivation. Rather, Alexander Hamilton promised in No. 29 that a standing army "can never be formidable to the liberties of the people while there is a large body of citizens, little if at all inferior to them in discipline and the use of arms, who stand ready to defend their own rights and those of their fellow-citizens." Further, James Madison in No. 46 defined the militia as "half a million citizens with arms in their hands", and he referred to "the advantage of being armed, which the Americans possess over the people of almost every other nation," and to the kingdoms of Europe where "the governments are afraid to trust the people with arms."

Aside from a reference to the Statute of Northampton (1328), which only prohibited the carrying of arms in a manner calculated to terrify the king's subjects,[104] *Tot* cites no other historical source. In sum, not a single original source quoted in *Tot* substantiates its assertion that the Second Amendment "was not adopted with individual rights in mind," and thus the later lower federal court decisions that rely on this unsupported decision constitute a house of cards with no valid foundation.

Most of the lower federal court opinions construing the gun-control legislation of 1968 actually hold nothing more than that possession of firearms *by felons* has no reasonable relationship to the preservation of a well regulated militia. Nor do these cases deny that all able-bodied, law-abiding citizens are in the militia or that the Second Amendment guarantees their individual right to keep and bear militia weapons.[105] *United States* v. *Synnes* (1971) recognized the existence of "the right to keep and bear arms,"[106] but correctly saw no conflict between the disarmament of felons "and the Second Amendment since there is no showing that prohibiting possession by felons obstructs the maintenance of a 'well regulated militia.' "[107] Felons may be disarmed not because the Second Amendment fails to protect individual rights, but because felons forfeit civil rights by engaging in crime. "In essence, since there is support for the proposition that it is eminently reasonable to categorize convicted aggressors as a separate class whose individual right to bear arms may be prohibited, there can be no violation of a constitutionally protected right of defendant under the Second Amendment,"—so held *United States* v. *Wiley* (1970).[108] The Second Amendment provides an individual right to the non-felon to possess common firearms regardless of any militia use. In the words of *United States* v. *Bowdach* (1976), "possession of the shotgun by a non-felon has no legal consequences. U. S. Const. Amend. II."[109]

The continuing public interest in individual marksmanship outside any organizational context, governmental or private, was attested to in *Gavett* v. *Alexander* (1979),[110] wherein the U.S. District Court for the District of Columbia upheld the constitutionality of the Civilian Marksmanship Program. Rejecting the view "that marksmanship has become an obsolete or useless skill," even in the nuclear age,[111] the court referred to "the governmental interest in the promotion of marksmanship" as "compelling."[112] Striking as unconstitutional, on due process and equal protection grounds, the federal statute's requirement that surplus military rifles could be sold at cost only to members of the National Rifle Association, the court reasoned that "it is obviously possible to become a competent marksman on an individual basis" and that "better marksmanship . . . a legitimate government objective, is capable of achievement outside an organizational framework. . . ."[113] In sum, *Gavatt* assumes as an empirical fact, based upon congressional legislative history of the statute, the social value of individual ownership of arms and of training in marksmanship.

Afterword: Public Policy and the Right to Keep and Bear Arms

"Our War of the Revolution was, in good measure, fought as a protest against standing armies. Moreover, it was fought largely with a civilian army, the militia," wrote Earl Warren in *The Bill of Rights and The Military* (1962).[1] Warren's remark came at a time when the role of the military again evoked public debate. The chief justice further explained that the people "were reluctant to ratify the Constitution without further assurances, and thus we find in the Bill of Rights Amendments 2 and 3, specifically authorizing a decentralized militia, guaranteeing the right to the people to keep and bear arms, and prohibiting the quartering of troops in any house in time of peace without the consent of the owner."[2]

According to Roscoe Pound, "nothing in the Bill of Rights can or ought to be ignored, though some provisions, such as the right to bear arms have a much altered significance under the conditions of popular uprisings against oppression under the conditions of military operations today."[3] This proposition is ambiguous—Pound apparently assumed that the Second Amendment encompasses the struggle against oppression, but he may have been over-awed by the superior military technology of government. The "much altered significance" of the citizen's right to bear arms, whatever Pound intended, becomes all the more crucial in a world of qualitatively more heavily armed and more oppressive governments. The victory of superiorly armed oppressors against truly "popular uprisings" of armed populaces is no more inexorable today than was the victory of the British in the American Revolution.[4] Nor does sophisticated military equipment guarantee victory over small arms, as Vietnam proved a decade ago.

Legal theorists heralding the obsolescence of the Second Amendment assume that the state's guns will be used exclusively for legitimate purposes when private individuals are unarmed. Roscoe Pound, in *Development of Constitutional Guarantees of Liberty* (1957), asserted: "In the urban industrial society of today a general right to bear efficient arms so as to be able to resist oppression by the government would mean that gangs could exercise an extra-legal rule which would defeat the whole Bill of Rights."[5] Yet the argument made by the Founding Fathers, that government may become a "gang" and defeat the Bill of Rights when the people are defenseless, remains unrefuted. And even if wrong or stupid, the Founding Fathers may be overruled only by a constitutional amendment.

In an uncharacteristic position Justice Douglas, dissenting in *Adams* v. *Williams* (1972),[6] put complete faith in the police: "There is no reason why all pistols should not be barred to everyone but the police."[7] Yet Douglas clarified this opinion to be based on his own arbitrary value judgment: "But if watering down is the mode of the day, I would prefer to water down the Second Amendment rather than the Fourth Amendment."[8] Curiously, Douglas also wrote in *The Bill of Rights is not Enough* (1963): "The closest the framers came to the *affirmative* side of liberty was in the right to bear arms. Yet this too has been greatly modified by judicial construction."[9] Douglas did not anticipate that, should his policy of disarming the people while leaving the police armed be implemented, a powerful police state ultimately could strike blows at the right of the people to be secure from unreasonable searches and seizures. Indeed, extensive arms searches in private dwellings were made by the British in their aggression against Scotland, Ireland and America.

The disastrous consequences to the right to be secure from unreasonable searches and seizures by legislative infringement on the right to keep arms was recognized in the dissenting opinion in *State* v. *Buzzard* (1843)[10]: "Can [the legislature,] directly or indirectly, invade the sanctuaries of private life and of personal security, by authorizing a public inquisition to search for either open or concealed weapons?"[11]

In *Miranda* v. *Arizona* (1966),[12] dissenting Justice White expressed concern for "those who rely on the public authority for protection and who without it can only engage in violent self-help with guns, knives and the help of their neighbors similarly situated."[13] However, America's founders not only concurred with this philosophy but also regarded guns as necessary for violent self-help *from* the "public authority." To them, the armed people may by natural law engage in self-defense against all criminals, whether public or private.[14]

One argument, articulated in Rohner's *The Right to Bear Arms: A Phenomenon of Constitutional History* (1966)[15] (a law review article cited by several courts) claims that the militia is obsolete and that "the people of the United States" accept the standing army and National Guard as the optimum for "security." This euphemistic language expresses a naive optimism for the armed state and a cynical pessimism for the armed people. His further contention that "the call for an armed citizenry seems confined to reactionary political groups"[16] expresses an assumption that requires further analysis.

While right-wing groups have defended the Second Amendment,[17] legal analysts who have expressed a social philosophy resting on traditional American revolutionary and libertarian thought have also argued for the original interpretation of the Second Amendment.[18] Although the National Rifle Association is often depicted as conservative, its philosophy is akin to radical libertarianism. As the anti-Second Amendment critic Robert Sherrill claimed, "The NRA's concept of Armed Citizenry heartily endorses the old anarchist saying, 'The state must never have a monopoly on the instruments of violence.' "[19] And if some NRA members hold that the best government governs least or not at all (especially in respect to gun control), the views of those who trust the police with guns, but not the people, more closely parallel the theory of fascism. Elitists dismiss as "reactionary" the espousal of Second Amendment rights. Yet under classical republican theory, those who would restrict access to firearms to members of the ruling class are truly the ones who espouse the "reactionary" view.

Overly restrictive interpretations of the Second Amendment are associated with reactionary concepts in several respects, including elitism, militarism, and racism. Thus, the claim invented in recent law review articles that the militia is identical with the National Guard, besides being historically false,[20] ignores the reality that the Guard fails to fulfill the role envisioned by the Founding Fathers. Specifically, the Second Amendment's framers anticipated a force of the whole armed populace, not a select group, to counter inroads on freedom by government, while the function of the Guard is to maintain the status quo. The shooting of unarmed anti-war demonstrators by National Guardsmen at Kent State University in 1970 has been compared with the Boston Massacre of 1770. The federalization of the Guard at the turn of the century "almost completely negated the original purpose of the militia, for the Founding Fathers saw the militia as a liberal agency that would act in defense of individual and local liberty against the power of the Federal Government."[21]

Straitjacket constructions of the Second Amendment associated with racism have been particularly associated with handgun bans. Ironically, the first general handgun ban in U.S. history was enacted in 1981 in a middle-class Chicago suburb—the Village of Morton Grove[22]—for prior to that ordinance, strict gun-control laws were mostly confined to urban areas with large black populations.[23] Even in the antebellum South, blacks were trusted to possess pistols temporarily, and even permanently if they had a license. "Degraded as are these individuals, as a class, by their social position, it is certain, that among them are many, worthy of all confidence, and into whose hands these weapons can be safely trusted, either for their own protection, or for the protection of the property of others confided to them."[24] It would appear that in Morton Grove today ordinary citizens are considered more degraded and less worthy of confidence than were free blacks in the antebellum South, who could obtain licenses to keep pistols in their homes lawfully.[25]

Earlier in this century, proposals to register or prohibit handguns were frankly intended to disarm blacks. In 1909, Virginia's most prestigious law review attacked the possession of the handgun by what it called the "son of Ham," as follows:

> It is a matter of common knowledge that in this state and in several others, the more especially in the Southern states where the negro population is so large, that this cowardly practice of "toting" guns has always been one of the most fruitful sources of crime. . . . There would be a very decided falling off of killings "in the heat of passion" if a prohibitive tax were laid on the privilege of handling and disposing of revolvers and other small arms, or else that every person purchasing such deadly weapons should be required to register. . . . Let a negro board a railroad train with a quart of mean whiskey and a pistol in his grip and the chances are that there will be a murder, or at least a row, before he alights.[26]

Regardless of whether the motives of contemporaries who would ban private ownership of some or all kinds of firearms is a fear of blacks or of all common citizens, whites included (other than the military and the police), certainly their efforts to pass legislation at the local and state level will continue to escalate. Since it is equally certain that their dedicated opponents would seem to have no intention of relenting, a showdown at the U.S. Supreme Court appears inevitable.

The peculiar philosophy implicit in the attack on the Second Amendment is also evident in gun control's creation of victimless crimes, that is, punishment for mere possession and not criminal use of firearms, and for prior restraint through seizing arms before a crime has been committed (the parallel to preventive detention is clear). Just as in the case of prohibition of alcohol, prohibition of guns results in "law enforcement excesses, discriminatory enforcement and police corruption, criminal profits, bureaucratic abuse, overloading courts and corrections, labeling and corrupting effects, diversion of resources, and loss of respect for law."[27]

The often state-sponsored violence against civil rights organizers in the South's second Reconstruction period during the 1950s and 1960s proved anew the utility of the right to keep and bear arms against state infringement.[28] The subsequent outbreak of the ghetto uprisings in the North in the 1960s, which resulted in massive searches and seizures for arms on dubious constitutional grounds by allegedly racist and murderous National Guardsmen and police forces, prompted the advocacy by many black leaders of the fundamental right to keep and bear arms. The "Program of the Organization of Afro-American Unity" (1964) provided:

The Constitution of the United States of America clearly affirms the right of every American citizen to bear arms. And as Americans, we will not give up a single right guaranteed under the Constitution. The history of unpunished violence against our people clearly indicates that we must be prepared to defend ourselves or we will continue to be a defenseless people at the mercy of a ruthless and violent racist mob.

We assert that in those areas where the government is either unable or unwilling to protect the lives and property of our people, that our people are within their rights to protect themselves by whatever means necessary.[29]

The widely circulated "Program of the Black Panther Party" (1966) expressed a common sentiment in the black community: "The Second Amendment to the Constitution of the United States gives a right to bear arms. We therefore believe that all black people should arm themselves for self-defense."[30]

As in Reconstruction, state legislatures, in response to the unrest of the last two decades, passed measures aimed at disarming what they saw to be a black threat. Congress, rather than guaranteeing the right to keep and bear arms as in the Fourteenth Amendment and in the Anti-KKK Act, passed the Gun Control Act of 1968, which, Robert Sherrill argues, was aimed at controlling blacks.[31]

The Fourteenth Amendment was meant to protect not only blacks but all citizens against state violence and deprivation of rights. Its framers considered the right to keep and bear arms as more fundamental than any other right because it guaranteed one's very existence and it served to protect freedom of speech and other liberties. They regarded arms possession as a fundamental right for protection against both private and official aggression, such as that sanctioned under color of law or committed by state agents. Since arms would always exist, including those in the hands of a potentially oppressive government, all people by the standards of the Second and Fourteenth Amendments may be armed for self-defense. In view of the logic of its own decisions and of the intent of the framers of the respective amendments, the United States Supreme Court would seem impelled to recognize the fundamental, private, and individual right to keep and bear arms as protected from both state and national infringement.

The Second Amendment to the U.S. Constitution explicitly provides that "the right of the people to keep and bear arms, shall not be infringed." The Bill of Rights was intended to remind not only the government, but also the people, of the rights of every individual. Regardless of what the nine justices of the Supreme Court may rule, it seems likely that millions of Americans will continue to exercise their constitutional right to keep and bear arms.

Notes

Preface

1. Quilici v. Village of Morton Grove, 532 F. Supp. 1169 (N.D. Ill. 1981), *aff'd*. 695 F.2d 261 (7th Cir. 1982), *cert. denied* 104 S.Ct. 194 (1983).
2. Smith v. Collin, 447 F. Supp. 676 (N.D. Ill.), *aff'd*. 578 F.2d 1197 (7th Cir.), *cert. denied* 439 U.S. 916 (1978). "The court has thus squarely rejected the theory that some ideas are too dangerous to permit their advocacy. . . ." 447 F. Supp. at 688.
3. 695 F.2d at 266.
4. *Id*. at 267.
5. *Id*. at 270 n. 8.
6. 578 F.2d at 1210.
7. 695 F.2d at 272.
8. *Id*. at 279.
9. *Id*. at 280.

Introduction:
Firearms Prohibition and Constitutional Rights

1. Moore v. East Cleveland, 431 U.S. 494, 539 (1977).
2. Burton v. Sills, 53 N.J. 86, 248 A.2d 521 (1968), *appeal dismissed*, 394 U.S. 812 (1969) *(mem.)*.
3. But see Engblom v. Carey, 677 F.2d 957, 961 (2d Cir. 1982). (The Third Amendment protects a tenant, as well as an owner, against peacetime quartering of troops.)
4. State constitutional provisions on the right to keep and bear arms are reproduced in Dowlut, *The Right to Arms*, 36 OKLA.L. REV. 65, 102 (1983). State legislative history may suggest that even where its wording differs, a state provision may be intended to provide a meaning identical with the Second Amendment. *E.g.*, PROCEEDINGS & DEBATES OF THE SENATE OF

VIRGINIA PERTAINING TO AMENDMENT OF THE CONSTITU-
TION 391–394 (1969–70).

5.   Federal laws are compiled in Bureau of Alcohol, Tobacco, and Firearms, FIREARMS: FEDERAL LAWS AND REGULATIONS (1979), and
National Rifle Association, FEDERAL FIREARMS LAWS (n.d.).

6.   Gun Control Act of 1968, 18 U.S.C. §§922(a) (5) and 924(a).

7.   D. Hardy, THE B.A.T.F.'S WAR ON CIVIL LIBERTIES (1979).

8.   26 U.S.C. §§5845, 5861, and 5871.

9.   18 U.S.C. §922. *See also,* Omnibus Crime Control and Safe Streets
Act of 1968, 18 U.S.C. Appendix, §§1201–02.

10.   State laws and local ordinances are partially reproduced annually in
the Code of Federal Regulations, pursuant to 18 U.S.C. §921(a)(19) and 27
C.F.R. Part 178; the same are published annually in Bureau of Alcohol,
Tobacco, and Firearms, FIREARMS: STATE LAWS AND PUBLISHED
ORDINANCES; and are summarized in a series of pamphlets published by
the National Rifle Association, YOUR STATE FIREARMS LAWS (n.d.).
See also, National Rifle Association, FIREARMS LAWS AND COURT DE-
CISIONS *passim* (Washington, D.C., n.d.).

11.   FLA. STAT. §§790.05, .06 and .25.

12.   CA. PENAL CODE §12031.

13.   FLA. STAT. §790.01, .25, which overruled Ensor v. State, 403 So.2d
349 (Fla. 1981) (derringer can be concealed *and* in plain view.)

14.   People v. Williams, 7 Cal. Rptr. 604, 184 C.A.2d 673 (1960).

15.   TEX. CODE ANN. §46.05.

16.   ORE. REV. STAT. §166.270(2)(b).

17.   MASS. ANN. LAWS ch. 269, §10.

18.   D. C. CODE §§6–1812, 6–1872, 6–1802(10).

19.   United States v. Miller, 307 U.S. 174 (1939).

Chapter 1
The Elementary Books of Public Right

1.   Jefferson, LIVING THOUGHTS 42 (J. Dewey ed. 1963).

2.   For general references on the influence of Aristotle, Cicero, Locke,
Sidney, and Trenchard and Gordon on the Founding Fathers, *see* B. Bailyn,
IDEOLOGICAL ORIGINS OF THE AMERICAN REVOLUTION (1967);
E. Corwin, THE "HIGHER LAW" BACKGROUND OF AMERICAN
CONSTITUTIONAL LAW (1955); C. Mullett, *Classical Influences on the
American Revolution*, 35 CLASSICAL JOUR. 93, 94 (1939–40).

3.   1 J. Adams, WORKS 26 (C. Adams ed. 1856).

4.   H. Granter, *The Machiavellianism of George Mason*, 17 W. & M. QUAR-
TERLY 239, 245–50 (2d Series 1937).

5.   1. G. Mason, PAPERS 231 (R. Rutland ed. 1970).

6.   5 J. Adams, WORKS at 183. For examples of long quotations from
Machiavelli favorably cited, *see* 4 *id.* at 57, 410, and 416–20.

7.   J. Pocock, THE MACHIAVELLELIAN MOMENT 528 (1975). The Machiavellian ideal that the citizen "should bear arms of his own" was transmitted by English theorists to the framers of the Second Amendment. Pocock, *Between Machiavelli and Hume,* EDWARD GIBBON AND THE DECLINE AND FALL OF THE ROMAN EMPIRE (Bowersock et al., eds. 1977).

8.   C. Robbins, *Algernon Sidney's Discourses . . .,* 4 W. & M. QUAR-TERLY 267, 269 (3d Series 1947).

9.   2 S. Adams, WRITINGS 210 (1906).

10.   *Id.* at 298–9.

11.   1 G. Mason, PAPERS at 279–80.

12.   C. Robbins, *Algernon Sidney's Discourses . . .,* 4 W. & M. QUAR-TERLY at 270.

13.   *E.g.,* see Pennsylvania Gazette, Ap. 13, 1788: Loyalists in the Revolution "objected to *associating, arming* and *fighting,* in defense of our liberties. . . . The people, as sovereigns of a country, are above all constitutions. . . . The contrary opinion is the doctrine of Hobbes. . . ."

14.   Plato, REPUBLIC 20 (B. Jowett transl. 1946).

15.   *Id.*

16.   Plato, REPUBLIC 139–40 (E. Cornford transl. 1945).

17.   *Id.* at 275. Plato's explanation seems appropriate regarding the Russian Revolution, which was based on a peasantry initially armed by the czar to fight an imperialist war.

18.   *Id.* at 280–81.

19.   *Id.* at 282.

20.   Plato recognizes the economic causes of wars of competing imperialisms at *id.* 61–62.

21.   *Id.* at 293.

22.   *Id.* at 295.

23.   *Id.* at 210.

24.   Plato, REPUBLIC 149 (B. Jowett transl. 1946); *cf.* Cornford transl. at 129.

25.   Cornford transl. at 125–29. *Cf.* Plato, *Critias* in 9 PLATO 271 (1929), which praises the ancient way of only two classes—the Guardians are the military class as well, and all others are workers.

26.   Plato would have admitted women into the royal or the warrior classes, advocating their training in bodily exercise and in "bearing arms and riding on horseback." *Id.* at 149. Plato also advances the abolition of legal actions for assault and outrage among the Guardians, "for we shall pronounce it right and honourable for a man to defend himself against an assailant of his own age, and in that way they will be compelled to keep themselves fit." *Id.* at 166. *Cf. id.* at 112–13.

27.   Plato, LAWS 218 (transl. T. Saunders, 1970). While Plato does not literally state such, Aristotle interpreted this to mean that "those bearing arms," that is, having citizenship, would be limited to five thousand in the *Laws* (and one thousand in the *Republic).* Aristotle, POLITICS 69 (transl. T. Sinclair 1962). Although Plato may not have held, as did Aristotle, that arms

bearing was necessary for full citizenship, clearly Plato anticipates that the great body of slaves and other workers would have neither arms nor citizenship.

28.   Plato, LAWS at 218.

29.   *Id.* at 282 and 305.

30.   *Id.* at 306. *Cf.* 280–82, 307 and 322–29.

31.   *Id.* at 324.

32.   *Id.* at 489. *Cf. id.* at 491–93 (punishment for abandonment of military weapons).

33.   *Id.* at 507. While providing for a right to self-defense, *id.* at 384–85 and 392–93, no such right would exist against the state. *Compare* Plato's APOLOGY, where Socrates justifies civil disobedience against the Thirty Tyrants, *with* his CRITO, which argues that the state must always be obeyed—even where it directs the unjustly convicted to drink hemlock.

34.   Aristotle, POLITICS at 68.

35.   *Id.* at 71. Emphasis added.

36.   *Id.* at 78.

37.   *Id.* at 79.

38.   *Id.* At the end of the critique of Hippodamus, reference is made to "the old laws and customs," including the following: "Greeks used to go about carrying arms. . . ." *Id.* at 82.

39.   *Id.* at 136.

40.   *Id.* at 142.

41.   *Id.* at 156. *Cf. id.* at 252 and 265.

42.   *Id.* at 158–58. *Compare id.* at 275 ("the separation of the fighting from the agricultural class") *with id.* at 287 ("one must be able to work and to fight").

43.   *Id.* at 177. *Cf. id.* at 276.

44.   *Id.* at 204 and 207.

45.   *Id.* at 218.

46.   *Id.* at 226. *And see id.* at 230.

47.   *Id.* at 248.

48.   *Id.*

49.   *Id.* at 272.

50.   *Id.* at 274.

51.   *E.g., id.* at 120 and 260.

52.   "The citizens had piled their arms when Peisistratus began to make a speech, and left them behind when they went up the hill." Aristotle, ATHENIAN CONSTITUTION 47n.b. (H. Rackham transl. 1935).

53.   *Id.* at 47. Peisistratus's disarming of the people was preceded by his own attempt to monopolize arms. "Peisistratus . . . inflicted a wound on himself with his own hand and then gave out that it had been done by the members of the opposite factions, and so persuaded the people to give him a bodyguard. . . . He was given the retainers called Club-bearers, and with their aid he rose against the people. . . . It is said that when Peisistratus asked for the guard Solon opposed the request . . . [because] Peisistratus was aiming at tyranny. . . ." *Id.* at 43–45.

54.   *Id.* at 57.

55. *Id.* at 103.
56. *Id.* at 105.
57. *Id.* at 107.
58. Aristotle, PARTS OF ANIMALS 373 (A. Peck transl. 1961). *And see* Xenophon, CYROPAEDIA 181 [II. ii. 9] (W. Miller transl. 1914): "And all [creatures] know how to protect themselves, too, against that from which they most need protection. . . ."
59. Dion. Hal., THE ROMAN ANTIQUITIES 119 (E. Cary transl. 1939).
60. *Id.* at 133.
61. I LIVY 148 n.2 (B. Foster transl. 1919).
62. *Id.* at 15. *Cf.* Cicero, *De Legibus* in 16 CICERO 465 (1928).
63. I LIVY 151.
64. Cicero, ON THE COMMONWEALTH 174–75 (Sabine and Smith transl. 1929). *Cf.* 2 Dion. Hal. 315–41 and 4 Dion. Hal. 317–25.
65. Servius Tullius introduced a property qualification for the levy *(dilectus)*, but military service came to be rejected by the citizens. Gaius Marius accepted the poorest, *capite censi*, whose livelihood was the military. "Thus the professional soldier replaced the citizen soldier." Julius Caesar, THE GALLIC WAR 595 (Cambridge, Mass. 1966) (comment of translator H. J. Edwards). "It was the extension of the Republic [through conquest] that professionalized the legionaires and made them the clients of Marius or Sulla, Pompey or Caesar." J. Pocock, *Between Machiavelli and Hume*, in G. Bowersock ed., EDWARD GIBBON AND THE DECLINE AND FALL OF THE ROMAN EMPIRE 108 (Cambridge, Mass. 1977). "The legions of the Republic were composed of citizens, those of the Empire of mercenaries. . . ." *Id.* at 109. Gaius Marius ordered his soldiers to murder candidates he disapproved. 3 James Burgh, POLITICAL DISQUISITIONS 359 (London 1774). *And see* comment of George Mason, *supra* note 5 and accompanying text.
66. Cicero, MURDER TRIALS 279 (M. Grant transl. 1975).
67. *Id.*
68. *Id.* at 280.
69. *Id.* at 281.
70. *Id.* at 285.
71. Cicero, SELECTED POLITICAL SPEECHES 79–81 (M. Grant transl. 1969).
72. *Id.* at 77.
73. *Id.* at 83.
74. *Id.* at 221.
75. *Id.* at 221–22.
76. *Id.* at 222. James Otis relied on this passage in arguing self-defense in a trial held in 1771. 1 John Adams, LEGAL PAPERS 160 n. 16 (1965). Most of the passage is quoted in William Eden, PRINCIPLES OF PENAL LAW 213–14 (London 1772), a work heavily relied on by Thomas Jefferson. Jefferson, THE COMMONPLACE BOOK 324–26 (1926).
77. *Id.* at 234.
78. *Id.*

79. Caesar, THE GALLIC WAR 309 (H. Edwards transl. 1966).

80. *Id.* at 204–5. *And see id.* at 481 ("All men whose age allowed them to bear arms") and 487 ("all who could bear arms").

81. *Id.* at 109.

82. *Id.* at 131.

83. *Id.* at 575.

84. *Id.* at 303.

85. Caesar, THE CIVIL WARS 5 (A. Peskett transl. 1966).

86. *Id.* at 13.

87. *E.g., id.* at 37, 207, and 347.

88. *Id.* at 149.

89. Cicero, DE OFFICIIS 359 (Harvard Loeb Classic ed. 1921).

90. *Id.* at 287 and 299.

91. *Id.* at 191–99.

92. Cicero, PHILIPPICS 237 (W. Ker transl. 1969).

93. *Id.* at 277.

94. *Id.* at 283.

95. *Id.* at 375.

96. *Id.* at 441.

97. *Id.* at 561.

98. *See* Plutarch, *Brutus* in 6 LIVES 189 (1918).

99. II Sat. I, 39 ff., in Horace, SATIRES AND EPISTLES 24–25 (J. Fuchs transl. 1977).

100. Artis Amatoriae III, 492 in 2 OVID 152–53 (J. Mozley transl. 1969). *And see* Halieuticon, in *id.* at 311: "The universe received the law; to all he did give arms, and reminded them of himself." There follows descriptions of natural weapons of living creatures.

101. Coke, THIRD INSTITUTE 162 (1628).

102. Ulpian, Lib. i §27, reaffirmed in 4 PANDECTAE JUSTINIANEAE 77 (Paris 1818–25).

103. Lucretius, OF THE NATURE OF THINGS [DE RERUM NATURA] 245 (W. Leonard transl. 1950). *And see id.* at 232 (natural weapons of animals.)

104. Galen, ON THE USEFULNESS OF THE PARTS OF THE BODY [DE UEU PARTIUM] 68–69 (M. May transl. 1968). *And see id.* at 71:

> Now just as man's body is bare of weapons, so is his soul destitute of skills. Therefore, to compensate for the nakedness of his body, he received hands, and for his soul's lack of skill, reason, by means of which he arms and guards his body in every way and equips his soul with all the arts. For if he has been born with a natural weapon, he would have that one alone for all time, and just so, if he had one natural skill, he would lack the others. But since it was better for him to make use of all weapons and all the arts, he was endowed with no one of them at birth.

105. Cicero, SELECTED POLITICAL SPEECHES at 222.

106. Justinian, INSTITUTES 505–6 (T. Sandars transl. 1970).

107. Justinian, INSTITUTES 205–6 (J. Moyle transl. 1913). Emphasis added.

108. *Id.* at 207.

109. Machiavelli, DISCOURSES 107 (L. Walker transl. 1970).

110. *Id.* at 121–22. *Cf. id.* at 251.

111. *Id.* at 168–69. *See also id.* at 445.

112. *Id.* at 205.

113. *Id.* at 218.

114. *Id.* at 279.

115. *Id.* at 282.

116. *Id.* at 308.

117. *Id.* at 309.

118. *Id.* at 309–10.

119. *Id.* at 330.

120. *Id.* at 353.

121. *Id.* at 373. *And see id.* at 479.

122. *Id.* at 374.

123. *Id.* at 474.

124. *Id.* at 114.

125. *Id.* at 492.

126. Machiavelli, THE ART OF WAR 18 (E. Farneworth transl. 1965).

127. *Id.* at 20. Cf. *id.* at 204.

128. *Id.* at 28–29.

129. *Cf. id.* at xi–xv and 25.

130. *Id.* at 29.

131. *Id.* at 30.

132. *Id.* at 31.

133. *Id.* at 32.

134. *Id.* at 33.

135. *Id.* at 33n.27 (note by Neal Wood). Emphasis added.

136. *Id.* at 36 and 38.

137. *Id.* at 39.

138. *Id.* at 40.

139. *Id.* at 41.

140. *Id.* at 46–47.

141. *Id.* at 47. Cf. *id.* at 73.

142. *Id.* at 59.

143. *Id.* at 60.

144 Machiavelli, THE PRINCE 73 (transl. L. Ricci, 1952).

145. *Id.* at 81.

146. *Id.* at 105.

147. *Id.* at 106.

148. *Id.* 108. This observation holds true from the American Revolution to contemporary revolutions.

149. *Id.* at 50.

150. *Id.* at 72. See further J. Pocock, THE MACHIAVELLIAN MO-MENT *passim* (1975).

151. I. Bodin, THE SIX BOOKES OF COMMONWEALE 38 (R. Knolles transl. 1606). The French edition was actually published at the end of the sixteenth century.

152. *Id.* at 106.

153. *Id.* at 542.

154. *Cf. id.* at 599 ("men that travel unarmed . . . encourage thieves to kill them. . . .").

155. *Id.* at 542.

156. *Id.* at 543.

157. *Id.* at 544. See also *id.* at 251 (overthrow by armed Swiss common-ers of the nobility).

158. *Id.* at 599.

159. *Id.* at 601.

160. *See also id.* at 398.

161. *Id.* at 601–5.

162. *Id.* at 389.

163. *Id.* at 610–11 and 614.

164. *Id.* at 615. Cf. *id.* at 620: "the Latins would rather take arms for their own liberty, than for anothers rule and empire."

165. I Hugonis Grotii, DE JURE BELLI ET PACIS 32–33 (W. Whewell transl. 1853).

166. *Id.* at 199.

167. *Id.* at 37.

168. *Id.* at 35 ("The laws permit taking up arms against armed persons.")

169. *Id.* at 54.

170. R. Filmer, PATRIARCHA *passim* (1680).

171. T. Hobbes, LEVIATHAN 85 (1964).

172. *Id.* at 117.

173. *Id.* at 86.

174. Embodied in "stateless societies are forms of armed aggression . . . but not organized offensive warfare to conquer people or territory." Thus, "conquest warfare . . . is not an inherent, inevitable feature of human social life—too many societies have existed in human history without it. . . . Is mod-ern war inherent and inevitable in the modern form of state organization?" Lesser, *War and the State,* in Fried *et al.,* WAR: THE ANTHROPOLOGY OF ARMED CONFLICT AND AGGRESSION 95 (1967). Cf. Edmund Burke, A VINDICATION OF NATURAL SOCIETY (1756) (government wars were the cause of innumerable deaths in history).

175. Hobbes at 88.

176. *Id.* at 89.

177. *Id.* at 85.

178. *Id.* at 95.

179. *Id.* at 115.

180. *Id.* at 121.

181.   *Id.* at 156. *Cf. id.* at 240: "For he that wants protection, may seek it any where. . . ."

182.   J. Harrington, POLITICAL WORKS 213 (J. Pocock ed. 1977).

183.   *Id.* at 425.

184.   *Id.* at 442–43. John Adams approvingly quoted these words in 1 DEFENSE OF THE CONSTITUTIONS OF GOVERNMENT OF THE UNITED STATES 168 (London 1787).

185.   J. Harrington, *supra* note 182, at 443.

186.   *Id.* at 454. In a tract which analyzed this work of Harrington, Henry Vance defined free citizens in part as those who by their faithfulness to "publick freedome, have deserved to be trusted with the keeping or bearing their own Armes in the publicke defense." *Id.* at 109.

187.   *Id.* at 696.

188.   J. Locke, SECOND TREATISE OF CIVIL GOVERNMENT 14 (Chicago 1955).

189.   *Id.* at 153–54.

190.   *Id.* at 114–15.

191.   *Id.* at 170.

192.   *Id.* at 174.

193.   *Id.* at 173.

194.   *Id.* at 177–93.

195.   *Id.* at 195.

196.   Algernon Sidney, DISCOURSES CONCERNING GOVERN-MENT 134 (1698).

197.   *Id.* at 146.

198.   *Id.* at 157.

199.   *Id.*

200.   *Id.* at 159.

201.   *Id.* at 163.

202.   *Id.* at 165.

203.   *Id.* at 167.

204.   *Id.* at 169.

205.   *Id.* at 170 ("Without arms, no life is secure."). *Cf. id.* at 386–91.

206.   *Id.* at 173.

207.   *Id.* at 175.

208.   *Id.* at 180–81.

209.   *Id.* at 266–67. *Cf. id.* at 282.

210.   *Id.* at 270. *Cf. id.* at 416.

211.   *Id.* at 347.

212.   *Id.* at 380.

213.   *Id.* at 395.

214.   *Id.* at 420. *Cf. id.* at 419 (previously, but presumably no longer, "Kings might safely be trusted . . . to confer the commands of the Militia. . . .").

215.   *Compare id.* at 320 with 406.

216.   *Id.* at 407.

217.   *Id.* at 434.

208	Notes to pages 32–34

218. *Id.* at 436.
219. J. Trenchard and T. Gordon, THE ENGLISH LIBERTARIAN
HERITAGE liv–lv (D. Jacobson ed. 1965).
220. *Id.* at 71–72.
221. *Id.* at 152. *And see id.* at 155 ("In free States, every Man being a
Soldier. . . .").
222. 1 Trenchard and Gordon, CATO's LETTERS 189 (London 1755).
On standing armies, *See* 3 *id.* at 234 ff.
223. Rousseau, THE SOCIAL CONTRACT 84 (anonymous transl. of
1762, 1947).
224. Rousseau, ON THE SOCIAL CONTRACT. . . . AND POLITI-
CAL ECONOMY 229 (J. Masters transl. 1978).
225. B. Bailyn, IDEOLOGICAL ORIGINS OF THE AMERICAN
REVOLUTION 41 (1967).
226. 2 J. Burgh, POLITICAL DISQUISITIONS 345 (London 1774).
227. *Id.* at 390.
228. *Id.* at 341ff.
229. *Id.* at 399.
230. *Id.* at 401.
231. *Id.* at 404.
232. *Id.* at 405.
233. *Id.* at 475–76.
234. A. Smith, II THE WEALTH OF NATIONS 309 (E. Cannan ed.,
n.d.).
235. *Id.* at 293–95.
236. *Id.* at 299.
237. *Id.* at 301.
238. *Id.* at 299.
239. *Id.* at 301.
240. *Id.* at 300.
241. *Id.* at 307.
242. *Id.* at 304 and 311. For discourses written at the end of the sixteenth
century on the military and political effects of the new firearms technology,
see J. Smyth and H. Barwick, BOW VERSUS GUN, ed. E. Heath (Yorkshire,
1973).
243. *Id.* at 304. On the discussion of the militia question by classical political economists, see further D. Winch, ADAM SMITH'S POLITICS 103 ff.
(1978); J. Western, THE ENGLISH MILITIA IN THE EIGHTEENTH
CENTURY (1965); E. Silberner, THE PROBLEM OF WAR IN THE
19TH CENTURY ECONOMIC THOUGHT (1946); and G. Neimanis,
MILITIA VS. STANDING ARMY IN THE HISTORY OF ECONOMIC
THOUGHT FROM ADAM SMITH TO FRIEDRICH ENGELS (Con-
ference of the History of Economic Society, University of Chicago, 21–23
May 1976) (refers to Jean-Bastiste Say, Antoine-Elisee Cherbuliez, and
Michael Chevalier).

244.   2 Montesquieu, THE SPIRIT OF THE LAWS 64 (T. Nugent transl. 1899).

245.   *Id.* at 59.

246.   *Id.* at 60.

247.   *Id.* at 79–80. Despite Paraguay's reputation as a commandist society, Montesquieu noted the following interconnected facts: "The Indians of Paraguay do not depend on any particular lord; they pay only a fifth of the taxes, and are allowed the use of firearms to defend themselves." 1 *id.* at 36.

248.   Beccaria, ON CRIMES AND PUNISHMENTS 87–88 (H. Paolucci transl. 1963). Thomas Jefferson copied this passage in full in his COMMON-PLACE BOOK 314 (G. Chinard ed. 1926), which was "the source book and repertory of Jefferson's ideas on government." *Id.* at 4. *And see* Wm. Wollaston, THE RELIGION OF NATURE 132 (1724): "Great part of the happiness of mankind depends upon those *means,* by which the innocent may be saved from their cruel invaders: among which the opportunities they have of *defending* themselves may be reckoned the chief."

249.   Beccaria's important influence on the Second and Eighth Amendments to the U.S. Constitution has been by and large ignored. *See* A. Caso, AMERICA'S ITALIAN FOUNDING FATHERS (1975).

Chapter 2
The Common Law of England

1.   Laws of Alfred §7 in I ENGLISH HISTORICAL DOCUMENTS c. 500–1042 at 375 (D. Douglas gen. ed. 1968).

2.   *Id.* §§19–19.2 at 376.

3.   *Id.* §19.3 at 376.

4.   *Id.* §38.1 at 379.

5.   Laws of Cnut §29.1, *Id.* at 422.

6.   *Id.* §60 at 427.

7.   *Id.* §60 at 430.

8.   I W. Stubbs, THE CONSTITUTIONAL HISTORY OF ENGLAND 470–71 (6th ed. 1873).

9.   II ENGLISH HISTORICAL DOCUMENTS, *supra* note 1, at 416.

10.   I W. Stubbs, *supra* note 8, at 633.

11.   *Id.* at 634.

12.   II ENGLISH HISTORICAL DOCUMENTS, *supra* note 9, at 417.

13.   *Id.* at 417.

14.   S. Grayzel, HISTORY OF THE JEWS 307 (New Am. Library 2d ed. 1968).

15.   S. Thorne *et al.,* THE GREAT CHARTER 137–41 (1965).

16.   *Id.* at 124 ff.

17.   I W. Stubbs, *supra* note 8, at 634.

18. II W. Stubbs, THE CONSTITUTIONAL HISTORY OF EN-GLAND 285 and 294 (4th ed. 1896).

19. Statute of Winchester, 13 Edw. I, c. 6 (1285). Brackets in original.

20. II W. Stubbs, *supra* note 18, at 294.

21. *Id.* at 290–91.

22. *Cf.* R. Held, THE AGE OF FIREARMS 61 (1978): "For the most part, guns were used in early Tudor England by the poorer classes of rustics who depended on wild fowl and venison" for sustenance. The "lower class fowlers and near paupers" were the "principal shooters" until around 1670. *Id.* at 92.

23. *Cf.* E. Heath, Introduction to J. Smyth and H. Barwick, BOW VERSUS GUN x–xi (1973).

24. I W. Holdsworth, A HISTORY OF ENGLISH LAW 107–8; *id.* at IV, 505–6.

25. An Acte Agaynst Unlawfull Hunting in Forest and Park, I Hen. VII c. 7 (1485).

26. D Balistis no Exercitand, 19 Hen. VII c. 4 (1503).

27. *Id.*

28. An Act Concerning Shooting in Longe Bowes, 3 Hen. VIII c. 3 (1511).

29. An Act Concerning Shooting in Crosbowes, 3 Hen. VIII c. 13 (1511).

30. Acte for Maytenanue of Archers, 6 Hen. VIII c. 2 (1514).

31. Acte Avoiding Shoting in Crosbowes, 6 Hen. VIII c. 13 (1514).

32. Thacte for Shotyng in Crosbowes and Handgonnes, 14 and 15 Hen. VIII c. 7 (1523).

33. An Acte for Shotyng in Crosbowes and Handgonnes, 25 Hen. VIII c. 17 (1533).

34. An Acte Concerninge Crosbowes and Handguns, 33 Hen. VIII ch. 6 (1541).

35. *Id.*.

36. *Cf.* L. Schwoerer, "NO STANDING ARMIES!" 83 (1974).

37. X W. Holdsworth, A HISTORY OF ENGLISH LAW 378 (7th ed. 1956).

38. 13 and 14 Car. II c.3 (1662).

39. An Act for the Better Preservation of the Game, 22 Car. II c. 25, §3 (1670).

40. *Id.* at §§5–7. This act was resorted to in order to justify breaking and entering houses to search for arms even after the Glorious Revolution. *See* Bowkley v. Williams, 2 Lutw. 1502, 124 Eng. Rep.828 (Common Pleas 1700); Lutwyche, REPORTS AND ENTRIES 484 (W. Nelson transl. 1718).

41. 2 Blackstone, COMMENTARIES *412.

42. See J. Malcom, *The Right of the People to Keep and Bear Arms: The Common Law Tradition*, 10 HASTINGS CONST. L.Q. 285 (1983). Judicial opinions on the acts of Henry VIII and Charles II are summarized in W. Nelson, THE LAWS CONCERNING GAME 137–47 (6th ed. 1762).

43.   2 MISCELLANEOUS STATE PAPERS FROM 1501–1726 407 (Phillip, Earl of Hardwicke compl. 1778).

44.   *Id.* at 410.

45.   *Id.* at 415.

46.   *Id.* at 416.

47.   *Id.* at 416.

48.   *Id.* at 417.

49.   *Id.* at 418..

50.   JOURNALS OF THE HOUSE OF COMMONS FROM DEC. THE 26TH 1688, to OCT. THE 26TH 1693 15, 22 (1742).

51.   *Id.* at 17.

52.   *Id.* at 21.

53.   *Id.* at 22.

54.   *Id.* at 25.

55.   *Id.*

56.   Referring to the words "suitable to their condition and such as are allowed by law," St. George Tucker distinguished the Second Amendment of the U.S. Constitution, whereby the right of the people to keep arms exists "without any qualification as to their condition or degree, as in the case of the British government." 1 Blackstone, COMMENTARIES *144 n.40, ed. St. Geo. Tucker (1st ed., 1803).

57.   An Act Declaring the Rights and Liberties of the Subject, 1 W. & M., Sess. 2, c.2, (1689).

58.   *Id.*

59.   I Blackstone *144.

60.   Parliament sought to break the executive's monopoly of arms by legislating "That no Papist or reputed Papist, so refusing [to take an oath] or making Default, as aforesaid, shall or may have or keep in his House, or elsewhere . . . any Arms, Weapons, Gunpowder, or Ammunition (other than such necessary Weapons, as shall be allowed to him by Order of the Justices of the Peace . . . for the Defense of his House or Person). . . ." An Act for the Better Securing the Government by Disarming Papists and Reputed Papists, 1 W.&M., Sess. 1, c.15, §4 (1689). While it placed Catholics into a position of unwarranted surveillance and could have introduced a new form of religious persecution, the act merely sought disbandment of the Catholic-dominated standing army of James II. It recognized the right even of Catholics who refused to take the oath to have and keep weapons for defense of the person and the home.

61.   W. Holdsworth, A HISTORY OF ENGLISH LAW 241 (7th ed. 1956).

62.   *Id.*

63.   G. Jellinek, THE DECLARATION OF THE RIGHTS OF MAN AND OF CITIZENS 49 (M. Farrand transl. 1901) (Emphasis aded). *And see id.* at 55–56.

64. L. Schwoerer, "NO STANDING ARMIES!" 162 ff. (1974).

65. J. Trenchard, AN ARGUMENT SHOWING THAT A STAND-
ING ARMY IS INCONSISTENT WITH A FREE GOVERNMENT (1697),
in 2 A COLLECTION OF STATE TRACTS PUBLISHED ON THE
OCCASION OF THE LATE REVOLUTION IN 1688 572 (London 1705).

66. *Id.* at 573–74.

67. A. Fletcher, POLITICAL WORKS 6 (1749).

68. *Id.* at 7. In his edition of Fletcher's *Works*, Robert Watson commented on this quotation by asking

> whether the inhabitants of this country ought to be classed amongst freemen or
> slaves.
>   Upon enquiry it will be found, that not one, out of ten, except such as are in
> the pay of government, is acquainted with the use of arms. . . . But why were
> the people disarmed and classed amongst slaves? . . . Is it true, that oppressive
> taxes have been extorted from the people, . . . for supporting the minister in
> disarming them; and carrying on cruel and unnecessary wars? If this really be our
> situation, surely the people ought to form themselves into associations, and learn
> the use of arms. In the mean time, every individual should procure arms for
> himself. . . ." R. Watson, *Notes*, in A. Fletcher, POLITICAL WORKS 227 (Lon-
> don 1798).

Cf. Opinion of Recorder of London (1780) (right individually and collectively
to possess and exercise in arms), in D. Caplan, *The Right of the Individual to
Bear Arms* 1982 (no. 4), DETROIT COLL. OF L. REV. 789, 800–3 (1982).

69. *Supra* note 67, at 35.

70. *Id.* at 27–28.

71. *Id.* at 29. Of Fletcher's use of the term "well-regulated militias,"
Robert Watson commented that "the American revolution furnished a memo-
rable proof of the superior bravery of militias, when general Burgoyne, with
the flower of the british troops, were compelled to lay down their arms to an
association of husbandmen. . . ." Watson, *supra* note 68, at 231.

72. *Supra* note 67, at 221. Fletcher proposed that any successor to the
crown agree, *inter alia*, "That all the sensible men of the nation, betwixt sixty
and sixteen, be, with all diligence possible, armed with bayonets, and firelocks all of a caliber, and continue always provided in such arms, with ammunition suitable." *Id.* at 205.

73. THE CLAIMS OF THE PEOPLE OF ENGLAND (1701), in 3 A
COLLECTION OF STATE TRACTS PUBLISHED ON THE OCCA-
SION OF THE LATE REVOLUTION IN 1688 8 (1705).

74. *Id.* at 10.

75. *Id.* at 12.

76. *Id.*.

77. *Id.* at 15.

78. *Rex* v. *Dewhurst*, 1 State Trials, New Series 529 (1820).

79. *Id.* at 601–2.

80. Statute of Northampton, 2 Edw. III c. 3 (1328).

81. *Id. Cf.* I Hawkins, A TREATISE OF THE PLEAS OF THE CROWN ch. 28, §10 (8th ed. 1824).

82. Coke, THIRD INSTITUTE 160*:*

83. *Id.* at 161–2.

84. By contrast, riding armed with others to commit murder, robbery, or kidnapping was a felony since ancient times. In the words of Henry Care, ENGLISH LIBERTIES 42 (1680): "And if percase any man of this Realm, Ride Armed covertly or secret with Men of Arms against any other to Slay him, or Rob him, or Take him, or Retain him till he hath made Fine and Ransom for to have his deliverance, it . . . shall be judged Felony or trespass, according to the Laws of the Land of old time used. . . ."

85. *Rex* v. *Knight,* 3 Mod. 117, 87 Eng. Rep. 75, 76 (K. B. 1686).

86. *Id.,* Comb. 38, 90 Eng. Rep. 330.

87. *Id.,* 3 Mod. 118, 87 Eng. Rep. 76. Emphasis added.

88. *Id.,* Comb. 38–39, 90 Eng. Rep. 330. The Americans incorporated the same elements in their reenactments of the Statute of Northampton. Virginia's Act Forbidding and Punishing Affrays (1786) recited that no man shall "go nor ride armed . . . in terror of the country. . . ." 2 T. Jefferson, PAPERS 519 (1951). In Massachusetts, the Act of 20 Jan. 1795 punished "such as ride or go armed offensively, to the fear or terror of the good citizens of this Commonwealth. . . ." 2 PERPETUAL LAWS OF THE COMMON-WEALTH OF MASSACHUSETTS 259 (1801).

89. I Hawkins, *supra* note 81, ch. 28, §9. *Cf. Chume* v *Piott,* 2 Bulst. 328, 329, 80 Eng. Rep. 1161, 1162 (K.B. 1616).

90. *Id.* at ch. 10, §14.

91. An Act Declaring the Rights and Liberties of the Subject, 1 W.&M., Sess. 2, c. 2 (1689). *See Rex* v. *Dewhurst,* 1 State Trials, New Series 529, 601–2 (1820).

92. *Rex* v. *Knight,* Comb. 38–39, 90 Eng. Rep. 330 (K. B. 1686); I Hawkins, *supra* note 89.

93. *Rex* v. *Smith,* 2 Ir. R. 190, 204 (K. B. 1914).

94. *Rex* v. *Meade,* 19 L. Times Repts. 540, 541 (1903).

95. 1 S. Maccoby, ENGLISH RADICALISM 493–95 (1955). XI W. Holdsworth, A HISTORY OF ENGLISH LAW 543–45, XIII at 267, and XVI at 92 (7th ed. 1956).

96. An Act for the Better Preservation of the Game, 6 Ann. c. 16 [5 and 6 Ann. c. 14 in common printed editions] (1706).

97. *Bluet* v. *Filer,* 1 Stra. 496, 93 Eng. Rep. 657 (K. B. 1722), relying on *Rex* v. *King,* East., Pas., 1 Sess. Ca. 93 (1717).

98. *Bluet* v. *Needs,* 2 Comyns. 522, 525, 92 Eng. Rep. 1189, 1190 (K. B. 1736).

99. *Rex* v. *Gardner,* 7 Mod. 279, 87 Eng. Rep. 1240 (K. B. 1739).

100. *Id.* at 279, 87 Eng. Rep. at 1241.

101. *Id.*

102. *Id.* at 280, 87 Eng. Rep. at 1241.

103. *Id.*

104. *Id.* at 2 Stra. 1098, 93 Eng. Rep. at 1056.

105. *Id.* at Andrews 255, 256–57, 95 Eng. Rep. at 386, 387, reprinted in II J. Chitty, A TREATISE ON THE GAME LAWS 1068, 1070 (1812).

106. *Supra* note 96.

107. An Act for the Better Preservation of the Game, 22 Car. II c. 25 (1670).

108. *Rex* v. *Gardner, supra* note 105, Andrews at 257, 95 Eng. Rep. at 388, II Chitty at 1071. Emphasis added.

109. *Malloch* v. *Eastly,* 7 Mod. 482, 87 Eng. Rep. 1370, II Chitty at 1093, 1103 (K. B. 1744).

110. *Wingfield* v. *Stratford,* 1 Wils. K. B. 315, 95 Eng. Rep. 637 (K. B. 1752).

111. *Id.*

112. *Id.*, Sayer 15, 16, 96 Eng. Rep. at 787 (K. B. 1752).

113. *Id.* at 17, 96 Eng. Rep. at 788. *And see Avery* v. *Hoole,* 2 Cowp. 825, 98 Eng. Rep. 1383 (K. B. 1778) (conviction affirmed).

114. *Rex* v. *Hartley,* Cald. 175, II Chitty, *supra* note 105, at 1178, 1183 (1782).

115. *Id.*, II Chitty at 1183.

116. *Rex* v. *Thompson,* 2 T. R. 18, 100 Eng. Rep. 10 (K. B. 1787).

117. *Id.* at 18, 100 Eng. Rep. at 11. *Cf.* the argument of defense counsel: "The act of keeping a gun is equivocal. . . ." *Id.* at 19, 100 Eng. Rep. at 11.

118. *Id.* at 21, 100 Eng. Rep. at 12. *See* I Chitty, *supra* note 105, at 83–84.

119. II Blackstone, COMMENTARIES *412.

120. I Blackstone, COMMENTARIES *144, n. 41 (St. Geo. Tucker ed. 1803).

121. *Id.* at *140–41.

122. *Id.* at *143–44.

123. R. Wilkinson-Latham, SWORDS 72–73 (New York, 1978) (citing the Disarming Act following the Scottish Rebellion of 1715 and the Act for the Abolition and Proscription of the Highland Dress of 1746, in response to the Rebellion of 1745); Kennett and Anderson, THE GUN IN AMERICA 20–22 (Westport, Conn., 1975) (citing the Act for the Better Security of the Government, by Disarming the Papists), 7 W. & M., c. 5 (Ireland 1695) and a supplementary act, 13 Geo. II, c. 6 (Ireland 1739); also citing the anti-Scottish acts, I Geo. I, c. 5 (1714), I Geo. I, c. 54 (1715), and 19 Geo. II, c. 39 (1746)).

Chapter 3
The American Revolution and the Second Amendment

1. An Act for the Safeguard and Defence of the Country Against the Indians, 28 Car. II, II Hening, STATUTES AT LARGE (VA.) 332 (1675–76).

2. *Id.* at 333.

3. *Id.* at 336.

4. *Id.* at 337.

5. *Id.* at 336.

6. H. Miller, THE CASE FOR LIBERTY 76 (1965).

7. J. Shy, A PEOPLE NUMEROUS AND ARMED xii (1976).

8. II Hening, STATUTES AT LARGE (VA.) 342 (note by Hening).

9. An Act for Carrying on a Warre Against the Barbarous Indians, Bacon's Laws, II Hening, STATUTES AT LARGE (VA.) 342 (1676).

10. An Act for the Releife of Such Loyall Persons as have Suffered Losse by the Late Rebells, 29 Car. II, II Hening, STATUTES AT LARGE 385 (1676–77).

11. *Id.* at 386.

12. BACON'S REBELLION 340 (J. Neville compl., Jamestown Foundation, n.d.). *And see id.* at 360, 363, and 366.

13. H. Miller, *supra* note 6, at 71.

14. *Id.* at 100.

15. O. Dickerson ed., BOSTON UNDER MILITARY RULE 61 (1936). On the *Journal's* wide circulation, *see id.* at ix.

16. *Id.* at 79.

17. I B. Bailyn, PAMPHLETS OF THE AMERICAN REVOLUTION 41–42 and 71–75 (1965).

18. *Rex* vs. *Wemms* (1770), III LEGAL PAPERS OF JOHN ADAMS 242 (1965).

19. See Ch. 1, n. 248 of this study.

20. III LEGAL PAPERS OF JOHN ADAMS 248. Hawkins' citation may be found in Ch. 2, n. 90 of this study.

21. *Rex* v. *Preston* (1770), III *id.* at 94. Representative cases are *Rex* vs. *Corbet* (1769), II *id.* at 326–33; *Rex* v. *Richardson* (1770), II *id.* at 411–15; and *Rex* v. *Wemms* (1770), III *id.* at 244–49.

22. II S. Adams, WRITINGS 119 (1906).

23. R. Frothingham, HISTORY OF THE SIEGE OF BOSTON 95 (6th ed. 1903). *And see* J. Alden, GENERAL GAGE IN AMERICA 255 (1948).

24. W. Moore, WEAPONS OF THE AMERICAN REVOLUTION viii (1967). *See* Allason Letter Book 1757–1770, f. 134, Virginia State Library: "we find it necessary to carry with us some defensive weapons . . . a pair of pistols. . . . let them be small, for the conveniency of carrying in a side pockett. . . ." According to G. Neumann, HISTORY OF WEAPONS OF THE AMERICAN REVOLUTION 150 (1967): "Among eighteenth-century civilians who traveled or lived in large cities, pistols were common weapons. Usually they were made to fit into pockets. . . ." *Id.* at 151.

25. Williamsburg Virginia Gazette, 2 July 1774, at 1, col. 3.

26. Documents Illustrative of the Formation of the Union of the American States, H. R. Doc. No. 398, 69th Cong., lst Sess. 14–15 (1927).

27. I Mason, PAPERS 210–11 (1970). On Virginia's independent voluntary companies, *see* E. Sanchez-Saavedra, A GUIDE TO VIRGINIA MILI-

TARY ORGANIZATIONS IN THE AMERICAN REVOLUTION 7 ff. (1978).

28.   Williamsburg Virginia Gazette, 27 Oct. 1774, at 2, col. 2.
29.   *Id.*, 1 Dec. 1774, at 2, col. 3.
30.   III S. Adams, WRITINGS 162–63, 172.
31.   J. Galvin, THE MINUTE MEN 102 (1967). Indeed, that summer Gage had written Dartmouth: "In Worcester they keep no terms; openly threatening resistance by arms; have been purchasing arms; preparing them; casting balls; and providing powder. . . ." *Id.* at 55.
32.   *Id.* at 65 (John Anderson's words). See also Howard Hamilton, *Culpeper Minute Men*, 75 SAR MAG. 8–9 (1981).
33.   Letter of 14 Dec. 1774, in Williamsburg Virginia Gazette, 8 June 1775, at 1, col. 2.
34.   I P. Force, AMERICAN ARCHIVES 1022 (1837–53).
35.   *Id.* at 1032.
36.   *Id.* at 1145; I Mason, PAPERS at 212. Emphasis added.
37.   I Mason, PAPERS at 215.
38.   *Id.* at 216.
39.   *Id.* at 229.
40.   *Id.* at 230.
41.   *Id.* at 229–30. *And see* "Shippen," Williamsburg Virginia Gazette, 25 Aug. 1774, at 2, col. 1: "Whilst Rome fought only against her *real enemies*, and from the just principles of self-defense, she raised herself to the highest pitch of human greatness; but when she carried her arms to distant nations, that never had molested her . . . she laid the foundation for her own destruction."
42.   III S. Adams, WRITINGS 213.
43.   *Id.* at 230.
44.   *Id.* at 251.
45.   R. Meade, PATRICK HENRY 28 (1969).
46.   *Id.* at 34. Emphasis added.
47.   *Id.* at 50–51.
48.   R. Meade, PATRICK HENRY at 53.
49.   J. Matthews, RICHARD HENRY LEE 30 (1978).
50.   I WRITINGS OF THOMAS PAINE 56 (Conway ed. 1894).
51.   *E.g.*, see 2 L. Cappon and S. Duff, VIRGINIA GAZETTE INDEX 1736–1780 (1950), which contains scores of references to such items as: "Arms, export from Great Britian prohibited . . . seized by Americans . . . seized by British . . . seizure ordered in American colonies. . . ." *Id.* at 30–31. "Pistols, captured by Americans . . . export . . . to British colonies, N. Am., forbidden . . . for sale. . . ." "Pistols, pocket, for sale. . . ." *Id.* at 884.
52.   Williamsburg Virginia Gazette, 14 Sept. 1776, at 1, cols. 1–2.
53.   *Id.*, 23 Oct. 1778, at 2, col. 1.
54.   *E.g., id.*, 1 May 1778, at 3, col. 1 ("a genteel pair of pocket pistols"); 10 July 1778, at 3, col. 3 ("three pair of four pound guns and carriages, and every other implement complete, 150 pair of pistols" for sale); 12 Feb. 1780, at 3, col. 2 ("Blunderbusses, pistols with swivels, muskets, cutlasses").

55. *E.g.,* B. Davis, THE COWPENS—GUILFORD COURTHOUSE CAMPAIGN 39 (1962): "When another Briton thrust at Washington, he was shot down with a pistol by a fourteen-year old Virginia buglar."

56. J. Shy, A PEOPLE NUMEROUS AND ARMED (1976); W. Marina, *Militia, Standing Armies, and the Second Amendment,* 2 LAW AND LIBERTY 1,4 (1976); and Marina, *Revolution and Social Change,* 1 LITERATURE OF LIBERTY 5, 21–27 (Ap./June 1978).

57. H. Lee, MEMOIRS OF THE WAR 90 (1869).

58. *Id.* at 163, 193.

59. *Id.* at 110. *Cf.* 167.

60. *Id.* at 187.

61. *Id.*

62. *Id.* at 260.

63. *Id.* at 85.

64. *Id.* at 168.

65. *Id.* at 173 and 317. *Cf.* Lee's praise of Algernon Sidney, *id.* at 117.

66. Virginia Declaration of Rights, XIII (1776).

67. Proposed Virginia Constitution (1776), I T. Jefferson, PAPERS 344 (J. Boyd ed. 1950).

68. Penn. Declaration of Rights, XIII (1776). While no objection to this provision can be found, a Resolution published in the Pennsylvania Evening Post (Philadelphia), 22 Oct. 1776, at 527, col. 1 deemed constitutional protection for hunting inappropriate. *Remarks on the Resolves, id.,* 5 Nov. at 554, cols. 1–2 replied that under English game laws, *"guns* have been seized. And though this was not legal, as guns are not engines appropriated to kill game," false testimony of poaching led to convictions. "Thus . . . are . . . the freeholders of moderate estates deprived of a natural right. Nor is this all; the body of the people kept from the use of guns are utterly ignorant of the arms of modern war, and the kingdom effectually disarmed, except of the standing force. . . ."

69. N. C. Declaration of Rights, XVII (1776).

70. Vt. Declaration of Rights, XV (1777).

71. Massachusetts Declaration of Rights, XVII (1780).

72. O. & M. Handlin eds., THE POPULAR SOURCES OF POLITICAL AUTHORITY: DOCUMENTS ON THE MASSACHUSETTS CONSTITUTION OF 1780 574 (1966).

73. *Id.* at 624. *And see id.* at 856.

74. *Infra,* this chapter, n. 167.

75. 3 J. Adams, A DEFENCE OF THE CONSTITUTIONS OF GOVERNMENT OF THE UNITED STATES OF AMERICA 475 (1787–88). The language of the Act of 20 Feb. 1787 further clarifies the meaning of the Massachusetts Declaration: "Whereas in a free government, where the people have a right to bear arms for the common defense . . . it is necessary for the safety of the State that the virtuous citizens thereof should hold themselves in readiness. . . ." 1 PERPETUAL LAWS OF THE COMMONWEALTH OF MASSACHUSETTS 366 (1801). Decades later, John Adams

continued to espouse a universal over a select militia, and endorsed a work
containing these words: "Here, every house is a castle. . . . Arms are in every
hand. . . ." W. Sumner, AN INQUIRY INTO THE IMPORTANCE OF
THE MILITIA TO A FREE COMMONWEALTH IN A LETTER . . .
TO JOHN ADAMS . . . WITH HIS ANSWER 21, 69–70 (Boston 1823).

    76.   Del. Declaration of Rights, XVIII (1776); Md. Declaration of Rights,
XXV (1776).

    77.   N. H. Bill of Rights, XXIV (1784).

    78.   Following B. Poore compl., THE FEDERAL AND STATE CON-
STITUTIONS (1877), Connecticut adopted no constitution at all until 1818,
I, §17 of which declared: "Every citizen has a right to bear arms in defense of
himself and the State." Rhode Island adopted its first constitution in 1842, I,
§22 of which declared: "The right of the people to keep and bear arms shall
not be infringed." The constitutions of Georgia (1777), New Jersey (1776),
New York (1777), and South Carolina (1776, 1778) contained no bills of rights.

    79.   New York and Rhode Island. See *infra*, n. 140–1 of this chapter. None
of the other four states suggested that a bill of rights be adopted.

    80.   Relevant state constitutional provisions at this time were as follows:
"That the people have a right to bear arms for the defence of themselves and
the state. . . ." Pennsylvania Declaration of Rights, XIII (1776); Vermont
Declaration of Rights, XV (1777), XVIII (1786). "That the people have a
right to bear arms, for the defence of the State. . . ." North Carolina Declaration of Rights, XVIII (1776). "The people have a right to keep and bear arms
for the common defence." Massachusetts Declaration of Rights, XVII (1780).
The following provision was adopted during the same period in which the
Bill of Rights to the U.S. Constitution was being ratified: "That the right of
the citizens to bear arms in defense of themselves and the State shall not be
questioned." Pennsylvania Declaration of Rights, XXI (1790); Kentucky Declaration of Rights, XII (1792).

    81.   3 J. Adams, A DEFENSE OF THE CONSTITUTIONS OF GOV-
ERNMENT OF THE UNITED STATES OF AMERICA 471–72 (1787–
88). Newspaper editorialists of the time also alluded to Rome's disarming of
conquered peoples. The *Massachusetts Centinel*, 11 April 1787 recalled "the
old Roman Senator, who after his country subdued the commonwealth of
Carthage, had made them deliver up . . . their arms . . . and rendered them
unable to protect themselves. . . ." 13 DOCUMENTARY HISTORY OF
THE RATIFICATION OF THE CONSTITUTION 79 (Kaminski and Saladino eds. 1981) (hereafter cited "DOCU. HY.").

    82.   J. Adams, *supra* note 81, at 474.

    83.   *Id.* at 475.

    84.   Letter to Wm. S. Smith, 1787, in Jefferson, ON DEMOCRACY 20
(S. Padover ed. 1939). In his influential Letter of 1788, Luther Martin stated:
"By the principles of the American revolution arbitrary power may, and ought
to be, resisted even by arms, if necessary." 1 J. Elliot, DEBATES IN THE
SEVERAL STATE CONVENTIONS 382 (2d ed. 1836). *And see New York
Journal*, 14 Aug. 1788, at 2, col. 4 (the people will resist arbitrary power). A

writer in the *Pennsylvania Gazette*, 23 Ap. 1788, in 2 DOCU. HY. (Mfm. Supp.) at 2483 (Jensen ed. 1976) critized "the loyalists in the beginning of the late war, who objected to *associating, arming* and *fighting*, in defense of our liberties, because these measures were not *constitutional.* A free people should always be left . . . with every possible power to promote their own happiness."

85.   Madison, Hamilton, and Jay, THE FEDERALIST PAPERS 180 (Arlington House ed. n.d.).

86.   *Id.* at 184–85.

87.   *Id.* at 294.

88.   *Id.* at 298.

89.   *Id.* at 299.

90.   *Id.* at 300. On arms regulation by the French monarchy to prevent democracy, see Kennett and Anderson, THE GUN IN AMERICA 5–16 (1975).

91.   "The state declarations of rights are not repealed by this Constitution, and, being in force, are sufficient," argued Roger Sherman in the federal convention. 5 J. Elliot, DEBATES 538 (1845). Hamilton averred in *The Federalist* No. 84 that a bill of rights "would contain various exceptions to powers which are not granted; and, on this very account, would afford a colorable pretext to claim more than were granted." THE FEDERALIST at 513. Hamilton's fear appears vindicated in view of the current restrictive interpretation that the Bill of Rights recognizes no individual right to bear arms.

92.   N. Webster, *An Examination into the Leading Principles of the Federal Constitution* (1787), in PAMPHLETS ON THE CONSTITUTION OF THE UNITED STATES 56 (P. Ford ed. 1888). *And see id.* at 48 & 51–52.

Decades later, in his famous dictionary, Webster would clarify the nature of the right to bear arms by defining "bear" as follows: "3. To wear; as, to *bear* a sword . . .; to *bear* arms in a coat." N. Webster, AN AMERICAN DICTIONARY OF THE ENGLISH LANGUAGE (New York 1828). Webster mentions no militia context in his definition, and his second example clearly means that carrying a pistol in a coat was "bearing arms."

93.   Coxe, "An American Citizen IV" (21 Oct. 1787), in 13 DOCU. HY. 433.

94.   *Id.* at 435, also in Coxe, *Examination of the Constitution* (1788), in PAMPHLETS ON THE CONSTITUTION OF THE UNITED STATES at 151.

95.   *Pennsylvania Gazette*, 20 Feb. 1788, 2 DOCU. HY. (Mfm. Supp.) at 1778–1780. *And see* Foreign Spectator, *Independent Gazetteer*, 21 Sept. 1787: "even the power of a veteran army could not subdue a partiotic militia ten times its number. . . ." 2 DOCU. HY. (Mfm. Supp.) at 384. A Supplement to the Essay on Federal Sentiments, *Independent Gazetteer*, 23 Oct. 1787: "The whole personal influence of the Congress, and their parricide army could never prevail over a hundred thousand men armed and disciplined, owners of the country. . . ." 2 DOCU. HY. (Mfm. Supp.) at 801.

Anti-Federalists agreed with this thesis. Thus, the *Freeman's Journal*, Feb.

27, 1788, stated that "it would require more troops than even the empress of Russia can command, to chain down the enlightened freeman. . . ." 2 DOCU. HY. (Mfm. Supp.) at 1829. And Detector, *Independent Gazetteer*, 11 Feb. 1788, gave the reason: "the sons of freedom . . . may know the despots have not altogether monopolized these *necessary articles* [powder and lead]." 2 DOCU. HY. (Mfm. Supp.) at 1695.

96.   *Pennsylvania Gazette*, 7 May 1788, 2 DOCU. HY. (Mfm. Supp.) at 2579.

97.   5 Elliot, DEBATES at 444.

98.   THE ANTIFEDERALIST PAPERS 75 (M. Borden ed. 1965).

99.   *Id.*

100.   *Id.* at 38.

101.   *Id.* at 19.

102.   E. Gerry, *Observations on the New Constitution* (1788), in PAMPHLETS ON THE CONSTITUTION OF THE UNITED STATES at 10.

103.   *Id.* at 11.

104.   *Pennsylvania Herald*, 17 Oct. 1787, 2 DOCU. HY. 196.

105.   *Id.* at 197. *And see* Z, *Freeman's Journal*, 5 Mr. 1788: "the people themselves freed America from foreign tyranny." 2 DOCU. HY (Mfm. Supp.) at 1925.

106.   R. Lee, *Letters of a Federal Farmer* (1787–88), in PAMPHLETS ON THE CONSTITUTION OF THE UNITED STATES 305–6.

107.   R. Lee, ADDITIONAL LETTERS FROM THE FEDERAL FARMER 53 (1788).

108.   *Id.* at 169.

109.   *Id.* at 170. Emphasis added.

110.   "A Slave," 6 Oct. 1787, 13 DOCU. HY. at 345. Aristocrotis, *The Government of Nature Delineated* 15–17 (1788) feared that the active militia would "quell insurrections that may arise in any parts of the empire on account of pretensions to support liberty, redress grievances, and the like." 2 DOCU. HY. (Mfm. Supp.) at 2524. "The second class or inactive militia, comprehends all the rest of the peasants; viz., the farmers, mechanics, labourers, & c. which good policy will prompt government to disarm. It would be dangerous to trust such a rabble as this with arms in their hands." *Id.* at 2526.

111.   Charleston *State Gazette*, 8 Sept. 1788. *And see id.*, 7 Aug 1788, at 3, col. 1–2 (militia as citizenry); Letter from New York, 31 Oct. 1787, 3 DOCU. HY. 390 (Jensen ed. 1978): "The militia [Art. I, §8, cl. 15] comprehends all the male inhabitants from sixteen to sixty years of age. . . . The Constitution . . . puts the utmost degree of confidence in the people. . . ."

112.   "On Tyranny, Anarchy, and Free Governments," *New York Morning Post*, 21 Aug. 1788, at 2, col. 2.

113.   "A Friend to Equal Liberty," Philadelphia *Independent Gazetteer*, 28 March 1788. The *Federal Gazette*, 12 March 1789, at 2, col. 3 opined: "if it is done, it is to be hoped the friends of *turtle* and *roast beef* will stand upon a clause in the bill of rights, to secure the perpetual enjoyment of those two excellent dishes."

114. *Independent Gazetter,* 30 April 1788. *And see* Thomas B. Wait to
George Thatcher, 15 Aug. 1788, Thatcher Papers, Vol. II, Boston Public
Library: "The same instrument that conveys the weapon, should refine the
shield—should contain not only the powers of the rulers, but also the defence
of the people." "Brutus" wrote in the *New York Journal,* 1 Nov. 1787: "Some
[natural rights] are of such a nature that they cannot be surrendered. Of this
kind are the rights of . . . defending life. . . ." 13 DOCU. HY. at 525.

115. As expressed in the Boston *Independent Chronicle,* 25 Oct. 1787, in a
"ship's news" satire on demands for a bill of rights: "[I]t was absolutely necessary to carry arms for fear of pirates, & c. and . . . their arms were all stamped
with peace, that they were never to be used but in case of hostile attack, that
it was in the law of nature to every man to defend himself, and unlawful for
any man to deprive him of those weapons of self defence." 13 DOCU. HY.
at 523.

116. 2 DOCU. HY. at 509.

117. Not only was the right to keep and bear private arms universally
acknowledged, but in Pennsylvania the right of individuals to keep *public*
arms was asserted. "Jacob Trusty" queried the editor of the *Freeman's Journal,*
19 Dec. 1787, 2 DOCU. HY. (Mfm. Supp.) at 1361 as follows:

> I wish you would inform me, through the channel of your paper, of the true
> meaning of disarming the Militia in this State at this solemn period: The county
> officer shows us an order of Council for to deliver them for cleaning; but we in
> our county have, upon second thought, resolved to clean them ourselves. Is this
> a trick for to push upon us the new plan of government whether we will or will
> not have it; no, Mr. Bailey, those gentlemen in your city who have planned it,
> are poor politicians, if they depend on our agreeing to give up our mush sticks.

"A Militia Man" responded in the *Pennsylvania Gazette,* 26 Dec. 1787, 2
DOCU. HY (Mfm. Supp.) at 1362 that the Supreme Executive Council had
merely directed the lieutenants "to collect all the public arms within their
respective counties, have them repaired, and make return to Council . . . for
payment." Jacob Trusty was then asserted to be mistaken "if he thinks the
militia will be duped into a broil by any antifederalist. . . ." To this, "Trusty"
responded in the *Independent Gazetteer,* 10 Jan. 1788, 2 DOCU. HY. (Mfm.
Supp.) at 1365 "that the militia of the country rather choose to repair and
clean their own *arms* at this critical juncture, than to deliver them up to any
one whatever." And "An Old Militia Officer of 1776" declared in the same
paper on 18 Jan., *id.* at 1369–70:

> The orders, issued by Council, enjoining the delivery of the public arms at
> this juncture, when a standing army is openly avowed to be necessary, has occa-
> sioned no small degree of apprehension. . . . These orders . . . amount . . . to a
> temporary disarming of the people. When the arms will be re-delivered, must
> depend upon the *discretion* of our rulers. . . . But if . . . these orders originate in
> that spirit of domination . . ., will it not be their indispensable duty, as men, as
> citizens, and as guardians of their own rights, immediately to arm themselves at

their own expence? This expedient will convince the enemies of liberty, that the people (their own defenders in the last resort) are prepared for the worst. . . .

And see id. at 1361–73, 1694–95, 1833, 2538–39, and 2923.

118. 2 DOCU. HY. at 336.
119. 2 Elliot, DEBATES at 74.
120. *Id.* at 97.
121. *Id.* at 404.
122. 4 Elliot at 203.
123. 3 Elliot at 45.
124. *Id.* at 48.
125. *Id.* at 50–51.
126. *Id.* at 386.
127. *Id.* at 168–169.
128. *Id.* at 380.
129. *Id.* at 425–26.
130. *E.g., id.* at 413.
131. *Id.* at 646.
132. 2 B. Schwartz, THE BILL OF RIGHTS 681 (1971).
133. Dissent of Minority, 2 DOCU. HY. 597–98, 623–24; E. Dumbauld, THE BILL OF RIGHTS AND WHAT IT MEANS TODAY 12 (1957). *And see id.* at viii–ix and 51–52. "The amendments proposed by the Pennsylvania minority bear a direct relation to those ultimately adopted as the federal Bill of Rights." 2 B. Schwartz, THE BILL OF RIGHTS at 628. *And see id.* at 665. While the cited provision explicitly supports an individual right to have arms for more than militia purposes, the minority was very concerned about the specter of a select militia. "The militia of Pennsylvania may be marched to New England or Virginia to quell an insurrection occasioned by the most galling oppression, and aided by the standing army, they will no doubt be successful in subduing their liberty and independency." 2 DOCU. HY. at 638.
134. 2 B. Schwartz, THE BILL OF RIGHTS at 761.
135. *Id.*
136. *Id.* at 758. "The right to bear arms, going back to the English Bill of Rights, received recognition in the Second Amendment to the Constitution. . . . Counting this article, seven out of twelve of New Hampshire's proposals were ultimately accepted." E. Dumbauld, THE BILL OF RIGHTS AND WHAT IT MEANS TODAY at 21 n.37.
137. A Foreign Spectator, "Remarks on the Amendments, No. XI," *Federal Gazette,* 28 Nov. 1788.
138. 3 J. Elliot, DEBATES 659 (1836). *And see* 3 Mason, PAPERS 1068–71 (1970).
139. E. Dumbauld, THE BILL OF RIGHTS AND WHAT IT MEANS TODAY at 21 and 51–52; 2 B. Schwartz, THE BILL OF RIGHTS at 765.
140. 1 J. Elliot, DEBATES at 327–28.
141. *Id.* at 335.

142.   4 *id.* at 244.

143.   R. Rutland, THE BIRTH OF THE BILL OF RIGHTS 206 (1955);
E. Dumbauld, THE BILL OF RIGHTS AND WHAT IT MEANS TODAY
at viii–ix, 21, and 51–52.

144.   1 ANNALS OF CONGRESS 434 (8 June 1789).

145.   Madison, Notes for Speech in Congress, 8 June 1789, 12 MADI-
SON PAPERS 193–94 (Rutland ed. 1979). In a letter to Edmund Pendleton,
20 Oct. 1788, Madison referred to proposed amendments as "those further
guards for private rights. . . ." 4 MADISON PAPERS 60. In a Rough Draft
of Proposed Bill of Rights that he would have presented had he not been
defeated for election by Madison, James Monroe proposed "a declaration in
favor of the equality of human rights; . . . of the right to keep and bear
arms. . . ." James Monroe Papers, N.Y. Public Library, Miscellaneous Papers.

The phrase "bear arms" means broadly to carry arms; it embodies no specific militia connotation. In 1785, Madison proposed a Bill for Preservation of
Deer to the Virginia legislature which would have imposed a recognizance on
"any person" who within a year of a game violation "shall bear a gun out of
his inclosed ground, unless whilst performing military duty. . . ." 2 Jefferson,
PAPERS 443–44 (Boyd ed. 1951). The measure failed to pass, even though
the common parlance of the day distinguished guns, pistols, or other firearms.
E.g., Act of 1684, 3 Hening, STATUTES (VA.) 13. Yet it demonstrates that,
to Madison and his contemporaries, to "bear" an arm was to carry it in one's
hands or on one's person for hunting, militia service, or any other purpose.

146.   Ames to Thomas Dwight, 11 June 1789, 1 WORKS OF FISHER
AMES 52–53 (1854).

147.   Ames to F. R. Minoe, 12 June 1789, *id.* at 53–54.

148.   12 June 1789, 3 PATRICK HENRY 391 (1951). Emphasis added.
And see Joseph Jones to Madison, 24 June 1789, 12 MADISON PAPERS 258
(the amendments are "calculated to secure the personal rights of the people. . . ."); William L. Smith to Edward Rutledge, 9 Aug. 1789, 79 SO. CAR.
HIST. MAG. 14 (1968) (the amendments "will effectually secure private
rights. . . .").

149.   *Federal Gazette,* June 18, 1789, at 2, col. 1. Madison's proposals had
been published two days before in the same paper. *Federal Gazette,* 16 June
1789, at 2, col. 2–3.

150.   Coxe to Madison, 18 June 1789, 12 MADISON PAPERS 239–40.

151.   Madison to Coxe, 24 June 1789, *id.* at 257.

152.   *E.g., New York Packet,* June 23, 1789, at 2, col. 1–2; *Massachusetts
Centinel* (Boston), July 4, 1789, at 1, col. 2. Coxe's "Remarks on the Second
Part of the Amendments," which appeared in the *Federal Gazette,* 30 June
1789, at 2 col. 1–2, exposited what is now the Ninth Amendment as follows:

It has been argued by many against a bill of rights, that the omission of some
in making the detail would one day draw into question those that should not be
particularized. It is therefore provided, that no inference of that kind shall be
made, so as to diminish, much less to alienate an ancient tho' unnoticed right,

nor shall either of the branches of the Federal Government argue from such omission any increase or extension of their powers.

In the next three decades, Coxe wrote many articles on the right to keep and bear arms. He referred to "the right to own and keep and use arms and consequently of *self-defense* and of the *public militia power*. . . ." Democratic Press (Philadelphia), 23 Jan. 1823, at 2, col. 2. "Arms" include muskets, rifles, pistols, and swords. *E.g.,* Democratic Press, 2 Feb. 1811, at 2. Coxe's prolific writings on this subject are analyzed by this author in a separate monograph.

153.   *Federal Gazette,* July 2, 1789, at 2, col. 1.

154.   1 ANNALS OF CONGRESS 750 (17 Aug. 1789). The committee on amendments made its report on 28 July. *Id.* at 672.

155.   *Id.* at 750 (17 Aug. 1789).

156.   *Id.*

157.   *Id.* at 750–51.

158.   *Id.* at 766 (20 Aug. 1789).

159.   *Id.* at 767. Actually, the opposite may be inferred by the eventual deletion of this part of the amendment, the purpose of which was to guarantee the individual "right" to keep and bear arms rather than to create a "duty" to do so. Arguably, this deletion was meant to preclude any constitutional power of the government to compel any person to bear arms rather than to exempt only the religiously scrupulous. *Cf.* J. Graham, A CONSTITUTIONAL HISTORY OF THE MILITARY DRAFT 45–50 (1971) (compulsory military service confined to the militia; individual right to keep and bear arms prevents military despotism).

160.   *Supra* note 158, at 767. Further insight into the attitudes of some of these same speakers toward an armed populace is revealed in debates on the militia bill. The proposal in that bill that every American "provide himself" with arms was, suggested Representative Parker, impractical for poor persons, who should thus be armed at the expense of the United States. 2 ANNALS OF CONGRESS 1804 (16 Dec. 1790).

Representative Jackson, who favored a self-armed people, opined that "the people of America would never consent to be deprived of the privilege of carrying arms. . . . In a Republic every man ought to be a soldier, and be prepared to resist tyranny and usurpation, as well as invasion, and to prevent the greatest of all evils—a standing army." *Id.* at 1806. "There are so few freemen in the United States who are not able to provide themselves with arms," added Representative Sherman. "[T]he people, if left to themselves, would provide such arms as are necessary. . . ." *Id.* at 1808.

The ultimate objection to a government-armed populace was expressed by Representative Wadsworth in the query, "Is there a man in this House who would wish to see so large a proportion of the community, perhaps one-third, armed by the United States, and liable to be disarmed by them?" *Id.* at 1809. This view prevailed, and as passed, the Militia Act of 8 May 1792 required every "free able bodied white male citizen" to "provide himself with a good musket or firelock. . . ."

161.   "Political Maxims" *New York Daily Advertiser,* 15 Aug. 1789, at 2, col. 1. *And see* Patrick Henry to Richard Lee, 28 Aug. 1789, 3 PATRICK HENRY at 398: "For Rights, without having power and might is but a shadow."

162.   Philadelphia *Independent Gazetteer,* 18 Aug. 1789, at 3, col. 1.

163.   From the Boston Independent Chronicle, Philadelphia *Independent Gazetteer,* 20 Aug. 1789, at 2, col. 2.

164.   Centinel, Revived, No. xxix, *Independent Gazetteer,* 9 Sept. 1789, at 2, col. 2.

165.   Senate Journal, MSS. by Sam A. Otis, Virginia State Library, Executive Communications, Box 13 (4 Sept. 1789) at 1; (8 Sept. 1789) at 7.

166.   *Id.* (8 Sept. 1789) at 7.

167.   *Id.* (9 Sept. 1789) at 1. Another alteration by the Senate may have also been significant. In changing the House's version that a militia was "the best security" to the version that a militia was "necessary to the security" of a free state, the Senate may have sought to answer the objections like that made by Representative Gerry in the House: "A well regulated militia being the best security of a free State, admitted an idea that a standing army was a secondary one." 1 ANNALS OF CONGRESS 751 (17 August 1789). It is noteworthy that Richard Henry Lee was a member of the Senate at that time.

168.   2 B. Schwartz, THE BILL OF RIGHTS at 1164 (25 Sept. 1789).

169.   "The lower house sent up amendments which held out a safeguard to personal liberty in great many instances. . . . " William Grayson to Patrick Henry, 29 Sept. 1789, 3 PATRICK HENRY at 406.

"The whole of that Bill [of Rights] is a declaration of the right of the people at large or *considered as individuals.* . . . [I]t establishes some rights of the individual as unalienable and which consequently, no majority has a right to deprive them of." (Emphasis added.) Albert Gallatin to Aexander Addison, 7 Oct. 1789, MS. in N.Y. Hist. Soc.—A.G. Papers, 2.

"But there are some rights too essential to be delegated—too sacred to be infringed. These each individual reserves to himself; in the free enjoyment of these the whole society engages to protect him. . . . All these essential and sacred rights, it would be difficult if not impossible, to recount, but some, in every social compact, it is proper to enumerate, as specimens of many others. . . ." An Idea of a Constitution, *Independent Gazetteer,* Dec. 28, 1789, at 3, col. 3.

And see The Scheme of Amendments, *Independent Gazetteer,* 23 March 1789, at 2, col. 1: "The project of muffing the press, which was publicly vindicated in this town [Boston], so far as to compel the writers against the government, to leave their names for publication, cannot be too warmly condemned." Registration of persons for exercise of basic freedoms was considered to be infringement.

170.   Patrick Henry "is pleased with some of the proposed amendments; but still asks for the great disideratum, the destruction of direct taxes." Edmund Randolph to James Madison, 18 Aug. 1789, 12 MADISON PAPERS 345. Jefferson was dissatisfied with the Bill of Rights, but did not object to the arms-bearing provision. Jefferson to Madison, 12 MADISON PAPERS

363–64. The Bill of Rights was "short of some essentials, as Election interference & Standing Army & C. . . . " Richard Henry Lee to Charles Lee, 28 Aug. 1789, 2 LETTERS OF RICHARD HENRY LEE 499 (Ballagh ed. 1914). Most of those in the Virginia House who opposed the adoption of the amendments "are not dissatisfied with the amendments as far as they go" but wanted delay to prompt an amendment on direct taxes. Hardin Burnley to Madison, 5 Nov. 1789, 12 MADISON PAPERS 460.

In the Virginia Senate, there was extensive criticism of the proposed free speech guarantee and other amendments as too narrow, but no one questioned the right to bear arms provision. Objections to Articles, VA. SEN. J. 61–65 (12 Dec. 1789). Virginia forestalled adoption of the Bill of Rights until the end of 1791. Nor did the Massachusetts General court, which rejected the Bill of Rights, object to the arms-bearing provison in its verbose Report of the Committee of the General Court on Further Amendments. *See* Report reprinted in MASSACHUSETTS AND THE FIRST TEN AMENDMENTS 25–29 (D. Myers ed. 1936).

171.   *Fayetteville Gazette*, Oct. 12, 1789, at 2, col. 1–2.

172.   *Gazette of the United States*, Oct. 14, 1789, at 211, col. 2.

173.   "A bill of rights for freemen appears to be a contradiction in terms. . . . [I]n a free country, every right of human nature, which are as numerous as sands upon the sea shore, belong to the quiet, peaceable citizen." *Federal Gazette*, 5 Jan. 1790, at 2, col. 3.

"The absurdity of attempting by a bill of rights to secure to freemen what they never parted with, must be self-evident. No enumeration of rights can secure to the people *all* their privileges. . . ." *Federal Gazette*, 15 Jan. 1790, at 3, col. 3. This article ridiculed a bill of rights as analogous to conveying a house and lot but excepting out of the grant an enumeration of other houses and lots retained by the seller.

174.   Speech of 7 Jan. 1790, Boston *Independent Chronicle*, 14 Jan. 1790, at 3.

175.   *Providence Gazette & Country Journal*, 30 Jan. 1790, at 1.

176.   19 March 1790. 3 PATRICK HENRY 417–18.

177.   "A Well regulated militia is the best defence to a free people, a standing army in time of peace are not equal to a well regulated militia." Political Maxims, *Independent Gazetteer*, 24 July 1790, at 2, col. 1. "Where a standing army is established, the inclinations of the people are but little regarded." Political Maxims, *Independent Gazetteer*, 31 July 1790, at 2, col. 2.

178.   *E.g.*, *Summary of the principal Amendments proposed to the Constitution*, post 29 May 1790 MSS, College of W. & M., Tucker-Coleman coll., Box 39b notebooks, Notebook VI, at 212–22.

179.   *Providence Gazette and Country Journal*, 5 June 1790, at 23.

180.   *Independent Gazetteer*, 29 Jan. 1791, at 2, col. 3.

181.   W. Rumble, *James Madison on the Value of Bills of Rights*, CONSTITUTIONALISM 122, 137 (Pennock and Chapman eds. 1979).

182.   2 B. Schwartz, THE BILL OF RIGHTS at 1112–13 (17 August 1789).

183.   R. Rohner, *The Right to Bear Arms: A Phenomenon of Constitutional History*, 16 CATHOLIC U.L. REV. 53, 55 (1966).

184.   Where "q" is true, the truth table of the hypothetical proposition shows the whole proposition to be true regardless of whether "p" is true:

p	q	p⊃q
T	T	T
T	F	F
F	T	T
F	F	T

The following Euler diagram further demonstrates that the linguistic form of the Second Amendment expresses the proposition that the right to keep and bear arms is broader than the needs of the militia:

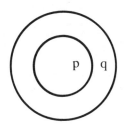

185.   2 B. Schwartz, THE BILL OF RIGHTS at 1031 (8 June 1789).

186.   B. Patterson, THE FORGOTTEN NINTH AMENDMENT 19 (Bobbs-Merrill Co. 1955).

187.   *Id. passim.*

188.   See Chapters 1 and 2 of this study.

Chapter 4
Antebellum Interpretations

1.   THE JEFFERSON CYCLOPEDIA 553 (1900).

2.   *Id.* at 551.

3.   "In a legal sense, arms may extend to any thing that a man wears for his own defense, or takes in his hand, and uses in anger, to strike, throw at, or wound another." W. Duane, A MILITARY DICTIONARY 14 (Philadelphia 1810). "Fire-Arms" of this description include "firelocks, rifles, fusils, carbines, guns, and pistols. . . ." *Id.* at 13. Also included was the "Blunderbuss, a well-known firearm, consisting of a wide, short, but very large bore, capable of holding a number of musket or pistol balls; very fit for doing great execution in a crowd, . . . defending the door of a house, staircase, etc. . . ." *Id.* at 55.

4. Biography of the Judges, 4 Va. (4 Call.) xxviii (1827). A colonel during the Revolution, St. George Tucker's "most brilliant exploit was his undertaking, at the instance of Governor Patrick Henry, an expedition to the West Indies, taking down indigo and bringing back much needed arms and ammunition." Hon. A. M. Dobie, Federal District Judges in Virginia Before the Civil War, 12 F.R.D. 451, 459 (4th Cir. 1951). Tucker's Blackstone was "unquestionably one of the most important law-books of its day. . . ." *Id.*at 460. Judge Dobie generally depicts Tucker as a giant on both state and federal benches.

5. I Blackstone, COMMENTARIES *143 n. 40 (St. Geo. Tucker ed. 1803).

6. *Id.* at 300 (App.). Tucker added:

> If, for example, a law be passed by congress, prohibiting the free exercise of religion, according to the dictates, or persuasions of a man's own conscience; or abridging the freedom of speech, or of the press; or the right of the people to assemble peaceably, or to keep and bear arms; it would, in any of these cases, be the province of the judiciary to pronounce whether any such act were constitutional, or not; and if not, to acquit the accused from any penalty which might be annexed to the breach of such unconstitutional act. . . . The judiciary, therefore, is that department of the government to whom the protection of the rights of the individual is by the constitution especially confided, interposing its shield between him and the sword of usurped authority, the darts of oppression, and the shafts of faction and violence. *Id.* at 357.

7. W. Rawle, A VIEW OF THE CONSTITUTION 125–26 (2d ed. 1829). *And see id.* at 153 ("In a people permitted and accustomed to bear arms, we have the rudiments of a militia. . . .").

8. I Henry St. Geo. Tucker, COMMENTARIES ON THE LAWS OF VIRGINIA 43 (1831). *And see* Tucker, LECTURES ON GOVERNMENT 37 (1844) (as sovereigns, the people have the right "to reform, to alter or abolish [the government], at their discretion."). In A FEW LECTURES ON NATURAL LAW 95 (1844), Tucker wrote:

> Now the natural right of self defence is nothing more than the liberty which the law of nature allows us of defending ourselves from an attack which is made upon our persons or of taking *such measures as may guard against any injuries* we are likely to suffer from another. . . .
>
> . . . [A]s the *law of nature allows us to defend ourselves, and imposes no limit upon the right,* the only limit we can impose is the necessity of the case. *Whatever means are necessary must be lawful;* for the rule is general, that where a right is absolutely given, the means of exercising it must also follow. [Emphasis added.]

And see id. at 10–11, 96–99.

John Randolph Tucker carried on the family tradition by averring of the Second Amendment: "this prohibition indicates that the security of liberty against the tyrannical tendency of government is only to be found in the right

of the people to keep and bear arms in resisting the wrongs of government."
II J. Tucker, CONSTITUTION OF THE UNITED STATES 671 (1899).

9. B. Oliver, THE RIGHTS OF AN AMERICAN CITIZEN 174
(1832).

10. *Id.* at 176.

11. *Id.* at 177.

12. *Id.* at 178.

13. *Id.*

14. *Id.* at 186. And see *id.* at 40: "Of those rights which are usually
retained in organized society . . . The first and most important of these rights,
is that of self-defence."

15. 3 J. Story, COMMENTARIES ON THE CONSTITUTION 746
(1833).

16. 2. Litt. (Ky.) 90, 13 Am. Dec. 251 (1822). See Powell v. McCormack,
395 U.S. 486, 547 (1969) ("the precendential value of these cases tends to
increase in proportion to their proximity to the Convention in 1787.").

17. 2 Litt. at 90.

18. *Id.* at 91–92.

19. *Id.* at 92. But see State v. Reid, 1 Ala. Reports 612, 616–17 (1840),
while holding that a statute prohibiting the carrying of concealed weapons
was not incompatible with the right to keep and bear arms in defense of self
and state, added: "A statute which, under the pretence of regulating, amounts
to a destruction of the right, or which requires arms to be so borne as to render them wholly useless for the purpose of defence, would be clearly unconstitutional."

20. 13 Tenn. Reports (5 Yerg.) 356 (1833).

21. A TREATISE OF THE PLEAS OF THE CROWN, Bk. 1, Ch.
28, sec. 4, regarding the Statute of Northampton, 2 Edw. 3, c. 3 (1328).

22. 13 Tenn. Reports (5 Yerg.) 358 (1833).

23. *Id.* at 359.

24. *Id.* at 360.

25. 2 Humph. (21 Tenn.) 154 (1840).

26. *Id.* at 158.

27. 4 Ark. 18 (1842).

28. *Id.* at 34.

29. *Id.* at 35 (Lacy, J., dissenting).

30. 1 Ga. 243 (1846).

31. *Id.* at 249.

32. *Id.* at 250.

33. *Id.* at 251.

34. *Id.*

35. 5 La. Ann. 489, 490 (1850). *And see* State v. Jumel, 13 La Ann. 399
(1858).

36. 24 Tex. 394 (1859).

37. *Id.* at 401.

38. *Id.* at 401–2.

39. 27 N.C. 203 (1844).
40. *Id.* at 204.
41. *Id.* at 207.
42. 4 Ga. 72 (1848).
43. *Id. And see* cases cited at 68 C.J. *Weapons*, §5 n. 19, 21, 22; §8, n. 37, 40 (1934).
44. 51 N.C. (6 Jones) 57 (1859).
45. *Id.*
46. *Id.*
47. 51 N.C. (6 Jones) 448 (1859).
48. *Id.* at 449.
49. 60 U.S. (19 How.) 393 (1857).
50. *Id.* at 417. Emphasis added.
51. *Id.* at 450.
52. *Id.* at 415.
53. *Id.* at 587.
54. *Id.* at 631, referring to the acts of 30 March 1802 (2 Stat. at L., 139) and 26 March 1804 (2 Stat. at L., 283).
55. *Supra* note 50 and accompanying text.
56. "What was the fourteenth article designed to secure? . . . [T]hat the privileges and immunities of citizens of the United States shall not be abridged or denied by the United States or by any State; defining also, what it was possible was open to some question after the Dred Scott decision, who were citizens of the United States." Sen. George F. Edmunds (R., Vt.), CONG. GLOBE, 40th Cong., 3d. Sess., pt. 1, 1000 (8 Feb. 1869).
57. *See, e.g.,* Aristotle, POLITICS 68–71 (Sinclair transl. 1962); Caesar, THE GALLIC WAR 131, 575 (Edwards transl. 1966); Cicero, PHILIPPICS 375 (Ker transl. 1969); Bodin, SIX BOOKES OF COMMONWEALE 38 (Knolles transl. 1606); Sidney, DISCOURSES CONCERNING GOVERN-MENT 270 (1698); 1 Montesquieu, SPIRIT OF THE LAWS 243 (Nugent transl. 1899).
58. Tucker, A DISSERTATION ON SLAVERY 19 (Philadelphia 1796).
59. *Id.* at 20, citing 1748 c. 31. Edit. 1794.
60. *Id.* at 22.
61. *Id.* at 30, 50.
62. *Id.* at 49.
63. 1 Blackstone, COMMENTARIES *144 (St. Geo. Tucker ed. 1803). Tucker's DISSERTATION ON SLAVERY was reprinted as an appendix to the COMMENTARIES.
64. Tucker at 55. This act was reenacted in 1705 and 1792.
65. *Id.* at 57.
66. *Id.* at 65.
67. *Id.* at 70–71.
68. *Id.* at 75.
69. *Id.* at 93. Tucker refers to Spirit of Laws, 12–15 and 1 Black. Com. 417. 1 Montesquieu, SPIRIT OF THE LAWS at 243–44 warned of the

"danger from the multitude of slaves" and "the danger of arming slaves . . . in republics." 1 Blackstone, COMMENTARIES 417 (St. Geo. Tucker ed. 1803) states that slaves, excluded from liberty, envy and hate the rest of the community, and thus warned "not to intrust those slaves with arms; who will then find themselves an overmatch for the freemen."

70. Tucker at 94–95

71. CONG. GLOBE, 35th Cong., 2d Sess. 983 (11 Feb. 1859).

72. *Id.*, 39th Cong., 1st Sess. 117 (1 Mr. 1866) (Rep. James F. Wilson [R., Iowa]). *And see id.* at 3027 (8 June 1866) (Sen. John B. Henderson [R., Mo.]).

73. W. Rawle, A VIEW OF THE CONSTITUTION 125–26 (2d ed. 1829).

74. CONG. GLOBE, 39th Cong., 1st Sess. 117–18 (1 Mr. 1866) (Rep. Wilson); *id.* at 1757 (4 Ap. 1866) (Sen. Lyman Trumbull [R., Ill.]); *id.* at 1832, 1836 (7 Ap. 1866) (Rep. William Lawrence [R., Ohio]).

75. H. Graham, *Early Antislavery Background of the Fourteenth Amendment*, WISC. L. REV. 479, 481 (1950).

76. *Id.* at 610, 647.

77. *Id.* at 658.

78. L. Levy, THE FOURTEENTH AMENDMENT AND THE BILL OF RIGHTS: THE INCORPORATION THEORY xiv–xv (New York 1970).

79. J. tenBroek, EQUAL UNDER LAW 126 (1965, enlarged ed. of ANTISLAVERY ORIGINS OF FOURTEENTH AMENDMENT, a work cited with approval in Lynch v. Household Finance Corp., 405 U.S. 538, 544 [1972]).

80. *Id.* at 110–13.

81. *Id.* at 146.

82. C. Shively, *Introduction*, 4 Spooner, COLLECTED WORKS 11 (1971). The American and Foreign Anti-Slavery Society provided copies of Spooner's UNCONSTITUTIONALITY OF SLAVERY to all members of Congress. *Id.*

83. Spooner, THE UNCONSTITUTIONALITY OF SLAVERY 66 (1860). Prior editions were published in 1845, 1847, 1853, and 1856.

84. *Id.* at 97.

85. *Id.* at 98. Similarly, William Goodell, citing *e.g.* the Mississippi Declaration of Rights provision that *"every* citizen has a right to bear arms for the defence of *himself* and the State," sought to show slavery incompatible with the state constitutions. Goodell, VIEWS OF AMERICAN CONSTITUTIONAL LAW 132 (1845). *And see* Goodell, THE AMERICAN SLAVE CODE 311 (1853): "For keeping a weapon or club, we have seen him subjected, by a cowardly code, to public whipping."

86. J. Tiffany, A TREATISE ON THE UNCONSTITUTIONALITY OF SLAVERY 117–18 (1849). While Tiffany contended that the entire Bill of Rights was applicable to the states, "Spooner stays closer to the Consti-

tution. He claims only two specific guarantees for the slaves," that is, the rights to bear arms and habeas corpus. Shively *supra* note 82, at 10. "Again Spooner is less sweeping than Tiffany. He emphasized the word 'Congress' in the First Amendment, but he thought that the Second Amendment at least applied to the states as well as the nation." tenBroek, *supra* note 79, at 111.

    87. THE WRITINGS OF CASSIUS MARCELLUS CLAY 257 (H. Greeley ed. 1848).

    88. Spooner, A DEFENCE FOR FUGITIVE SLAVES 27–28 (1850). *And see* Spooner, ADDRESS OF THE FREE CONSTITUTIONALISTS 25 (1860):

> When the government fails to protect the people against robbers, kidnappers, and murderers, it is not only a legal right, but an imperative moral duty, of the people to take their mutual defence into their own hands. And the constitution recognizes this right, when it declares that "the right of the people to keep and bear arms shall not be infringed;" for "the right of the people to keep and bear arms" implies their right to use them when necessary for their protection.

Spooner's most well-known legal work, AN ESSAY ON THE TRIAL BY JURY 17–18 (1852), which was referred to in Reconstruction debates, includes the following:

> This right of resistance is recognized by the constitution of the United States, as a strictly legal and constitutional right. It is so recognized, first by the provision that "the trial of all crimes, except in cases of impeachment, shall be by jury"—that is, by the country—and not by the government; secondly, by the provision that "the right of the people to keep and bear arms shall not be infringed." This constitutional security for "the right to keep and bear arms," implies the right to use them—as much as a constitutional security for the right to buy and keep food would have implied the right to eat it. The constitution, therefore, takes it for granted that the people will judge of the conduct of the government, and that, as they have the right, they will also have the sense, to use arms, whenever the necessity of the case justifies it. . . .
>
> In the American *State* constitutions also, this right of resistance to the oppressions of the government is recognized, in various ways, as a natural, legal, and constitutional right. . . . [I]t is recognized by many of them, as, for example, those of Massachusetts, Maine, Vermont, Connecticut, Pennsylvania, Ohio, Indiana, Michigan, Kentucky, Tennessee, Arkansas, Mississippi, Alabama, and Florida, by provisions expressly declaring that the people shall have the right to bear arms. In many of them also, as, for example, those of Maine, New Hampshire, Vermont, Massachusetts, New Jersey, Pennsylvania, Delaware, Ohio, Indiana, Illinois, Florida, Iowa, and Arkansas, by provisons, in their bills of rights, declaring that men have a natural, inherent, and inalienable right of *"defending* their lives and liberties." This, of course, means that they have a right to defend them against any injustice *on the part of the government,* and not merely on the part of private individuals; because the object of all bills of rights is to assert the rights of individuals and the people, *as against the government,* and not as against private persons. It would be a matter of ridiculous supererogation to assert, in a constitu-

tion of government, the natural right of men to defend their lives and liberties against private trespassers.

89.   2 Douglass, LIFE AND WRITINGS 201 (Foner ed. 1950). Douglass in 1851 announced his break with the Garrisonian abolitionist argument that the Constitution was proslavery. *Id.* at 155–56. See also *id.* at 201, 5 *id.* at 285.

90.   5 *id.* at 375.

91.   2 *id.* at 420.

92.   *Id.* at 286–87. Douglass noted newspaper reports that "colored persons are pricing and buying fire arms, such as pistols, revolvers, & c." to resist return to slavery. *Id.* at 164.

93.   *Id.* at 457–58. *And see* 5 *id.* at 181, 206.

94.   2 *id.* at 460.

95.   *Id.* at 351. Douglass was in sympathy with John Brown, who argued that "the practice of carrying arms would be a good one for the colored people to adopt, as it would give them a sense of their manhood." DuBois, JOHN BROWN 106 (1909).

96.   CONG. GLOBE, 39th Cong., 1st Sess., pt. 1, 674 (6 Feb. 1866). *But see id.* at pt. 4, 3215 (16 June 1866) (allegation by Rep. William E. Niblack (D., Ind.) that the majority of Southern blacks "either adhered from first to last to the rebellion or aided and assisted by their labor or otherwise those who did so adhere.")
Of course, many factors contributed to Northern victory, See D. Donald ed., WHY THE NORTH WON THE CIVIL WAR (1960). While all may be fair in love and war, experiences during the conflict suggest that deprivation of one right is coupled with deprivation of others. When the secession movement began, Lincoln suspended *habeas corpus* and enstated the disarming of citizens and military arrests in Maryland and Missouri. In the latter state, one military order provided: "All persons who shall be taken with arms in their hands within these lines shall be tried by court-martial, and if found guilty will be shot." 3 WAR OF THE REBELLION, ser. 1, 467 (Fremont's Declaration of Marial Law, 30 Aug. 1861). Gen. Marsh's Gen. Order No. 19 provided: "All arms and ammunition of whatever kind and wherever found, not in the hands of the loyal militia, will be taken possession of by the latter and used for the public defense." 13 *id.* at 506. The resultant searches and seizures of arms provided the occasion for general looting. R. Brownlee, GRAY GHOSTS OF THE CONFEDERACY 85, 170 (1958). Deprivation of rights in the North was sufficiently commonplace that the Democratic Platform of 1864, 4th Resolution, denounced "the subversion of the civil by military law in States not in insurrection; the arbitrary military arrests . . .; the suppression of freedom of speech and of the press; . . . and the interference with and denial of the right of the people to bear arms in their defence. . . ." E. Pollard, THE LOST CAUSE 574 (1867). *And see* J. Marshall, AMERICAN BASTILE *passim* (1875).

97.   J. McPherson, THE NEGRO'S CIVIL WAR 72–73 (1965).

98.   Before the war, plantation slaves "who are accustomed to handling fire-arms either accompany their young master a-hunting, or borrowing the guns belonging to the latter, go hunting themselves. . . ." D. Hundley, SOCIAL RELATIONS IN OUR SOUTHERN STATES 361 (1860). *And see* State v. Hannibal, 51 N.C. 57 (1859); State v. Harris, 51 N.C. 448 (1859) (despite the slave codes, whites trusted blacks with firearms for hunting and defense). J. Otto, *A New Look at Slave Life*, 88 NATURAL HISTORY 8, 20 (1979) relates:

> We were surprised to find indications that the slaves owned firearms. Lead shot, a gunflint, and a percussion cap all lay in the midden. Such evidence of slave-owned firearms—admittedly indirect—has also appeared at other slave cabin sites excavated on the Georgia and Florida coasts, and we know that the state of Georgia never enacted any laws prohibiting slave ownership of firearms.

Thus, blacks were experienced enough in the use of arms to play a significant, though unofficial, role as Confederate soldiers, some even as sharpshooters. H. Blackberry, BLACKS IN BLUE AND GRAY 1–40 (1979); J. Obatala, *Black Confederates*, PLAYERS 13 ff. (April 1979). In Louisiana, the only state in the Union to include blacks in the militia, substantial numbers of blacks joined the rebellion furnishing their own arms. M. Berry, *Negro Troops in Blue and Gray*, 8 LOUISIANA HISTORY 165–66 (1967).

99.   61 THE WAR OF THE REBELLION, ser. 1, pt. 2, 1068 & 1315 (1880–1901); R. Durden, THE GRAY & THE BLACK 250 (1972).

100.   Durden at 169.

101.   CONG. GLOBE, 38th Cong., 2d Sess., pt. 1, 171 (9 Jan. 1865).

102.   *Id.* at 289 (18 Jan. 1865).

Chapter 5
Freedmen, Firearms, and the Fourteenth Amendment

1.   T. Farrar, MANUAL OF THE CONSTITUTION 59, 145 (1867).

2.   II J. Bishop, COMMENTARIES ON THE CRIMINAL LAW §124 (1865). *And see* cases cited at 68 Corpus Juris *Weapons* §4 n. 60 (1934). Bishop was cited in debate on the Civil Rights Bill of 1866 by Rep. William Lawrence (D. Ohio). CONG. GLOBE, 39th Cong., 1st Sess., pt.2, 1837 (7 Ap. 1866).

3.   II J. Bishop at 120 n. 6.

4.   *Id.* at 125 n. 2.

5.   That is, with the exception of Indians. Though beyond the scope of this study, the history of the prohibition of arms possession by native Americans presents a parallel example of the use of gun control to suppress or exterminate nonwhite ethnic groups. While legal discrimination against blacks in

respect to arms was abolished during Reconstruction, the sale of arms and ammunition to "hostile" Indians remained a prohibition. *E.g.*, 17 Stat. 457, 42d Cong., 3d Sess., ch. 138 (1873). *See also Sioux Nation of Indians* v. *United States*, 601 F.2d 1157, 1166 (Ct. Cl. 1979), *aff'd*, 448 U.S. 371 (1980): "Since the Army had taken from the Sioux their weapons and horses, the alternative to capitulation to the government's demands was starvation. . . ." The federal government's special restrictions on selling firearms to native Americans were abolished finally in 1979. Wahington Post, 6 Jan. 1979, §A, at 11, col. 1.

    6.   W. DuBois, BLACK RECONSTRUCTION IN AMERICA 167, 172–73, 223 (1962); E. Coulter, THE SOUTH DURING RECONSTRUCTION 40 (1947). Coulter at 49 states: "To possess a gun and be followed by a dog which he could call his own greatly helped the freedman to enjoy his new freedom; and to carry a pistol distinguished the 'young colored gentleman' from the 'gun-toting' generality of Negroes who sometimes carried their [long] guns to the fields to produce a thrill or to shoot a rabbit."

    7.   Laws of Miss., 1865, at 165 (29 Nov. 1865); 1 DOCUMENTARY HISTORY OF RECONSTRUCTION 289–90 (W. Fleming ed. 1906). J. Burgess, RECONSTRUCTION AND THE CONSTITUTION, 1866–1876 47, 51–52 (1902) states of the Mississippi Act:

This is a fair sample of the legislation subsequently passed by all the "States" reconstructed under President Johnson's plan. . . . The Northern Republicans professed to see in this new legislation at the South the virtual re-enslavement of the negroes.

    8.   CONG. GLOBE, 39th Cong., 1st Sess., pt. 1, 40 (13 Dec. 1865).
    9.   J. Burgess, *supra* note 7, at 64.
    10.   Sen. Exec. Doc. No. 2, 39th Cong., 1st Sess., 36 (19 Dec. 1865).
    11.   *Id.* at 85.
    12.   *Id.* at 93–95.
    13.   *Id.* at 96.
    14.   Civil Rights Act, 14 Stat. 27 (1866). A portion of this act survives as 42 U.S.C. §1982: "All citizens of the United States shall have the same right, in every State and Territory, as is enjoyed by white citizens thereof to inherit, purchase, lease, sell, hold and convey real and personal property."
    15.   CONG. GLOBE, 39th Cong., 1st Sess., pt. 1, 474 (29 Jan. 1866).
    16.   *Id.* at 478.
    17.   *Id.* at 517 (30 Jan. 1866). See also *supra* note 12 and accompanying text.
    18.   *Id.* at 651 (5 Feb. 1866).
    19.   Exec. Doc. No. 70, 39th Cong., 1st Sess., 233, 236 (1866).
    20.   CONG. GLOBE, 39th Cong., 1st Sess., pt. 1, 941 (20 Feb. 1866).
    21.   *Id.*
    22.   S.R. No. 30, CONG. GLOBE, 39th Cong., 1st Sess. 806; H.R. No. 63, *id.* at 813 (13 Feb. 1866).

23. *Id.* at 1033–34 (26 Feb. 1866).

24. *Id.* at 1088 (28 Feb. 1866). *And see* further comments of Bingham at 1089 ("the existing Amendments") and 1094 ("the law in its highest sense").

25. *Id.* at 1088.

26. *Id.*, pt. 2, 1266 (8 Mr. 1866).

27. *Id.* at 1629 (24 Mr. 1866).

28. *Id.*

29. *Id.* at 1838 (7 Ap. 1866).

30. *Id.*

31. *Id.*

32. *Id.*

33. *Id.* at 1839. Ironically, Clarke's home state, Kansas, adopted measures to prohibit former Confederates from possessing arms. Kennett & Anderson, THE GUN IN AMERICA 154 (1975).

34. CONG. GLOBE, 39th Cong., 1st Sess. 2459 (8 May 1866).

35. *Id.* at 2539 (10 May 1866).

36. *Id.* at 2542–43.

37. H. Flack, THE ADOPTION OF THE FOURTEENTH AMENDMENT 80 (1908). See *infra* note 60.

38. CONG. GLOBE, 39th Cong., 1st Sess., pt. 3, 2765 (23 May 1866). Emphasis added.

39. *Id.* at 2766.

40. I. Brant, THE BILL OF RIGHTS 337 (1965).

41. Republican Centennial Com., THE STORY OF SHAFTSBURY 14–15 (1954).

42. CONG. GLOBE, 39th Cong., 1st Sess. 2961 (5 June 1866). Emphasis added.

43. *See* Flack, *supra* note 37, at 91.

44. 1 Report of the Joint Select Committee on the Condition of Affairs in the Late Insurrectionary States, 42nd Cong., 2d Sess. 35 (1872).

45. CONG. GLOBE, 38th Cong., 1st Sess. 1490 (9 Ap. 1864).

46. *Eg., id.* at 839 (2 Feb. 1864).

47. *Id.*, 39th Cong., 1st Sess. 318 (19 Jan. 1866).

48. "No negro or mulatto shall come into, or settle in, the state after the adoption of this constitution." Ind. Const., Art. XIII, §1 (1851).

49. *Id.* at Art. I, §32.

50. CONG. GLOBE, 39th Cong., 1st Sess., pt. 3, 2939 (4 June 1866).

51. *Id.* at 3039 (8 June 1866).

52. *Id.* at 3042.

53. *Id.* at 3041.

54. 60 U.S. 393, 15 L. Ed. 691, 705 (1857). Johnson's oral argument in *Dred Scott* has not been preserved. *See* 3 LANDMARK BRIEFS AND ARGUMENTS OF THE SUPREME COURT OF THE UNITED STATES (1978).

55. CONG. GLOBE, 39th Cong., 1st Sess. 504 (30 Jan. 1866).

56. *Id.* at 40 (13 Dec. 1865). Johnson was a member of the Joint Committee on Reconstruction, which reported numerous instances of freedmen being disarmed. H.R. Rep. No. 30, 39th Cong., 1st Sess. *passim* (1866).

57. *Id.*, pt. 4, 3210 (16 June 1866). The pertinent Florida statute made it "unlawful for any Negro, mulatto, or person of color to own, use, or keep in possession or under control any bowie-knife, dirk, sword, firearms, or ammunition of any kind, unless by license of the county judge or probate, under a penalty of forfeiting them to the informer, and of standing in the pillory one hour, or be whipped not exceeding thirty-nine stripes, or both, at the discretion of the jury." Dubois, *supra* note 6, at 172.

The South Carolina law provided: "Persons of color constitute no part of the militia of the State, and no one of them shall, without permission in writing from the district judge or magistrate, be allowed to keep a firearm, sword, or other military weapon, except that one of them, who is the owner of a farm, may keep a shot-gun or rifle, such as is ordinarily used in hunting, but not a pistol, musket, or other firearm or weapon appropriate for purposes of war . . . and in case of conviction, shall be punished by a fine equal to twice the value of the weapon so unlawfully kept, and if that be not immediately paid, by corporal punishment." *Id.* at 172–173.

58. Flack, *supra* note 37, at 80.

59. *Id.* at 94.

60. *Id.* at 96. All of the above quotations are from pages of Flack cited as authority in Lynch v. Household Finance Corp., 405 U.S. 538, 544 (1972).

61. 1 DOCUMENTARY HISTORY OF RECONSTRUCTION 208 (Fleming ed. 1906). The proclamation's recognition of the same right of ex-Confederates as for freedmen was apparently in response to such situations as the following:

> Mr. Ferebee [N.C.] . . . said that in his county the white citizens had been deprived of arms, while the negroes were almost all of them armed. . . .
>
> Gen. Dockery . . . stated that in his county the white residents had been disarmed, and were at present almost destitute of means to protect themselves against robbery and outrage. *Id.* at 90; ANNUAL CYCLOPEDIA 627 (1865).

62. *The Loyal Georgian* (Augusta), 3 Feb. 1866, at 1, col. 2.

63. *Id.* at 2, col. 2.

64. *Id.* at 3, col. 4.

65. Circular No. 5, Freedmen's Bureau, 22 Dec. 1865. *See, e.g.*, issues of *Loyal Georgian* for 20, 27 Jan., 3 Feb. 1866.

66. D. Sterling, THE TROUBLE THEY SEEN: BLACK PEOPLE TELL THE STORY OF RECONSTRUCTION 394 (1976). Sterling documents numerous incidences of blacks using firearms for self-defense as well as searches and seizures of firearms from blacks.

67. *E.g.*, "The Constitutional Amendment in the Senate," *The Loyal Georgian*, 24 Feb. 1866, at 2, cols. 3–4.

68. *Harper's Weekly*, 13 Jan. 1866, at 3, col. 2.

69. *New York Times*, 24 May 1866, at 1, col. 6.

70. *New York Herald*, 24 May 1866, at 1, col. 3.

71. *National Intelligencer*, 24 May 1866, at 3, col. 2.

72. *Philadelphia Inquirer*, 24 May 1866, at 8, col. 2.

73. H. Flack, THE ADOPTION OF THE FOURTEENTH AMEND-MENT 142 (1908).

74. *New York Times*, 25 May 1866, at 4, col. 4.

75. *Chicago Tribune*, 29 May 1866, at 2, col. 3.

76. *Baltimore Gazette*, 24 May 1866, at 4, col. 2.

77. *Boston Daily Journal*, 24 May 1866, at 4, col. 4; *Boston Daily Advertiser*, 24 May 1866, at 1, col. 6; *Springfield Daily Republican*, 24 May 1866, at 3, col. 1.

78. *Daily Richmond Examiner*, 25 May 1866, at 2, col. 3.

79. *Id.*, 26 May 1866, at 1, col. 6.

80. Charleston *Daily Courier*, 28 May 1866, at 1, col. 2, and at 4, col. 2; *id.*, 29 May 1866, at 1, cols. 1–2 (comment on Howard's speech). The revolver ads are found in every issue.

81. Kendrick, JOURNAL OF THE JOINT COMMITTEE ON RE-CONSTRUCTION 265 (1914).

82. Report of the Joint Committee on Reconstruction, H.R. Rep. No. 30, 39th Cong., 1st Sess., pt. 2, 219 (1866).

83. *Id.* at 229.

84. *Id.* at 240–41. *And see id.* at 229, 239, 246; pt. 3, at 30–32 (utility of firearms for killing game and varmints and for self-defense).

85. *Id.*, pt. 3, at 142. *Cf. id.*, pt. 4, at 160: "The majority of them [freed-men] are armed, and entitled to bear arms under the existing laws of the southern States."

86. Drake, RADICALISM VINDICATED: LETTER OF SENATOR DRAKE OF MISSOURI, TO SENATOR JOHNSON, OF MARYLAND 9 (Washington, D.C.: Union Republican Congressional Committee, 2d ed., 1867). Sen. Johnson himself was equally fervent in supporting the citizen's right to keep and bear arms.

87. H. Wilson, HISTORY OF THE RECONSTRUCTION MEA-SURES 134–35 (1868).

88. Wilmington *Weekly Journal*, 25 Sept. 1868.

89. "He wondered if the noble Anglo-Saxon would submit to having their arms taken from them. No! they would not; they know their rights and the negroes were learning from them rapidly." Speech of Richard H. Cain, Charleston, *New York Times*, 21 July 1876.

"The right of an American citizen to possess and bear arms is guaranteed him by the constitution. The right of a merchant to sell and of an individual to buy arms, is beyond all question." "The Arms Seizure," New Orleans *Picayune*, 10 Sept. 1874, at 1, col. 4.

90. WISC. SEN. J. 32 (1867).

91. MASS. H. R. DOC. No. 149, at 3 (1867).

92. *Id.* at 4. Emphasis added.

93. *Id.* at 25.

94. I Brant, THE BILL OF RIGHTS 343 (1965).

95. JOUR. OF TEX. STATE CONVENTION 82 (1866). Emphasis in original.

96. *Id.* at 88.

97. TEX. SEN. J. 420 (1866). Emphasis added.

98. TEX. CONST. I, §13 (1866).

99. TEX. H. J. 578 (1866).

100. CONG. GLOBE, 39th Cong., 1st Sess., pt. 1, 81 (19 Feb. 1866) (speech of Sen. George F. Edmunds [R., Vt.] against Southern militias).

101. WISC. SEN. J. 106 (1867). Inexplicibly, passages like this are cited to reject the incorporation theory in Fairman, *Does the Fourteenth Amendment Incorporate the Bill of Rights?*, 2 STAN. L. REV. 5, 109 (1949). Fairman's premise throughout the article is that incorporation was asserted, but not frequently enough; therefore incorporation was not intended, even though never denied. Not only has each and every citation by Fairman of state records been rechecked in a fruitless effort to find a single speech or report which substantiates his thesis, but those state records (particularly Southern ratifications) ignored by Fairman have been checked with the same result. Worse still, Fairman completely ignores the well-recorded debates on the Southern state constitutions adopted in 1868 pursuant to the congressional requirement that they be amended consistent with the Fourteenth Amendment.

102. PA. LEG. REC. App. 59 (1867). (Mr. Ewing).

103. *Id.* at 65 (Mr. Day).

104. *Id.* at 94 (Mr. Allen).

105. *Id.* at 25 (Mr. Burnett).

106. *Id.* at 67 (Mr. Deise).

107. BREVIER LEG. REPTS. 80 (1867) (Mr. Ross).

108. *Id.* (Mr. Bird).

109. *Id.* at 81.

110. *Id.* at 90.

111. Act of 2 Mr. 1867, 14 Stat. 428 (1867).

112. Ala. Const., Art. I, §23 (1819, 1865), §28 (1867), §27 (1875).

113. State v. Reid, 1 Ala. Repts. 612, 616–17 (1840).

114. OFFICIAL JOURN. OF CONST. CONV. OF THE STATE OF ALA. . . . COMMENCING NOV. 5, 1867 144 (1868).

115. Ark. Const., I, §21 (1836). *See* JOURN. OF PROCEEDINGS (Ark.) 16 (1836).

116. State v. Buzzard, 4 Ark. 18 (1842). "Again, the term 'arms' . . . includes guns or firearms of every description. . . ." *Id.* at 21.

117. Ark. Const., I, §21 (1861). *See* JOURN. OF BOTH SESSIONS OF THE CONV. OF THE STATE OF ARK. 430 (1861). This was consistent with the governor's urging of an alliance with the Indians "because of the utter incapacity on the part of the Indians to resist alone the occupation of their country by federal troops or federal agents." *Id.* at 156.

118.   Ark. Const., I, §21 (1864). JOURN. OF THE CONV. OF DELE-
GATES OF THE PEOPLE OF ARK. OF 1864 (1870) is unenlightening on
this matter.
119.   REPORT OF THE JOINT COMMITTEE ON RECONSTRUC-
TION, 39th Cong., 1st Sess., pt. 3, 81 (1866). *And see id.* at 86.
120.   Ark. Const., I, §5 (1868).
121.   DEBATES AND PROCEEDINGS OF THE CONVENTION
(ARK.) (1868). *E.g.,* "When the present proposed Amendments to the Constitution of the United States shall have been adopted, then, under that Constitution, these colored friends will be citizens. . . ." (Mr. Duvall) *(id.* at 128,
after discussion of Fourteenth Amendment at 125–26). Mr. Langley found
the miscegnation statute "unconstitutional. I read from the Fourteenth Article of Amendment to the Constitution of the United States. . . ." After reading §1, he continued, "It is part of the condition precedent to our admission
into the Union." *Id.* at 377. "I wish to read, also, Section 1 of the Article
known as the Fourteenth Article of Amendment," began Mr. Hodges on the
same subject. *Id.* at 502.
For the progress of the arms provision in Committee Reports, *see id.* at 354,
584.
122.   Fife v. State, 31 Ark. 455, 460–1 (1876).
123.   *Id.* at 458. *And see* Wilson v. State, 33 Ark. 557, 34 Am. Rep. 52,
54–55 (1878), reversing conviction for carrying a revolver:

> But to prohibit the citizen from wearing or carrying a war arm . . . is an unwar-
> ranted restriction upon his constitutional right to keep and bear arms.
>   If cowardly and dishonorable men sometimes shoot unarmed men with army
> pistols or guns, the evil must be prevented by the penitentiary and gallows, and
> not by a general deprivation of a constitutional privilege.

124.   Fla. Const. I, §21 (1838, 1861). *See* JOURNAL OF PROCEED-
INGS OF A CONVENTION (Fla.) 1838–1839 17 (1839).
125.   Fla. Const., I, §1 (1865); JOURN. OF PROCEEDINGS OF THE
CONVENTION OF FLA. 30, 135 (1865).
126.   *Id.* at 99.
127.   W. E. B. DuBois, BLACK RECONSTRUCTION IN AMERICA
172 (1962).
128.   CONG. GLOBE, 39th Cong., 1st Sess., pt. 4, 3210 (16 June 1866)
(Rep. George W. Julian [R., Ind.]).
129.   FLA. SEN. J. 13 (1866). That the U.S. Constitution was referred
to is clear because *(a)* it is the U.S. Constitution that was being referred to in
the page before and *(b)* Florida then had no right to arms provision in its
constitution. The nonenforcement of the statute was verified by black politi-
cian John Wallace as follows:

> For instance, the law prohibiting colored people handling arms of any kind with-
> out a license, was a dead letter, except in some cases where some of the freedmen

would go around plantations hunting, with apparently no other occupation, such a person would be suspected of hunting something that did not belong to him and his arms would be taken away from him. We have often passed through the streets of Tallahassee with our gun upon our shoulder, without a license, and were never disturbed by any one during the time this law was in force.

J. Wallace, CARPET BAG RULE IN FLORIDA 35 (1885); 1 DOCUMENTARY HISTORY OF RECONSTRUCTION 272 (Fleming ed. 1906).

130. "The Thirteenth Amendment, just adopted, could be interpreted as giving Congress the power to punish inequalities in civil rights and in criminal punishments, as the incidents of slavery and involuntary servitude. . . ." J. Burgess, RECONSTRUCTION AND THE CONSTITUTION 1866–1876 65 (1902).

131 Fla. Const., Dec. of Rights, §22 (1868). See JOURNAL OF PROCEEDINGS OF THE CONSTITUTIONAL CONVENTION (Fla.) 5, 73 (1868).

132. 1 Ga. 243, 250 (1846).

133. *Id.* at 251.

134. Cooper v. Savannah, 4 Ga. 72 (1848).

135. Ga. Const., I, §4 (1865); JOUR. OF THE PROCEEDINGS OF THE CONVENTION (Ga.) 182, 366 (1910).

136. Ga. Const., I, §14 (1868).

137. JOUR. OF PROCEEDINGS OF THE CONST. CONVENTION (Ga.) 168 (1868) (emphasis added).

138. Hill v. State, 53 Ga. 472 (1874); Strickland v. State, 137 Ga. 1, 72 S.E. 260, 267 (1911).

139. However, the antebellum constitution of Louisiana included a provison making the bearing of arms a duty. It read: "The free white men of the State shall be armed and disciplined, for its defence; but those belonging to religious societies whose tenets forbid them to carry arms, shall not be compelled so to do. . . ." La. Const., III, §22 (1812), §60 (1845), §59 (1852). Despite the reference to white men, free men of color volunteered and provided their own arms for defense of New Orleans in the War of 1812 and again in 1861 for Confederate service. R. McConnell, NEGRO TROOPS OF ANTEBELLUM LOUISIANA (1968). In 1864, the provision was altered as follows: "All ablebodied men in the State shall be armed and disciplined for its defence." La. Const., IV, §67 (1864).

140. 5 La. Ann. 489, 490 (1850). *Accord,* State v. Jumel, 13 La. Ann. 399 (1858) (concealed carry prohibition consistent with Second Amendment).

141. OFFICIAL JOUR. OF PROCEEDINGS OF THE CONVENTION (La.) 37 (1867–1868).

142. *Id.* at 41.

143. *Id.* at 84. The unenumerated rights guarantee became La. Const., I, §14 (1868).

144. *Id.* at 263, 275–79, 290–93.

145. State v. Bias, 37 La. Ann. 259, 260 (1885). "When we see a man

with a musket to shoulder, or carbine slung on back, or pistol belted to his side, or such like, he is bearing arms in the constitutional sense." *Id.*

146.   Miss. Const., I, §23 (1817, 1832). Abolitionist William Goodell cited this provison to show the illegality of slavery under the state constitutions. Goodell, VIEWS OF AMERICAN CONSTITUTIONAL LAW 132 (1845).

147.   Laws of Miss. 165 (1865).

148.   JOUR. OF PROCEEDINGS IN THE CONST. CONVENTION (Miss.) 84, 156 (1868).

149.   *Id.* at 231.

150.   Miss. Const., I, §15 (1868).

151.   N.C. Const., XVII (1776).

152.   State v. Huntley, 25 N.C. 418, 422–23 (1843).

153.   27 N.C. 203, 204 (1844).

154.   *Id.* at 207.

155.   JOUR. OF THE CONST. CONVENTION (N.C.) 165, 212, 215, 229 (1868).

156.   N.C. Const., I, §24 (1868).

157.   *E.g.,* JOUR. at 175, 485 (controversy on whether whites and blacks to be enrolled in the same militia companies).

158.   JOUR. OF CONVENTION OF STATE OF NORTH CARO-LINA 261 (1875).

159.   State v. Speller, 86 N.C. (11 Kenan) 697, 700 (1882); State v. Kerner, 181 N.C. 574, 107 S.E. 222, 223–25 (1921).

160.   S.C. Const. (1776, 1778, 1790, 1865).

161.   PROCEEDINGS OF THE CONST. CONVENTION OF SOUTH CAROLINA 85 (1868).

162.   *Id.* at 258; S.C. Const., I, §28 (1868).

163.   PROCEEDINGS, *supra* note 161 at 257, 259.

164.   *Id.* at 341–49.

165.   *Id.* at 346–47.

166.   *Id.* at 349–50 (conscientious objection to being "compelled" to bear arms); 407, 571 (militia, "volunteer companies"); 671–75, 751–52 ("independent companies").

167.   *Id.* at 343.

168.   *Id.* at 357.

169.   *See* State v. Johnson, 16 S.C. 187 (1881) (concealed carry prohibition valid "as far as may be consistent with the right of the citizen to bear arms").

170.   Tenn. Const., I, §26 (1834).

171.   Simpson v. State, 13 Tenn. (5 Yerg.) 356, 360 (1833).

172.   Aymette v. State, 21 Tenn. (2 Hump.) 154, 158 (1840). *And see* Smith v. Ishenhour, 43 Tenn. (3 Cold.) 214, 217 (1866) (collection of arms by Confederate government): "This is the first attempt, in the history of the Anglo-Saxon race, of which we are apprised, to disarm the people by legislation."

173.   JOUR. OF PROCEEDINGS OF CONVENTION (Tenn.) 72 (1870).

174. *Id.* at 20, 63.

175. *Id.* at 106.

176. Tenn. Const., I, §26 (1870). "That the sure and certain defense of a free people is a well-regulated militia" was provided in §24.

177. An Act to Preserve the Peace and Prevent Homicide, 11 June 1870. Tenn. Laws 28–29 (2d Sess. 1869–1870).

178. Andrews v. State, 3 Heisk. 165, 8 Am. Repts. 8, 13 (1871).

179. *Id.* The use of arms "will properly train and render [the citizen] efficient in defense of his own liberties as well as of the State." 8 Am. Repts. at 14.

180. *Id.* at 15.

181. Tex. Const., I, §13 (1845, 1866, 1868), §23 (1876).

182. Cockrum v. State, 24 Tex. 394, 401–2 (1859). The function of the Second Amendment was that "the people cannot be effectually oppressed and enslaved, who are not first disarmed." *Id.*

183. 1 JOUR. OF THE RECONSTRUCTION CONVENTION, WHICH MET AT AUSTIN, TEX. 953–55 (1870). In the opinion of the Attorney General on the Supremacy of the U.S. Constitution, he reiterated the state's obligations under the Military Reconstruction Act, adding that the " 'Vagrant,' 'Fire-Arms,' . . . & c., 'laws,' amount to a cunningly devised system, planned to prevent equality before the law, and for the restoration of African slavery in a modified form, in fact, though not in name." *Id.* at 975.

184. *Id.* at 195.

185. *Id.* at 195–97.

186. 2 *id.* at 111. This situation led to a resolution that the law abiding "will be compelled, in the exercise of the sacred right of self defence, to organize for their own protection." 1 *id.* at 111.

187. 2 *id.* at 387.

188. 1 *id.* at 152.

189. *Id.* at 235. *And see id.* at 236: "we declare that everything in this 'Bill of Rights' is excepted out of the general powers of government, and shall forever remain inviolate. . . ."

190. *Id.* at 233.

191. English v. State, 35 Tex. 473, 477 (1872).

192. *Id.* at 475, citing 2 Bishop, CRIMINAL LAW §124.

193. Va. Const., I, §13 (1776, 1870).

194. Henry St. Geo. Tucker, COMMENTARIES ON THE LAWS OF VIRGINIA 43 (1831).

195. 1 VA. CONVENTION OF 1867–1868, DEBATES AND PROCEEDINGS 350 (1868).

196. *Id.* at 519; ADDRESS OF CONSERVATIVE MEMBERS at 5–6; Va. Const. IX (1870).

197. 1 VA. CONVENTION OF 1867–1868 at 421. *And see id.* at 634: "the rights declared in the Bill of Rights are natural and inherent rights, rights which previously existed. . . ." (Edward K. Snead).

198. For instance, the Radical Snead read extensively from St. Geo.

Tucker's essay on slavery, *id.* at 535–40, and the Dred Scott decision was discussed. *Id.* at 622.

199.   *Id.* at 166. Advocates of the right of revolution undoubtedly recognized the same utility of an armed people. *See id.* at 356, 403 ff.

200.   Fairman, *Does the Fourteenth Amendment Incorporate the Bill of Rights?*, 2 STAN. L. REV. 5 (1949) argues that since some states failed to guarantee a right to indictment (Fifth Amendment) or jury trial in civil cases where over twenty dollars is in controversy (Seventh Amendment), the Bill of Rights could not have been intended to apply to the states through the Fourteenth Amendment. Of course, no complaints were made during Reconstruction about violations of these merely procedural rights, and thus there was little debate about them. Northern state constitutions which lacked some of the more important substantive rights of the federal Bill of Rights during Reconstruction reveal no intent *not* to incorporate these rights into the Fourteenth Amendment because: (1) many of these states had no occasion to call a constitutional convention, (2) many viewed the Fourteenth Amendment as an ideal which the defeated Southerners should be forced meticulously to follow, but which needed no emphasis on the "saintly" Northern victors, and (3) the enumeration in the federal Bill of Rights of basic freedoms was deemed sufficient.

Even ignoring that everyone during Reconstruction who mentioned the subject at all agreed that incorporation was intended, it must be remembered that the right to keep and bear arms, freedom from unreasonable search and seizure, and similar guarantees were very much on the minds of the Fourteenth Amendment's supporters. At a minimum, selective incorporation of these more significant rights follows from Fairman's test of total consistency between Bill of Rights provisions and comparable state provisions.

201.   *See* THE FEDERAL AND STATE CONSTITUTIONS (B. Poore compl. 1877).

202.   Ala., I, §28 (1867); Conn., I, §17 (1818); Fla., I, §22 (1868); Ind., I, §32 (1851); Ky., XIII (1850); Mich., XVIII, §7 (1850); Ore., I, §28 (1857); Penn., I, §21 (1838,1873); Tex., I, §13 (1868); Vt., I, §16 (1796).

203.   Ark., I, §5 (1868); Me., I, §16 (1820); Mass., I, 17 (1780); S.C., I, §28 (1868); Tenn., I, §26 (1870).

204.   Kan., I, §4 (1859); Miss., I, §15 (1868); Ohio, I, §4 (1851).

205.   Colo., I, §13 (1876); Mo., II, §17 (1875).

206.   Ga., I, §14 (1868); N.C., I, §24 (1868).

207.   R.I., I, §22 (1842).

208.   DEBATES OF THE MD. CONVENTION OF 1867 151 (1867).

209.   CONG. GLOBE, 39th Cong., 1st Sess., pt. 1, 914 (19 Feb. 1866).

210.   *Id.* at 914–15.

211.   *Id.* at 915.

212.   *Supra* notes 7 and 8.

213.   *Supra* note 16.

214.   CONG. GLOBE, 39th Cong., 1st Sess., pt. 2, 1100 (1 Mr. 1866).

215.   *Id.*, 2d Sess. 1848 (26 Feb. 1867).

216.   *Id.* at 1575–76 (19 Feb. 1867).

217. *Id.* at 1576.

218. *Id.*

219. *Id.*

220. *Id.* at 1848 (26 Feb. 1867).

221. *Id.* A supporter of the Fourteenth Amendment, *id.*, 1st Sess. 3042 (8 June 1866), Sen. Willey later advocated enforcement of "the rights and privileges and immunities of that race [blacks] . . . not only in the District of Columbia, but all over the whole country. . . ." *Id.*, 40th Cong., 2d Sess. 1125 (12 Feb. 1868). Further, Willey clearly distinguished "the right [of every citizen] to bear arms" in the above speech, from being "compelled to bear arms in defense of the Government," a concept he alluded to in defense of black suffrage. *Id.*, 3d Sess. 911 (6 Feb. 1869).

222. *Id.*, 39th Cong., 2d Sess. 1849 (16 Feb. 1867).

223. *Id.* Emphasis added.

224. *Id.* Emphasis added.

225. *Id.*

226. *Id.*

227. *Id.*

228. Act of 2 Mr. 1867.

229. An analysis of roll-call voting behavior comparing voting for and against the Fourteenth Amendment and the bill to disband the state militia organizations indicates that 82 percent (18 of 22) of the senators who voted for the Fourteenth Amendment (and who were present during voting on the militia bill) also voted for the militia disbanding bill, and 18 percent (4 of 22) voted against it. Obviously those who voted for both the Fourteenth Amendment and the militia disbanding bill must have perceived the Second Amendment as protecting an individual right to keep and bear arms to all persons (including freedmen) and not a state right to maintain militias. Of the four persons who were Fourteenth Amendment supporters but militia bill opponents, all were Republicans, one of whom (Willey) interpreted the Second Amendment as protecting individual rights during the militia debates, and the remainder likely concurred, but for constitutional or policy reasons voted against the militia bill.

All senators who voted against the Fourteenth Amendment also voted against disbanding the militia if present on the latter vote, or likely would have done so had they been present. These senators, among whom numbered Hendricks and Saulsbury, probably all believed the Second Amendment protected a citizen's right to keep and bear arms, and also believed the militia clause of the Second Amendment in conjunction with the powers reserved to the states under the Tenth Amendment protected the right of states to form militias.

The voting records on the Fourteenth Amendment and the militia bill are located respectively in CONG. GLOBE, 39th Cong., 1st Sess. 3042 (8 June 1866) and *id.*, 2d Sess. 1849 (26 Feb. 1867).

230. CONG. GLOBE, 39th Cong., 2d Sess., pt. 2, 1249 (14 Feb. 1867).

231. *Id.* at 1349 (19 Feb. 1867). Emphasis added.

232. *Id.*
233. *Id.* at 1350.
234. *Id.* at 1355.
235. *Id.* at 1400 (20 Feb. 1867).
236. *Id.*
237. *Id.* at pt. 3, 1592 (26 Feb. 1867).
238. *Id.*, 1706 (1 Mr. 1867), 1733, 1752, and Appendix 217–28 (2 Mr. 1867).
239. CONG. GLOBE, 40th Cong., 3d Sess., pt. 1, 80 (15 Dec. 1868).
240. *Id.*
241. *Id.*
242. *Id.*
243. *Id.* at 81.
244. *Id.*
245. *Id.* at 83–84.
246. *Id.* at 84.
247. *Id.* at 84–85. *Cf.* Houston v. Moore, 18 U.S. 1, 16–17 (1820): "But as state militia, the power of the state governments to legislate on the same subjects, having existed prior to the formation of the constitution, and not having been prohibited by that instrument. . . ."
248. CONG. GLOBE, 40th Cong., 3d Sess., pt. 1, 86 (15 Dec. 1868).
249. *Id.* at 84.
250. *Id.* at 115 (16 Dec. 1868).
251. *Id.*
252. *Id.*
253. *Id.* at 121 (17 Dec. 1868).
254. Act of 14 Jan. 1869, in *id.*, Appendix at 301.
255. CONG. GLOBE, 40th Cong., 3d Sess., pt. 2, 1819 (2 Mr. 1869).
256. Act of 3 Mr. 1869, in *id.*, Appendix at 325.
257. H. R. Report No. 22 on Memorial of Victoria C. Woodhull, 41st Cong., 3d Sess., pt. 2, 8–9 (1 Feb 1871). The report also refers to definitions of "citizenship" in Aristotle's *Politics* and the *Dred Scott* case, both of which included the right to keep and bear arms in the term "citizenship."
258. 1464 H. R. REP. No. 37, 41st Cong., 3d Sess. 3 (20 Feb. 1871).
259. CONG. GLOBE, 42d Cong., 1st Sess., pt. 1, 174 (20 Mr. 1871). Introduced as "an act to protect loyal and peaceable citizens in the South . . .", H. R. No. 189.
260. H. R. REP. No. 37, *supra* note 258, at 7–8.
261. CONG. GLOBE, 42d Cong., 1st Sess., pt. 1, 154 (18 Mr. 1871).
262. *Id.* at 196 (21 Mr. 1871).
263. *Id.* at 321 (28 Mr. 1871).
264. *Id.*, pt. 2, Appendix, 68. Passed as the Enforcement Act, 17 Stat. 13 (1871), §1 survives as 42 U.S.C. §1983: "Every person who, under color of any statute, ordinance, regulation, custom, or usage, of any State or Territory, subjects, or causes to be subjected, any citizen of the United States or other person within the jurisdiction thereof to the deprivation of any rights,

privileges, or immunities secured by the Constitution and laws, shall be liable to the party injured in an action at law, suit in equity, or other proper proceedings for redress."

The present-day action for conspiracy to deprive persons of rights or privileges under 42 U.S.C. §1985 derives from the same act.

265. CONG. GLOBE, 42d Cong., 1st Sess., pt. 1, 337 (29 Mr. 1871).
266. *Id.* at 339.
267. *Id.* at 385 (1 Ap. 1871).
268. *Id.*, pt. 2, Appendix, 84 (31 Mr. 1871).
269. *Id.*, pt. 1, 413 (3 Ap. 1871).
270. *Id.* at 422 (3 Ap. 1871).
271. *Id.*
272. *Id.*
273. *Id.* at 445 (4 Ap. 1871).
274. *Id.* at 453.
275. *Id.* at 459.
276. *Id.* at 475–76 (5 Ap. 1871). Emphasis added.
277. *Id.*, pt. 2, Appendix, 314.
278. 17 Stat. 13, 42d Cong., 1st Sess., ch. 22 (1871).
279. 1 Report of the Joint Select Committee on the Condition of Affairs in the Late Insurrectionary States, H.R. 22, S.R. 41, 42d Cong., 2d Sess. 35 (19 Feb 1872). The committee was in session between 20 Ap. 1871 and 19 Feb. 1872.
280. *Id.* at 261–62.
281. *Id.* at 263.
282. *Id.* at 426.
283. 2 *id.* at 301. The war between the white Home Guards and the Lowrys, who had resisted conscription into forced labor camps during the Civil War, is related in W. Evans, TO DIE GAME: THE STORY OF THE LOWRY BAND, INDIAN GUERRRILLAS OF RECONSTRUCTION (1971). The following comment by Evans at 5, relying on U.S. War Dept., Records of the Army Commands (Record Group 393, National Archives), Hearings, 7–8, exemplifies the centrality of firearms prohibition to racial domination:

> In 1835 the North Carolina legislature had designated the Indians along the Lumber River as "free persons of color," and had taken away their right to bear arms, as well as their right to vote. From time to time the substantial planters who sat on the Robeson County Court would grant a permit to some Negro or Indian to own a firearm for such a legitimate purpose as shooting crows. But no permit had ever been issued to Calvin Lowry. Furhermore the whites would not have been pleased to learn that on his father's place, buried beneath the peas in the corncrib, was the stock of another unregistered gun, and hidden at various places about the farm were the remaining parts, not to mention a gourd of powder.

284. 3 Report of the Joint Select Committee, *supra* note 279, at 77.

285.   8 *id*. at 75–76.

286.   9 *id*. at 683.

287.   *Id*. at 689.

288.   *Id*. at 723.

289.   *Id*. at 743.

290.   *Id*. at 862–63.

291.   *Id*. at 1166–67.

292.   *Id*. at 1233.

293.   *E.g., id*. at 928–31, 1162, 1165. *And see id*. at 779, 813, 914–15, 917, 927, and 1195.

294.   Ex-Confederate Gen. N. B. Forrest testified that the KKK "arose about the time the militia were called out, and Governor Brownlow [Tennessee] issued his proclamation stating that the troops would not be injured for what they should do to rebels. . . ." 13 *id*. 6. While claiming that "the organization was formed for self-protection," *id*. at 9, Forrest had been a supporter of the Fourteenth Amendment, *id*. at 20, which explains why, two years before, he denounced the Klan because "the order was being used . . . to disarm harmless negroes having no thought of insurrectionary movements, and to whip both whites and blacks." C. Bowers, THE TRAGIC ERA 311 (1929). The outrages in turn allegedly furnished "a plausible pretext for the organization of State militias to serve the purpose of Radical politics." *Id*. at 311. Carpetbagger-controlled militias were deeply involved in political violence to influence elections, and were blamed for infringing their opponents' constitutional rights to free speech and to keep and bear arms, among numerous other abuses. *E.g., id*. at 439 and *passim;* O. Singletary, NEGRO MILITIA AND RECONSTRUCTION 35–41, 74–75 (1963).

295.   United States v. Avery, 5 Report of the Joint Select Committee at 1672 (4th Cir. 1871). The Act of 31 May 1870 exists today at 18 U.S.C. §§241, 242.

296.   *Id*. at 1670.

297.   *Id*. at 1672.

298.   Now 42 U.S.C. §1984.

299.   71 U.S. 277, 321.

300.   CONG. GLOBE, 42d Cong., 2d Sess., pt. 1, 762 (1 Feb. 1872).

301.   *Id*., pt. 6, Appendix 25–26 (6 Feb. 1872). *See also* 2 CONG. REC., 43d Cong., 1st Sess., pt. 1, 384–85 (5 Jan. 1874) (statement by Rep. Robert Q. Mills (D., Tex.) that the Fourteenth Amendment adopts Bill of Rights privileges).

302.   CONG. REC., 43d Cong., 1st Sess., pt. 6, Appendix, 241–42 (4 May 1874). Emphasis added.

303.   *Id*. at 242. Emphasis added.

304.   In discussion concerning the Civil Rights Act of 1875, Sen. James A. Alcorn (R., Miss.) defined the militia in these terms: "The citizens of the United States, the *posse comitatus*, or the militia if you please, and the colored man composes part of these." *Id*. at 304 (22 May 1874). The antebel-

lum exclusion of blacks from the armed people as militia was commented on by Sen. George Vickers (D., Md.), who recalled a 1792 law passed by Congress: "That every free able-bodied white male citizen shall be enrolled in the militia." Vickers added that as late as 1855 New Hampshire "confined the enrollment of militia to free white citizens." CONG. GLOBE, 41st Cong., 2d Sess., pt. 2, 1558–59 (25 Feb. 1870). The word "white" was stricken from the U.S. militia law in 1867. CONG. GLOBE, 39th Cong., 2d Sess., Appendix 196 (2 March 1867). When this change came to be reflected at the state level, the following apprehension was expressed by Rep. Michael C. Kerr (D., Ind.): "Are the civil laws of Alabama to be enforced by this negro militia? Are white men to be disarmed by them?" CONG. GLOBE, 40th Cong., 2d Sess., pt. 3, 2198 (28 Mr. 1868).

While having arms in the general militiaman's capacity was at times commented on during Reconstruction, more often than not keeping and bearing arms was depicted as a right infringed on by militias or by Klansmen. The practical utility of this right was expressed towards the end of Reconstruction in testimony by Professor R. T. Greener as follows: "Every leading man, during this [Republican election] campaign, carried a pistol. I never carried one before but I surely wouldn't have been without one in traveling through that upcountry. It wouldn't have been safe. . . . I never felt certain whether I was going to get back alive or not." Denial of the Elective Franchise in S.C. at the election of 1875 and 1876, Sen. Misc. Document No. 48, 44th Cong., 2d Sess., in D. Sterling, THE TROUBLE THEY SEEN: BLACK PEOPLE TELL THE STORY OF RECONSTRUCTION 470 (1976).

Chapter 6
The Supreme Court Speaks

1. 71 U.S. 277 (1867).
2. *Id.* at 321. Emphasis added.
3. Sen. Matthew H. Carpenter (R., Wis.), CONG. GLOBE, 42d Cong., 2d Sess., pt. 1, 762 (1 Feb 1872). See *supra* Chapter 5, note 300 and accompanying text.
4. 307 U.S. 175 (1939).
5. 32 U.S. 243 (1833).
6. 35 Tex. 473 (1872).
7. *Id.* at 477.
8. *Id.* at 475, citing 3 Bishop, CRIMINAL LAW ¶124.
9. Butchers' Benevolent Ass'n v. Crescent City Live-Stock Landing & Slaughter-House Co., 83 U.S. 36 (1873).
10. 92 U.S. 542 (1876).
11. United States v. Avery (4th Cir. 1871), 5 Report of the Joint Select Committee on the Condition of Affairs in the Late Insurrectionary States, 42d Cong., 2d Sess. 1670–72 (19 Feb. 1872).

12.   16 Stat. 140, today's 18 U.S.C. §241, 242.

13.   United States v. Cruikshank, 25 Fed. Cas. 707 (D. La. 1874).

14.   *Id*. at 714–15. Emphasis added.

15.   *See* Brief for the United States. *Contrast* the lengthy oral argument on this issue by the U.S. attorney at the KKK trials in Charleston, S.C., the transcript of which was printed in the congressional report on the Klan, *supra* note 11.

16.   Brief of R. H. Marr at 26.

17.   *E.g.*, Jones v. Mayer Co., 392 U.S. 409, 441 n. 78 (1968).

18.   S. Morrison, *Does the Fourteenth Amendment Incorporate the Bill of Rights?* 2 STAN. L. REV. 140, 145–46 (1949).

19.   92 U.S. 542, 552.

20.   *Id*. at 553.

21.   *Id*. at 551. Emphasis added.

22.   *Id*. at 553–54.

23.   *Id*. at 554.

24.   L. Kennett & J. Anderson, THE GUN IN AMERICA 155 (1975).

25.   W. E. B. DuBois, BLACK RECONSTRUCTION IN AMERICA 482, 489, & 691 (1977).

26.   University of California Regents v. Bakke, 438 U.S. 265, 391 (1978). *And see* E. Dumbauld, THE BILL OF RIGHTS AND WHAT IT MEANS TODAY 61 (1957): "The Supreme Court, in an effort to minimize the impact of 'Reconstruction' after the war of 1861–65, struck down prosecution for interferring with the right of peaceable assembly and the right to bear arms. . . ."

Ironically, antebellum judicial opinion interpreted the Second Amendment among other Bill of Rights provisions as applicable to the states while the Supreme Court interpreted the Bill of Rights as inapplicable to the states even after the adoption of the Fourteenth Amendment. Still, even after *Barron* and *Cruikshank* the right to have arms continued to be considered an individual right. Citing the Second Amendment, J. Bishop, COMMENTARIES ON THE LAW OF STATUTORY CRIMES §792 (3d ed. rev. by M. Early 1901) states: "This one is declaratory of personal rights, so also are some of the others which are adjudged not to extend to the states; and, contrary perhaps to some former views, it is now settled in authority that this provision has no relevancy to state legislation."

27.   116 U.S. 252 (1886).

28.   *Id*. at 265.

29.   *Id*. at 267. The nineteenth century court's view that assembly for purpose of petition was inapplicable to the states has been long since overruled. See cases cited in Hague v. C.I.O., 307 U.S. 496, 519 (1939) (Stone, J., separate opinion).

30.   The issue of whether an organized militia may be constituted only by a government is beyond the scope of this study, but the court's proscription fails to take account of who may act against despotic government and who may keep their own private arms for that purpose. See 3 J. Story, COMMENTARIES ON THE CONSTITUTION 746 (1833).

31.   116 U.S. 265. Emphasis added.

32.   D. Caplan, *The Right of the Individual to Bear Arms*, DETROIT COL-LEGE OF L. REV. 789, 794–808 (1982).

33.   In the trials stemming from the famous Haymarket riot, *Lehr und Wehr Verein* (the group Presser led in a march through Chicago) was described as "an armed proletarian corps" which formed after "the shooting down of peaceably inclined wage-workers by the bloodhounds of 'law and order'. . . ." The same source alleged that the militia law which proscribed armed marches (under which Presser was convicted) was expressly passed to suppress *Lehr und Wehr Verein*. Spies v. People, 122 Ill. 1, 12 N.E. 865, 886 (1887). The Illinois Supreme Court found this "armed socialistic organization" to be an unlawful conspiracy, but never questioned the right to keep and bear arms per se. *Id.* at 921-24. Although the Second Amendment was not an issue in the case, it is interesting that John Randolph Tucker argued before the U.S. Supreme Court in the same case that the first ten amendments apply to the states through the fourteenth. Ex Parte Spies, 123 U.S. 131, 150-51 (1887). *Cf.* Hayes, *The Right to Bear Arms, A Study in Judicial Misinterpretation*, 2 WM. & MARY L. REV. 381, 405 (1960): "The *Presser* and *Cruikshank* decisions were the children of the War Between the States and 'Black Republican Reconstructionism' "—this suggests the sociological explanation that the decisions were reactions to Southern and black threats to Northern and white political power.

34.   Brief of Attorney General of Illinois at 4, citing and paraphrasing Houston v. Moore, 18 U.S. (5 Wheat.) 1, 16–17 (1820) (Story, J.), which stated: "But as state militia, the power of the state governments to legislate on the same subjects, having existed prior to the formation of the constitution, and not having been prohibited by that instrument. . . . "

35.   *Id.* at 8. The brief also relies on Dunne v. People, 94 Ill. 120, 34 Am. Dec. 213 (1879), which construed the same statute as *Presser. Dunne* based the state right to maintain a militia on the Tenth Amendment:

> It might be well in this connection to call to mind that "powers not delegated to the United States by the Constitution, nor prohibited by it to the States, are reserved to the States respectively, or to the people." The power of State governments to legislate concerning the militia existed and was exercised before the adoption of the Constitution of the United States, and as its exercise was not prohibited by that instrument, it is understood to remain with the States. . . . 34 Am. Dec. at 216.

Regarding the right contended for, to parade with arms in cities, the Illinois Supreme Court added: "The right of the citizen to 'bear arms' for the defense of his person and property is not involved, even remotely, in this discussion." *Id.* at 228.

36.   S. Morrison, *Does the Fourteenth Amendment Incorporate the Bill of Rights?* 2 STAN. L. REV. 140, 147 (1949).

37.   153 U.S. 535 (1894).

38. *Id.* at 538.

39. *Id.*

40. This explains why State of Arkansas v. Kansas & T. Coal Co., 96 F. 353, 362 (W.D. Ark. 1899), *rev'd on other grounds* 183 U.S. 185 (1901) apparently held the Fourteenth Amendment to protect the crossing of state lines by a group of armed men. Under their constitution, the citizens of Arkansas "have the right to keep and bear arms; and it is also seen from the [second] amendment to the constitution of the United States that the federal government is denied the power to deprive the people of the right to keep and bear arms. . . . If this right belongs to the citizens of this state under the fourteenth amendment, can the state pass any law which shall deprive citizens of other states of the same right, under the same circumstances?"

41. 165 U.S. 275 (1897).

42. *Id.* at 281–82.

43. The dissenting opinion of Justice Harlan, by arguing that specific guarantees preclude infringement via exceptions, would by implication prohibit legislation even against carrying concealed weapons. *See id.* at 293, 302.

44. 158 U.S. 550 (1895).

45. *Id.* at 552.

46. *Id.* at 558.

47. *Id.* at 560.

48. *Id.* at 563.

49. *Id.* at 564.

50. 232 U.S. 138 (1914).

51. *Id.* at 144.

52. *Id.* at 143.

53. *Id.*

54. The U.S. Supreme Court has on several occasions reiterated the federal common-law right of arming for self-defense. Gourko v. United States, 153 U.S. 183, 191 (1894) held that if "the defendant had reasonable grounds to believe, and in fact believed, that the deceased intended to take his life, or to inflict upon him great bodily harm, and, so believing, armed himself solely for necessary self-defense . . . , the jury were not authorized to find him guilty of murder because of his having deliberately armed himself, provided he rightfully so armed himself for purposes simply of self-defense. . . ." And see Thompson v. United States, 155 U.S. 271, 278 (1894) ("the purpose of the defendant in arming himself was for self-defense"); Rowe v. United States, 164 U.S. 546, 547–48 (1896) (self-defense where "after deceased began cutting defendant the latter drew his pistol and fired"); and Brown v. United States, 256 U.S. 335, 342 (1921) (in view of deceased's threats defendant "had taken a pistol with him, and had laid it in his coat upon a dump").

"As to the duty of the able-bodied citizen to aid in suppressing crime," Justice Cardozo, concurring in Hamilton v. University of California, 293 U.S. 245, 265 n.1 (1934) recalled an earlier opinion he had written. Under English law, the duty of the citizen in the hue and cry to pursue felons implied "a duty to provide himself with instruments sufficient for the task." In 1285, these included a breastplate of iron, sword, knife, and horse. "Still, as in the days of Edward I, the citizenry may be called upon to enforce the justice of the state . . . with whatever implements . . . are convenient and at hand." Babington v. Yellow Taxi Corp., 250 N.Y. 14, 164 N.E. 726, 727 (1928).

55. 307 U.S. 174 (1939).

56. 26 U.S.C. §1132c, *as amended*, 26 U.S.C. §5801 (1976).

57. 26 F. Supp. 1002, 1003 (W.D. Ark. 1939).

58. "But I think we owe somewhat less deference to a decision that was rendered without benefit of a full airing of all the relevant considerations." Monell v. Dep't. of Social Services of City of New York, 436 U.S. 658, 709 n.6 (1978) (Powell, J., concurring) (overruling of Monroe v. Pape, 365 U.S. 167 [1961] after reexamination of Reconstruction debates).

59. United States v. Miller, 307 U.S. at 178 (1939). Emphasis added. *Cf.* Burks v. State, 162 Tenn. 406, 36 S.W. 2d 892, 894 (1931) (factual determination that shotgun with 12 ½" barrel a constitutionally protected "arm").

60. *See* Arnold v. United States, 115 F.2d 523, 525 (9th Cir. 1940).

61. 2 Hump. (21 Tenn.) 154 (1840).

62. *Id.* at 158.

63. Art. I, §8, cl. 15, 16.

64. 307 U.S. at 178.

65. *Id.* at 179.

66. *Id.* Emphasis added.

67. See Blackstone, COMMENTARIES, 409: "It seems universally agreed by all historians, that King Alfred first settled a national militia in the kingdom, and by his prudent discipline made all the subjects of his dominion soldiers. . . ."

68. 5 WEALTH OF NATIONS ch. 1, *quoted in* 307 U.S. at 179.

69. 1 Osgood, THE AMERICAN COLONIES IN THE 17TH CENTURY, ch. XIII. 307 U.S. at 179–80. Emphasis added.

70. January Session, 1784, cited in 307 U.S. at 180.

71. Act of 4 April 1786, cited in 307 U.S. at 180–181.

72. October 1785 (12 Hening's Statutes), cited in 307 U.S. at 181–82.

73. 307 U.S. at 183.

74. *Id.* at 183 n.3.

75. 116 U.S. 252 (1886).

76. 165 U.S. 275 (1897).

77. Presser v. Illinois, 116 U.S. 252, 265, 267 (1886).

78. Robertson v. Baldwin, 165 U.S. 275, 281–82 (1897).

79. 31 Ark. 455 (1876).

80. 33 Ga. 347 (1862).

81. Art. I, §9, ¶13.

82. 72 Kan. 230, 83 P. 619 (1905).

83. 253 Mich. 537, 235 N.W. 245 (1931).

84. 219 Mich. 635, 189 N.W. 927 (1922).

85.   2 Hump. (21 Tenn.) 154 (1840).

86.   42 Tex. 455 (1875).

87.   35 W. Va. 367, 14 S.E. 9 (1891).

88.   Cooley, THE GENERAL PRINCIPLES OF CONSTITUTIONAL LAW 281–82 (2d ed. 1891) (emphasis added). The Court in *Miller* (1939) cited 1 Cooley, CONST. LIMITATIONS 646 (5th ed.).

89.   153 U.S. 535, 538 (1894).

90.   Chicago B. & Q.R. Co. v. Chicago, 166 U.S. 226 (1897). Reliance on the specific guarantees of the Bill of Rights in defining rights protected by the Fourteenth Amendment gave the Court a more objective standard than it had employed previously. The earlier cases spoke of "fundamental rights" based on national citizenship. Slaughterhouse Cases, 83 U.S. 36, 74, 76 (1873), quoting Corfield v. Coryell, 4 Washington Circuit Court 371 (1823); United States v. Cruikshank, 92 U.S. 542, 554 (1876); Presser v. Illinois, 116 U.S. 252, 267 (1886). These vague rights were seen as protected by the privileges and immunities clause of the Fourteenth Amendment, the due process clause of which extended only to guaranteeing procedural fairness. Under the new approach, substantive rights are guaranteed by the due process clause of the Fourteenth Amendment. The centrality of a Bill of Rights provision to "ordered liberty" warrants its incorporation into the Fourteenth Amendment. Palko v. Connecticut, 302 U.S. 319, 325 (1937); Griswold v. Connecticut, 301 U.S. 479, 499 (1965) (Harlan, J., concurring).

91.   Prudential Ins. Co. v. Cheek, 259 U.S. 530, 543 (1922).

92.   Gitlow v. New York, 268 U.S. 652 (1925); Fiske v. Kansas, 274 U.S. 380 (1927).

93.   Palko v. Connecticut, 302 U.S. 319, 328 (1938) (Fifth Amendment—double jeopardy).

94.   367 U.S. 643 (1961).

95.   Gideon v. Wainwright, 372 U.S. 335 (1963); Escobedo v. Illinois, 378 U.S. 478 (1964).

96.   Malloy v. Hogan, 378 U.S. 1 (1964).

97.   Miranda v. Arizona, 384 U.S. 436 (1966).

98.   Klopfer v. North Carolina, 386 U.S. 213 (1967).

99.   Washington v. Texas, 388 U.S. 14 (1967).

100.   Duncan v. Louisiana, 391 U.S. 145 (1968).

101.   Benton v. Maryland, 395 U.S. 784 (1969).

102.   Maloy v. Hogan, 378 U.S. 1 (1963); Hurtado v. California, 110 U.S. 516 (1884).

103.   See Griswold v. Connecticut, 381 U.S. 479 (1965).

104.   10 U.S.C. §311(a) (1970).

105.   Cases v. United States, 131 F.2d 916 (1st Cir. 1942), *cert. denied* 319 U.S. 770 (1943), *rehearing denied* 324 U.S. 889 (1945).

106.   Justice Black, *The Bill of Rights*, 35 N.Y.U.L.REV. 865, 873 (1960); W. Rawle, A VIEW OF THE CONSTITUTION 125 (1825).

107.   Sprecher, *The Lost Amendment*, 51 A.B.A.J. 554, 665, 666 (1965) and Comment, *The Right To Bear Arms*, 31 ALBANY L. REV. 74, 79–80 (1967).

108. Santee, *The Right to Keep and Bear Arms*, 26 DRAKE L. REV. 423, 433–36 (1976–77).

109. 367 U.S. 497, 541–43 (1961).

110. 381 U.S. 479 (1965).

111. 431 U.S. 494, 539 (1977).

112. *Id.* at 538–39.

113. *Id.* at 564–65.

114. 445 U.S. 55 (1980).

115. *Id.* at 65.

116. *Id.* at 65 n. 8.

117. *Id.* at 65.

118. 403 U.S. 388 (1971).

119. *Id.* at 395.

120. *Id.* at 399.

121. *But see* Tritsis v. Backer, 501 F.2d 1021 (7th Cir. 1974), a *Bivens* action against agents of Bureau of Alcohol, Tobacco and Firearms for deprivation of rights guaranteed by the Fourth, Fifth, Sixth, Ninth, Tenth, and Fourteenth Amendments. Suit was brought after dismissal of charges for illegally transferring a firearm in violation of 26 U.S.C. §5861(e). Summary judgment was granted defendants on submission of affidavits supporting reasonable good faith.

A cause of action for damages for deprivation by state agents of the right to bear arms was anticipated in 1871 by Rep. W. C. Whitthorne (D., Tenn.) in debate over the Civil Rights Act, now 42 U.S.C. §1983. *Infra* note 156. *Bivens* thus in effect extended the §1983 action to lawsuits against federal agents.

122. 442 U.S. 228 (1979).

123. 446 U.S. 14 (1980).

124. *Id.* at 18. *And see id.* at 23 ("violations of citizens constitutional rights, . . . violation by federal officials of federal constitutional rights").

125. Ex Parte Baine, 121 U.S. 1, 12 (1887). *See* Cohens v. Virginia, 19 U.S. (6 Wheat.) 264, 418 (1821) (Marshall, J.) ("Great weight has always been attached, and very rightly attached, to contemporaneous exposition."); South Carolina v. United States, 199 U.S. 437, 448 (1905) ("The Constitution is a written instrument. As such its meaning does not change. That which it meant when adopted it means now."); Eisner v. Macomber, 252 U.S. 189, 220 (1920) (Holmes, J., dissenting) (The amendments "should be read in 'a sense most obvious to the common understanding at the time of its adoption.' For it was for public adoption that it was proposed."); Report No. 21, Senate Judiciary Committee, 42d Cong., 2d Sess. 2 (25 Jan. 1872) ("In construing the Constitution we are compelled to give it such interpretation as will secure the result which was intended to be accomplished by those who framed it and the people who adopted it."); I J. Story, COMMENTARIES ON THE CONSTITUTION §400 (2d ed. 1851) ("The first and fundamental rule in the interpretation of all instruments is, to construe them according to the sense of the terms, and the intention of the parties."); Cooley, CONSTITUTIONAL LIMITATIONS 69 (6th ed. 1890) ("The object of construction, as applied to

a written constitution, is to give effect to the intent of the people in adopting it.").

126.   334 U.S. 1, 10–11 (1947).

127.   378 U.S. 1, 4n.2 (1964) (citations omitted). Actually, *Cruikshank* and *Presser* stated that both the First Amendment and the Second Amendment did not *directly* apply to the states.

128.   *Id.* at 5. *And see* Powell v. McCormack, 395 U.S. 486, 546–47 (1969): "That an unconstitutional action has been taken before surely does not render that same action any less unconstitutional at a later date."

129.   391 U.S. 145, 166–67 (1968).

130.   Lynch v. Household Finance Corp., 405 U.S. 538, 545 (1972). "The statutory descendants of §1 of the Civil Rights Act of 1871 must be given the meaning and sweep that their origins and their language dictate." *Id.* at 549.

131.   436 U.S. 658, 665 (1978). "But I think we owe somewhat less deference to a decision that was rendered without benefit of a full airing of all the relevant considerations." *Id.* at 709 n.6 (Powell, J., concurring).

132.   Specifically, Monroe v. Pape, 365 U.S. 167 (1961).

133.   Monell v. Dept. of Social Services of City of New York, 436 U.S. at 686–87.

134.   CONG. GLOBE, 42nd Cong., 1st Sess., pt. 2, Appendix 84 (31 Mr. 1871).

135.   436 U.S. at 685 n. 45. The Court proceeded to quote Bingham's references to some of the Bill of Rights freedoms protected by the amendment.

136.   *Id.*

137.   CONG. GLOBE, 42d Cong., 1st Sess., pt. 1, 475–76 (Ap. 5, 1871). *Monell* approves these pages without quoting from the speech.

138.   Jones v. Mayer, 392 U.S. 409, 424 n. 31 (1968) (emphasis added). This case relies largely on congressional debates and reports to demonstrate the original understanding of the Civil Rights Act of 1866, 42 U.S.C. §1982, as a prohibition of badges of slavery under the Thirteenth Amendment. *Id.* at 422–47.

139.   Robinson v. Memphis and Charleston R.R., 109 U.S. 3, 27 L. Ed. 836, 851 (1883). *And see* C. Collins, THE FOURTEENTH AMENDMENT AND THE STATES 143 (1912): "The Fourteenth Amendment expressed no new ideals of law and justice. . . . At the time of the adoption of the Amendment these constitutional ideals were expressed in every State constitution in the Union. . . ."

140.   359 U.S. 121 (1959).

141.   *Id.* at 124–25.

142.   *Id.* at 125. *See* Appendix comparing the state constitutions, *id.* at 140–49.

143.   Benton v. Maryland, 395 U.S. 84 (1969).

144.   This is a conservative figure, in that some other states included provisions which guaranteed the right to defend life and property or which declared in favor of a militia composed of the armed people. Further, some states had no bill of rights. Quoted statistics are derived from comparing states

with explicit guarantees for bearing arms in *supra* Ch. 5, notes 202–207, with the thirty-five states which ratified the Fourteenth Amendment.

145. 73 L.Ed. 2d 172 (1982).
146. *Id.* at 179.
147. *Id.* at 179–80. The Court cites Cong. Globe, 42d Cong., 1st Sess. 476 (1871). Emphasis added.
148. Cong. Globe, *supra* note 147, at 475–76. Emphasis added.
149. 73 L.Ed. 2d at 180.
150. Cong. Globe, *supra* note 147, at 332, 334.
151. *Id.* at 375.
152. *Id.* at 448–49.
153. H. R. REP. No. 37, 41st Cong., 3d Sess. 3 (20 Feb. 1871).
154. Cong. Globe, 42d Cong. 1st Sess. 459 (1871). The Court relies on this page of Coburn's speech as authority four times. 73 L.Ed. 2d at 180 n.6, 180, and 181.
155. 73 L.Ed. 2d at 180 n.6. Emphasis added.
156. Cong. Globe, 42d Cong., 1st Sess. 337 (1871). The Court relies on this page of Whitthorne's speech in both notes 6 and 7 of the opinion.
157. *Id.*, App. at 46.
158. *Id.* at 47.
159. *Id.* at 216, 243.
160. 73 L.Ed. 2d at 180 n.6, 181 n.7 and 182, n.9.
161. *Id.* at 180 n.6.
162. Cong. Globe, 42d Cong., 2d Sess., App. 25–26 (1872).
163. 73 L.Ed. 2d at 181 n.8.
164. *Supra* note 162.
165. *Supra* note 156, App. at 85. This page is cited as authority in 73 L.Ed. 2d at 182.
166. *Id.*

Chapter 7
State and Federal Judicial Opinions

1. 35 Tex. 473 (1872).
2. 42 Tex. 455 (1875).
3. Barron v. Baltimore, 32 U.S. 243 (1833).
4. 42 Tex. at 458.
5. 31 Ark. 455 (1876).
6. *Id.* at 460–61.
7. *Id.* at 458. *Cf.* Wilson v. State, 33 Ark. 557, 560, 34 Am. Rep. 52 (1878): "If cowardly and dishonorable men sometimes shoot unarmed men with army pistols or guns, the evil must be prevented by the penitentiary and gallows, and not by a general deprivation of a constitutional privilege."
8. 35 W. Va. 367, 14 S.E. 9 (1891).

9.   14 S.E. at 11.
10.   8 Idaho 597, 70 P. 609 (1902).
11.   *Id.*
12.   75 Vt. 295, 55 A. 610 (1903).
13.   55 A. at 610.
14.   *Id.* at 610–11.
15.   72 Kan. 230, 83 P. 619 (1905).
16.   83 P. at 620. The only case cited in support of this interpretation actually held only that "no independent military company has a constitutional right to parade with arms in our cities. . . ." Commonwealth v. Murphy, 166 Mass. 171, 173, 44 N.E. 138 (1896).
17.   83 P. at 620.
18.   Strickland v. State, 137 Ga. 1, 72 S.E. 260, 262 (1911).
19.   4 Ark. 18 (1842).
20.   139 N.Y.S. 277, 154 App. Div. 413, 29 N.Y. Cr. 74 (1913).
21.   139 N.Y.S. at 284.
22.   *Id.* at 285.
23.   181 N.C. 574, 107 S.E. 222 (1921).
24.   *Id.* at 575, 107 S.E. 223.
25.   *Id.* at 576, 107 S.E. 224.
26.   *Id.*
27.   *Id.* at 577, 107 S.E. 224.
28.   *Id.*
29.   *Id.* at 577–78, 107 S.E. 225.
30.   *Id.*
31.   205 Mich. 260, 171 N.W. 428, 430 (1919).
32.   219 Mich. 635, 189 N.W. 927 (1922).
33.   *Id.* at 638–39, 189 N.W. at 928.
34.   *Id. And see* People v. Nakamura, 99 Colo. 262, 62 P. 2d 246 (1936) (rejection of collectivist argument).
35.   193 Cal. 633, 226 P. 914 (1924).
36.   226 P. at 921–22.
37.   69 Cal. App. 466, 231 P. 601 (1924).
38.   231 P. at 604.
39.   253 Mich. 537, 235 N.W. 245 (1931).
40.   *Id.* at 540, 235 N.W. at 246.
41.   N.Y.S. 2d 63, 267 App. Div. 64, *aff'd* 294 N.Y. 699 (1945).
42.   45 N.Y.S. 2d 66.
43.   *Id.*
44.   *Id.* at 69.
45.   51 N.Y.S.2d. 202, 268 App.Div. 202 (1944), *reargument denied* 63 N.Y.S.2d 840, 270 App.Div. 1046 (1946), *aff'd* 73 N.E. 2d 41, 296 N.Y. 926 (1947).
46.   *Id.* at 205.
47.   205 N.Y.S.2d 526, 24 Misc. 949 (1960).

48. 205 N.Y.S.2d at 529.
49. *Id.*
50. *Id.* at 531.
51. 272 N.C. 535, 159 S.E.2d 1 (1962).
52. 159 S.E.2d at 8.
53. *Id.* at 9, citing Hill v. State, 53 Ga. 472.
54. *Id.* at 11.
55. *Id.* at 14.
56. *Id.* at 15.
57. *Id.*, referring to Palko v. Connecticut, 302 U.S. 319 (1937).
58. 99 N.J.Super. 459, 240 A.2d 432, *aff'd* 53 N.J. 86, 248 A.2d 521, *appeal dismissed* 394 U.S. 812 (1969) *(mem.).*
59. 248 A.2d at 525.
60. *Id.* at 526–27.
61. *See* United States v. Miller, 307 U.S. 174, 179 (1939) ("the Militia comprised all males physically capable of acting in concert for the common defense. . . . These men were expected to appear bearing arms supplied by themselves. . . ."). Thus, Burton v. Sills departed from *Miller* while purporting to follow it. 248 A.2d at 526–27.
62. Harris v. State, 83 Nev. 404, 432 P.2d 929, 930 (1967) (possession of tear gas gun without permit a felony); State v. Bolin, 200 Kan. 369, 436 P.2d 978, 979 (1968) (convicted burglar may not have pistol); Photos v. Toledo, 19 Ohio Misc. 147, 250 N.E.2d 916, 926 (1969) (identification may be required for handgun owners); People v. Marques, 179 Colo. 86, 498 P.2d 929 (1972) (upheld conviction of felon, earlier convicted of assualt with a deadly weapon, for carrying a concealed weapon); Nebraska v. Skinner, 189 Neb. 457, 203 N.W.2d 161 (1973) (upheld conviction of possession of handgun by felon); People v. Evans, 115 Cal.Rptr. 304, 307, 40 C.A.3d 582 (1974) ("An ex-felon's right to defend himself remains, but he is prevented from the use of firearms"); Mosher v. Dayton, 48 Ohio St. 2d 243, 2 Ohio Op. 3d 403, 358 N.E.2d 540, 543 (1976) (upheld ordinance requiring identification card and demonstration of need to acquire handgun, stating where individual rights are supreme, constitutional "language authorizing such intention must be clear and unambiguous.") *(But see* dissent at 544 that "legislation which seeks to restrict one of the fundamental civil rights" should be reasonable and necessary); Commonwealth v. Davis, 369 Mass. 886, 343 N.E.2d 847, 848–50 (1976) upheld statute providing a maximum of life imprisonment for possession of a shotgun with a barrel less than eighteen inches in length); State v. Sanne, 116 N.H. 583, 364 A.2d 630 (1976) (carrying pistols without license); Milligan v. State, 554 S.W.2d 192 (Tex. Crim. App. 1977) (state may prohibit possession of pistol by one convicted of violent felony who is off his premises [a comparatively lenient statute]); and State v. Sanders, 357 So.2d 492 (La. 1978) (upheld conviction of felon carrying concealed pistol).
63. Guida v. Dier, 375 N.Y.S.2d 826, 828, 84 Misc.2d 110 (1975), modified on other grounds 387 N.Y.S.2d 720, 722, 54 App. Div. 2d 86 (1976).

64.   398 N.E.2d 1339 (1980).
65.   *Id.* at 1341.
66.   *Id.*
67.   614 P.2d 94 (Or. 1980).
68.   *Id.* at 95.
69.   *Id.* at 98.
70.   *Id.*
71.   *Id.*
72.   And see, Connecticut v. Anonymous, 179 Ct. 516, 427 A.2d 403, 405 (1980):

> The defendant argues that without proof, beyond a reasonable doubt, that he did not possess a permit, a finding of guilty is improper. He cites the constitutional right to bear arms; Conn. Const. art. 1 §15; U.S. Const.Amend. II; and stresses that carrying a weapon is not criminal per se, but only becomes criminal if the weapon is carried without a proper permit. We agree.

And see also, Rabbitt v. Leonard, 36 Conn. Sup. 108, 110, 413 A.2d 489, 491 (Conn. Supr. Ct. 1979) (Under Connecticut consitution, a citizen has a "fundamental right to bear arms in self-defense. . . .").
73.   Selective Training and Service Act of 1940, 50 U.S.C. §§301–18.
74.   36 F.Supp. 739 (D. Or. 1940).
75.   Here the court cites *Miller* and "The Militia Clause of the Constitution," 54 Har. L. Rev. 181–220. 36 F. Supp. at 742 n.9.
76.   36 F. Supp. at 742.
77.   1 Stat. 271. 36 F. Supp. at 742 n.10.
78.   50 U.S.C. Appendix, §301(a), 36 F.Supp. at 743 n.16.
79.   *Id.* at 743.
80.   131 F.2d. 916, *cert. denied* 319 U.S. 770 (1942), *rehearing denied* 324 U.S. 889 (1945).
81.   §2 (e) and (f), Federal Firearms Act, 52 Stat. 1250, 15 U.S.C. §901–09.
82.   131 F.2d at 921.
83.   165 U.S. 275 (1897).
84.   131 F.2d at 922.
85.   *Id.*
86.   131 F.2d 261 (3d Cir. 1942), *rev'd on other grounds* 319 U.S. 463 (1943).
87.   *Cf.* Quilici v. Morton Grove, 532 F.Supp. 1169 (N.D. I11. 1981), *aff'd* 695 F.2d 261 (7th Cir. 1982), *cert. denied* 104 S.Ct. 194 (1983). The intent of the framers of the Second and Fourteenth Amendments was so overwhelmingly against its opinion that the Circuit Court held that intent to be "irrelevant."
88.   United States v. Johnson, 497 F.2d 548, 550 (4th Cir. 1974) relies on Cody v. United States, 460 F.2d 34 (8th Cir. 1972) and United States v. Miller, 307 U.S. 174 (1939) to conclude that "the Second Amendment only confers a collective right" although such language never appears in those two cases.

Equally exaggerative of *Miller* is the citation thereof in Stevens v. United States, 440 F.2d 144 (6th Cir. 1971) to support the claim that the Second Amendment right "applies only to the right of the State to maintain a militia and not to the individual's right to bear arms. . . ." United States v. Warin, 530 F.2d 103, 106 (6th Cir. 1976), *cert. denied* 426 U.S. 948 (1976) agrees with *Cases* in questioning the U.S. Supreme Court's *Miller* decision and string cites to *Stevens, Johnson, Cody* and *Tot* to conclude: "It is clear that the Second Amendment guarantees a collective rather than an individual right." Aside from a reference to the English Bill of Rights in *Warin*, not one of these cases refers to any original source, and thus their validity is entirely contingent on the accuracy of the historical account presented in *Tot*.

89. 131 F.2d at 266 n.13.
90. 5 J. Elliot, DEBATES 445 (Philadelphia 1845).
91. *Id.* at 444.
92. 1 *id.* at 371.
93. *Id.* at 372.
94. 4 *id.* at 203.
95. *Id.* at 250–51.
96. *Id.* at 244.
97. Emery, *The Constitutional Right to Keep and Bear Arms*, 28 HARV. L. REV. 473, 476 (1915).
98. *Id.*
99. McKenna, *The Right to Keep and Bear Arms*, 12 MARQ. L. REV. 138, 145 (1928).
100. *Id.* at 149.
101. *Id.* at 144, 146.
102. Haight, *The Right to Keep and Bear Arms*, 2 BILL OF RIGHTS REV. 31, 42 (1941).
103. 131 F.2d at 266 n.14.
104. *Supra* Ch. 2, notes 80–94 and accompanying text.
105. *See* Cody v. United States, 460 F.2d 34, 36–37 (8th Cir., 1972); United States v. Lauchli, 444 F.2d 1037, 1041 (7th Cir. 1971); United States v. Gross, 313 F. Supp. 1330, 1334 (S.D. Ind. 1970), *aff'd* 451 F.2d 1355 (7th Cir. 1971); United States v. Synnes, 438 F.2d 764, 771 (8th Cir. 1971), *vacated on other grounds*, United States v. Bass, 404 U.S. 336 (1971); United States v. Three Winchester 30-30 Caliber Lever Action Carbines, 363 F.Supp. 322, 323, *aff'd.* 504 F.2d 1288 (7th Cir. 1974).
106. 438 F.2d at 771 n.9.
107. *Id.* at 772.
108. 309 F.Supp 141, 144 (D. Minn. 1970), *aff'd* 438 F.2d 773 (8th Cir. 1971).
109. 414 F.Supp. 1346, 1353 and n.11 (S.D. Fla. 1976), *reh. denied* 565 F.2d 163 (5th Cir. 1977).

Several federal cases on the 1968 legislation are related to Fifth, not Second Amendment claims, and yet these too assume the right of the common citizen to have arms. See United States v. Weatherford, 471 F.2d 47, 50 (7th Cir. 1972) (reasonable under Fifth Amendment to prohibit felons from transporting weapons and ammunition in interstate commerce); Marchese v. State of California, 545 F.2d 645, 647 (9th Cir. 1976) ("a legislature reasonably may decide that persons with criminal convictions have more of a tendency to commit a crime of violence than persons without criminal records."); United States v. Ransom, 515 F.2d 885, 891 (5th Cir. 1975) ("the legislative classification applying to felons is rational").

110.   Gavett v. Alexander, 477 F.Supp. 1035 (D.D.C. 1979).
111.   *Id.* at 1046.
112.   *Id.* at 1048.
113.   *Id.*

Afterword:
Public Policy and the Right to Keep and Bear
Arms

1.   Warren, *The Bill of Rights and The Military*, 37 N.Y.U.L.R. 181, 184 (1962).

2.   *Id.* at 185.

3.   Pound, *Introduction* to B. Patterson, THE FORGOTTEN NINTH AMENDMENT vi (1955).

4.   On the "childish notion" expressed by Engels that the oppressor's superior military technology guarantees victory over the inferiorly armed oppressed, see F. Fanon, THE WRETCHED OF THE EARTH 63–64 (1963).

5.   Pound, DEVELOPMENT OF CONSTITUTIONAL LIBERTY 91 (1957).

6.   407 U.S. 143 (1972).

7.   *Id.* at 150–51.

8.   *Id.* at 152.

9.   Douglas, *The Bill of Rights is Not Enough*, 38 N.Y.U.L. REV. 207, 233 (1963).

10.   4 Ark. 18 (1842).

11.   *Id.* at 37.

12.   384 U.S. 436 (1966).

13.   *Id.* at 542.

14.   John Locke, SECOND TREATISE OF CIVIL GOVERNMENT, §228 (1689), compares government officials who usurp power to "robbers or pirates" and defends the right of violent resistance against them.

15.   R. Rohner, *The Right to Bear Arms*, 16 CATHOLIC U.L.REV. 53 (1966).

16.   *Id.* at 72.

17.   P. Courtney, GUN CONTROL MEANS PEOPLE CONTROL, (Littleton, Colo., 1974). Yet such "reactionaries" have a higher consciousness of the existence of the ruling elite than the ideologists of the status quo who ignore its existence altogether. *See, e.g.,* Carl Bakal, THE RIGHT TO BEAR ARMS (1966) (latter reissued as NO RIGHT TO BEAR ARMS.)

18.   S. Hayes, *The Right to Bear Arms: A Study in Judicial Misinterpretation,* 2 W&M. L. REV. 381 (1960); J. Whisker, OUR VANISHING FREEDOM: THE RIGHT TO KEEP AND BEAR ARMS (1973). *But see* Feller and Gotting, *The Second Amendment: A Second Look,* 61 N.W.U. L. REV. 46 (1966).

19.   Robert Sherrill, THE SATURDAY NIGHT SPECIAL 228 (New York 1973). On the N.R.A. philosophy, see Robert J. Kukla, GUN CONTROL, ed. Harlon B. Carter (1973); THE RIGHT TO BEAR ARMS: AN ANALYSIS OF THE SECOND AMENDMENT 9 (N.R.A. Institute for Legislative Action, n.d.) states: "The guardians of our basic liberties are not formal bodies of police or military. . . . The guardians of civil liberty are those, each individual, who would enjoy that liberty."

20.   See Ch. 3 of this study. Also, Burroughs v. Peyton, 57 Va. (16 Gratt.) 470, 482 (1864) ("the militia embraces the whole armsbearing population. . . ."); State v. Grayson, 163 S.W. 2d 335, 337 (Mo. 1943) ("The term 'militia' was not [historically] used as restricted to the National Guard.").

21.   S. Ambrose, *The Armed Forces and Civil Disorder,* THE MILITARY AND AMERICAN SOCIETY 241, 245 (1972). The above summary recapitulates Amborse's article. Ambrose continues: "The Founding Fathers . . . went to great lengths to insure that the Federal Government would not have a monopoly on violence. On an individual level, they guaranteed citizens the right to have arms. . . ." *Id.* The role of the *Guarda Nacional* in Central America, where the peasants have no right to have firearms and are routinely abused and murdered, highlights the inconsistency of the "collecitivist" view of the Second Amendment with the ideal to secure a "free state." *And see* M. Derthick, THE NATIONAL GUARD IN POLITICS 16 (1965) (the "National Guard" a response to labor riots of 1877).

22.   Village of Morton Grove Ordinance #81–11.

23.   *E.g.,* D.C. Code §§6–2312(4), 6–2376, and 22–3206; East St. Louis Ordinance #81-10043; Atlanta Code §§17-4001 et seq.; New York City Code §§436–5.0 et seq.; Dade County Code §§21–19.1 et seq. As U.S. Attorney General, Edward H. Levi proposed more stringent firearms prohibitions for areas beset with high crime rates, that is, inner cities. *But see* MASS. ANN. LAWS, ch. 269, §10 (mandatory one-year imprisonment for unlicensed carrying of handgun).

Just prior to the passage of Chicago's recent restrictive measure, Russ Meek argued in a leading black newspaper that the proposal was akin to black codes; and pointed out that Chicago is 40% Black, 14% Hispanic, and 11% Oriental, native American, and other minorities. "The right to keep and bear arms is in the Constitution, and it does not say *'For whites only!'* It says *'The people,'* and that means US!" Chicago Defender, 17 Oct. 1981, at 11. *And see Washington*

Post, 11 July 1977, view of Black United Front that gun control is " 'illegal and white man's law' calculated to disarm urban blacks."

24. State v. Lane, 30 N.C. 256, 257 (1848).

25. Even the infamous black codes in such states as Florida, Alabama, Mississippi, and South Carolina made licenses to possess pistols and other firearms available to black freedmen. See DuBois, BLACK RECONSTRUCTION IN AMERICA 172–73 (1962). By not even making licenses available for individual keeping of handguns in the home, the Morton Grove Ordinance would be more inconsistent with the Fourteenth Amendment than were the black codes it was adopted to nullify.

26. Comment, *Carrying Concealed Weapons*, 15 VA. L. REG. 391–92 (1909). The registration requirement and special tax on handguns advocated was later passed, Acts of Assembly (Va.) 285–87 (1926) and subsequently declared unconstitutional. Commonwealth v. O'Neal, 13 VA. L. REG. 746 (Hustings Ct.—Roanoke, 1928).

"The Southern States have very largely furnished the precedents. It is only necessary to observe that the race issue there has extremely intensified a decisive purpose to entirely disarm the negro, and this policy is evident upon reading the opinions." State v. Nieto, 101 Ohio State 409, 130 N.E. 663, 669 (1920) (Wamamaker, J., dissenting) (Mexican convicted of carrying concealed pistol). In holding an act prohibiting the unlicensed carrying of a pistol contrary to the Second Amendment and the Flordia Constitution, Buford, J., concurring, noted that "The Act was passed for the purpose of disarming the negro laborers. . . . The statute was never intended to be applied to the white population. . . ." Watson v. Stone, 4 So. 2d 700, 703 (Fla. 1941).

27. R. Kessler, *Enforcement Problems of Gun Control: A Victimless Crimes Analysis*, 16 CRIM. L. BULL. 131, 137 (1980).

28. R. Williams, NEGROES WITH GUNS (1962) (black armed defense against violence supported or tolerated by local police and F.B.I.); D. Kates, *Why a Civil Libertarian Opposes Gun Control*, CIVIL LIBERTIES REVIEW, June/July 1976, 24–32, & Aug./Sept. 1976, 44–59 (armed self-defense by civil rights organizers against Klan attacks); D. Kates, RESTRICTING HANDGUNS: THE LIBERAL SKEPTICS SPEAK OUT *passim* (1979).

29. MALCOLM X 337, J. Clarke ed. (New York, 1969).

30. B. Seale, SEIZE THE TIME 68 (1970).

31. R. Sherrill, THE SATURDAY NIGHT SPECIAL 280 (1973). *See* Gun Control Act, 18 U.S.C. §§921–28 (1968); Omnibus Crime Control and Safe Streets Act, 18 U.S.C. Appendix §§1201–03 (1968); and particularly the ironically entitled Civil Rights Act, 18 U.S.C. §§231–33 (1968) (the contrast with civil rights acts of a century before, which in part enhanced the right of blacks to protect themselves with arms, is striking).

Senators Dodd and Kennedy and other supporters of the 1968 legislation made sensational references to the Black Muslims and Black Panthers and to the riots in Tampa, Newark, and Detroit in support of disarming urban blacks. See citations in R. Kukla, GUN CONTROL 89, 93–96, 243, 251–59 (1973).

In contrast with racist hysteria, Stanford Research Institute's FIREARMS, VIOLENCE AND CIVIL DISORDERS concluded that "violence by fire- arms on the part of the participants in the disorders of 1967 was substantially exaggerated by the communications media and by public officials," and that most firing was by "trigger-happy Guardsmen" who often exchanged fire with the police rather then with conjured up "snipers." See Kukla at 251–59.

Index

Case Index

Slaughter-House Cases, 156
State v. Buzzard, 94–95, 181, 194
State v. Chandler, 96, 127
State v. Dawson, 185
State v. Duke, 168, 179
State v. Hannibal, 97
State v. Harris, 97
State v. Kerner, 181–83
State v. Kessler, 186–87
State v. Newsom, 97, 128–29
State v. Rosenthal, 180
State v. Workman, 168, 180

Stone v. Christenson, 187
Tot v. United States, 189–91
United States v. Bowdach, 191
United States v. Cruikshank, 156–62, 173
United States v. Miller, 6, 156, 164–69, 172, 187–89, 260n88
United States v. Synnes, 191
United States v. Wiley, 191
Weeks v. United States, 173
Wingfield v. Stratford, 52

Subject Index

abolitionists, 99–104
abridgment, 94, 113
absolutism, 7, 8, 24–32
Adams, John, 7, 8, 32, 58, 65, 66
Adams, Samuel, 8, 59, 60, 62, 74, 79
A Discourse of Government with Relation to Militias, 47
A Dissertation on Slavery: With a Proposal for the Gradual Abolition of it, in the State of Virginia, 99
administrative privilege, 186
affray, 50, 51, 94
A Journal of the Times, 58
Alabama, 124
Alfred, king of England, 37
Ames, Adelbert, 144
Ames, Fisher, 76
"An American Citizen," 68
An Argument Showing that a Standing Army is Inconsistent with a Free Government, 46
antifederalists, 66, 70
Aristotle, 7, 11–14, 26, 33, 66
Arizona, 194
Arkansas, 94, 124, 179
armed populace, 15, 21, 61, 93. *See also* militia arms, types of, 14, 19, 20, 42, 94, 227n3; courts influenced by, 164, 165, 179–84, 187–89; government and popular, 156, 193; states and, 126, 130, 168. *See also* concealed weapons
arsenals, 74
Art of Lawgiving, The, 28

Art of War, The, 22
assassination, 16, 20
assault, 17, 58
assembly, 31, 37, 48, 49, 57, 158
Assize of Arms, 38, 39
Athenian Constitution, 13
A View of the Constitution, 101

Barclay, 29
Bayard, Senator, 178
Bayne, Thomas, 133
bearing arms, 93, 158; citizenship and, 11, 92, 127; definitions for, 219n92, 223n145; private armies and, 160; restrictions on, 78; state power to regulate, 95, 127, 130
Beccaria, Cesare, 7, 32, 34, 35, 58
Berkeley, William, 55, 56, 57
Bill of Rights, 7, 171; popular understanding of, 72, 76, 77, 112, 121, 125; states and the, 64, 65, 81, 117, 128, 156, 170–78
Bill of Rights and The Military, The, 193
Bill of Rights is not Enough, The, 194
Bill of Rights Review, 190
Bill of Rights, the English, 44–48
Bingham, John A., 101, 110, 112, 146, 174, 178
Bishop, Joel P., 107, 133, 156
black codes, 108
Black, Justice, 174
Blackstone: English law and, 43, 45, 53,